## この一冊で難関校合格

# 過去問で覚える英単語スピードマスター

### 必勝 2000

嶋津幸樹 著
Shimazu Koki

Jリサーチ出版

# 受験生へのメッセージ

## そうだったのか！
## 実戦的かつ単語学習が面白くなる単語集

　私は高校2年（17歳）で塾を創設し、大学に通いながら小学生から高校生まで500人以上の塾生を指導してきました。その高校2年だったときに気がついたのが、語源の驚異です。英語は主にラテン語とギリシャ語から成り立っています。そこでラテン語の辞書を買いあさり、1語1語調べ始めてみると、1つの語源で20〜30もの単語に派生できるということに気がつきました。

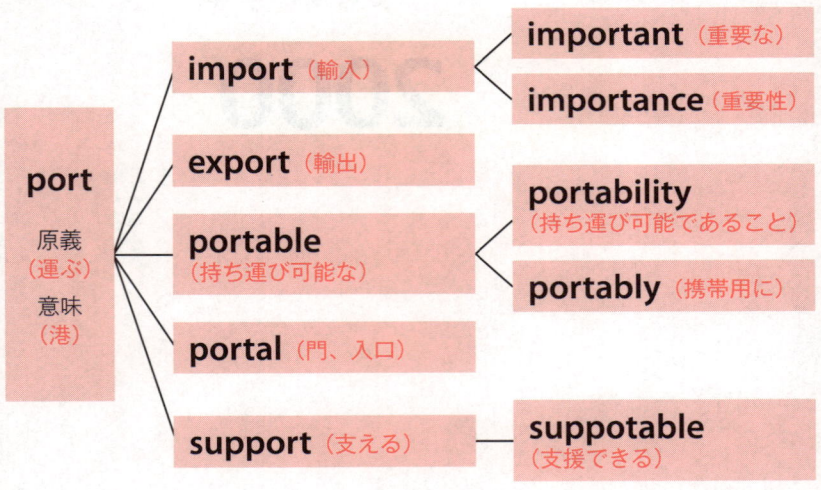

　私は高校時代にはこの語源の知識のおかげで全国統一模試で偏差値80を達成、教えていた高校生の塾生は東大をはじめ難関大学に続々合格、さらに中学生の塾生が英検準1級に合格するなど、グングン英語力が伸びていくのを目の当たりにしてきました。

本書は、私のこうした経験をすべて詰め込んだ単語集です。掲載した単語はすべてが最新の大学入試の出題傾向に基づく頻出単語です。
　①過去問を解く➡②正解を見抜く➡③連鎖式に語彙を増やす、という3つのステップで本書は構成されています。過去問を解き、実戦力をつけたいと思う読者の方なら、難関大学合格に必要な語彙を他のどんな単語集よりも効果的に、また、楽しく身につけることができるはずです。連鎖式に語彙を増やすページでは、トピック（話題）ごとに語源やイラスト、コロケーションで深い語彙力を身につけることが可能です。「なるほど」「そうだったのか」と思わず膝を打ちたくなる発見がいくつも出てきます。発見や驚きこそ、学習の醍醐味であり、大学に合格する秘訣です。

## 「使える語彙」を増やすことが合格への近道

　語彙力には2つの種類があります。「知っている語彙」と「使える語彙」です。従来の日本の英語教育では「知っている語彙」ばかりが求められ、「使う」という観点が軽視されてきたことが否めません。しかし、これからは違います。スピーキングテストがあるTOEFLが大学入試や国家公務員試験で注目されています。それは1つのトピックに関して自分の意見や見解を英語で述べる力（英語での自己表現力）が求められているということです。英語で意見を述べることの根底にあるものが、豊富な語彙力です。いま学ぼうとしている単語はいつか社会で使う可能性がある。そう思うだけでイキイキと学習できるはずです。大学合格はもちろん、さらにその先の人生で役立つ英語力を、本書で身につけていただくことを願っています。

嶋津幸樹

# CONTENTS

受験生へのメッセージ ……………………………………………… 2
本書の特長 ………………………………………………………… 6
本書の利用法 ……………………………………………………… 10

## Chapter 1　Nature

- UNIT 1　自然・起源 ………………………………………… 14
- UNIT 2　環境・状況 ………………………………………… 18
- UNIT 3　天気・気候 ………………………………………… 22
- UNIT 4　災害・破壊 ………………………………………… 26
- UNIT 5　耕作・農業 ………………………………………… 30
- UNIT 6　動物・人生 ………………………………………… 34
- UNIT 7　行動・本能 ………………………………………… 38
- UNIT 8　感情・性格 ………………………………………… 42
- UNIT 9　会社・仲間 ………………………………………… 46
- UNIT 10　依存・独立 ………………………………………… 50

## Chapter 2　Education

- UNIT 11　教育・育成 ………………………………………… 56
- UNIT 12　能力・才能 ………………………………………… 60
- UNIT 13　教科・専攻 ………………………………………… 64
- UNIT 14　成績・進歩 ………………………………………… 68
- UNIT 15　音楽・作曲 ………………………………………… 72
- UNIT 16　知識・思考 ………………………………………… 76
- UNIT 17　理解・習得 ………………………………………… 80
- UNIT 18　記憶・意識 ………………………………………… 84
- UNIT 19　集中・強調 ………………………………………… 88
- UNIT 20　我慢・忍耐 ………………………………………… 92
- UNIT 21　文字・文学 ………………………………………… 96

| UNIT 22 | 辞書・定義 | 100 |
| UNIT 23 | 出版・人口 | 104 |
| UNIT 24 | 表示・公表 | 108 |
| UNIT 25 | 諺・名言 | 112 |

## Chapter 3 Science

| UNIT 26 | 医薬・医療 | 118 |
| UNIT 27 | 病気・病院 | 122 |
| UNIT 28 | 感染・接触 | 126 |
| UNIT 29 | 傾向・流行 | 130 |
| UNIT 30 | 習慣・伝統 | 134 |
| UNIT 31 | 発明・達成 | 138 |
| UNIT 32 | 生産・利益 | 142 |
| UNIT 33 | 電話・会話 | 146 |
| UNIT 34 | 維持・保持 | 150 |
| UNIT 35 | 動作・活動 | 154 |

## Chapter 4 Society

| UNIT 36 | 輸送機間 | 160 |
| UNIT 37 | 交通・渋滞 | 164 |
| UNIT 38 | 場所・範囲 | 168 |
| UNIT 39 | 旅行・予約 | 172 |
| UNIT 40 | 観光・景色 | 176 |
| UNIT 41 | 地域・社会 | 180 |
| UNIT 42 | 政治・憲法 | 184 |
| UNIT 43 | 選挙・重要 | 188 |
| UNIT 44 | 要求・必要 | 192 |
| UNIT 45 | 原因・結果 | 196 |
| UNIT 46 | 企業・労働 | 200 |

| UNIT 47 | 雇用・解雇 | 204 |
| UNIT 48 | 経営・会議 | 208 |
| UNIT 49 | 設立・建設 | 212 |
| UNIT 50 | 観客・顧客 | 216 |
| UNIT 51 | 給料・税金 | 220 |
| UNIT 52 | 料金・費用 | 224 |
| UNIT 53 | 通貨・銀行 | 228 |
| UNIT 54 | 破産・借金 | 232 |
| UNIT 55 | 価値・感謝 | 236 |
| UNIT 56 | 合法・違法 | 240 |
| UNIT 57 | 裁判・訴訟 | 244 |
| UNIT 58 | 犯罪・処罰 | 248 |
| UNIT 59 | 証拠・保証 | 252 |
| UNIT 60 | 主張・基準 | 256 |
| UNIT 61 | 時間・世代 | 260 |
| UNIT 62 | 期限・厳守 | 264 |
| UNIT 63 | 連続・継続 | 268 |
| UNIT 64 | 永遠・遺産 | 272 |
| UNIT 65 | 最新・最初 | 276 |
| UNIT 66 | 尊敬・軽蔑 | 280 |
| UNIT 67 | 関係・関連 | 284 |
| UNIT 68 | 表現・印象 | 288 |
| UNIT 69 | 許可・容認 | 292 |
| UNIT 70 | 拒否・否定 | 296 |
| UNIT 71 | 問題・迷惑 | 300 |
| UNIT 72 | 誘惑・障害 | 304 |
| UNIT 73 | 謝罪・責任 | 308 |
| UNIT 74 | 危険・恐怖 | 312 |
| UNIT 75 | 遠慮・失礼 | 316 |
| UNIT 76 | 強制・義務 | 320 |

| UNIT 77 | 制限・禁止 | 324 |
| UNIT 78 | 廃止・停止 | 328 |
| UNIT 79 | 国境・区別 | 332 |
| UNIT 80 | 所有・占領 | 336 |

## Chapter 5 Intention

| UNIT 81 | 選択・優先 | 342 |
| UNIT 82 | 変化・変形 | 346 |
| UNIT 83 | 説得・援助 | 350 |
| UNIT 84 | 影響・評価 | 354 |
| UNIT 85 | 決意・解決 | 358 |
| UNIT 86 | 成功・機会 | 362 |
| UNIT 87 | 偶然・事故 | 366 |
| UNIT 88 | 献身・貢献 | 370 |
| UNIT 89 | 目的・期待 | 374 |
| UNIT 90 | 自信・勇気 | 378 |
| UNIT 91 | 使用・消費 | 382 |
| UNIT 92 | 調査・実験 | 386 |
| UNIT 93 | 反対・苦情 | 390 |
| UNIT 94 | 明確・曖昧 | 394 |
| UNIT 95 | 類似・相違 | 398 |
| UNIT 96 | 適切・調整 | 402 |
| UNIT 97 | 不足・十分 | 406 |
| UNIT 98 | 増加・減少 | 410 |
| UNIT 99 | 参加・部分 | 414 |
| UNIT 100 | 勝敗・平等 | 418 |

# 本書の特長

| 1ページ目 | 2ページ目 | 3～4ページ目 |
|---|---|---|
| 過去問（4問）を解く | 答えあわせ<br>選択肢の単語もチェック | 関連する語を<br>イモヅル式に覚える |

## 1テーマ4ページ完結のシンプル構成

　過去に大学入試で出題された問題を整理し、テーマ別に集めてあります。各テーマは4ページで完結。1ページ目に4問の過去問が掲載されていますので、まずはそれに取り組んでください。隣のページの2ページ目に英文の日本語訳と選択肢の意味が紹介しています。選択肢の単語についても、しっかり理解しておくと後々役に立つでしょう。

　3ページ目と4ページ目は同じテーマで大学入試でよく問われる単語がリストアップされています。語源から覚え、複数の関連語をイモヅル式に覚えることができますので、たいへん効率的であり、ここで頭に入れたことが本番でも効果を発揮します。

## なぜ過去問を解きながら覚える？

　問題を解くということは、正解を導くためにその問題文の隅々まで目を配し、意識をグッと集中させるため、頭がヒートアップします。鉄は熱いうちに打て、という言葉があるように、ヒートアップした頭（記憶）のまま答えあわせをすると、強く長く記憶残ることが科学的にも実証されています。

その熱せられた頭のまま、3〜4ページ目の同じテーマの単語とその使い方を一気に学習してしまいましょう。たった1つの単語が他の関連語（各テーマ14〜25語）をイモヅル式に思い出させるのにも一役買ってくれるはずです。

## 集中力がケタ外れに高まる！

　本書のメソッドは実際の英語塾で活用され、東大をはじめ、有名大学合格者を次々に輩出しています。合格者たちが選んだ学習法なので、その効果は抜群。それは「過去問を解く」ときの集中力は、ケタ外れに高くなるからです。学校でさまざまなテストを受けてきた皆さんも、それは実感されていると思います。従来の単語集のように覚えているつもりで実はただ眺めているだけの集中力とはケタ外れに違ってきます。

## センター試験から難関私大に必須の2000語を完全カバー

　およそ2000語の単語が本書の中で登場します。センター試験から早慶上智など難関私立大学に合格できるように、最新傾向に則して紹介します。

## 発音・リスニング問題を補完する工夫

　大学入試でも年々重視傾向にある発音やリスニング問題にも対応できるように、すべての単語と例文を音声で収録しています（無料音声ダウンロード）。本文にも 発 や ア というマークで、入試でねらわれやすいポイントを示してありますので、志望校の傾向に合わせてぜひ活用してください。

# 本書の利用法

本書は大きく「Nature」「Education」「Science」「Society」「Intention」の5つのChapter（章）で構成され、その下に100のテーマがあります。1テーマが4ページ完結というシンプルな設計にしてありますので、「今日は2つのテーマ（計8ページ）をやってみよう」「本番まであと4カ月（約120日）だから1日1テーマずつやって、あとは復習に時間を割こう」など、学習計画が立てやすくなっています。

UNIT 1 自然・起源　STEP 1 過去問を解く

1　1回目 ○△×　2回目 ○△×

I told you over and over again, but you still failed to understand the ( ) of your task.　上智大学

1. nature
2. center
3. means
4. duty

4. resources

stors of humanity ( ) in　亜細亜大学

014

2 正解を見抜く

1 I told you over and over again, but you still failed to understand the nature of your task.　正解 1

訳 君には何度も伝えたが、君は仕事の本質を理解していない。

nature 名 自然
center 名 中央
means 名 本質
duty 名 義務

natureには「自然」以外に「本質」という意味があります

2 Many of the animals that are native to Australia, like the kangaroo and the koala, are very unusual species.　正解 3

訳 カンガルーやコアラなどのオーストラリア特有の動物の多くが、非常に珍しい種の動物である。

contrary 形 正反対の　equivalent 形 同等の
native 形 特有の　similar 形 類似の

3 Gold and diamonds are two of South Africa's most valuable natural resources.　正解 4

訳 金とダイアモンドは南アフリカの最も貴重な天然資源である。

affair 名 出来事
matter 名 物質
phenomenon 名 現象
resource 名 資源

4 Most scientists believe that the ancestors of humanity originated in Africa.　正解 3

訳 ほとんどの科学者が人類はアフリカに起源があると信じている。

plan 動 計画する
preserve 動 保存する
originate 動 起こる
own 動 所有する

Chapter1 Nature 015

## ワンポイントアドバイス

問題を解くヒントが解説されています。

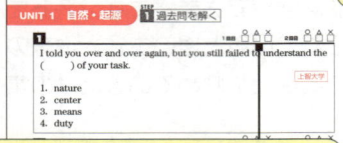

## 正解・不正解・勘が当たった

問題に正解したら○、不正解には×、勘が当たった場合は△にしるしを付け、繰り返し学習する際に利用してください。

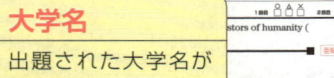

## 大学名

出題された大学名が記載してあります。

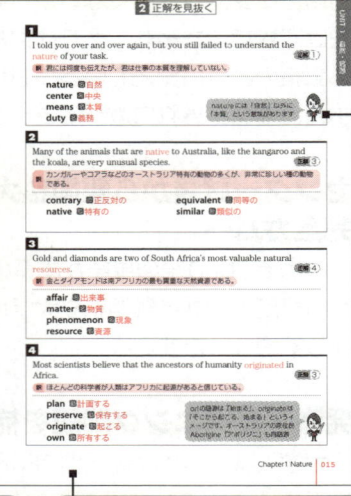

## 各テーマの1ページ目

過去問が4問あります。出題形式は穴埋め問題か正誤問題のどちらかです。穴埋め問題は（　）に当てはまる語を一つ選んでください。正誤問題は下線が引かれた語を正しく訂正する語を一つ選んでください。

## 各テーマの2ページ目

問題に対する正解と日本語訳、選択肢で登場したすべての単語の意味が紹介されています。

## 語源
単語のコアなイメージがわかります。

## チェックボックス
覚えた単語・熟語をチェックしましょう。

## ヘッドフォンマーク 🎧
音声について（ダウンロードの手順はP.12）
2種類の音声ファイルが用意されています。
①英語のみ
②日本語の意味→英語

## コロ マーク
コロケーション
（入試によくでる連語）

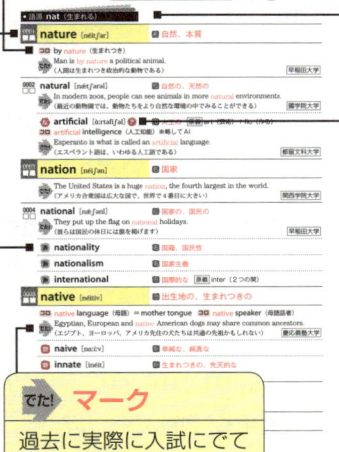
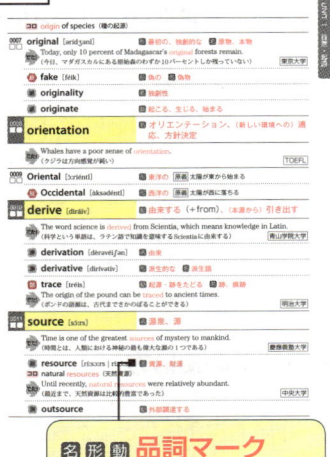

## でた! マーク
過去に実際に入試にでてきた英文を紹介。

## 派 類 反 マーク
入試によくでる派生語、類義語、反意語を紹介。見出し語と一緒に覚えると効率的。

## 発 ア マーク
入試でよくねらわれる発音・アクセント。

## 名 形 動 品詞マーク
品詞の種類を示します。
（記号についてはP.12へ）

## 音声ファイルダウンロードの手順

### ①パソコン、タブレット端末、スマートフォンからインターネットで専用サイトにアクセス

　Jリサーチ出版のホームページから『過去問で覚える英単語スピードマスター』の表紙画像を探してクリックしていただくか、下記のURLを入力してください。

　http://www.jresearch.co.jp/isbn978-4-86392-145-0/

### ②【音声ダウンロード】というアイコンをクリック

### ③ファイルを選択し、ダウンロード開始

### ④ファイルの解凍、再生

　音声ファイルは「ZIP形式」に圧縮された形でダウンロードされます。圧縮を解凍し、デジタルオーディオ機器でご利用ください。

---
ご注意を！

音声ファイルの形式は「MP3」です。再生にはMP3ファイルを再生できる機器が必要です。ご使用の機器等に関するご質問は、使用機器のメーカーにお願い致します。また、本サービスは予告なく終了されることがあります。

---

## 赤シートの使い方
・赤シートを当てると単語の意味が消えます。
・意味を覚えたかどうか確認するのにご利用ください。

## 記号・用語について
[品詞]

- 動 動詞
- 名 名詞
- 形 形
- 副 副詞
- 派 派生語
- 類 類義語
- 反 反意語

# Chapter 1
# Nature

# UNIT 1 自然・起源

## STEP 1 過去問を解く

### 1

I told you over and over again, but you still failed to understand the ( ) of your task.

上智大学

1. nature
2. center
3. means
4. duty

### 2

Many of the animals that are ( ) to Australia, like the kangaroo and the koala, are very unusual species.

立命館大学

1. contrary
2. equivalent
3. native
4. similar

### 3

Gold and diamonds are two of South Africa's most valuable natural ( ).

南山大学

1. affairs
2. matters
3. phenomena
4. resources

### 4

Most scientists believe that the ancestors of humanity ( ) in Africa.

亜細亜大学

1. planned
2. preserved
3. originated
4. owned

## STEP 2 正解を見抜く

### 1

I told you over and over again, but you still failed to understand the nature of your task.

正解 ①

**訳** 君には何度も伝えたが、君は仕事の本質を理解していない。

- nature 名自然
- center 名中央
- means 名本質
- duty 名義務

natureには「自然」以外に「本質」という意味があります

### 2

Many of the animals that are native to Australia, like the kangaroo and the koala, are very unusual species.

正解 ③

**訳** カンガルーやコアラなどのオーストラリア特有の動物の多くが、非常に珍しい種の動物である。

- contrary 形正反対の
- native 形特有の
- equivalent 形同等の
- similar 形類似の

### 3

Gold and diamonds are two of South Africa's most valuable natural resources.

正解 ④

**訳** 金とダイアモンドは南アフリカの最も貴重な天然資源である。

- affair 名出来事
- matter 名物質
- phenomenon 名現象
- resource 名資源

### 4

Most scientists believe that the ancestors of humanity originated in Africa.

正解 ③

**訳** ほとんどの科学者が人類はアフリカに起源があると信じている。

- plan 動計画する
- preserve 動保存する
- originate 動起こる
- own 動所有する

oriの語源は「始まる」、originateは「そこから起こる、始まる」というイメージです。オーストラリアの原住民 Aborigine「アボリジニ」も同語源

Chapter1 Nature | 015

## STEP 3 連鎖式に語彙を増やす 01

● 語源 nat (生まれる)

### 0001 nature [néitʃər] 名 自然、本質

- コロ by nature（生まれつき）
- でた! Man is by nature a political animal.
（人間は生まれつき政治的な動物である） 早稲田大学

### 0002 natural [nǽtʃərəl] 形 自然の、天然の

- でた! In modern zoos, people can see animals in more natural environments.
（最近の動物園では、動物たちをより自然な環境の中でみることができる） 國学院大学

- 反 artificial [ὰːrtəfíʃəl] ア 形 人工の 原義 art（芸術）＋ fic（作る）
- コロ artificial intelligence（人工知能）※略してAI
- でた! Esperanto is what is called an artificial language.
（エスペラント語は、いわゆる人工語である） 都留文科大学

### 0003 nation [néiʃən] 名 国家

- でた! The United States is a huge nation, the fourth largest in the world.
（アメリカ合衆国は広大な国で、世界で4番目に大きい） 関西学院大学

### 0004 national [nǽʃənl] 形 国家の、国民の

- でた! They put up the flag on national holidays.
（彼らは国民の休日には旗を掲げます） 早稲田大学

- 派 nationality 名 国籍、国民性
- 派 nationalism 名 国家主義
- 派 international 形 国際的な 原義 inter（2つの間）

### 0005 native [néitiv] 形 出生地の、生まれつきの

- コロ native language（母語）＝ mother tongue コロ native speaker（母語話者）
- でた! Egyptian, European and native American dogs may share common ancestors.
（エジプト、ヨーロッパ、アメリカ先住の犬たちは共通の先祖かもしれない） 慶応義塾大学

- 類 naive [nɑːíːv] 形 単純な、純真な

- 類 innate [inéit] 形 生まれつきの、先天的な
- コロ innate intelligence（生まれながらの知性）

● 語源 ori (始まる)

### 0006 origin [ɔ́ːrədʒin, ǽr- | ɔ́r-] 名 起源、生まれ

**コロ** origin of species（種の起源）

### 0007 original [ərídʒənl]
**形** 最初の、独創的な　**名** 原物、本物

でた！ Today, only 10 percent of Madagascar's original forests remain.
（今日、マダガスカルにある原始森のわずか10パーセントしか残っていない）　[東京大学]

**反** fake [féik]　**形** 偽の　**名** 偽物

**派** originality　**名** 独創性

**派** originate　**動** 起こる、生じる、始まる

### 0008 orientation
**名** オリエンテーション、（新しい環境への）適応、方針決定

でた！ Whales have a poor sense of orientation.
（クジラは方向感覚が鈍い）　[TOEFL]

### 0009 Oriental [ɔ̀:riéntl]
**形** 東洋の　[原義] 太陽が東から始まる

**反** Occidental [àksədéntl]　**形** 西洋の　[原義] 太陽が西に落ちる

### 0010 derive [diráiv]
**動** 由来する（＋from）、（本源から）引き出す

でた！ The word science is derived from Scientia, which means knowledge in Latin.
（科学という単語は、ラテン語で知識を意味するScientiaに由来する）　[青山学院大学]

**派** derivation [dèrəvéiʃən]　**名** 由来

**派** derivative [dirívətiv]　**形** 派生的な　**名** 派生語

**類** trace [tréis]　**動** 起源・跡をたどる　**名** 跡、痕跡

でた！ The origin of the pound can be traced to ancient times.
（ポンドの語源は、古代までさかのぼることができる）　[明治大学]

### 0011 source [sɔ́:rs]
**名** 源泉、源

でた！ Time is one of the greatest sources of mystery to mankind.
（時間とは、人類における神秘の最も偉大な源の1つである）　[慶應義塾大学]

**派** resource [rí:sɔ:rs | rizɔ́:s]　**名** 資源、財源

**コロ** natural resources（天然資源）

でた！ Until recently, natural resources were relatively abundant.
（最近まで、天然資源は比較的豊富であった）　[中央大学]

**派** outsource　**動** 外部調達する

Chapter1 Nature

# UNIT 2　環境・状況　STEP 1　過去問を解く

## 1

Today people throughout the world generally support (　　　) policies.

青山学院大学

1. environment friend
2. environmental friend
3. environmentally friend
4. environmentally friendly

## 2

I would like to go (　　　) by refusing plastic bags at the supermarket.

青山学院大学

1. black
2. blue
3. green
4. orange

## 3

The government asked the car makers to sell more (　　　) friendly cars this year.

学習院大学

1. accurately
2. certainly
3. environmentally
4. technically

## 4

That extra shot of adrenaline brought on by nervousness will help you to think faster, to talk more easily, and to speak with greater emphasis, than under normal (　　　).

上智大学

1. crises
2. observations
3. circumstances
4. ways

## STEP 2 正解を見抜く

### 1

Today people throughout the world generally support environmentally friendly policies.

正解 ④

訳 今日、世界中の人たちが環境に優しい政策を一般に支持している。

**environmentally friendly** 環境に優しい

environmental friendly とも言います

### 2

I would like to go green by refusing plastic bags at the supermarket.

正解 ③

訳 スーパーではビニール袋を断ってエコを心掛けたい。

**go green** エコを心掛ける

greenは「環境」を表します。日本語の「エコ」は英語のecology（生態系）からきています

### 3

The government asked the car makers to sell more environmentally friendly cars this year.

正解 ③

訳 政府は今年、より環境に配慮した車を販売するように自動車メーカーに要請した。

**accurately** 副 正確に
**certainly** 副 確実に
**environmentally** 副 環境保護に関して
**technically** 副 技術的には

### 4

That extra shot of adrenaline brought on by nervousness will help you to think faster, to talk more easily, and to speak with greater emphasis, than under normal circumstances.

正解 ③

訳 緊急のために過剰に分泌されるアドレナリンによって、人は普通の状況下よりも思考が速くなり、話し方が流暢になりより説得力のある話ができるようになる。

**crisis** 名 危機　　**observation** 名 観察
**circumstance** 名 状況　　**way** 名 方法

under normal circumstances で「普通の状況下で」と訳します

Chapter1 Nature

## STEP 3 連鎖式に語彙を増やす 02

### 0012 environment [inváiərənmənt] ア
名 環境

でた! An important cultural difference can be found in the attitude to the environment.
（ある重要な文化的差異は、環境に対する態度の中に見いだせる事が出来る） 早稲田大学

派 **environmental** 形 環境の
コロ environmental problems （環境問題）

でた! I am concerned about the environmental effects in Cambodia specifically.
（私は、特にカンボジアの環境効果に関心がある） 東北大学

派 **environmentally** 副 環境保護に関して
コロ environmentally friendly （環境に優しい）

### 0013 circumstance [sə́:rkəmstæns | -stəns]
名 環境、状況、事情  原義 周りに立つ
コロ under these circumstances （これらの状況下で）

### 0014 surrounding [səráundiŋ]
名 環境（-s）

でた! Humans have always needed information about their surroundings.
（人間は、周囲の環境における情報を必要としてきた） 同志社大学

派 **surround** 動 取り囲む

### 0015 condition [kəndíʃən]
名 状況、条件
コロ living conditions （生活状況）

派 **conditional** 形 条件付きの

### 0016 ecology [ikálədʒi | ikɔ́l-]
名 生態系、生態学

でた! A fundamental principle of ecology is that everything is connected to everything.
（生態学の基本原則は、全てのものは繋がっているという事である） 桜美林大学

派 **ecological** 形 生態の、環境保護の
類 **ecosystem** 名 生態系

### 0017 material [mətíəriəl]
名 素材、材料、資料  形 物理的な
コロ raw materials （原料）

### 0018 substance [sʌ́bstəns]
名 物質、実質、本質

でた! Salt may seem a strange substance to use as money.
（塩をお金として使うことは、変に思えるかもしれない） 桜美林大学

派 **substantial** [səbstǽnʃəl] 形 実質的な、たくさんの

## 0019 fuel [fjúːəl] 名 燃料

- コロ fossil fuel（化石燃料）
- 類 petroleum [pətróuliəm] 名 石油
- 類 fossil [fάsəl] 名 化石　形 化石の
  - でた! He developed his own legends, based on local discoveries of dinosaur fossils.
  （地元で発見された恐竜の化石をもとに、彼は独自の伝説を展開した） 〔慶應義塾大学〕

## 0020 exhaust [igzɔ́ːst] 動 使い果たす、疲れ果てさせる

- 類 use up 使い切る
- 派 exhausted 形 疲れ果てている
- 派 exhaustion [igzɔ́ːstʃən] 名 使い果たすこと、疲労困憊

## 0021 supply 名 供給　動 供給する

- コロ supply and demand（需要と供給）

## 0022 oxygen [άksidʒən | ɔ́k-] 名 酸素

- でた! Trees give off oxygen and absorb carbon dioxide.
（木は酸素を放出し、二酸化炭素を吸収する）
- コロ carbon dioxide（二酸化炭素）

## 0023 hydrogen [háidrədʒən] 名 水素　原義 hydro（水）＋gen（生む）

## 0024 radiation [rèidiéiʃən] 名 放射線

- コロ ultraviolet radiation（紫外線）
- でた! Nuclear fuel gives off radiation.
（核燃料は、放射能を放出する）

## 0025 glacier [gléiʃər | glǽsjə] 名 氷河

- でた! Global warming is causing many glaciers to shrink in size.
（地球温暖化が原因で、多くの氷河が小さくなっている） 〔立教大学〕
- 派 glacial 形 氷河の

Chapter1 Nature　021

# UNIT 3 天気・気候

**STEP 1** 過去問を解く

## 1

Save money for a ( ) day.

1. rainy
2. snowy
3. fine
4. windy

奈良大学

## 2

The ( ) was so thick that my flight was cancelled.

1. conduct
2. estate
3. fog
4. temper

立命館大学

## 3

In a desert the ( ) is very low. Everything is dry.

1. temperature
2. pressure
3. humidity
4. wind

法政大学

## 4

The weather forecast promises a sunny morning, but there may be a ( ) or two in the afternoon.

1. rain
2. fall
3. shower
4. drop

慶應義塾大学

## STEP 2 正解を見抜く

### 1

Save money for a rainy day. 正解 ①

**訳** 万が一に備えて貯金しておきなさい。

- **rainy** 形 雨の
- **snowy** 形 雪の多い
- **fine** 形 晴天の
- **windy** 形 風の強い

「雨の日のために」＝「万が一に備えて」という表現です

### 2

The fog was so thick that my flight was cancelled. 正解 ③

**訳** 霧がとても濃かったので飛行機は欠航になった。

- **conduct** 名 行為
- **estate** 名 財産
- **fog** 名 霧
- **temper** 名 機嫌

fog「霧」はmistより濃い霧です。「濃い霧」はthick fog, dense fogと言いますが、deep fogとは言えません

### 3

In a desert the humidity is very low. Everything is dry. 正解 ③

**訳** 砂漠では湿度がとても低いです。全てが乾燥しています。

- **temperature** 名 気温
- **pressure** 名 気圧
- **humidity** 名 湿度
- **wind** 名 風

Everything is dryに注目。乾燥からhumidity「湿度」が連想できます

### 4

The weather forecast promises a sunny morning, but there may be a shower or two in the afternoon. 正解 ③

**訳** 天気予報によれば、明け方は天気が良いが、午後ににわか雨が1、2度降るかもしれないとのことである。

- **rain** 名 雨
- **shower** 名 にわか雨
- **fall** 名 秋
- **drop** 名 しずく

showerは「お風呂のシャワーを浴びる」の他に「にわか雨」という意味があります。rainには冠詞のaが付きません

## STEP 3 連鎖式に語彙を増やす 03

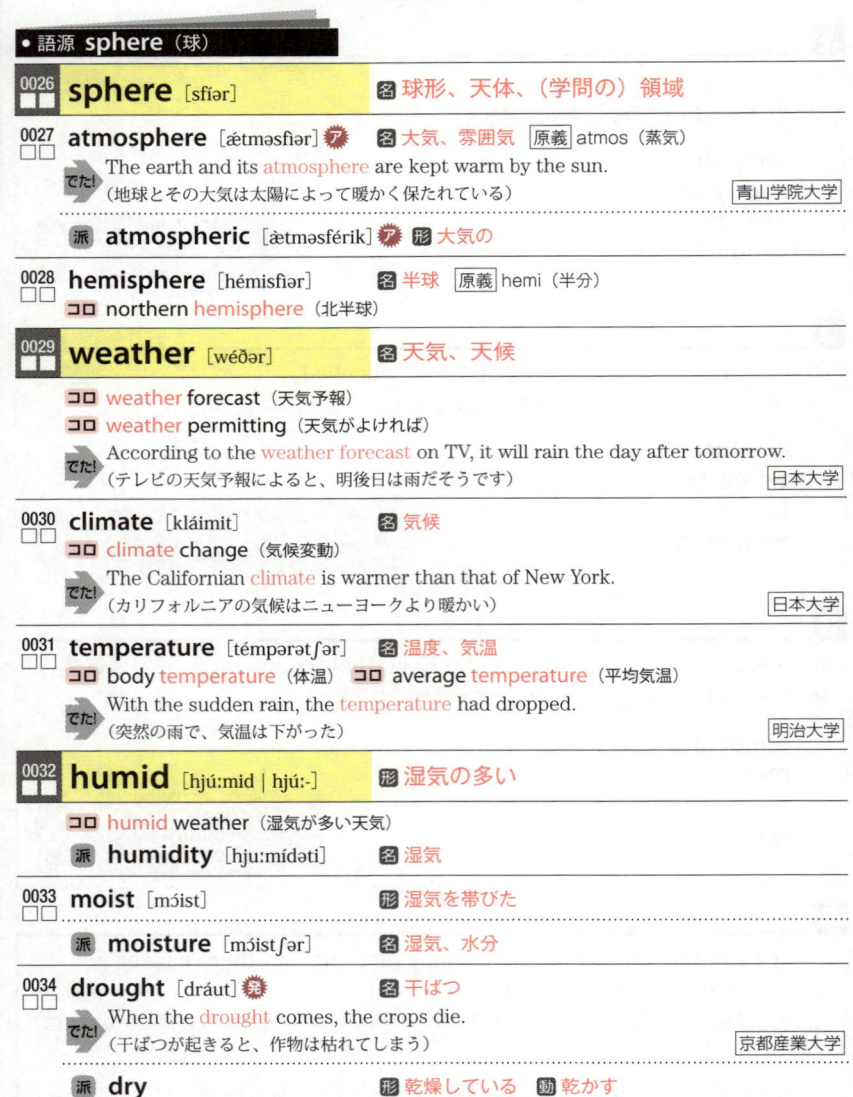

● 語源 sphere（球）

| 0026 | **sphere** [sfíər] | 名 球形、天体、（学問の）領域 |

| 0027 | **atmosphere** [ǽtməsfìər] | 名 大気、雰囲気　原義 atmos（蒸気） |

でた! The earth and its atmosphere are kept warm by the sun.
（地球とその大気は太陽によって暖かく保たれている） 〔青山学院大学〕

派 **atmospheric** [ætməsférik] 形 大気の

| 0028 | **hemisphere** [hémisfìər] | 名 半球　原義 hemi（半分） |

コロ northern hemisphere （北半球）

| 0029 | **weather** [wéðər] | 名 天気、天候 |

コロ weather forecast （天気予報）
コロ weather permitting （天気がよければ）

でた! According to the weather forecast on TV, it will rain the day after tomorrow.
（テレビの天気予報によると、明後日は雨だそうです） 〔日本大学〕

| 0030 | **climate** [kláimit] | 名 気候 |

コロ climate change （気候変動）

でた! The Californian climate is warmer than that of New York.
（カリフォルニアの気候はニューヨークより暖かい） 〔日本大学〕

| 0031 | **temperature** [témpərətʃər] | 名 温度、気温 |

コロ body temperature （体温）　コロ average temperature （平均気温）

でた! With the sudden rain, the temperature had dropped.
（突然の雨で、気温は下がった） 〔明治大学〕

| 0032 | **humid** [hjúːmid | hjúː-] | 形 湿気の多い |

コロ humid weather （湿気が多い天気）
派 **humidity** [hjuːmídəti] 名 湿気

| 0033 | **moist** [mɔ́ist] | 形 湿気を帯びた |

派 **moisture** [mɔ́istʃər] 名 湿気、水分

| 0034 | **drought** [dráut] | 名 干ばつ |

でた! When the drought comes, the crops die.
（干ばつが起きると、作物は枯れてしまう） 〔京都産業大学〕

派 **dry** 形 乾燥している　動 乾かす

## 0035 shower [ʃáuər]  　名 にわか雨

I was caught in a shower on my way home.
(家に帰る途中に、にわか雨にあった)　　青山学院大学

**類 pour** [pɔ́ːr] 発　　動 土砂降りに降る、注ぐ

It never rains but it pours.
(降ればいつも土砂降り＝二度ある事は三度ある)　　芝浦工業大学

**コロ** pour A into B（AをBに注ぐ）

She poured warm milk into the bottle.
(彼女は温かい牛乳をびんに注いだ)　　早稲田大学

**類 rainfall** [réinfɔ̀ːl]　　名 降水量

**コロ** ample rainfall（十分な降水量）

## 0036 flood [flʌ́d] 　　名 洪水　動 溢れる

Media content floods in and swirls around us, affecting the way we think and act and dream.（メディアコンテンツは我々の考え方、行動、夢に影響を与えながら、我々の周りに溢れ渦巻いている）　　同志社大学

## 0037 shade [ʃéid]　　名 日陰

If the sun is too hot, perhaps you would like to sit in the shade.
(日光が暑すぎると、きっとあなたは日陰で座っていたいと思うかもしれない)　　センター試験

**類 shadow** [ʃǽdou]　　名 影

## 0038 thunder　　名 雷

The children were afraid of the loud thunder during the bad weather.
(悪天候の間中、子供らは大きな雷に恐れていた)　　昭和女子大学

**類 lightning** [láitniŋ]　　名 稲妻

**類 thunderstorm** [θʌ́ndərstɔ̀ːrm]　名 雷雨

## 0039 fog [fɔ́ːg | fɔ́g]　　名 霧

Toward noon the fog began to disappear, and the sun broke through.
(昼ごろ、霧は晴れ始め、太陽が顔を出した)　　センター試験

**派 foggy**　　形 霧の多い、混乱した

# UNIT 4　災害・破壊

**STEP 1 過去問を解く**

## 1

( ) are not likely to be caused by seismic activity.

上智大学

1. Volcanoes
2. Typhoons
3. Tsunami
4. Earthquakes

## 2

Thunder is a natural ( ).

青山学院大学

1. emotion
2. habit
3. phenomenon
4. phantom

## 3

After Jim watched the report on the news about an earthquake, he started to think about how to prepare for a similar ( ) in his area. He bought food, water, and other supplies.

英語検定2級

1. parade
2. disaster
3. reward
4. luxury

## 4

The ( ) of the ozone layer is one of the greatest problems facing mankind.

立命館大学

1. destruction
2. discovery
3. procedure
4. purchase

## STEP 2 正解を見抜く

### 1

Typhoons are not likely to be caused by seismic activity.

正解 ②

訳 台風は、地震の活動からは引き起こされない。

- **volcano** 名 火山
- **typhoon** 名 台風
- **tsunami** 名 津波
- **earthquake** 名 地震

seismicは「地震の」という形容詞です。地震によってnot likely to be causedなものは地面と接触がないTyphoons「台風」が正解

### 2

Thunder is a natural phenomenon.

正解 ③

訳 雷は自然現象である。

- **emotion** 名 感情
- **habit** 名 習慣
- **phenomenon** 名 現象
- **phantom** 名 幻想

natural phenomenon「自然現象」、複数形はphenomena

### 3

After Jim watched the report on the news about an earthquake, he started to think about how to prepare for a similar disaster in his area. He bought food, water, and other supplies.

正解 ②

訳 ジムが地震に関しての報道を見た後、どのように自分の地域で同様の災害に備えるか考え始めた。彼は食料、水、その他の必需品を購入した。

- **parade** 名 パレード
- **reward** 名 報酬
- **disaster** 名 災害
- **luxury** 名 贅沢品

disasterの原義はdis（分離）+aster（星）「悪い星」

### 4

The destruction of the ozone layer is one of the greatest problems facing mankind.

正解 ①

訳 オゾン層破壊は、人類が直面する最大級の問題の1つです。

- **destruction** 名 破壊
- **discovery** 名 発見
- **procedure** 名 手続き
- **purchase** 名 購入

## STEP 3 連鎖式に語彙を増やす 04

**0040 disaster** [dizǽstər | -zάːs-] 名 災害、惨事 原義「悪い星」

- コロ natural disaster（天災）
- でた! The slightest mistake may lead to a fatal disaster.
  （わずかな誤りでも、致命的な惨事に繋がるかもしれない） 青山学院大学
- 派 **disastrous** [dizǽstrəs] 形 災害を引き起こす、悲惨な ※スペル注意

**0041 catastrophe** [kətǽstrəfi] 名 （突然の）大惨事、大失敗

- でた! The play was so bad that our whole evening was a catastrophe.
  （その劇はあまりにもつまらなかったので、私達の夜は散々たるものになった） 関西外国語大学
- 派 **catastrophic** [kæ̀təstrάfik] 形 大惨事の、破壊的な
- 類 **calamity** [kəlǽməti] 名 不幸、惨事、災難

**0042 phenomenon** [finάmənὰn | -nɔ́minən] 名 現象 ※複数形 phenomena

- コロ natural phenomenon（自然現象）

**0043 pollution** [pəlúːʃən] 名 汚染

- コロ air pollution（大気汚染）
- でた! We need to take steps now to reduce pollution.
  （我々は汚染を減らすための措置を今講じる必要がある） 明治大学
- 派 **pollute** 動 汚染する

**0044 contamination** [kəntæ̀mənéiʃən] 名 汚染

- 派 **contaminate** [kəntǽmənèit] 動 （不純物・放射性物質で）汚染する
  原義 con（共に）＋ tam（接触）＝触って感染する
- コロ contaminated water（汚染水）

**0045 volcano** [vɑlkéinou | vɔl-] 名 火山

**0046 earthquake** [ə́ːrθkwèik] 名 地震
- コロ earthquake of magnitude 7（マグニチュード7の地震）

● 語源 serv（奉仕する）

**0047 conservation** [kὰnsərvéiʃən | kɔ̀n-] 名 保護、保存

- 派 **conserve** [kənsə́ːrv] 動 保存する、保護する
- コロ conserve the environment（自然を保護する）

| | | | |
|---|---|---|---|
| | 派 **conservative** [kənsə́ːrvətiv] | 形 保守的な、控えめな | 名 保守的な人 |
| | 類 **protect** [prətékt] | 動 保護する、保持する | |
| | コロ protect A from ~ing (Aを〜から守る) | | |
| | 類 **protection** | 名 保護 | |
| | コロ importance of envionmental protection（環境保護の重要性） | | |
| 0048 | **preserve** [prizə́ːrv] | 動（形・性質を）保存する、保護する | |
| | コロ preserve forests（森を守る） | | |
| | でた! We must preserve our precious ecological system.<br>（我々は貴重な生態系を守らなければならない） 関西学院大学 | | |
| | 派 **preservative** | 形 保存力のある、防腐用の | 名 防腐剤 |
| | 派 **preservation** | 名 保存、保護 | |
| 0049 | **observe** [əbzə́ːrv] | 動 観察する、（法律・規則を）順守する | |
| | 派 **observation** | 名 観察 | |
| | 派 **observance** | 名 順守 | |
| 0050 | **service** [sə́ːrvis] | 名 サービス | |
| | 派 **serve** | 動 仕える、奉仕する | |
| | 派 **servant** [sə́ːrvənt] | 名 召し使い、使用人 | |
| 0051 | **reservation** [rèzərvéiʃən] | 名（ホテルや乗り物等の）予約 | |
| | 派 **reserve** | 動 予約する、保留する、取っておく | |
| | 派 **reserved** | 形 予約してある、予備の、控えめな | |
| 0052 | **deserve** [dizə́ːrv] | 動 価値がある、値する | |
| 0053 | **destroy** [distrɔ́i] | 動 破壊する　原義 de（分離）＋st（立てる） | |
| | でた! About half of all mangrove forests in the world already have been destroyed.<br>（世界全てのマングローブの森の約半分はすでに破壊されている） 九州大学 | | |
| | 派 **destruction** | 名 破壊 | |
| | 派 **destructive** | 形 破壊的な | |
| 0054 | **ruin** [rúːin] | 動 修復不可能なほどに破滅する　名 荒廃 | |
| 0055 | **collapse** [kəlǽps] | 動 崩壊する、墜落する、倒れ込む　名 崩壊 | |

UNIT 4　災害・破壊

Chapter1 Nature

# UNIT 5　耕作・農業

**STEP 1** 過去問を解く

## 1

This is wonderful (　　). Anything will grow in it.

1. soil
2. field
3. floor
4. landscape

同志社大学

## 2

When David went to college, he decided to study (　　). He wanted to learn how to help farmers.

1. agriculture
2. literature
3. animation
4. linguistics

英語検定2級

## 3

It is important for children to (　　) their mind by reading many books.

1. cultural
2. culture
3. cultivate
4. culturally

法政大学

## 4

One of the earliest (　　) in the world started around 5,000 years ago in Egypt.

1. civilizations
2. scholars
3. facilities
4. degrees

英語検定2級

## STEP 2 正解を見抜く

### 1

This is wonderful soil. Anything will grow in it.

正解 ①

**訳** これは素晴らしい土壌です。ここなら何でも育つでしょう。

- **soil** 名 土壌
- **field** 名 畑
- **floor** 名 床
- **landscape** 名 風景

### 2

When David went to college, he decided to study agriculture. He wanted to learn how to help farmers.

正解 ①

**訳** デイビッドは大学に行ったとき、彼は農業を勉強することを決めた。彼は農民をどう支援するか学びたかった。

- **agriculture** 名 農業
- **literature** 名 文学
- **animation** 名 アニメーション
- **linguistics** 名 言語学

farmer を help したいという文章から agriculture「農業」が連想できます

### 3

It is important for children to cultivate their mind by reading many books.

正解 ③

**訳** 子供は知性を育てるために多くの書物を読むことが大切である。

- **cultural** 形 教養の
- **culture** 名 文化
- **cultivate** 動 育成する
- **culturally** 副 文化的に

It is 形容詞 for 人 to 動詞の原形に当てはめても分かる問題です。cultivate the mind「知性を育てる」で覚えましょう

### 4

One of the earliest civilizations in the world started around 5,000 years ago in Egypt.

正解 ①

**訳** 世界最古の文明は5000年前にエジプトで始まった。

- **civilization** 名 文明
- **scholar** 名 学者
- **facility** 名 設備、施設
- **degree** 名 程度

## STEP 3 連鎖式に語彙を増やす 05

● 語源 cult（耕す）

### 0056 culture [kʌ́ltʃər]　名 文化、教養　原義 耕す

でた! Language is the greatest tool that makes human culture possible.
（言語は、人間の文化を可能にする最も優れた道具である） 明治学院大学

派 cultural　形 文化の
コロ cultural differences（文化の違い）

### 0057 cultivate [kʌ́ltəvèit] ア　動 耕す、育成する、(才能を)洗練する
コロ cultivate the mind（精神を磨く）

派 cultivation　名 栽培、育成

### 0058 agriculture [ǽgrikʌ̀ltʃər] ア　名 農業　原義 agri（畑）

でた! Archaeologists now think that agriculture might not have begun just by accident.
（現在考古学者は、農業は単なる偶然で始まったのではないかもしれないと考えている） 東京大学

派 agricultural　形 農業の
コロ agricultural chemical（農薬）

でた! Agricultural people had to move from place to place to plant crops.
（農耕民族は作物を植えるためにあちこちを移動しなければならなかった） TOEFL

### 0059 colony [kάləni | kɔ́l-]　名 植民、植民地

でた! Algeria is a former French colony.
（アルジェリアは旧フランス植民地である） 青山学院大学

派 colonial　形 植民地の
コロ colonial period（植民地時代）

派 colonize　動 植民地にする

でた! The Inuits colonized the polar coasts of the Arctic.
（イヌイットは北極の沿岸を植民地化した） TOEFL

### 0060 civilization [sìvəlizéiʃən | -laiz-]　名 文明

コロ Western civilization（西洋文明）

### 0061 civil [sívəl]　形 市民の、公民の、民事の
コロ civil war（市民戦争、内戦）　コロ civil servant（公務員）

### 0062 harvest [hάːrvist]　名 収穫　動 収穫する

でた! Favorable weather is crucial to a good harvest.
（好天が豊作には不可欠である） TOEFL

**0063 seed** [síːd] 名 種
- コロ plant seeds (種をまく)
- でた! The seeds which we planted are finally beginning to grow.
  (我々が植えた種がようやく育ち始めた) 〔立命館大学〕

類 **reap** [ríːp] 動 収穫する

類 **sow** [sóu] 動 まく 活 sow-sowed-sown
- でた! You must reap what you have sown.
  (自分でまいた種は自分で収穫しろ＝自業自得)

leap (飛躍する) と混同注意

**0064 fertile** [fə́ːrtl | -tail] 形 肥沃な

派 **fertilize** 動 肥沃にする

派 **fertility** 名 肥沃

**0065 fertilizer** [fə́ːrtəlàizər] 名 肥料
- コロ chemical fertilizer (化学肥料)
- でた! Fertilizers are used on crops to increase yield.
  (肥料は収穫を増やすために作物に使われる) 〔TOEFL〕

**0066 barren** [bǽrən] 形 不毛な、子供を産まない
- コロ barren lands (不毛の土地)

**0067 desert** [dézərt] [dizə́ːrt] 名 砂漠 動 見捨てる
- でた! He survived in the desert for a week on water.
  (彼は水を飲んで砂漠で一週間生き延びた) 〔一橋大学〕

dessertと混同注意

派 **deserted** 形 見捨てられた、人通りのない

**0068 grain** [gréin] 名 穀物、粒子

**0069 wheat** [hwíːt | wíːt] 名 小麦

**0070 crop** [krάp | krɔ́p] 名 農作物

**0071 soil** [sɔ́il] 名 土、土壌、土地
- コロ rich soil (肥えた土地)
- でた! The soil lost its ability to retain rainwater.
  (その土地は雨水を保つ能力を失った) 〔TOEFL〕

UNIT 5 耕作・農業

Chapter1 Nature

# UNIT 6　動物・人生　STEP 1 過去問を解く

## 1

Snakes and lizards are kinds of (　　).

早稲田大学

1. dinosaurs
2. mammals
3. plants
4. reptiles

## 2

Passenger pigeons, <u>kin</u> of the dove, were once the most numerous of all birds with a population of 5 billion.

青山学院大学

1. couple
2. king
3. offspring
4. family

## 3

Swim is to fish as run is to (　　).

上智大学

1. water
2. seaweed
3. drown
4. walk
5. hare

## 4

Christopher Columbus was an Italian (　　) birth.

中央大学

1. by
2. for
3. from
4. on

034

## STEP 2 正解を見抜く

### 1

Snakes and lizards are kinds of reptiles.　　　正解 ④

訳 ヘビやトカゲは爬虫類である。

- **dinosaur** 名 恐竜
- **mammal** 名 哺乳類
- **plant** 名 植物
- **reptile** 名 爬虫類

> mammal「哺乳類」、reptile「爬虫類」の他にもamphibian「両生類」、primate「霊長類」がよく出ます

### 2

Passenger pigeons, family of the dove, were once the most numerous of all birds with a population of 5 billion.　　　正解 ④

訳 ハトの仲間のリョコウバトは、かつて全ての鳥の中で最も数が多く50億羽も生息していた。

- **couple** 名 カップル
- **offspring** 名 子孫
- **king** 名 王様
- **family** 名 家族

### 3

Swim is to fish as run is to hare.　　　正解 ⑤

訳 魚が泳ぐように野うさぎは走る。
※ A is to B as C is to D. (AとBの関係はCとDの関係と同じ)

- **water** 名 水
- **drown** 動 溺れる
- **hare** 名 野うさぎ
- **seaweed** 名 海草
- **walk** 動 歩く

### 4

4　Christopher Columbus was an Italian by birth.　　　正解 ①

訳 クリストファー・コロンブスは生まれはイタリア人だった。

- **by birth** 生まれは

> by nature（生まれながら）という表現も重要

Chapter1 Nature

## STEP 3 連鎖式に語彙を増やす 06

**0072 birth** [bə́:rθ]　名 誕生
- by birth（生まれは）　 birth rate（出生率）
- give birth to A（Aを生み出す）
- His wife gave birth to twin boys.
（彼の妻は双子の男の子を産んだ）　〔慶應義塾大学〕

**0073 marriage** [mǽridʒ]　名 結婚
- 派 marry　動 結婚する
- be married to A（Aと結婚している）

**0074 divorce** [divɔ́:rs]　名 離婚　動 離婚する
- According to the latest survey, one in five marriages ends in divorce.
（最新の調査によると、5組に1組は離婚に終わっている）　〔東京理科大学〕

**0075 residence** [rézədəns]　名 住宅、居住
- 派 resident　名 住民
- permanent resident（永住民）
- More than a third of New York's residents are foreign-born.
（ニューヨークの住民の3分の1以上は、外国生まれだ）　〔明治大学〕
- 派 residential [rèzədénʃəl]　形 住宅の

**0076 commodity** [kəmɑ́dəti | -mɔ́d-]　名 日用品、商品(-es)
- commodity prices（物価）
- 類 utensil [ju:ténsəl]　名 台所用品

**0077 neighbor** [néibər]　名 隣人　動 接近する
- 派 neighborhood　名 近所

**0078 bath** [bǽθ | bɑ́:θ]　名 風呂
- 派 bathe [béið] 発　動 水浴びをする、入浴する

**0079 shelter** [ʃéltər]　名 避難所
- take shelter from A（Aから避難する）
- Meteorologists warned people to take shelter from the approaching hurricane.
（気象学者は、接近中のハリケーンから避難するように人々に警告した）　〔関西外国語大学〕

**0080 animal** [ǽnəməl]　名 動物

**0081 human** [hjú:mən | hjú:-]　名 人間　形 人間の
- human beings（人間性）

| | | |
|---|---|---|
| 派 humanity | 名 人類 | |
| 類 mankind [mænkáind] | 名 人類 | |

**0082 species** [spíːʃiːz]　名 (生物・植物の) 種　＊単複同形
コロ rare species (希少種)
でた! About thirty million species of animals and plants live on the earth.
(地球上には約3000万の異なる種の動植物が生きている)　〔日本大学〕

**0083 mature** [mətjúər | -tjúə]　形 成熟した、大人の

| | |
|---|---|
| 派 maturity | 名 成熟 |
| 類 grown-up | 形 成人の　名 大人 |
| 反 immature [ìmətʃúər] | 形 未熟な |

**0084 ripe** [ráip]　形 熟した
派 ripen　動 熟す
類 come of age (成人になる)
コロ a coming-of-age ceremony (成人式)
でた! His daughter came of age last year.
(彼の娘は去年成人した)　〔駒澤大学〕

**0085 ancestor** [ǽnsestər]　名 (個人としての) 祖先
原義 an (反対に) ＋cest (進む)

派 ancestry　名 (集団としての) 祖先

**0086 descendant** [diséndənt]　名 子孫
派 descend　動 降りる、下る
派 descent　名 降下
類 posterity [pɑstérəti]　名 子孫
類 offspring [ɔ́ːfspríŋ]　名 子孫

**0087 kin** [kín]　名 血縁、親族
派 kinship　名 親戚関係

# UNIT 7 行動・本能

**STEP 1 過去問を解く**

## 1

A ( ) is a up and down movement of the head used in many countries to show that you agree with or understand something.

センター試験

1. nod
2. pat
3. shake
4. wink

## 2

When the cat ( ), I could see her sharp teeth.

立命館大学

1. operated
2. peeled
3. translated
4. yawned

## 3

The scientist went to India to study how tigers ( ) when the weather is hot. He found that they often go swimming to stay cool.

英語検定2級

1. interpret
2. approve
3. behave
4. delay

## 4

Many birds that live in Canada during the spring and summer ( ) to warmer areas when the weather gets cold.

英語検定2級

1. devote
2. migrate
3. commit
4. indicate

## STEP 2 正解を見抜く

### 1

A <u>nod</u> is a up and down movement of the head used in many countries to show that you agree with or understand something.　　　正解 ①

**訳** うなずきとは、何かに同意する時、理解する時に示される多くの国で使われる頭の上下の動きである。

- **nod** 图 うなずき
- **shake** 图 振ること、握手、震え
- **pat** 图 軽くたたくこと
- **wink** 图 瞬き、ウインク

### 2

When the cat <u>yawned</u>, I could see her sharp teeth.　　　正解 ④

**訳** 猫があくびをした時、鋭い歯が見えた。

- **operate** 動 作動する、処理する、手術する
- **peel** 動 むく
- **translate** 動 翻訳する
- **yawn** 動 あくびをする

> sharp teeth「鋭い歯」を見せるという動作から「あくび」が連想できます

### 3

The scientist went to India to study how tigers <u>behave</u> when the weather is hot. He found that they often go swimming to stay cool.　　　正解 ③

**訳** 科学者は気候が暑いときに、虎がどんな行動をするかを研究しにインドに行きました。彼は、虎が涼しさを保つためにしばしば泳ぎに行くのがわかりました。

- **interpret** 動 通訳する
- **behave** 動 振る舞う
- **approve** 動 認める
- **delay** 動 遅らせる

### 4

Many birds that live in Canada during the spring and summer <u>migrate</u> to warmer areas when the weather gets cold.　　　正解 ②

**訳** カナダに住む多くの鳥は春から夏にかけて気候が寒くなるときより暖かい場所に移動する。

- **devote** 動 捧げる
- **commit** 動 犯す
- **migrate** 動 移住する
- **indicate** 動 示す

## STEP 3 連鎖式に語彙を増やす 07

### 0088 **behavior** [bihéivjər] 名 振る舞い、行儀、行動

でた! Only certain dogs can learn the right behavior.
(ある特定の犬のみが、正しい行動を学習できる) 早稲田大学

派 **behave** [bihéiv] 動 振る舞う
コロ behave oneself (行儀よくする)

### 0089 attitude [ǽtitjùːd | -tjùːd] 名 態度

でた! World conditions are constantly changing, and attitudes must change with them.
(世界の状況は絶えず変化している。そして態度もそれとともに変化しなければならない)

### 0090 **instinct** [ínstiŋkt] 名 本能、直感

コロ by instinct (本能的に)　コロ maternal instinct (母性本能)

派 **instinctive** [instíŋktiv] 形 本能的な
でた! Fear is instinctive and requires no conscious thought.
(恐怖とは本能的なものであり、意識的な思考を必要としない) 慶應義塾大学

### 0091 nod [nάd | nɔ́d] 動 うなずく、居眠りする 名 うなずき、居眠り
コロ nod one's head (同意する)

### 0092 yawn [jɔ́ːn] 動 あくびをする
でた! We are likely to yawn when we see other people do so.
(我々は、他の人があくびをするのを見ると、自分もあくびをする傾向がある) 慶應義塾大学

### 0093 sweat [swét] 動 汗をかく 名 汗
でた! Unlike humans, dogs and cats can't sweat to cool themselves.
(人間と違って犬や猫は体温を下げるための汗をかけない) 同志社大学

### 0094 tear [tíər] 名 涙、裂け目
[tɛ́ər] 動 引き裂く 活 tear-tore-torn
コロ burst into tears (突然泣き出す)
でた! As soon as she heard the news, she busrt into tears.
(その知らせを聞くと、彼女はすぐに泣き始めた) 早稲田大学

### 0095 laugh [lǽf | lάːf] 動 笑う (+ at)
コロ burst into laughing (突然笑い出す)

派 **laughter** [lǽftər | lάːf-] 名 笑い

### 0096 embrace [imbréis] 動 抱きしめる、受け入れる
でた! It is acceptable in some countries for men to embrace each other and for women to hold hands.
(男性同士が互いに抱き合ったり、また女性同士が手を握り合うことが容認される国がある)

| 類 **hug** [hʌ́g] | 動 抱きしめる |

0097 **scream** [skríːm] 動 (恐怖や危険に恐れて) 叫ぶ、悲鳴をあげる
でた! A grown-up should know better than to scream.
(大人は金切り声をあげないくらいの分別を持つべきだ)　　関西学院大学

| 類 **yell** [jél] | 動 大声で叫ぶ (+at) |
| 類 **roar** [rɔ́ːr] | 動 うなる |

• 語源 **migr** (移る)

0098 **migrate** [máigreit]　動 移住する、(鳥・魚などが)移動する、渡る

派 **migration**　名 移住
でた! The Asian migration hypothesis is today supported by most of the scientific evidence. (アジアの移民仮説は今日、多くの科学的根拠によって支持されている)　TOEFL

派 **migrant**　形 出稼ぎの　名 移住民
でた! Some migrants are highly skilled workers such as professors or bankers.
(教授や銀行家のようなとても才能がある労働者もいる)　北海道大学

0099 **immigrate** [íməgrèit]　動 外国から移住する

派 **immigrant**　名 外国からの移民、移住者
でた! Upon arrival, immigrants are called aliens by law.
(到着するとすぐに、移民は法律によって外国人と呼ばれる)　慶應義塾大学

派 **immigration**　名 移住、入国、入植
でた! Immigration happens nowadays as well.
(移住は今でも起きている)　同志社大学

0100 **emigrate** [émigrèit]　動 外国へ移住する
でた! Germanic tribes emigrated to England.
(ゲルマン民族がイギリスに移住した)　TOEFL

派 **emigrant**　名 外国への移民

派 **emigration**　名 外国への移住、出稼ぎ

Chapter1 Nature | 041

# UNIT 8 感情・性格

**STEP 1** 過去問を解く

## 1

When Tim was told to leave, he was so (    ) that he kicked the chair and left.

立命館大学

1. calm
2. content
3. furious
4. peaceful

## 2

She is so (    ) that she cried for days when her rabbit died.

センター試験

1. impressed
2. impressive
3. sensible
4. sensitive

## 3

The national (    ) is, at least in part, a product of the culture.

同志社大学

1. individuality
2. character
3. person
4. personality

## 4

It was very (    ) of him to reject the bride.

名古屋外国語大学

1. sensitive
2. sensible
3. sense
4. sensibly

## STEP 2 正解を見抜く

### 1

When Tim was told to leave, he was so furious that he kicked the chair and left.

正解 ③

**訳** ティムが出て行けと言われたとき、彼はひどく立腹し、いすを蹴って出て行った。

- calm 形 穏やかな
- content 形 満足して
- furious 形 ひどく立腹した
- peaceful 形 平和な

### 2

She is so sensitive that she cried for days when her rabbit died.

正解 ④

**訳** 彼女はとても傷つきやすいのでウサギが死んでから数日間泣き続けた。

- impressed 形 感動して
- impressive 形 印象的な
- sensible 形 分別のある
- sensitive 形 敏感な、傷つきやすい

> sensitiveは「他人の感情や問題を理解できるほど敏感な」という意味と、「他人の言うことに影響されやすい」という意味があります

### 3

The national character is, at least in part, a product of the culture.

正解 ②

**訳** 国民性とは少なくとも部分的には文化の産物である。

- individuality 名 個性
- character 名 性格
- person 名 人
- personality 名 性格

### 4

It was very sensible of him to reject the bride.

正解 ②

**訳** 彼がその賄賂を拒否したのは非常に賢明なことだった。

- sensitive 形 敏感な
- sensible 形 分別のある、賢明な
- sense 名 感覚
- sensibly 副 分別よく

## STEP 3 連鎖式に語彙を増やす 08

● 語源 sent, sens（感じる）

### 0101 sense [séns]　图 感覚、センス、意味　動 感じる、感知する

- in a sense（ある意味では）
- sense of direction（方向感覚）
- common sense（一般常識）
- Of the five senses, the most important to nearly all animals is smell.
（五感のうち、ほとんど全ての動物にとって最も重要なのは臭覚である） センター試験
- make sense（意味をなす）
- His letter was so confusing that I could hardly make any sense of it at all.
（彼の手紙はとても混乱していたので、私はほとんど全く意味を理解する事が出来なかった） 慶應義塾大学

派 **nonsense**　图 ナンセンス、ばかげた考え

### 0102 sensitive [sénsətiv]　形 敏感な、傷つきやすい（+ to）

A leader must be sensitive to the needs of other people.
（指導者は他の人の要求に敏感でなければならない） 法政大学

派 **sensitivity**　图 感受性

### 0103 sensible [sénsəbl]　形 分別のある、賢明な

It was sensible of her to have decided not to join the plot.
（その陰謀に加わらないと決めた彼女は賢明である） 桜美林大学

派 **sensibility**　图 感受性

### 0104 sentiment [séntəmənt]　图 感情、情緒

派 **sentimental**　形 感情的な

feelingより堅く、外的な刺激に対する感覚。

### 0105 sensation [senséiʃən]　图 感覚、大評判

派 **sensational**　形 衝撃的な、扇情的な

### 0106 consensus [kənsénsəs]　图 意見の一致、世論

- reach a consensus（合意に達する）
- Decisions in Japanese companies tend to be made by group consensus.
（日本の企業における決定は、集団の総意によってなされる傾向にある） 玉川大学

派 **consent** [kənsént]　動 同意する　原義 con（共に）
※agreeよりも重大なことに対して使う。

I took it for granted that he would consent.
（彼が承諾するのは当然のことだと思った） 横浜市立大学

044

## 0107 **emotion** [imóuʃən]

名 感情　原義 e（外に）＋mot（動く）

派 **emotional**　形 感情的な

でた！ The study of psychology begins with distinguishing different kinds of emotional states.（心理学の研究は、様々な感情の状態を識別することから始まる）　九州大学

## 0108 **sympathy** [símpəθi]

名 同情、共感　原義 sym（同じ）＋pathy（感情）

コロ have sympathy for A（Aに同情する）

派 **sympathize**　動 同情する

派 **sympathetic**　形 同情的な、思いやりのある

でた！ I was scolding her, but I was sympathetic, too.
（私は彼女を叱っていたが、同情もしていた）　センター試験

反 **antipathy** [æntípəθi]　名 反感　原義 anti（反対）＋pathy（感情）

## 0109 **anger** [ǽŋgər]

名 怒り

派 **angry**　形 怒っている

でた！ I am angry with him for his neglect.（私は、彼が無視した事に怒っている）　東京学芸大学

## 0110 **rage** [réidʒ]

名 怒り　動 激怒する、荒れ狂う

コロ raging storm（大嵐）

でた！ His amazement turned to shock and rage when he heard the news.
（彼がその知らせを聞いたとき、彼の驚きはショックと憤りに変わった）　早稲田大学

派 **outrage**　名 憤慨、不法行為　動 憤慨させる

派 **outrageous**　形 非道な、無法な、風変わりな

## 0111 **fury** [fjúri]

名 怒り、激怒、猛威

派 **furious**　形 怒っている

でた！ Tom slammed the door with all his strength because he was furious.
（彼は激怒していたのでドアを力強く閉めた）　青山学院大学

## 0112 **temper** [témpər]

名 機嫌、気性

コロ short temper（短気）　コロ keep one's temper（怒りを抑える）
コロ lose one's temper（腹を立てる）

でた！ Mary loses her temper easily.
（メアリーは簡単に腹を立てる）　京都大学

派 **temperament** [témpərəmənt]　名 気性

# UNIT 9 会社・仲間

**STEP 1 過去問を解く**

## 1

Our trip to Kyoto was just great. Among other things, I enjoyed your (　　).

上智大学

1. company
2. friend
3. partner
4. togetherness

## 2

That man standing by the door is one of my <u>colleagues</u>.

東海大学

1. enemies
2. fans
3. co-workers
4. critics

## 3

May I <u>come along with</u> you?

中央大学

1. accompany
2. get
3. help
4. leave
5. take

## 4

My brother's wife is away for the week, so I thought I'd go over and <u>keep him company</u>.

日本大学

1. be with him
2. find him a job
3. make him work overtime
4. surprise him

046

## STEP 2 正解を見抜く

UNIT 9 会社・仲間

### 1

Our trip to Kyoto was just great. Among other things, I enjoyed your company.　　正解 ①

訳 京都への旅は実に素晴らしかったです。とりわけ、ご一緒できて楽しかったです。

- **company** 名 同伴、会社
- **friend** 名 友達
- **partner** 名 パートナー
- **togetherness** 名 一体感

### 2

That man standing by the door is one of my co-workers.　　正解 ③

訳 ドアのそばに立っている男性は、私の仕事仲間のひとりです。

- **enemy** 名 敵
- **fan** 名 ファン
- **co-worker** 名 同僚
- **critic** 名 批評家

> colleagueは「同じ立場の同僚」、co-workerは「同じ職場の同僚」

### 3

May I accompany you?　　正解 ①

訳 あなたに同行しても良いですか。

- **accompany** 動 同行する、付き添う
- **get** 動 得る
- **help** 動 助ける
- **leave** 動 去る
- **take** 動 取る

> companyの原義は「共にパンを食べる」です。accompanyのacは「方向」を表す接頭語なので、パンを食べる仲間についていくイメージ

### 4

My brother's wife is away for the week, so I thought I'd go over and be with him.　　正解 ①

訳 私の兄の奥さんは一週間不在なので私は彼のところに行って兄と一緒にいようと思った。

- **be with him** 彼と一緒にいる
- **find him a job** 彼に仕事を見つける
- **make him work overtime** 彼を残業させる
- **surprise him** 彼を驚かす

Chapter1 Nature

## STEP 3 連鎖式に語彙を増やす 09

**0113 company** [kÁmpəni] 名 仲間、会社、同行　原義 com（共に）＋pan（パン）

**0114 accompany** [əkÁmpəni] 動 同行する、伴う
- コロ be accompanied by A（Aが伴う）
- でた！ Environmental protection is accompanied by some inconvenience.
（環境保護はある程度の不便を伴う）　法政大学

派 **accompaniment** 名 同行、伴うもの

**0115 companion** [kəmpǽnjən] 名 仲間、連れ、付き添い
派 **companionship** 名 友達付き合い
- コロ get along with A（Aと仲良くする）
- でた！ I am afraid that they don't get along very well.
（残念ながら彼らは仲が良くないと思います）　慶應義塾大学
- コロ make friends with A（Aと友達になる）
- でた！ A party is a good place to make friends with other people.
（パーティーは、他の人と友達になるのに良い場所である）　関西学院大学

**0116 term** [tə́:rm] 名 間柄、専門用語、期間、条件（-es）
- でた！ The term "play" has many meanings.
（「play」という単語には多くの意味がある）　同志社大学
- コロ in terms of A（Aの観点からすると）
- コロ be on good terms with A（Aと仲が良い）
- でた！ Jack is on very good terms with our children.
（ジャックは、私たちの子供ととても仲が良い）　関西学院大学

派 **terminal** 形 末期の、終点の

派 **terminate** 動 終わらせる

派 **terminology** [tə̀:rmənálədʒi] 名 専門用語

**0117 colleague** [káli:g | kɔ́l-] 名 同僚
- でた！ He could not get along well with his colleagues.
（彼は、同僚とうまくやっていけなかった）　中央大学

類 **co-worker** [kóu-wə́:rkər] 名 同僚

類 **peer** [píər] 名 仲間、同輩　動 じっと見る、凝視する

類 **crew** [krú:] 名 乗組員

**0118 acquaintance** [əkwéintəns] ⚡ 名 知人、面識
- でた！ He made the acquaintance of a young lady.
（彼は若い女性と知り合った）　防衛大学

048

| 派 | acquaint | 動 知らせる |

コロ be acquainted with A（Aの知識がある、Aを知っている）

でた! He got acquainted with a young lady.
（彼は若い女性と知り合った） 〔防衛大学〕

## 0119 store [stɔ́:r]
動 貯める、蓄える　名 店、蓄え

派 stock [stάk | stɔ́k] 　名 株、在庫
コロ out of stock（在庫切れ）

## 0120 restore [ristɔ́:r]
動 回復させる、修復する、復興する、復旧する

派 restoration [rèstəréiʃən]　名 回復、修復
コロ Meiji restoration（明治維新）

● 語源 firm（固い）

## 0121 firm [fə́:rm]
名 会社　形 固い

## 0122 confirm [kənfə́:rm]
動 確認する

でた! The postal clerk confirmed my identity before handing me the express letter.
（郵便局員は、私に速達の手紙を手渡す前に私の身分を確認した） 〔立命館大学〕

派 confirmation 　名 確認
コロ confirmation button（確認ボタン）

## 0123 affirm [əfə́:rm]
動 断言する

派 affirmative 　形 肯定的な

反 negative 　形 否定的な

派 affirmation 　名 断言

類 assert [əsə́:rt]　動 断言する

派 assertive 　形 断定的な

UNIT 9　会社・仲間

Chapter1 Nature　049

# UNIT 10　依存・独立

**STEP 1** 過去問を解く

## 1

He totally depends (　　) his parent.

青山学院大学

1. in
2. on
3. at
4. against

## 2

When she was in trouble, she had no choice but to (　　) her family for help.

上智大学

1. reach out
2. depend of
3. turn to
4. run into

## 3

After he started to live (　　), Kevin realized just how much his mother used to look after him.

英語検定2級

1. repeatedly
2. possibly
3. independently
4. restlessly

## 4

I have always found her to be an efficient and <u>reliable</u> assistant.

桜美林大学

1. lazy
2. capable
3. dependable
4. cooperative

## STEP 2 正解を見抜く

### 1

He totally depends on his parent.

正解 ②

**訳** 彼は完全に親に依存している。

**depend on** 依存する

> dependの語源はde（下に）+ pend（ぶら下がる）＝誰かにぶら下がって依存する

### 2

When she was in trouble, she had no choice but to turn to her family for help.

正解 ③

**訳** 彼女は困ったとき、家族に助けを求めるしかなかった。

**turn to** 依存する

### 3

After he started to live independently, Kevin realized just how much his mother used to look after him.

正解 ③

**訳** 彼が独立して生活し始めた後、ケビンはどれだけ彼の母親が彼を世話していたか気づいた。

**repeatedly** 副 繰り返して
**independently** 副 独立して
**possibly** 副 ひょっとして
**restlessly** 副 落ち着きがなく

### 4

I have always found her to be an efficient and dependable assistant.

正解 ③

**訳** 私はいつも、彼女が有能で信頼できる助手だと思っていた。

**lazy** 形 怠惰な
**capable** 形 有能な
**dependable** 形 信頼できる
**cooperative** 形 協力的な

UNIT 10 依存・独立

Chapter1 Nature

## STEP 3 連鎖式に語彙を増やす 🎧10

### ● 語源 pend (ぶら下がる)

**0124 pendant** [péndənt] 　　名 ペンダント

**0125 pendulum** [péndʒuləm | -dju-] 　名 振り子

**0126 depend** [dipénd]
動 依存する、次第である (+ on)
原義 de (下に) + pend (ぶら下がる)

> でた! Asian farmers depend on the rain that comes with monsoons.
> (アジアの農民は、モンスーンに伴う雨に依存している) 〔慶應義塾大学〕

> でた! It depends on the circumstances whether they go on strike.
> (彼らがストライキをするかどうかは、状況次第だ) 〔中央大学〕

**0127 dependent** [dipéndənt] 　形 依存している (+ on)

　派 **dependence** 　　　名 依存

　派 **dependable** 　　　形 信頼できる

　反 **independent** [ìndipéndənt] 形 独立している (+ of)
　コロ Independent nation (独立国家)
> でた! All men are by nature equally free and independent.
> (すべての人間は、生まれながらにして等しく自由で、独立である)

　派 **independently** 　　副 独立して

　派 **independence** 　　名 独立
　コロ Independence Day (独立記念日)

pendは、
ぶら下がっている感じ

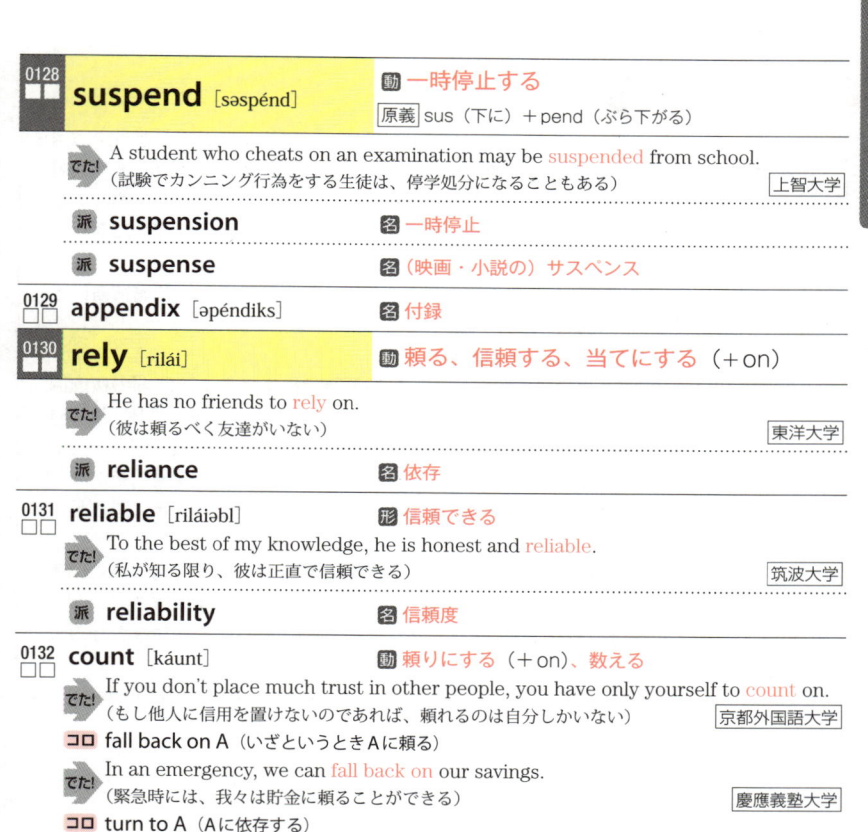

## 0128 suspend [səspénd]

動 一時停止する
原義 sus（下に）＋pend（ぶら下がる）

でた! A student who cheats on an examination may be suspended from school.
（試験でカンニング行為をする生徒は、停学処分になることもある）
上智大学

派 suspension　　名 一時停止

派 suspense　　名 （映画・小説の）サスペンス

## 0129 appendix [əpéndiks]　　名 付録

## 0130 rely [rilái]

動 頼る、信頼する、当てにする（＋on）

でた! He has no friends to rely on.
（彼は頼るべく友達がいない）
東洋大学

派 reliance　　名 依存

## 0131 reliable [riláiəbl]　　形 信頼できる

でた! To the best of my knowledge, he is honest and reliable.
（私が知る限り、彼は正直で信頼できる）
筑波大学

派 reliability　　名 信頼度

## 0132 count [káunt]

動 頼りにする（＋on）、数える

でた! If you don't place much trust in other people, you have only yourself to count on.
（もし他人に信用を置けないのであれば、頼れるのは自分しかいない）
京都外国語大学

コロ fall back on A （いざというときAに頼る）

でた! In an emergency, we can fall back on our savings.
（緊急時には、我々は貯金に頼ることができる）
慶應義塾大学

コロ turn to A （Aに依存する）

でた! In my anguish, I turned to my father for help.
（苦痛のあまり、私は援助を求めて父に頼った）
上智大学

コロ up to A （A次第）

### coffee break ☕ 適切な学習法

　英語を勉強する上で一番大切なことは学習方略（strategy）です。どういう目標を立てて、どうやって取り組んでいくかを計画することが大切であり、それを続けることが成功への道です。言語習得ほど忍耐（patience）を要する学問はありません。難しい学問ではありませんが継続すること（continue）が非常に難しい学問です。

　つまり言語習得には時間がかかります。大学受験生にとっても、言語習得者にとっても時間の使い方が大切です。

　ここでは時間の概念を一変するお話をします。

　まず1日は24時間と限られています。私が高校時代に考えていた時間の概念は8＋8＋8＝24時間というものです。24時間を大切な3つ（食事、睡眠、勉強）で割ります。時間の概念を変えて行動の切り替えを上手くすれば勉強時間は十分に確保できます。8時間で食事などの日課（routine）を行い、8時間睡眠をとっても、8時間勉強時間が残ります。有効に時間を活用すれば1日を有意義に過ごせます。

　受験勉強や言語習得は自分との戦いです。携帯電話で無駄な時間を過ごしていませんか？現実逃避（procrastination）していませんか？良い大学にはもっと楽しい生活が待っています。学習方略（strategy）をしっかり立てて成功をつかみ取ってください！

# Chapter 2
# Education

# UNIT 11 教育・育成

## STEP 1 過去問を解く

### 1

He was born and brought (　　) in New York.

青山学院大学

1. to
2. in
3. up
4. over

### 2

Peter was (　　) by his uncle.

駒澤大学

1. educated
2. cultivated
3. raised
4. trained

### 3

It is important to (　　) good relationships with your colleagues.

立命館大学

1. alert
2. foster
3. lick
4. terrify

### 4

Some experts say that parents today (　　) their children by giving them anything they want.

英語検定2級

1. trade
2. encounter
3. conduct
4. spoil

## STEP 2 正解を見抜く

### 1

He was born and brought up in New York.

正解 ③

訳 彼はニューヨークで生まれ育った。

**bring up** 育てる

> bring upは「育てる」という熟語。受動態の形でwas brought「育てられた」=「育った」と意訳できます

### 2

Peter was raised by his uncle.

正解 ③

訳 ピーターは彼の叔父に育てられた。

**educate** 動 教育する
**cultivate** 動 耕作する
**raise** 動 育てる
**train** 動 訓練する

### 3

It is important to foster good relationships with your colleagues.

正解 ②

訳 あなたの同僚との良い関係を築くのは、重要なことです。

**alert** 動 警報を出す
**foster** 動 育成する
**lick** 動 なめる
**terrify** 動 怖がらせる

### 4

Some experts say that parents today spoil their children by giving them anything they want.

正解 ④

訳 最近の親は子供に欲しいものを何でも与えて甘やかしている、と言う専門家もいる。

**trade** 動 貿易する
**encounter** 動 遭遇する
**conduct** 動 行う
**spoil** 動 甘やかす

Chapter2 Education | 057

## STEP 3 連鎖式に語彙を増やす

### 0133 education [èdʒukéiʃən]
名 教育　原義 e（外に）＋duc（導く）

でた! Education involves both learning and teaching.
（教育は、学ぶことと教えることの両方を含む）　滋賀大学

派 educate [édʒukèit] ア　動 教育する

派 educational　形 教育的な
コロ reform the Japanese educational system（日本の教育制度を改革する）

### 0134 form [fɔ́ːrm]
動 形成する、構成する

でた! Most of the world's existing lakes were formed by glacier action.
（世界に現存する湖の大半は、氷河活動によって形成された）　東京理科大学

派 formal　形 公式的な

でた! Walt had little formal education but loved to draw.
（ウォルトは正式な教育をあまり受けていなかったが、絵を描くのが好きだった）　慶應義塾大学

派 informal　形 非公式的な、形式ばらない　原義 in（否定）

### 0135 formula [fɔ́ːrmjulə]
名 公式

派 formulate　動 公式化する

派 formulation　名 公式化

### 0136 discipline [dísəplin] ア
名 しつけ、訓練、規律
動 訓練する、しつける　原義「教える」

コロ strict discipline（厳しい規律）

でた! All parents face the problems of freedom and discipline.
（全ての両親は、放任と規律の問題に直面する）　慶應義塾大学

### 0137 doctrine [dáktrin | dɔ́k-]
名 教義、主義　原義 doc（教える）

類 dogma [dɔ́ːgmə]　名 教義

### 0138 docile [dásəl | dóusail]
形 教えやすい　原義 doc（教える）

### 0139 grow [gróu]
動 成長する、上がる（＋up）、増える
活 grow-grew-grown

派 growth　名 成長

### 0140 raise [réiz]
動 育てる、上げる、増やす

## 0141 rear [ríər]
動 （成人になるまで）育てる 名 後部 形 後方の
コロ bring up（育てる）
でた! Because his parents had died when he was young, his uncle brought him up.
（幼いころに両親が亡くなったので、彼の叔父が彼を育てた） センター試験

## 0142 foster [fɔ́ːstər | fɔ́s-]
動 （才能等を）育成する、養育する、助長する
コロ foster parents（里親）
でた! The industrial revolution fostered the rise of the middle class.
（産業革命は中流階級の繁栄を助長した） TOEFL

## 0143 nurture [nə́ːrtʃər]
動 育む、大事に育てる 名 養育、教育

> nature or nurture（生まれか育ちか）
> natureはinhevited abilities（生まれつきの能力）、
> nurtureはacquired abilities（習得した能力）を表します。

## 0144 spoil [spɔ́il]
動 だめにする、甘やかす
派 spoilage 名 損傷
でた! Food packaging also reduces spoilage.
（食品の包装によって、食品の腐敗も減少する） 大阪外国語大学

## 0145 indulgence [indʌ́ldʒəns]
名 甘やかすこと
でた! The Japanese are given to indulgence in their relations.
（日本人は、人間関係において甘える癖がある） 上智大学

派 indulgent 形 甘い、寛大な

---

UNIT 11 教育・育成

> 育成のイメージは、educate the mind of a child（一般的な教育のイメージ）、cultivate a skill（教育するというより洗練するイメージ）、raise a large family（成長を手助けするイメージ）、train a tiger（鍛錬するイメージ）

Chapter2 Education

# UNIT 12 能力・才能

**STEP 1 過去問を解く**

## 1

She is always able to answer the teacher's questions. She is such a ( ) girl.

センター試験

1. dependent
2. lazy
3. shy
4. smart

## 2

The new city hall has a seating ( ) of 5,000.

青山学院大学

1. ability
2. admission
3. reception
4. capacity

## 3

The chimpanzee is an intelligent creature, ( ) of solving simple problems.

センター試験

1. able
2. enable
3. capable
4. possible

## 4

Mr. Wright told Sue that she should study harder for her math exams. He said that she has the ( ) to do well but she needs to spend more time preparing.

英語検定2級

1. objection
2. potential
3. variety
4. audience

## STEP 2 正解を見抜く

### 1

She is always able to answer the teacher's questions. She is such a smart girl.

正解 ④

**訳** 彼女はいつも先生の質問に答えることができる。彼女はそんな頭のいい女の子である。

- **dependent** 形 依存している
- **shy** 形 恥ずかしい
- **lazy** 形 怠惰な
- **smart** 形 賢い

### 2

The new city hall has a seating capacity of 5,000.

正解 ④

**訳** 新しい市民ホールは5000人を収容するだけの席がある。

- **ability** 名 才能
- **admission** 名 入場料
- **reception** 名 受付
- **capacity** 名 収容能力

### 3

The chimpanzee is an intelligent creature, capable of solving simple problems.

正解 ③

**訳** チンパンジーは知的な動物で、簡単な問題を解くことができる。

- **able** 形 できる(+to)
- **enable** 動 可能にする
- **capable** 形 できる(+of)
- **possible** 形 可能な

### 4

Mr. Wright told Sue that she should study harder for her math exams. He said that she has the potential to do well but she needs to spend more time preparing.

正解 ②

**訳** ライトさんは、彼女が数学の試験のために、より一生懸命勉強すべきであるとスーに言いました。彼は、彼女には順調である可能性があると言っていましたが、彼女はより多くの時間を費やす必要があります。

- **objection** 名 反対
- **variety** 名 多様性《発音注意》
- **potential** 名 可能性
- **audience** 名 聴衆

UNIT 12 能力・才能

Chapter2 Education

## STEP 3 連鎖式に語彙を増やす 12

● 語源 able（可能）

### 0146 ability [əbíləti]
名 能力、手腕

でた！ I really feel that the ability to communicate in English is important.
（英語でのコミュニケーション能力は大切であると非常に実感しています） 同志社大学

派 **able** 形 できる

反 **unable** [ʌnéibl] 形 できない

でた！ As they grow old, many people become unable to look after themselves.
（多くの人は歳をとるにつれて、自分自身の世話が出来なくなる） センター試験

### 0147 enable [inéibl]
動 可能にする

コロ enable A to B （AがBすることを可能にする）

でた！ A college education will enable you to get a broader view of the world.
（大学教育は世界についてのより広い視野を得ることを可能にする） センター試験

### 0148 disable [diséibl]
動 不可能にする

コロ disabled people （身体障害者）

派 **disability** [dìsəbíləti] 名 障害

### 0149 possible [pásəbl | pɔ́s-]
形 可能な

でた！ Is it possible for you to come to the office an hour earlier than usual tomorrow?
（明日あなたがいつもより1時間早くオフィスに来ることは可能でしょうか） センター試験

反 **impossible** 形 不可能な

派 **possibility** 名 可能性
コロ rule out the possibilities （可能性を排除する）

### 0150 probable [prábəbl | prɔ́b-]
形 起こりそうな

コロ it is probable that S V （たぶんSVであろう）

派 **probability** 名 確率、見込み

派 **probably** [prábəbli] 副 おそらく

### 0151 capacity [kəpǽsəti]
名 能力、才能

派 **capable** [kéipəbl] 形 出来る、可能な、能力がある
コロ be capable of A （Aが出来る）

でた！ The face is capable of around 7,000 different expressions.
（顔は、約7,000もの異なる表情を見せることができる） 中央大学

派 **capability** [kèipəbíləti] 名 能力、性能

062

## 0152 accommodate [əkάmədèit | əkɔ́m-] 動 収容する、適応させる
- 派 **accommodation** 名 収容、適応
- コロ accommodation available（宿泊可能）

## 0153 potential [pəténʃəl] 名 可能性、潜在能力　形 潜在的な

## 0154 skill [skíl] 名 技能、能力
- コロ skilled worker（熟練した働き手）= skillful worker

## 0155 talent [tǽlənt] 名 才能
- 派 **talented** 形 才能がある
- コロ exceptionally talented（際立って才能のある）
- 類 **gifted** [gíftid] 形 才能のある

## 0156 faculty [fǽkəlti] 名（ある分野の）才能、（身体の）機能、（大学の）学部
- コロ faculty of education（教育学部）
- 派 **facility** [fəsíləti] 名 才能、施設(-es)、容易さ、便利さ
- 派 **facilitate** 動 容易にする、促進する

## 0157 intelligent [intélədʒənt] 形（本来生まれ持った）知識・知性が高い
- 派 **intelligence** 名 知能、知性

## 0158 intellect [íntəlèkt] ア 名 知性
- 派 **intellectual** [ìntəléktʃuəl] 形 知的な
- コロ intellectual property rights（知的財産権）

## 0159 smart [smάːrt] 形（理解力が早く知識を吸収する）要領が良い

## 0160 clever [klévər] 形（頭の回転さ、機敏さ、器用さがあり）賢い、ずる賢い

## 0161 wise [wáiz] 形（長年培ってきた知識や経験の豊富さがあり）賢い
- 派 **wisdom** [wízdəm] 名 知恵
- コロ wisdom teeth（親知らず）

UNIT 12　能力・才能

Chapter2 Education

# UNIT 13　教科・専攻　STEP 1 過去問を解く

## 1

I am so interested in (　　) that I studied a number of past events.

駒澤大学

1. science
2. history
3. mathematics
4. physics

## 2

My uncle specializes (　　) Ancient Greek History.

関東学院大学

1. of
2. on
3. in
4. with

## 3

I tried to change the (　　), but they went on talking about politics.

南山大学

1. subject
2. object
3. project
4. reject

## 4

Emily (　　) to six law schools and was accepted at four of them.

中央大学

1. dwelled
2. criticized
3. involved
4. applied
5. harmed

## STEP 2 正解を見抜く

### 1

I am so interested in history that I studied a number of past events.

正解 ②

**訳** 私は歴史に大変興味があるので、過去の多くの出来事を研究しました。

- **science** 名科学
- **history** 名歴史
- **mathematics** 名数学
- **physics** 名物理学

> a number of past events「過去の多くの出来事」からhistory「歴史」が連想できます

### 2

My uncle specializes in Ancient Greek History.

正解 ③

**訳** 私の叔父は古代ギリシャの歴史を専攻しています。

- **specialize in** 専攻する

> specialize inはイギリス英語で、アメリカ英語ではmajor inを使います

### 3

I tried to change the subject, but they went on talking about politics.

正解 ①

**訳** 私は話題を変えようとしたが、彼らは政治について話し続けた。

- **subject** 名話題
- **object** 名目的
- **project** 名計画、企画
- **reject** 動拒絶する

> subjectは重要多義語です。STEP3で確認しましょう

### 4

Emily applied to six law schools and was accepted at four of them.

正解 ④

**訳** エミリーは6つの法律学校に申し込みそれらのうちの4つに合格した。

- **dwell** 動住む
- **involve** 動巻き込む
- **harm** 動害する
- **criticize** 動批判する
- **apply** 動申し込む

UNIT 13　教科・専攻

Chapter2 Education

## STEP 3 連鎖式に語彙を増やす 🎧13

### 0162 subject [sʌ́bdʒikt] 　名 学科、話題、主題　動 従属させる

- でた! She is changing the subject of the professor's talk.
（彼女は教授の話の話題を変えている） 〔TOEFL〕
- でた! After 1976, education became the subject of fierce argument.
（1976年以降、教育が激しい議論の主題となった） 〔上智大学〕
- コロ be subject to A（Aを受けやすい）
- でた! All prices are subject to change.
（全ての価格は変更される事があります） 〔青山学院大学〕
- でた! Man as well as the other creatures is subject to the laws of nature.
（他の生き物だけでなく、人間も自然の法則に従わなければならない） 〔東京理科大学〕

- 派 **subjective**　形 主観的な

### 0163 major [méidʒər]　動 専攻する（+in）《米》　形 主要な

- でた! If they admit me to the university, I think I will major in economics.
（もし大学に入学出来たら、経済学を専攻しようと思っています） 〔首都大学東京〕
- でた! Pollution of the oceans by humans has become a major problem.
（人間による海の汚染が大きな問題になっている） 〔獨協大学〕

- 派 **majority** [mədʒɔ́:rəti]　名 大多数、大部分
- でた! The vast majority of modern Native Americans have type O blood.
（現代のネイティブアメリカ人の大多数はO型の血液型である） 〔TOEFL〕

### 0164 specialize [spéʃəlàiz]　動 専攻する（+in）《英》

- でた! Mr. Kimura specialized in commerce when he was in university.
（木村さんは大学時代、商業を専攻していた） 〔中央大学〕

- 派 **specialist**　名 専門家、スペシャリスト
- 派 **specialty** [spéʃəlti]　名 専門、名産、特産品

### 0165 enter [éntər]　動 入る

- コロ get in A（Aに入る）
- 派 **entrance**　名 入学、入り口
- コロ entrance ceremony（入学式）
- 類 **enroll** [inróul]　動 入学する、名前を登録する
- 派 **enrollment** [inróulmənt]　名 入学、登録

### 0166 graduate [grǽdʒuèit] [grǽdʒuət] 動 卒業する（＋from） 名 大学院、卒業生

でた！ I want to get a job with an international organization after I graduate from university.（大学を出たら、私は国際機関に就職したい） 法政大学

派 **undergraduate** 名 学部生

派 **postgraduate** 名 大学院生

派 **graduation** 名 卒業
コロ graduation ceremony（卒業式）

類 **commencement** [kəménsmənt] 名 卒業、開始

freshman（1年生）
sophomore（2年生）
junior（3年生）
senior（4年生）

### 0167 senior [síːnjər] 形 上級の、先輩の

派 **seniority** [siːnjɔ́ːrəti] 名 年功序列

### 0168 junior [dʒúːnjər] 形 年少の、後輩の

### 0169 apply [əplái] 動 適応する、当てはまる（＋to）、申し込む（＋for）

コロ apply A to B（A（理論）をBに応用する）

でた！ When are you going to apply for the job?
（いつその仕事に申し込むつもりですか） 中央大学

でた！ Applicants are requested to apply in person.
（応募者は本人自身が直接申し込むようになっている） 慶應義塾大学

派 **application** 名 申し込み、アプリケーション
コロ fill out the application form（申込書に記入する）

派 **applicant** [ǽplikənt] 名 申込者、志願者

UNIT 13 教科・専攻

---

学問に関する単語一覧

| math 数学 | English 英語 | art 芸術、美術 | science 科学 | social studies 社会科 |
|---|---|---|---|---|
| history 歴史 | physics 物理学 | psychology 心理学 | philosophy 哲学 | biology 生物学 |
| botany 植物学 | geography 地理 | anthropology 人類学 | archeology 考古学 | chemistry 化学 |
| linguistics 言語学 | statistics 統計学、統計 | economic 経済学 | astronomy 天文学 | neuroscience 脳科学 |

Chapter2 Education

# UNIT 14 成績・進歩

**STEP 1** 過去問を解く

## 1

Your attendance will ( ) your final grade.

拓殖大学

1. defect
2. perfect
3. effect
4. affect

## 2

Professor Kim ( ) his students by both their attendance and their coursework in addition to the final exam.

明治大学

1. trains
2. marks
3. grades
4. educates

## 3

At first, Tommy wasn't very good at tennis. However, his skills ( ) improved until he became the best player at our school.

英語検定2級

1. gradually
2. currently
3. eagerly
4. slightly

## 4

They are making good ( ) with the highway construction.

青山学院大学

1. pay
2. progress
3. jump
4. play

## STEP 2 正解を見抜く

### 1

Your attendance will affect your final grade.　正解 ④

訳 あなたの出席は、あなたの最終的な成績評価に影響するでしょう。

- defect 名 欠点
- perfect 形 完全な
- effect 名 効果
- affect 動 影響する

> affectは「直接的に影響する」、effect「間接的な影響」で動詞としてはあまり使いません

### 2

Professor Kim grades his students by both their attendance and their coursework in addition to the final exam.　正解 ③

訳 キム教授は彼の生徒を、最終テストに加え出席とコースワークで成績を付ける。

- train 動 訓練する
- mark 動 印をつける
- grade 動 成績付けする
- educate 動 教育する

### 3

At first, Tommy wasn't very good at tennis. However, his skills gradually improved until he became the best player at our school.　正解 ①

訳 最初はトミーはテニスがそれほど上手ではありませんでした。しかしながら彼の技能は徐々に向上し、彼がわが校の最高の選手になりました。

- gradually 副 徐々に
- eagerly 副 熱心に
- currently 副 現在では
- slightly 副 わずかに

### 4

They are making good progress with the highway construction.　正解 ②

訳 彼らは高速道路建設を順調に進展させている。

- pay 動 支払う
- progress 名 進歩
- jump 名 ジャンプ
- play 名 劇

> progressの語源はpro（前に）+gress（進む）=進歩。make progressで「進歩する」

UNIT 14 成績・進歩

Chapter2 Education

**STEP 3 連鎖式に語彙を増やす** 🎧14

● 語源 grad gres (進む)

### 0170 grade [gréid]  名 成績  動 成績をつける

でた！ The test will influence the final grade.
（テストは最終成績に影響するだろう） [TOEFL]

### 0171 upgrade [ápgréid]  動 改良する  名 グレードアップ

反 **downgrade** [dáungréid]  動 格下げする

反 **degrade** [digréid]  動 身分・品格を下げる

### 0172 gradually [grǽdʒuəli]  副 徐々に

でた！ The Japanese economy has been recovering gradually.
（日本経済は徐々に回復している） [明海大学]

派 **gradual**  形 徐々の
でた！ A gradual modification of life-style can make a dramatic difference.
（生活様式を徐々に変える事で劇的な差を生む可能性がある） [法政大学]

コロ **by degrees**（徐々に）
でた！ The sound faded away by degrees.
（音は徐々に消えていった） [埼玉大学]

コロ **little by little**（徐々に）

### 0173 degree [digríː]  名 程度、温度、学位

でた！ Without a greenhouse effect, the earth would be about 60 degrees colder on average.
（もし温室効果がなければ、地球は平均して60度くらい今より寒いだろう） [早稲田大学]

### 0174 progress [prágres | próu-]  名 進歩、前進  動 進歩する

でた！ Most of the teachers at that university care about their students' progress.
（その大学のほとんどの先生が、学生の進歩について気にかけている） [早稲田大学]

コロ **make progress**（進歩する）
でた！ He worked very hard, but could make little progress.
（彼は一生懸命働いたが、ほとんど進歩しなかった） [東京大学]

コロ **in progress**（進行中で）

派 **progressive**  形 進歩的な、革新的な

### 0175 aggressive [əgrésiv]  形 攻撃的な

派 **aggression**  名 攻撃、侵略

## 0176 digress [digrés] 動 脱線する、(わき道へ)それる

でた! He is not very organized and he digresses a lot in the lecture.
(彼は几帳面ではないので、講義の間、よくわきへそれる) [TOEFL]

派 digression 名 脱線、逸脱

## 0177 advance [ædvæns | ədvá:ns] 名 前進 動 進む

コロ in advance (前もって、事前に)

でた! Information technology has advanced rapidly over the last ten years.
(情報技術は、この十年で急速に進歩した) [亜細亜大学]

### advantage [ædvæntidʒ | ədvá:n-] 名 利点、長所

コロ take advantage of A (Aを利用する)

でた! He took advantage of the good weather to do some gardening.
(彼は好天を利用して庭いじりをした) [学習院大学]

類 merit 名 長所、利点

## 0178 disadvantage [dìsədvæntidʒ | -vá:n-] 名 不利、短所

でた! She argued advantages and disadvantages.
(彼女は利点と不利点を議論した) [TOEFL]

類 demerit 名 短所、欠点

## 0179 accelerate [æksélərèit, ək-] ア 動 加速させる、促進する

派 acceleration 名 加速、促進

## 0180 evolution [èvəlú:ʃən | ì:v-] 名 進化

コロ Darwin's theory of evolution (ダーウィンの進化論)

でた! Mass extinctions were important to evolution.
(大量絶滅は進化には重要であった) [TOEFL]

派 evolve 動 進化する、徐々に進展する

派 evolutionary 形 進化の

でた! Feathers are among the most unusual evolutionary changes.
(羽は最も珍しい進化的変化の一つである) [TOEFL]

UNIT 14 成績・進歩

Chapter2 Education

# UNIT 15 音楽・作曲

**STEP 1** 過去問を解く

## 1

A : I love this piece of music. It's very dramatic.
B : I'm not sure who (　　) it, but I think he was German.

英語検定2級

1. composed
2. determined
3. managed
4. constructed

## 2

A violin is an instrument (　　) of a broad range of notes.

中央大学

1. accessible
2. accountable
3. capable
4. changeable
5. permissible

## 3

This piano is out of (　　). It has to be fixed immediately.

南山大学

1. tone
2. tune
3. sound
4. condition

## 4

Will you please (　　) down the stereo? It's too loud.

学習院大学

1. make
2. go
3. switch
4. turn

## STEP 2 正解を見抜く

### 1

A: I love this piece of music. It's very dramatic.
B: I'm not sure who composed it, but I think he was German.

正解 ①

**訳** A：私はこの音楽がとても好きです。それは非常に印象的です。
B：私は、それをだれが作曲したかがよくわかりませんが、ドイツ人だったと思います。

- **compose** 動 作曲する
- **manage** 動 管理する
- **construct** 動 組み立てる
- **determine** 動 決定する

composeの語源はcom（共に）＋pose（置く）＝音符を置いて楽譜を作るイメージ

### 2

A violin is an instrument capable of a broad range of notes.

正解 ③

**訳** バイオリンは、広い音域の音を奏でることができる楽器です。

- **accessible** 形 近づきやすい
- **accountable** 形 説明する義務のある
- **capable** 形 有能な、才能のある
- **changeable** 形 変わりやすい
- **permissible** 形 許される

### 3

This piano is out of tune. It has to be fixed immediately.

正解 ②

**訳** このピアノは音程が狂っています。すぐに調律してもらわなくてはなりません。

- **out of tune** 調子が狂って

### 4

Will you please turn down the stereo? It's too loud.

正解 ④

**訳** ステレオの音を下げてくれませんか。音が大きすぎます。

- **turn down** ボリュームを下げる

Chapter2 Education

## STEP 3 連鎖式に語彙を増やす

### 0181 music [mjúːzik]
**名** 音楽  語源 muse「凝視する」

本来音楽は「聞くもの」ではなく「見るもの」でした。iPodやaudio playerの影響で「見る」という概念が薄れ、音楽は「聞くもの」であるという概念に変わっていきました。

派 **musical**　**形** 音楽の　**名** ミュージカル

でた! The biwa is a musical instrument that was used in Japan as early as the eight century. (「琵琶」というのは、早くも8世紀に日本で使われた楽器である)　センター試験

### 0182 museum [mjuːzíːəm]
**名** 美術館、博物館

でた! The idea of galleries and museums that anyone can visit is quite a modern one. (誰でも行くことが出来る画廊や美術館という発想は、極めて現代的なものである)　センター試験

### 0183 amusement [əmjúːzmənt]
**名** 娯楽

派 **amuse**　**動** 楽しませる

派 **amusing**　**形** 楽しい、愉快な

でた! His amusing comment made everyone laugh. (彼の愉快なコメントは、みんなを笑わせた)　TOEFL

### 0184 compose [kəmpóuz]
**動** 作曲する　原義 com（共に）+ pose（置く）

でた! Wolfgang Amadeus Mozart was born in 1757, composed some of the world's greatest pieces of classical music, and died young in 1791. (ヴォルフガング・アマデウス・モーツァルトは1757年に生まれ世界で最も有名なクラシック音楽をいくつか作曲し、1791年に若くして亡くなった)　立教大学

派 **composition**　**名** 作曲、作文

コロ English composition（英作文）

でた! She compared different types of musical composition. (彼女は違ったタイプの音楽作品を比較した)　TOEFL

派 **composer**　**名** 作曲家

### 0185 instrument [ínstrəmənt]
**名** 楽器、器具

コロ musical instrument（楽器）

でた! Learning to play an instrument can help children improve math, science, and language skills. (楽器の演奏を学ぶことは、子供が数学、理科、言語の能力を発達させる手助けとなる)　立教大学

## 0186 rhythm [ríðm]　名 リズム
でた! Gradually, you will develop your own sense of rhythm.
（少しずつ自分なりのリズムのセンスが生まれるようになる）　東京大学

## 0187 tone [tóun]　名 音調、トーン
コロ tone of voice（声のトーン）

## 0188 tune [tjúːn]　名 旋律、調子
でた! A slight alternation is made in the tune.
（旋律における僅かな変化がなされる）　TOEFL

## 0189 volume [vάljum]　名 音量、1巻
コロ turn down the volume of the radio（ラジオの音を小さくする）

# UNIT 16 知識・思考　STEP 1 過去問を解く

## 1

Don't tell me that you didn't know it was illegal. (　　) of the law is no excuse.

英語検定準1級

1. Awareness
2. Avoidance
3. Tolerance
4. Ignorance

## 2

I hadn't seen her for more than 20 years, but I still (　　) her right away.

慶応義塾大学

1. realized
2. recognized
3. resembled
4. resented

## 3

The bus driver was (　　) enough to let me know when we reached the place where I wanted to get off.

英語検定2級

1. separate
2. considerate
3. continuous
4. suspicious

## 4

Mari has made (　　) improvement in English since I last talked to her.

獨協大学

1. artificial
2. imitation
3. permanent
4. considerable

## STEP 2 正解を見抜く

### 1

Don't tell me that you didn't know it was illegal. Ignorance of the law is no excuse.

正解 ④

訳 違法だと知らなかったなんて言うな。法律を知らないことは言い訳にならない。

- awareness 名 気づき
- avoidance 名 回避
- tolerance 名 忍耐
- ignorance 名 無知

### 2

I hadn't seen her for more than 20 years, but I still recognized her right away.

正解 ②

訳 彼女に20年以上会っていなかったが、まだすぐに彼女を認識した。

- realize 動 悟る
- recognize 動 認識する
- resemble 動 似ている
- resent 動 憤慨する

### 3

The bus driver was considerate enough to let me know when we reached the place where I wanted to get off.

正解 ②

訳 そのバスの運転手は、私が降りたい場所にいつ着いたのかを知らせてくれるほど親切でした。

- separate 形 分かれた
- continuous 形 連続的な
- considerate 形 思いやりのある
- suspicious 形 疑い深い

### 4

Mari has made considerable improvement in English since I last talked to her.

正解 ④

訳 マリは私が最後に彼女と話したとき以来、英語がかなり向上しています。

- artificial 形 人工の
- imitation 名 模倣
- permanent 形 永久的な
- considerable 形 相当の

UNIT 16 知識・思考

Chapter2 Education

## STEP 3 連鎖式に語彙を増やす (16)

● 語源 kn, gn（知る）

### 0190 knowledge
[nɑ́lidʒ | nɔ́l-] 発
名 知識

コロ gain knowledge（知識を得る）

でた! Only by using knowledge of the past and present we can solve the problems.
（過去と現在の知識を使うことによってのみ、私達は問題を解決することが出来る） 早稲田大学

### 0191 acknowledge [æknɑ́lidʒ, ək- | -nɔ́l-] 発 動 認める

派 acknowledgement　　名 承認

### 0192 ignore [ignɔ́:r]
動 無視する、知らないふりをする
原義 i（否定）+ gn（知る）

でた! I think it is wrong to ignore the patient's wishes.
（患者の希望を無視するのは、間違っていると思う） 東洋大学

派 ignorance　　名 無知

### 0193 recognize [rékəgnàiz]
動 認識する
原義 re（再び）+ co（共に）+ gn（知る）+ ize（動詞化語尾）

派 recognition　　名 認識

### 0194 cognition [kɑgníʃən | kɔg-]　　名 認知

派 cognitive　　形 認知の

### 0195 identify [aidéntəfài]　　動 分かる、確認する、見極める

でた! He has difficulty identifying what is important information.
（彼は、何が重要な情報なのか見極めるのに苦労した） TOEFL

派 identity　　名 身元、アイデンティティ

派 identical　　形 同一の、一卵性の
コロ identical twins（一卵性双生児）

派 identification　　名 身元確認

### 0196 inform [infɔ́:rm]　　動 知らせる（+ of）

コロ inform A of B（AにBを知らせる）

でた! To be informed is to know simply that something is a fact.
（知識があるということは、ある事が事実であることを知っているに過ぎないのである） 成城大学

派 information　　名 情報
コロ information technology（IT=技術革新）　　コロ exchange information（情報交換する）

- 語源 ast sider (星)

## 0197 consider [kənsídər]
**動** よく考える、みなす
**原義** con (共に) + sider (星)

She considers herself to be a good writer.
(彼女は自分自身が良い作家であると考えている)
TOEFL

## 0198 consideration
**名** 熟考
**コロ** take A into consideration (Aを考慮する)
You must take all these facts into consideration.
(これらの事実を全て考慮しなければなりません)
慶應義塾大学

## 0199 considerable [kənsídərəbl]
**形** 相当の、ずいぶん多くの
**コロ** considerable amount of money (多額のお金)
Every morning, he spends considerable time reading all the pages of three newspapers.
(毎朝、彼は3つの新聞全てのページを読むのにかなりの時間を費やす)

> 語源が「星」なので数が多いことを連想できます。

中央大学

### 派 considerably
**副** かなり、ずいぶん
Since 1987, the popularity of different types of packaged soft drinks in Japan has changed considerably. (1987年以降、日本ではパッケージされた清涼飲料のタイプの人気が大きく変わっている)
センター試験

## 0200 considerate [kənsídərət]
**形** 思いやりのある (+ to, of)
I've always understood one should try and be considerate of others. (私はいつも人は他人に対して思いやりを持つように心がけるべきだと理解している)
立命館大学

### 類 kind
**形** 親切な **名** 種類

### 類 sort [sɔ́ːrt]
**名** 種類 **動** 分類する

## 0201 asterisk [ǽstərìsk]
**名** 星形

## 0202 astronomy [əstrάnəmi | -trɔ́n-]
**名** 天文学

## 0203 astronaut [ǽstrənɔ̀ːt]
**名** 宇宙飛行士

## 0204 constellation [kὰnstəléiʃən | kɔ̀n-]
**名** 星座

## 0205 sidereal [saidíəriəl]
**形** 星の

### 類 planet [plǽnit]
**名** 惑星

UNIT 16 知識・思考

Chapter2 Education

# UNIT 17　理解・習得　STEP 1 過去問を解く

## 1

I got a letter from Pierre, but it was so badly written that I couldn't (　　) out what it said.

英語検定2級

1. get
2. make
3. take
4. go

## 2

(　　) a foreign language is no problem for some people, but it's a challenging task for others.

獨協大学

1. Gripping
2. Mentioning
3. Mastering
4. Occupying

## 3

Appropriate praise helps a child (　　) an appropriate sense of pride.

立命館大学

1. acquire
2. assign
3. delegate
4. digest

## 4

Upon leaving his ships, Christopher Columbus soon (　　) that his voyage across the Atlantic Ocean had not taken him to Asia.

慶應義塾大学

1. returned
2. reached
3. remembered
4. realized

## STEP 2 正解を見抜く

### 1

I got a letter from Pierre, but it was so badly written that I couldn't make out what it said.

正解 ②

訳 ピエールから手紙をもらったが、字が汚くて何と書いてあるか理解できなかった。

**make out** 理解する

### 2

Mastering a foreign language is no problem for some people, but it's a challenging task for others.

正解 ③

訳 外国語を習得するのは、ある人達には問題のないことですが、他の人達にとっては難しいがやりがいのある仕事です。

**grip** 動 しっかりつかむ
**master** 動 習得する
**mention** 動 言及する
**occupy** 動 占領する

### 3

Appropriate praise helps a child acquire an appropriate sense of pride.

正解 ①

訳 適切な褒め言葉は、子供が自尊心を習得する手助けとなります。

**acquire** 動 習得する
**assign** 動 割り当てる
**delegate** 動 委任する
**digest** 動 要約する

> acquireの語源はac（方向）+ quire（求める）＝向かって求める＝獲得する、習得する

### 4

Upon leaving his ships, Christopher Columbus soon realized that his voyage across the Atlantic Ocean had not taken him to Asia.

正解 ④

訳 船を降りるとクリストファー・コロンブスは、大西洋を横断してきたこの航海の末、アジアに辿り着いたわけではなかったとすぐに悟った。

**return** 動 戻る
**remember** 動 覚えている
**reach** 動 到着する
**realize** 動 悟る

UNIT 17 理解・習得

Chapter2 Education

## STEP 3 連鎖式に語彙を増やす 17

### 0206 understand [ʌ́ndərstǽnd]
動 理解する

- make oneself understood（分からせる）
  - My English is not very good, but I was able to make myself understood when I was in America.（私の英語はそれほど良くはありませんが、アメリカにいたとき私は自分のことを理解させることができました） 早稲田大学
- figure out（理解する）
  - I can't figure out why you don't like jazz.（なぜあなたがジャズを嫌いなのか理解できない） 関西大学
- make out（理解する）
  - I could not make out what he was saying.（彼が言っている事が私には理解できなかった） 日本大学
- take in A（Aを理解する、取り入れる、欺く）
  - I couldn't take in the lecture at all.（その講義が全く理解できなかった） 慶應義塾大学

### 0207 comprehend [kàmprihénd | kɔ̀m-] ⑦
動 理解する、包む

She is trying to comprehend a difficult question.（彼女は難問を理解しようとしている） TOEFL

派 **comprehensive** 形 包括的な、理解力のある

The research is a comprehensive study of North American mammal species.（その研究は、北アメリカの哺乳類に関する包括的な調査である） 同志社大学

派 **comprehensible** 形 理解できる

派 **comprehension** 名 理解力

### 0208 master [mǽstər | mάːs-]
動 習得する 名 マスター、主人、修士

- masters degree（修士号） ※doctorate degree（博士号）
  - We master the ability to express and read emotion very early in life.（我々は生まれて間もなく、感情を表現したり、読み取ったりする能力を身につける） 明治学院大学

### 0209 acquire [əkwáiər]
動 習得する

Most of us acquire a second language only with conscious effort.（私たちのほとんどは、意識的な努力だけで第二言語を習得する） 亜細亜大学

派 **acquisition** 名 習得
- second language acquisition（第二言語習得）

## 0210 learn [lə́:rn] 動 学ぶ

派 learning 名 学習
コロ brush up A (A (忘れかけた外国語・知識など) を磨き直す)
でた! You'd better brush up your English before you go to Los Angeles this summer.
(この夏ロサンゼルスに行く前に、英語力を磨き直しておいた方がいいですよ) 上智大学
コロ pick up A (Aを身につける)
でた! She picked up French just by living in Paris for a year.
(一年間パリで生活しただけで、彼女はフランス語を身につけた) 学習院大学

## 0211 grasp [grǽsp | grɑ́:sp] 動 理解する、つかむ 名 理解、把握、つかむこと

## 0212 taste [téist] 名 好み、味 動 味見する

でた! My wife has strange taste in furniture.
(私の妻には変わった家具の趣味がある) 慶應義塾大学

派 tasty 形 味が良い  tastyの方が上品。

類 delicious [dilíʃəs] 形 おいしい

## 0213 realize [rí:əlàiz | ríəl-] 動 悟る、実現する
原義 real (現実) + ize (動詞化語尾) = 現実化する

コロ realize a dream (夢を実現する)
でた! I didn't realize she was such an expert.
(彼女がそのような専門家だと気づかなかった) 上智大学
コロ come true (願いが叶う、実現する)
でた! The desire he has had for years has come true.
(彼の何年もの願いが叶った) 慶應義塾大学

派 realization 名 理解、実現

派 reality 名 現実
でた! Mary's dream of going to abroad finally became a reality.
(外国に行くというメアリーの夢はついに現実となった) 南山大学

## 0214 grant [grǽnt | grɑ́:nt] 動 認める、与える
コロ take A for granted (Aを当然のことと思う)
コロ take it for granted that S V (SVを当然と思う)
でた! I took it for granted that he had received the letter.
(私は、彼がその手紙を受け取ったのは当然だと思った) 上智大学

UNIT 17 理解・習得

# UNIT 18 記憶・意識　STEP 1 過去問を解く

## 1

A: Do you remember your first date?
B: Yes, I (　　) remember it.

北海学園大学

1. virtually
2. vividly
3. visually
4. variously

## 2

I know the face, but I can't (　　) his name.

日本大学

1. tell
2. show
3. recall
4. notice

## 3

Please (　　) me to ring up the client after lunch.

中央大学

1. remember
2. remind
3. regain
4. recognize
5. refer

## 4

I'm sorry, but that doesn't really (　　).

青山学院大学

1. ring my bell
2. ring a bell
3. ring the bell
4. ring one bell

## STEP 2 正解を見抜く

### 1

A: Do you remember your first date?
B: Yes, I vividly remember it.

正解 ②

**訳** A：最初のデートを覚えているかい。
B：ええ、鮮明に覚えているわ。

- **virtually** 副 実質的には
- **visually** 副 視覚的に
- **vividly** 副 鮮明に
- **variously** 副 多様に

### 2

I know the face, but I can't recall his name.

正解 ③

**訳** その顔は知っているけど、名前が思い出せない。

- **tell** 動 伝える
- **show** 動 見せる
- **recall** 動 思い出す
- **notice** 動 気づく

### 3

Please remind me to ring up the client after lunch.

正解 ②

**訳** 昼食が終わったら、私に依頼人に電話をかけることを思い出させてください。

- **remember** 動 覚えている
- **remind** 動 思い出させる
- **regain** 動 取り戻す
- **recognize** 動 認識する
- **refer** 動 参照する

### 4

I'm sorry, but that doesn't really ring a bell.

正解 ②

**訳** すみませんが、本当にそれには聞き覚えがありません。

- **ring a bell** 思い出させる

> ring the bellの場合はbellを指す特定のtheがあるので「ベルを鳴らす」となります

UNIT 18 記憶・意識

Chapter2 Education

## STEP 3 連鎖式に語彙を増やす 18

### 0215 remind [rimáind] 動 思い出させる
- remind A of B (AにBを思い出させる)
- This picture always reminds me of those happy days.
  (この写真を見るたびに、その楽しかったころを思い出す) 横浜市立大学
- 派 **reminder** 名 思い出させるもの、記念の品
- ring a bell (思い出させる、以前に聞いたことがある)

### 0216 memory [méməri] 名 記憶、思い出
- Memory begins to get weaker around 30 years old.
  (記憶力は30歳頃に衰え始める) 上智大学
- 派 **memorize** [méməràiz] 動 暗記する
- learn A by heart (Aを暗記する)
- As a child, I learned lots of poems by heart.
  (幼少期、私はたくさんの詩を暗記した) 立命館大学
- 派 **memorial** 形 記念の

### 0217 recall [rikɔ́ːl] 動 (意識的に努力して)思い出す
- recall clearly (明確に思い出す)
- Most people cannot recall anything that happened before the age of two.
  (2歳以前に起きたことは、ほとんどの人が思い出せない) 早稲田大学

### 0218 conscious [kɑ́nʃəs] 形 意識がある (+of)
- 反 **unconscious** [ʌnkɑ́nʃəs] 形 無意識の
- After the car hit the boy, he remained unconscious for two days.
  (少年は車にひかれた後、2日間意識不明のままであった) センター試験
- 派 **consciously** 副 無意識に
- 派 **consciousness** 名 意識
- recover consciousness (意識を取り戻す)
- come to (意識を取り戻す)
- She fainted but came to after a few minutes.
  (彼女は意識を失ったが、数分後意識を取り戻した) 慶應義塾大学

### 0219 aware [əwéər] 形 気づいている (+of)
- She is now aware that her original idea had a weakness.
  (彼女は最初の考えは弱点があったと今気づいている) TOEFL
- 派 **awareness** 名 気づいていること

- 語源 viv（生きる）

**0220 survive** [sərváiv] 　動 生き残る

でた！ Human beings have survived so far but could now be risking their future.
（人類は今までのところ生き延びていたが、今その未来を危険にさらしているかもしれない）

センター試験

派 **survival** 　名 生き残ること、サバイバル

**0221 revive** [riváiv] 　動 生き返らせる　原義 re（再び）＋viv（生きる）

派 **revival** 　名 復活

**0222 vivid** [vívid] 　形 鮮やかな、鮮明な、生き生きとした

コロ vivid color（鮮やかな色）

派 **vividly** 　副 鮮明に、はっきりと

でた！ I remember vividly the last time I cried.
（最後に泣いたときのことを鮮明に覚えている）

摂南大学

UNIT 18　記憶・意識

## coffee break 　エビングハウスの忘却曲線

　皆さんは英単語が覚えられないと葛藤にかられた経験はないですか？覚えたとしても使えない。使えたとしても伝わらない。私もそんな経験をしたうちの一人でした。ここでは「記憶」についてお話しします。

　100年以上前にドイツの心理学者ヘルマン・エビングハウスが記憶の忘却に関する研究を行いました。

　この研究で分かったのは「人間は学習した物を翌日には74％忘れる」ということです。１週間後には77％、１ヶ月後には79％忘れるのが人間なのです。つまり覚えようとするのではなく、忘れないようにすることが大切です。

　最初の３日間が一番忘れやすい！つまり３日間、同じ事を繰り返します。３日間連続して学習すると忘却の曲線がなだらかになります。次は３週間後、そして３ヶ月後！これで３年記憶を維持できます。３という数字が付く言葉は人間に深い意味があるのです。継続できない人に対して使う三日坊主、辛抱すれば３年後には報われる石の上にも三年など、「３」という数字は人間の根底に深く根付いているのかもしれません。英単語をたくさん知っている人はただ単に頭が良いのではなく、忘れないようにしているだけなのです。

Chapter2 Education

# UNIT 19 集中・強調  STEP 1 過去問を解く

## 1

She is good at (　　) on what she is doing even in a noisy room.

立命館大学

1. breathing
2. concentrating
3. depending
4. matching

## 2

He was (　　) in a book and didn't seem to hear me.

獨協大学

1. absorbed
2. considered
3. estimated
4. obtained

## 3

My boss (　　) the importance of finishing the report over the weekend, since he wanted to discuss it at the meeting on Monday morning.

英語検定2級

1. embarrassed
2. emphasized
3. employed
4. encouraged

## 4

This <u>passion</u> for pets is raising interest in the humane treatment of all animals.

同志社大学

1. search
2. enthusiasm
3. suffering
4. frustration

## STEP 2 正解を見抜く

### 1

She is good at concentrating on what she is doing even in a noisy room.

正解 ②

訳 彼女は、騒がしい部屋の中でも、自分がやっていることに集中することが得意である。

- breathe 動 息をする
- concentrate 動 集中する
- depend 動 依存する
- match 動 合わせる

### 2

He was absorbed in a book and didn't seem to hear me.

正解 ①

訳 彼は本に夢中であり、私の話を聞いているようには思えませんでした。

- absorb 動 熱中させる
- consider 動 よく考える
- estimate 動 見積もる
- obtain 動 得る

### 3

My boss emphasized the importance of finishing the report over the weekend, since he wanted to discuss it at the meeting on Monday morning.

正解 ②

訳 私の上司は月曜日の朝ミーティングでレポートについて議論したがっていたので、彼は週末の間にレポートを終える重要性を強調しました。

- embarrass 動 恥をかかせる
- employ 動 雇う
- emphasize 動 強調する
- encourage 動 励ます

### 4

This enthusiasm for pets is raising interest in the humane treatment of all animals.

正解 ②

訳 ペットに対する熱意のおかげで動物全てに対する人道的な扱いについての関心が高まっている。

- search 名 追求
- suffering 名 苦悩
- enthusiasm 名 熱中
- frustration 名 欲求不満

UNIT 19 集中・強調

Chapter2 Education

## STEP 3 連鎖式に語彙を増やす 19

### 0223 center [séntər]
名 中心、中央、注目の的　動 集中させる

コロ center of the universe（宇宙の中心）

でた! On the afternoon of 10 October 1964, the world's attention was centered on a young athlete in the Olympic stadium in Tokyo.
（1964年の10月10日の午後、世界中の注目が東京オリンピック競技場にいる一人の若い陸上選手に集まっていた）
上智大学

### 0224 concentrate [kánsəntrèit | kɔ́n-]
動 集中する（＋on）

でた! I cannot concentrate on reading while people around me are talking.
（私の周りの人が話している時に、私は読書に集中できません）
関西大学

派 concentration　名 集中
コロ lose one's concentration（集中力を失う）

類 focus [fóukəs]　名 焦点　動 集中する、焦点をあてる（＋on）

でた! The focus of the international conference shifted from global warming to the education of women.
（国際会議の焦点は、地球温暖化から女子教育に移行した）
拓殖大学

### 0225 emphasize [émfəsàiz]
動 強調する

コロ emphasize the importance of A（Aの重要性を強調する）

でた! Nature has been emphasized as a social value.
（自然は社会的価値として強調されてきた）

派 emphasis　名 強調　複 emphases
コロ put an emphasis on A（Aを強調する）

### 0226 stress [strés]
動 強調する　名 ストレス、強調

コロ stress the importance（重要性を強調する）

### 0227 exaggerate [igzǽdʒərèit]
動 大げさに言う、誇張する

派 exaggeration　名 誇張

### 0228 absorb [æbsɔ́ːrb, -zɔ́ːrb | əb-]
動 吸収する

コロ be absorbed in A（Aに夢中になる）

でた! He is absorbed in scientific work.
（彼は科学の仕事に熱中している）
慶應義塾大学

派 absorption [æzɔ́ːrpʃən]　名 吸収、夢中、没頭

| 0229 | **enthusiasm** [inθúːziæzm | -θju-] 発 名 熱狂 |
|---|---|
| | コロ with enthusiasm（熱中して） |

| | 派 **enthusiastic** [inθùːziǽstik] 形 熱狂的な、熱狂した |
|---|---|
| | コロ be crazy about A（Aに熱中した）|

| 0230 | **keen** [kíːn] 形 鋭い、熱心な |
|---|---|
| | コロ be keen on ~ing（～することに熱中している）|
| でた! | She seems to be very keen on music.<br>（彼女は音楽にとても熱中しているように見える） 立命館大学 |

| | 派 **keenly** 副 熱心に |
|---|---|

| 0231 | **eager** [íːgər] 形 熱望している、熱心な（＋to） |
|---|---|
| | コロ be eager to A（しきりにAしたがる）|

| | 派 **eagerly** 副 熱心に |
|---|---|

| | 派 **eagerness** 名 熱望、熱心 |
|---|---|
| でた! | He is impressed with her eagerness to continue.<br>（彼は彼女が継続しようとする熱意に感銘を受けている） TOEFL |

| 0232 | **addict** [ǽdikt] 名 中毒者、常習犯　動 中毒になる（＋to） |
|---|---|

| | 派 **addiction** 名 中毒 |
|---|---|

| 0233 | **passion** [pǽʃən] 名 情熱、感情 |
|---|---|
| でた! | He has no control over his passion.<br>（彼には感情を抑える力がない） 青山学院大学 |

| | 派 **passionate** 形 情熱的な（＋about） |
|---|---|
| でた! | Mary is very passionate about tennis now. She spends every weekend playing.<br>（メアリーは今テニスに燃えている。彼女は毎週末テニスに時間を費やしている） 英語検定2級 |

| | 派 **compassion** 名 同情　原義 com（共に）＋passion（情熱）|
|---|---|

UNIT 19 集中・強調

Chapter2 Education

# UNIT 20 我慢・忍耐

**STEP 1 過去問を解く**

## 1

The traffic here is very slow. We can't (　　) it any longer.

専修大学

1. stand
2. lose
3. wheel
4. run

## 2

I can't (　　) children shouting while I'm studying.

学習院大学

1. cut down on
2. get through to
3. put up with
4. stand up to

## 3

It is important to teach young people to be (　　). This is one of the most important values in an open society.

上智大学

1. crude
2. sentimental
3. tolerant
4. fundamental

## 4

I couldn't <u>bear</u> the thought of being separated from my best friend.

玉川大学

1. carry
2. endure
3. produce
4. support

## STEP 2 正解を見抜く

### 1

The traffic here is very slow. We can't stand it any longer.  　　正解 ①

**訳** ここの交通は非常に遅いです。私たちは、もうそれに耐えることができません。

- **stand** 動 耐える
- **lose** 動 失う
- **wheel** 動 動かす
- **run** 動 走る

### 2

I can't put up with children shouting while I'm studying.  　　正解 ③

**訳** 私が勉強している時に子供たちが騒いでいるのには耐えられない。

- **put up with** ～を我慢する

### 3

It is important to teach young people to be tolerant. This is one of the most important values in an open society.  　　正解 ③

**訳** 若者に寛大になることを教えることは重要である。これは開かれた社会で最も重要な価値の1つだ。

- **crude** 形 天然の
- **tolerant** 形 寛大な
- **sentimental** 形 感傷的な
- **fundamental** 形 根本的な

### 4

I couldn't endure the thought of being separated from my best friend.  　　正解 ②

**訳** 私は、私の親友から切り離されるという考えに耐えられませんでした。

- **carry** 動 運ぶ
- **endure** 動 耐える
- **produce** 動 生産させる
- **support** 動 支える

UNIT 20　我慢・忍耐

Chapter2 Education

## STEP 3 連鎖式に語彙を増やす 20

● 語源 dur (硬くする)

### 0234 endure [endjúər]
動 (長期的に) 耐える　原義「硬くする」

Creative people must be able to endure loneliness.
(創造的な人は孤独に耐えることが出来るに違いない)　関西学院大学

派 **endurance**　名 辛抱、忍耐

The endurance displayed by the athlete gave evidence of his rigorous training.
(アスリートによって見せられた忍耐力が、彼の厳しい訓練の証拠となった)　TOEFL

### 0235 during [djúəriŋ | djúər-]
前 〜の間

Robin suddenly began to feel nervous during the interview.
(ロビンは面接中に、突然緊張し始めた)　センター試験

派 **duration** [djuréiʃən]　名 持続、耐久

派 **durable** [djúərəbl]　形 耐久性のある、丈夫な
コロ durable refrigerator (丈夫な冷蔵庫)

Memory is perhaps one's most durable characteristic as an individual.
(記憶は、その本人の最も持続性のある特徴かもしれない)　東京大学

### 0236 stand [stǽnd]
動 立つ、耐える　活 stand-stood-stood
コロ put up with A (Aを我慢する)

I can't put up with his rudeness.
(彼の無礼には耐えられない)　立教大学

### 0237 bear [béər]
動 耐える、生む　活 bear-bore-born
コロ bear the pain (痛みに耐える)
コロ bear in mind (心に留めておく)

Bear in mind what I am going to say.
(私がこれから言うことを、心に留めておきなさい)　名古屋大学

### 0238 tolerate [tάləreit | tɔ́l-]
動 我慢する、大目に見る

I can't tolerate his rudeness.
(彼の無礼には耐えられない)　立教大学

派 **tolerance**　名 忍耐、我慢、寛容

Mr. Brown seems to have little tolerance for people of other religions.
(ブラウンさんは、他の宗教を信じる人たちに対して寛容さをほとんど持ち合わせていないようだ)　慶應義塾大学

派 **tolerant**　形 耐性がある、寛大な

## 0239 withstand [wiðstænd] 動 耐える、抵抗する
でた! She cannot withstand the pressures of her job.
(彼女は仕事のプレッシャーに耐えられない) TOEFL

## 0240 resist [rizíst] 動 耐える、抵抗する 原義 re(反対に)+sist(立つ)
でた! I cannot resist the smell of curry. It's my favorite dish.
(私は、カレーのにおいがすると我慢できません。それは私の好物です) 法政大学

でた! The nation resists the recent trend of democratization.
(その国は最近の民主化の傾向に抵抗している) 群馬大学

派 resistant 形 抵抗力のある

派 resistance 名 抵抗

### coffee break ☕ マシュマロテスト

　マシュマロテストはアメリカのスタンフォード大学の心理学者によって実施されました。アメリカの4歳の子供186人に対し行われました。「子供は1つのマシュマロを与えられ、15分間我慢できたらもう1つもらえる」という我慢試しの実験です。結果、我慢してマシュマロを食べなかったのは3分の1でした。その後、追跡調査を行うと、我慢できた子供たちはアメリカの大学入試SATで210点の相違が認められました。

　マシュマロを食べず我慢できた4歳の子供にはそれぞれの戦略的方略がありました。マシュマロを食べてしまった子供はマシュマロを触ったり匂いを嗅いだりしてしまい、対照的に我慢できた子供は手で目を伏せたりしてマシュマロを見ないようにし、注意を逸らそうとする行為が見られました。

　自分自身の戦略を見直せば我慢することや、集中することは、容易なのかもしれません。

UNIT 20 我慢・忍耐

Chapter2 Education

# UNIT 21 文字・文学

**STEP 1 過去問を解く**

## 1

When you write your name, you have to start not with a small letter but with a ( ) letter.

センター試験

1. capital
2. great
3. grand
4. large

## 2

The name of the Italian cheese that you are eating is Dolcelatte, and it ( ) means "sweet milk."

拓殖大学

1. eventually
2. inevitably
3. literally
4. unlikely

## 3

( ) people make up about 98 percent of the whole population.

横浜市立大学

1. Literal
2. Literary
3. Literature
4. Literate

## 4

Education experts stress that ( ) is the key to learning. Every effort should be made to see that no student leaves elementary school without being able to read and write.

英語検定準1級

1. clarity
2. literacy
3. dignity
4. urgency

## STEP 2 正解を見抜く

### 1

When you write your name, you have to start not with a small letter but with a capital letter.

正解 ①

**訳** 名前を書くとき、小文字で書き始めるのではなく、大文字で書き始めなければなりません。

**capital letter** 大文字

> small letterは「小文字」、write in capital letters「大文字で書く」で覚えましょう

### 2

The name of the Italian cheese that you are eating is Dolcelatte, and it literally means "sweet milk."

正解 ③

**訳** あなたが食べているイタリアのチーズの名前はDolcelatteです、そして、それは文字通り「sweet milk」を意味します。

**eventually** 副 結局は
**literally** 副 文字通り
**inevitably** 副 必然的に
**unlikely** 形 ありそうもない

### 3

Literate people make up about 98 percent of the whole population.

正解 ④

**訳** 読み書きのできる人々は、全体の人口の約98パーセントを占めています

**literal** 形 文字の
**literary** 形 文学の
**literature** 名 文学
**literate** 形 読み書きのできる

> il は「否定」を表す接頭語で反意語はilliterate「読み書きができない」

### 4

Education experts stress that literacy is the key to learning. Every effort should be made to see that no student leaves elementary school without being able to read and write.

正解 ②

**訳** 教育の専門家は学習において読み書きの能力がカギになると強調している。どの生徒も読み書きができずに小学校レベルで取り残されないようにあらゆる努力がなされるべきだ。

**clarity** 名 透明性
**dignity** 名 威厳
**literacy** 名 読み書きの能力
**urgency** 名 差し迫ったこと

Chapter2 Education

## STEP 3 連鎖式に語彙を増やす 21

### ● 語源 liter（文字）

**0241 letter** [létər]　　名 手紙、文字、文学（-s）

- コロ capital letter（大文字）

**0242 literature** [lítərətʃər]　　名 文学、文献

でた! One of the oldest themes in literature is the love triangle.
（文学における最も古いテーマの一つは三角関係である） 〔成城大学〕

派 **literary**　　形 文学の

**0243 literacy** [lítərəsi]　　名 読み書きの能力

でた! Lack of literacy does not mean the people were uneducated.
（読み書きの能力が欠けていることは、教養がないことを意味しない） 〔静岡大学〕

派 **literate**　　形 読み書きのできる、教養がある

でた! No one in the English-speaking world can be considered literate without a basic knowledge of the Bible.
（聖書の基本的な知識がないと英語圏では誰も教養があると思われない） 〔上智大学〕

反 **illiterate** [ilítərət]　　形 読み書きのできない

派 **literally**　　副 文字通り

でた! The bottom line for a corporation is literally its bottom line.
（企業にとって要点は文字通り最終損益額である） 〔早稲田大学〕

### ● 語源 scrib（書く）

**0244 describe** [diskráib]　　動 描写する、説明する
原義 de（下に）＋ scrib（書く）

でた! Describe the type of teacher you would like to study with.
（あなたが一緒に勉強したい先生のタイプを説明してください） 〔青山学院大学〕

派 **descriptive**　　形 記述的な、描写して

派 **description**　　名 描写、説明

- コロ beyond description（言葉に出来ない）

でた! The grief that I underwent was beyond description.
（私が経験した悲しみは、言葉に言い表せなかった） 〔関西学院大学〕

**0245 inscribe** [inskráib]　　動 刻み込む、記入する　原義 in（中に）＋ scrib（書く）

派 **inscription**　　名 刻むこと

| 0246 | scribble [skríbl] | 動 殴り書きする（+ down）　名 乱筆 |
|---|---|---|
| 0247 | script [skrípt] | 名 台本 |
| 0248 | manuscript [mǽnjuskrìpt] ア | 名 原稿、写本　原義 manu（手）+ script（書く） |

でた! The oldest surviving manuscripts of Greek plays date from around the tenth century.（ギリシャ劇の現存する最も古い原稿は十世紀頃のものである） [TOEFL]

| 0249 | **subscribe** [səbskráib] | 動 定期購読する（+ to） |
|---|---|---|

でた! I subscribe to a daily newspaper.
（私は日刊新聞を定期購読している） [TOEFL]

| | 派 subscription | 名 定期購読 |
|---|---|---|
| 0250 | postscript [póustskrìpt] | 名 追伸 |
| 0251 | legend [lédʒənd] | 名 伝説 |
| | 派 legendary | 形 伝説の |
| 0252 | biography [baiágrəfi \| -ɔ́g-] | 名 伝記 |
| 0253 | autobiography | 名 自伝 |
| 0254 | graffito [grəfíːtou] | 名 落書き　複 graffiti |
| 0255 | calligraphy [kəlígrəfi] | 名 達筆、書道 |

でた! As we examine ancient manuscripts, we are impressed with the calligraphy of scribes.（古代の文書を調べると、写字生たちの達筆さに感銘を受ける） [慶應義塾大学]

UNIT 21　文字・文学

Chapter2 Education

# UNIT 22 辞書・定義

**STEP 1 過去問を解く**

## 1

I don't know what this word means. I'll look it (　　) in the dictionary.

センター試験

1. about
2. for
3. through
4. up

## 2

Keep a dictionary on the desk so that you can (　　) it whenever necessary.

青山学院大学

1. look
2. refer
3. regard
4. consult

## 3

If you don't know what a word means, you can find the (　　) in a dictionary.

立命館大学

1. decision
2. definition
3. determination
4. direction

## 4

Do you mean that literally or is it just a (　　)?

上智大学

1. style
2. meaning
3. sense
4. metaphor

## STEP 2 正解を見抜く

### 1

I don't know what this word means. I'll look it up in the dictionary.

正解 ④

**訳** 私はこの単語の意味がわかりません。 私は辞書でそれを調べるつもりです。

**look up** 辞書で調べる

> look it upのように代名詞の場合はlook upの間に入ります。the wordの場合はlook up the wordとなります

### 2

Keep a dictionary on the desk so that you can consult it whenever necessary.

正解 ④

**訳** 必要な時にいつでも調べられるように、机の上に辞書を置いておきなさい。

**look** 動見る（＋at）
**refer** 動参照する（＋to）
**regard** 動みなす
**consult** 動調べる

### 3

If you don't know what a word means, you can find the definition in a dictionary.

正解 ②

**訳** もし単語の意味が分からなかったら、辞書でその定義を見つけることが出来ます。

**decision** 名決定
**definition** 名定義
**determination** 名決心
**direction** 名方向

### 4

Do you mean that literally or is it just a metaphor?

正解 ④

**訳** あなたは文字通りそれを言っていますか、それともただの比喩ですか？

**style** 名様式
**meaning** 名意味
**sense** 名感覚
**metaphor** 名比喩

## STEP 3 連鎖式に語彙を増やす

### ● 語源 dic（言う）

**0256 dictionary** [díkʃənèri | -ʃənəri]
名 辞書
コロ consult a dictionary（辞書を引く）

**0257 predict** [pridíkt]
動 予言する、予測する  [原義] pre（前に）＋ dict（言う）
コロ predict the future（未来を予測する）

predict（正確な情報に基づいて予言する）、foretell（方法、手段を問わずに予言する）、prophesy（神秘的な知識や霊感などで予言する）

派 **predictable** 形 予測可能な
反 **unpredictable** 形 予測できない
派 **prediction** 名 予言、予測

**0258 prophesy** [práfəsài] 発
動 予言する
派 **prophecy** [práfəsi] 名 予言
派 **prophet** 名 予言者  [原義] 神の意志を代弁する
類 **forecast** [fɔ́:rkæst | kɑ́:st] 動 予想する、予報する  名 予想、予報
(活) forecast-forecast-forecast

**0259 dictate** [díkteit]
動 書き取る
派 **dictation** 名 書き取り
派 **dictator** 名 独裁者

でた! Adolf Hitler was a German dictator.（アドルフ・ヒトラーはドイツの独裁者だった）

**0260 indicate** [índikèit] 7
動 指し示す、指摘する

でた! She indicates that money alone never makes great school.
（彼女はお金だけでは良い学校は作れないと指摘する） 亜細亜大学

派 **indication** 名 指示、表示
コロ point out A（Aを指摘する）

でた! One of the climbers pointed out how dangerous the route was.
（登山者の1人がそのルートが如何に危険かを指摘した） 中央大学

**0261 contradict** [kàntrədíkt | kɔ̀n-] 7
動 矛盾する

でた! His replies contradicted his previous testimony.
（彼の答えは以前の証言と矛盾していた） 北里大学

## 派 contradiction　名 矛盾
でた！ It is difficult for liars to make up a story without contradictions.
（嘘つきの人が矛盾しない話をでっちあげることは難しい）　同志社大学

## 派 contradictory　形 矛盾した

### 0262 consult [kənsʌ́lt]　動 辞書で調べる、相談する
でた！ We should consult a lawyer on that matter.
（私達はその件について弁護士に相談すべきである）　中央大学
- コロ unknown word（未知語）
- コロ look up（辞書で調べる）

でた！ Look up the word in your dictionary.
（その単語を辞書で調べなさい）　関西大学

### 0263 refer [rifə́:r]　動 参照する、言及する（＋ to）

## 派 reference　名 参照、言及
- コロ reference book（参考書）

### 0264 mention [ménʃən]　動 言及する、述べる
- コロ Don't mention it.（どういたしまして）

### 0265 translate [trænsléit, trænz-]　動 翻訳する
- コロ translate A into B（AをBに翻訳する）

## 派 translation　名 翻訳
でた！ Translation has played a central role in human interaction.
（翻訳は人間の交流の中で中心的な役割を果たしてきた）　愛媛大学

### 0266 interpret [intə́:rprit]　動 通訳する、解釈する
でた！ The ambiguous speech was very difficult to interpret.
（その曖昧な演説は解釈するのが難しかった）　TOEFL

## 派 interpretation　名 通訳、解釈

## 派 interpreter　名 通訳者
でた！ The Prime Minister made a short speech in America through an interpreter.
（首相はアメリカで通訳を通して短い演説をした）　センター試験

### 0267 vocabulary [voukǽbjulèri | -ləri]　名 語彙

### 0268 usage [júːsidʒ, -zidʒ]　名 使用法、語法

### 0269 metaphor [métəfɔ̀:r]　名 比喩

Chapter2 Education

# UNIT 23 出版・人口

**STEP 1 過去問を解く**

## 1

Professor Edwards has just finished writing a book. He is looking forward to it being (　　).

英語検定準2級

1. published
2. invented
3. achieved
4. expressed

## 2

Books that are anonymous do not mention the (　　) of the authors.

上智大学

1. publisher
2. name
3. nationality
4. methodology

## 3

On the same day that the pop star's CD was released, it sold over a million (　　).

英語検定2級

1. prints
2. scripts
3. texts
4. copies

## 4

Ten years ago few people lived in the town, but its population (　　) after a new highway was built.

英語検定2級

1. proposed
2. lengthened
3. consumed
4. exploded

## STEP 2 正解を見抜く

### 1

Professor Edwards has just finished writing a book. He is looking forward to it being published.

正解 ①

**訳** エドワーズ教授は、ちょうど本を書き終えたところです。彼はそれが発行されるのを楽しみにしています。

- publish 動 出版する
- achieve 動 成し遂げる
- express 動 表現する
- invent 動 発明する

本を書き終えた（finished writing a book）とあるので何を楽しみにしている（looking forward to）のかを考えればpublish「出版する」が選択できます

### 2

Books that are anonymous do not mention the name of the authors.

正解 ②

**訳** 匿名の本は、著者の名前を記していない。

- publisher 名 出版社
- name 名 名前
- nationality 名 国籍
- methodology 名 方法論

books that are anonymous「匿名の本」からname of the authors（著者の名前）を挙げないがイコール関係

### 3

On the same day that the pop star's CD was released, it sold over a million copies.

正解 ④

**訳** そのポップスターがCDをリリースした日に、100万枚以上売れた。

- print 名 印刷
- script 名 スクリプト
- text 名 本文
- copy 名 コピー、枚

### 4

Ten years ago few people lived in the town, but its population exploded after a new highway was built.

正解 ④

**訳** 町には、10年前にはわずかな人々しか住んでいませんでしたが、新しい高速道路が建設された後に、人口が急増しました。

- propose 動 提案する
- consume 動 消費する
- explode 動 急増する
- lengthen 動 長くする

ほとんど人がいない（few people）が主語で、しかし人口が（population）がどうしたのか考えればexploded（爆発した）が連想できます

UNIT 23 出版・人口

Chapter 2 Education

## STEP 3 連鎖式に語彙を増やす 23

• 語源 pop pub（人々）

### 0270 publish [pÁbliʃ]
**動** 出版する、発行する、公表する
原義 pub（人々）

でた! The editors have been advised to defer publishing the article.
（編集者らはその記事を公表するのを延期するように忠告された） 慶應義塾大学

コロ **come out**（出版する、出てくる）

でた! Bill's new book will be coming out at the end of this month.
（ビルさんの新しい本は今月末に出版される予定です） 中央大学

派 **publisher** **名** 出版社、発行者

派 **publication** **名** 出版、出版物

### 0271 population [pàpjuléiʃən | pɔ̀p-]
**名** 人口

コロ **population** density（人口密度）

派 **populate** **動** 住まわせる

### 0272 explode [iksplóud]
**動** 爆発する、増加する

派 **explosive** **形** 爆発的な

派 **explosion** **名** 爆発

コロ **go off**（爆発する）

### 0273 popular [pɑ́pjulər | pɔ́p-]
**形** 人気のある

派 **popularity** **名** 人気

### 0274 public [pÁblik]
**形** 公共の

コロ **public** telephone（公衆電話）

派 **publicity** **名** よく知られていること

反 **private** [práivət] **形** 私的な

派 **privacy** **名** プライバシー、私生活、秘密

類 **republic** [ripÁblik] **名** 共和国

コロ the **Republic** of Korea（大韓民国）

### 0275 author [ɔ́:θər]
**名** 著者 原義 au（増す）
※ auction の au と同語源。auction は値段が増えること。

でた! Anyone who has access to a computer can be an author.
（コンピュータを利用できる人は誰でも著者になれる） 上智大学

派 **authority** [əθɔ́:rəti] **名** 権威、当局（-es）

| 派 | **authorize** [ɔ́:θəràiz] | 動 権威を与える |

| 派 | **royalty** [rɔ́iəlti] | 名 印税 (-es)、王族 |

| 派 | **royal** | 形 王の |
| コロ | royal family (皇室) | |

**0276 encyclopedia** [insàikləpí:diə] 名 百科事典

| 類 | **picture book** (絵本) |

**0277 poem** [póuəm] 名 (個人的に) 詩

| 派 | **poetry** | 名 (集合的に) 詩 |
| 派 | **poet** | 名 詩人 |

**0278 tale** [téil] 名 物語
コロ fairy tale (おとぎ話)

**0279 article** [ɑ́:rtikl] 名 記事、条項、品物
コロ newspaper article (新聞記事)

でた! The article describes possible risks associated with the use of cellphones.
(その記事は携帯電話使用に関連した潜在的な危険性について描写している)　青山学院大学

**0280 fiction** [fíkʃən] 名 作り話

**0281 print** [prínt] 名 印刷　動 印刷する

でた! The first banknotes were printed over 1,000 years ago.
(最初の紙幣は1000年以上前に印刷された)　中央大学

**0282 edit** [édit] 動 編集する

| 派 | **edition** | 名 版 |
| 派 | **editor** | 名 編集者 |

**0283 quote** [kwóut] 動 引用する　名 引用文

| 派 | **quotation** | 名 引用 |

**0284 cite** [sáit] 動 引用する

| 派 | **citation** | 名 引用 |

**0285 phrase** [fréiz] 名 句

| 派 | **phrasal** | 形 句の |
コロ phrasal noun (名詞句)

UNIT 23　出版・人口

Chapter2 Education

# UNIT 24 表示・公表

**STEP 1** 過去問を解く

## 1

Every bank must (　　　) its financial information to the public this year.

立命館大学

1. crush
2. defeat
3. disclose
4. encourage

## 2

The symbol "x" usually <u>stands for</u> an unknown quantity in mathematics.

青山学院大学

1. includes
2. represents
3. decreases
4. increases

## 3

John didn't know how to (　　　) to his wife that he quit his job.

南山大学

1. speak
2. ask
3. explain
4. request

## 4

The company recently (　　　) that it will utilize human protein in its new formula.

慶應義塾大学

1. dissolved
2. discussed
3. disclosed
4. dismissed

## STEP 2 正解を見抜く

### 1

Every bank must disclose its financial information to the public this year.

正解 ③

**訳** 今年はどの銀行も大衆に財務情報を発表しなければならない。

- crush 動 押しつぶす
- defeat 動 打ち負かす
- disclose 動 発表する
- encourage 動 励ます

### 2

The symbol "x" usually represents an unknown quantity in mathematics.

正解 ②

**訳** xという記号は通常数学で未知数を表す。

- include 動 含む
- represent 動 表す
- decrease 動 減る
- increase 動 増える

### 3

John didn't know how to explain to his wife that he quit his job.

正解 ③

**訳** ジョンはなぜ仕事をやめたのか妻にどう説明すればよいかわからなかった。

- speak 動 話す
- ask 動 尋ねる
- explain 動 説明する
- request 動 求める

### 4

The company recently disclosed that it will utilize human protein in its new formula.

正解 ③

**訳** その会社は人間のタンパク質を新しい手法で使用すると最近発表した。

- dissolve 動 溶かす、解く
- discuss 動 討論する
- disclose 動 発表する
- dismiss 動 解雇する

UNIT 24 表示・公表

Chapter2 Education

## STEP 3 連鎖式に語彙を増やす 24

### 0286 represent [rèprizént] 動 表す、代表する

The olive branch represents peace.
(オリーブの枝は平和を象徴している) 〔学習院大学〕

- stand for A (Aを表す)

What do the letters U.N. stand for?
(U.N.は何を表していますか) 〔関西学院大学〕

派 representative [rèprizéntətiv] 名 代表者 形 代表する
- on behalf of A (Aを代表して)

He made a speech on behalf of the committee.
(彼は委員会を代表して演説をした) 〔青山学院大学〕

派 representation 名 表現、代表

### 0287 display [displéi] 動 表示する 名 表示

Most zoos are public parks, which display animals for recreational or educational purposes. (ほとんどの動物園は公共の公園であり、憩いの場、教育目的のために動物を展示している) 〔慶應義塾大学〕

### 0288 exhibit [igzíbit] 動 展示する 名 展示

The art gallery will exhibit some of Picasso's paintings.
(その画廊はピカソの絵画を何点か展示する予定である) 〔関西外国語大学〕

派 exhibition [èksəbíʃən] 名 展覧会

### 0289 demonstrate [déməstrèit] 動 実証する、実際にやってみて説明する

Pasteur demonstrated that life comes only from life.
(パスツールは生命は生命からのみ生まれることを証明した) 〔滋賀医科大学〕

派 demonstration 名 実演、説明、デモ

### 0290 illustrate [íləstrèit] 動 実例で説明する

派 illustration 名 実例、図解

## 0291 explain [ikspléin]

**動** 説明する
**原義** 「平(plain)にする」＝平にして分かりやすくする

- explain A to B（AをBに説明する）
- Examining the language can help to explain why people laugh.
  （言語を調べることは人々がなぜ笑うか説明する手助けとなりうる）〔上智大学〕
- account for A（Aを説明する、A（割合）を占める）
- Can you account for all the money you spent on your trip?
  （旅行で使った全てのお金の説明はつきますか）〔慶應義塾大学〕

**派** explanation **名** 説明

## 0292 declare [dikléər]

**動** 宣言する

**派** declaration [dèkləréiʃən] **名** 宣言、声明文
- the Declaration of Independence（独立宣言）

## 0293 reveal [rivíːl]

**動** 明らかにする

- reveal the fact（真実を明らかにする）
- Close investigation will reveal the truth.
  （詳細な調査で真実が明らかになるだろう）〔立命館大学〕

**派** disclose [disklóuz] **動** 暴露する、明らかにする、発表する
**原義** dis（否定）＋close（閉める）＝隠すことをしない＝暴露する

**派** disclosure [disklóuʒər] **名** 暴露

**類** uncover [ʌnkʌ́vər] **動** 明らかにする、発掘する、暴露する
- Laboratory studies have uncovered several mechanisms that might explain chocolate's heart-healthy benefits.（チョコレートには心臓の健康利点があることを明白にするいくつかのメカニズムが実験室の研究によって明らかになった）〔同志社大学〕

## 0294 conceal [kənsíːl]

**動** 隠す

- conceal the evidence（証拠を隠す）
- Tears will flow in spite of our efforts to conceal.
  （涙は隠そうと努力しても流れ出るものだ）〔東洋大学〕

**派** concealment **名** 隠すこと

**類** hide [háid] **動** 隠れる、隠す
- hide and seek（かくれんぼ）

UNIT24 表示・公表

Chapter2 Education | 111

# UNIT 25 諺・名言

**STEP 1 過去問を解く**

## 1

A rolling stone (　　) no moss.

成蹊大学

1. stands
2. gathers
3. picks
4. grows

## 2

There is a proverb, "A (　　) in the hand is worth two in the bush."

駒澤大学

1. butterfly
2. lion
3. bird
4. baby

## 3

The newspaper is capable of storing millions of (　　) of information.

東京都市大学

1. counts
2. numbers
3. levels
4. pieces

## 4

Her sister bought three (　　) of stockings yesterday.

関東学院大学

1. cakes
2. pairs
3. pieces
4. sheets

## STEP 2 正解を見抜く

### 1

A rolling stone gathers no moss.　　　正解 ②

訳 転がる石は苔をむさない。

- stand 動立つ
- gather 動集める
- pick 動拾う
- grow 動成長する

### 2

There is a proverb, "A bird in the hand is worth two in the bush."　　　正解 ③

訳 "掌中の一羽は叢中の二羽に値する"という諺があります。

- butterfly 名蝶
- lion 名ライオン
- bird 名鳥
- baby 名赤ん坊

### 3

The newspaper is capable of storing millions of pieces of information.　　　正解 ④

訳 新聞は、何百万もの情報を格納できる。

- count 名数え
- number 名数
- level 名水準
- piece 名部分

### 4

Her sister bought three pairs of stockings yesterday.　　　正解 ②

訳 彼女の姉は昨日3足のストッキングを買った。

- cake 名ケーキ
- pair 名1対、1組
- piece 名部分
- sheet 名1枚

UNIT 25　諺・名言

Chapter2 Education

## STEP 3 連鎖式に語彙を増やす 25

**0295 verb** [vˈɜːrb]　　名 動詞

派 **verbal**　　形 言葉の、口の、動詞の
コロ verbal communication（言葉での意思疎通）

類 **adverb** [ˈædvɜːrb]　　名 副詞

**0296 proverb** [prάvɜːrb | prˈɔv-]　　名 諺　原義 pro（前の）＋verb（言葉）
コロ as the proverb goes（諺にあるように）
でた! Proverbs can tell us a lot about a particular culture.
（ことわざは我々に特定の文化について多くを教えてくれる）　　早稲田大学

類 **saying** [séiiŋ]　　名 諺

### 諺一覧

- Rome was not built in a day, as the saying goes.
  （諺にあるように、ローマは一日にして成らず）
- A drawing man will catch at a straw.「溺れる者はわらをもつかむ」
- A friend in need is a friend indeed.「まさかの時の友こそ真の友」
- A good medicine tastes bitter.「良薬口に苦し」
- Birds of a feather flock together.「類は友を呼ぶ」
- When in Rome, do as the Romans do.「郷に入っては郷に従え」
- Don't count your chickens before they are hatched.「捕らぬたぬきの皮算用」
- Even Homer sometimes nods.「弘法も筆の誤り」「猿も木から落ちる」
- Heaven helps those who help themselves.「天は自らを助くる者を助く」
- It is no use crying over split milk.「覆水盆に返らず」
- Kill two birds with one stone.「一石二鳥」
- Practice makes perfect.「習うより慣れろ」
- Seeing is believing「百聞は一見に如かず」
- So many men, so many minds.「十人十色」
- Strike while the iron is hot.「鉄は熱いうちに打て」
- The early bird catches the worm.「早起きは三文の得」
- There is no royal road to learning.「学問に王道なし」
- You must reap what you have sown.「自業自得」

### 入試問題にチャレンジ　（　）に入る語は何でしょうか？

① （　）is no use（　）over spilt milk.
② It is（　）（　）（　）to cry over spilt milk.
③ It is（　）to cry over spilt milk.　　東京外国語大学

答 ① It／crying ② of no use ③ useless

## coffee break ☕ 数字の語源

試験によくでる単語も、語源さえ押さえておけば、瞬間的に意味をつかむことができるでしょう。

語源　uni＝1
　　　uniform　制服
　　　unicorn　一角獣
　　　unit　単位
　　　unicycle　一輪車
語源　bi＝2
　　　bicycle　自転車
　　　bilingual　二カ国語を話す人
語源　tri＝3
　　　triangle　三角形
　　　triceratops　トリケラトプス
　　　tricycle　三輪車
　　　trio　3人組
　　　tripod　三脚
　　　triple　三倍の

〔文法用語に関連する単語〕

| | |
|---|---|
| **noun** | 名 名詞 |
| コロ countable noun（可算名詞） | |
| コロ uncountable noun（不可算名詞） | |
| **pronoun** | 名 代名詞 |
| **verb** | 名 動詞 |
| **adverb** | 名 副詞 |
| **adjective** | 名 形容詞 |
| **preposition** | 名 前置詞 |
| **conjunction** | 名 接続詞 |
| **article** | 名 冠詞 |
| **singular** | 名 単数形 |
| **plural** | 名 複数形 |
| **subject** | 名 主語 |
| **objective** | 名 目的語 |
| **complement** | 名 補語 |
| **present tense** | 名 現在形 |
| **past tense** | 名 過去形 |
| **future tense** | 名 未来形 |
| **present progressive tense** | 名 現在進行形 |
| **pas progressive tense** | 名 過去進行形 |
| **present perfect tense** | 名 現在完了形 |
| **paragraph** | 名 段落 |
| **context** | 名 文脈、文章の前後関係 |
| **summarize** | 動 要約する |
| でた! Briefly summarize the problem the speakers are discussing.<br>（スピーカーが議論している問題を簡潔に要約しなさい） | TOEFL |
| 類 **sum** | 名 合計、総額 |
| コロ sum up（要約する） | |
| 派 **summary** | 名 要約 |
| **conclude** | 動 結論付ける 原義 con（共に）＋clud（閉める） |
| でた! We concluded that the new learning method was quite effective.<br>（我々はその新しい学習法がとても効果的であると結論付けた） | 早稲田大学 |
| 派 **conclusion** | 名 結論 |
| コロ in conclusion（結論として） | |
| でた! Darwin came to the conclusion that species change.<br>（ダーウィンは種は変化するという結論に達した） | 青山学院大学 |
| 派 **conclusive** | 形 決定的な |

# Chapter 3
# Science

# UNIT 26 医薬・医療
## STEP 1 過去問を解く

### 1

Be sure to (　　) vitamin tablets every morning.

法政大学

1. drink
2. eat
3. feed
4. take

### 2

Tom had lost so much blood that the doctor gave him (　　).

上智大学

1. a transcript
2. a circulation
3. a transfusion
4. an infection

### 3

The (　　) is a teaspoonful, to be taken three times a day. You must not exceed it.

慶應義塾大学

1. dose
2. measure
3. medicine
4. quantity

### 4

Thanks to (　　), my blood pressure was lowered to a normal level.

慶應義塾大学

1. menagerie
2. mediocrity
3. medication
4. mediation

## STEP 2 正解を見抜く

### 1

Be sure to take vitamin tablets every morning.

正解 ④

訳 毎朝必ずビタミン錠を飲みなさい。

- drink 動 飲む
- eat 動 食べる
- feed 動 えさを与える
- take 動 薬を飲む

> 薬を飲む時にはdrinkではなくtakeを用います。粉薬はpower、tabletは錠剤、一般的な薬はmedicine

### 2

Tom had lost so much blood that the doctor gave him a transfusion.

正解 ③

訳 トムは失血がひどかったので、医者は輸血を行った。

- transcript 名 複写
- circulation 名 血液循環
- transfusion 名 輸血
- infection 名 伝染

### 3

The dose is a teaspoonful, to be taken three times a day. You must not exceed it.

正解 ①

訳 1回の服用量は小さじ一杯で、一日3回服用してください。それ以上は摂り過ぎてはいけません。

- dose 名 一回の服用量
- medicine 名 薬
- measure 名 寸法
- quantity 名 量

> trans（横切る）＋ fuse（注ぐ）

### 4

Thanks to medication, my blood pressure was lowered to a normal level.

正解 ③

訳 薬物治療のおかげで、私の血圧は標準の値に下がった。

- menagerie 名 動物園
- mediocrity 名 平凡
- medication 名 投薬治療
- mediation 名 調停

Chapter3 Science

# STEP 3 連鎖式に語彙を増やす 26

## ● 語源 med (治療する)

### 0297 medicine [médəsin | médsin]
名 薬

- コロ take medicine（薬を飲む）
- コロ dose of medicine（一回分の薬）
- でた! The new medicine saved him from the illness.
（その新しい薬が彼を病気から救った） 〔北里大学〕

**派 medical** — 形 医学の
- コロ medical check-up（健康診断）

**派 medication** — 名 薬物治療、薬、薬剤

**類 pill** [píl] — 名 錠剤

**類 drug** [dráɡ] — 名 薬、麻薬

### 0298 remedy [rémədi]
名 治療法、医薬品　動 治療する

- でた! The use of traditional remedies is increasing in advanced countries.
（伝統的な治療法の使用は先進国で増えている） 〔桜美林大学〕

**派 remedial** — 形 治療の

**類 therapy** [θérəpi] — 名 (薬の使用や手術を行わない) 治療、セラピー

**派 therapist** — 名 治療専門家、セラピスト

### 0299 symptom [símptəm]
名 症状、兆候

- でた! Experienced doctors would never miss symptoms of such illnesses.
（経験豊富な医者ならそのような病気の症状を見落とさないだろう） 〔早稲田大学〕

### 0300 transfusion [trænsfjúːʒən]
名 輸血

- でた! The first blood transfusion was recorded in 1628.
（最初の輸血は1628年に記録されている） 〔九州大学〕

**派 transfuse** — 動 輸血する

### 0301 transplant [trænsplænt]
動 移植する、移住させる
- コロ transplant A into B（AをBに移植する）

**派 transplantation** — 名 移植、移住

### 0302 organ [ɔ́ːrɡən]
名 臓器、オルガン
- コロ organ transplant（臓器移植）

**派 organic** — 形 有機的な

| | | |
|---|---|---|
| 派 | **organism** | 名 生物 |

**0303 prescribe** [priskráib] 　　動 処方する、指示する

派 **prescription** 　　名 処方箋

**0304 cure** [kjúər] 　　動 治す　名 治療

コロ cure A of B（A（人）のBを治す）

でた! They believe that plants and herbs have the power to cure sickness.
（彼らは植物やハーブが病気を治す力を持っていると信じている）　　関西大学

**0305 treat** [trí:t] 　　動 治療する、奢る、扱う

でた! Pets should be treated like family members.
（ペットは家族の一員のように扱われるべきだ）　　TOEFL

派 **treatment** 　　名 治療、扱い

コロ go Dutch（割り勘にする）　コロ split the bill（割り勘にする）

**0306 recover** [rikʌ́vər] 　　動 回復する

派 **recovery** 　　名 回復

コロ recovery from heart disease（心臓病からの回復）

**0307 operate** [ápərèit | ɔ́p-] 　　動 手術する、操作する

コロ operate a machine（機械を操作する）

でた! Do not drive or operate machinery while taking this medication.
（この薬を服用している間は車を運転したり機械を操作したりしないこと）　　青山学院大学

派 **operation** 　　名 手術

コロ oprtation room（手術室）

**0308 mortal** [mɔ́:rtl] 　　形 致命的な、死ぬ運命にある

派 **mortality** 　　名 死ぬ運命、死亡数

コロ mortality rate（死亡率）

反 **immortal** 　　形 不死の

**0309 circulate** [sə́:rkjulèit] 　　動 循環する、流布する、伝わる

でた! The news of the president's visit circulated quickly throughout the city.
（大統領訪問のニュースは瞬く間に町中に伝わった）　　TOEFL

派 **circulation** 　　名 循環、発行部数

**0310 digest** [daidʒést, did-] ア　　動 消化する、要約する　名 要約

派 **digestion** 　　名 消化

UNIT 26 医薬・医療

Chapter3 Science

# UNIT 27 病気・病院

## STEP 1 過去問を解く

### 1

The boy seems to be suffering from an unknown <u>disease</u>.

東海大学

1. sickness
2. despair
3. silence
4. advantage

### 2

The <u>invalid</u> is now getting better.

上智大学

1. affiction
2. infant
3. patient
4. sorrow
5. torment

### 3

A: Did the doctor figure out what's wrong with your back?
B: Not yet. He said he'll have to run some more tests before he can make an exact (     ).

英語検定準1級

1. maneuver
2. diagnosis
3. supervision
4. apprehension

### 4

The doctors have decided to (     ) Bill after an intensive medical checkup.

法政大学

1. hospitality
2. hospitalize
3. hospitalism
4. hospital

## STEP 2 正解を見抜く

### 1

The boy seems to be suffering from an unknown sickness. 正解 ①

訳 その少年は未知の病気に苦しんでいるようだ。

- **sickness** 名 病気
- **despair** 名 絶望
- **silence** 名 静けさ
- **advantage** 名 利点

### 2

The patient is now getting better. 正解 ③

訳 その病人は良くなってきている。

- **affiction** 名 苦悩
- **infant** 名 幼児
- **patient** 名 患者
- **sorrow** 名 悲しみ
- **torment** 名 苦痛

> invalidは「病人」を表します。ラテン語でvaliは「強い」という意味。iは「否定」を表すので、「強くない」=「病人」

### 3

A: Did the doctor figure out what's wrong with your back?
B: Not yet. He said he'll have to run some more tests before he can make an exact diagnosis. 正解 ②

訳 A: その医師はあなたの背中に何か異常があるのか分かりましたか。
B: いいえ、まだです。確実な診断をくだすにはもっと検査する必要があると、彼は言いました。

- **maneuver** 名 巧妙な手段、策略
- **supervision** 名 監督、管理
- **diagnosis** 名 診断
- **apprehension** 名 懸念

### 4

The doctors have decided to hospitalize Bill after an intensive medical checkup. 正解 ②

訳 その医師は、集中的な健康診断の後にビルを入院させることに決めました。

- **hospitality** 名 もてなし
- **hospitalize** 動 入院させる
- **hospitalism** 名 施設病、ホスピタリズム
- **hospital** 名 病院

> izeは動詞化語尾です

Chapter3 Science

## STEP 3 連鎖式に語彙を増やす 27

**0311 disease** [dizíːz] 発 　　名 病気
- chronic disease（慢性病）
- They're suffering from life-threatening diseases like diabetes.
（彼らは糖尿病のような生命を脅かす病気で苦しんでいる）〔明治学院大学〕
- suffer from A（Aに苦しむ）
- People are suffering from a shortage of water this summer.
（人々は今年の夏、水不足に苦しんでいる）〔中央大学〕
- go to the doctor（通院する）

**0312 ill** [íl]　　形 病気である
- speak ill of A（Aの悪口を言う）
- Sandy speaks ill of her colleagues very often.
（サンディーはとても頻繁に同僚の悪口を言う）〔日本大学〕

派 **illness**　　名 病気

**0313 fever** [fíːvər]　　名（病気による）熱

**0314 cough** [kɔ́ːf | kɔ́f] 発　　名 咳　動 咳をする

**0315 flu** [flúː]　　名 インフルエンザ
- get a flu shot（インフルエンザのワクチンを打ってもらう）

**0316 cancer** [kǽnsər]　　名 がん
- lung cancer（肺がん）
- My uncle died of lung cancer.
（私の叔父は肺がんが原因で亡くなった）〔関西学院大学〕

**0317 allergy** [ǽlərdʒi]　　名 アレルギー

**0318 diabetes** [dàiəbíːtis, -tiːz]　　名 糖尿病

派 **diabetic** [dàiəbétik]　　形 糖尿病の

**0319 obesity** [oʊbísɪti]　　名 肥満

派 **obese** [oʊbíːs]　　形 肥満した

**0320 famine** [fǽmin] 発　　名 飢餓

**0321 starve** [stɑ́ːrv]　　動 餓死する

派 **starvation**　　名 飢餓

**0322 plague** [pléig] 発　　名 ペスト、疫病
- The plague was prevalent in Europe.
（ペストはヨーロッパで流行していた）〔TOEFL〕

| 類 syndrome [síndroum] | 名 症候群 |

**0323 diagnosis** [dàiəgnóusis] 🔥　名 診断　(複) diagnoses

派 diagnose [dáiəgnòus]　動 診断する
コロ take care of（世話をする、面倒を見る）

**0324 patient** [péiʃənt]　名 患者　形 忍耐強い

でた! I agree with the idea that doctors should do their best to help patients.
（医者は患者を助けるために全力を尽くすべきだという考えに私は賛成です）　慶應義塾大学

類 invalid [ínvəlid] 🔥 [invəlíd]　名 病人　形 病弱な
反 impatient　形 忍耐のない
派 patience　名 忍耐

**0325 ambulance** [ǽmbjuləns]　名 救急車

• 語源 **nurt**（養う）

**0326 nurse** [nə́:rs]　名 看護師　動 介護する
**0327 nurture** [nə́:rtʃər]　名 養育、教育　動 育てる
**0328 nutrition** [nju:tríʃən | nju:-]　名 栄養

派 nutritious　形 栄養がある
反 malnutrition　名 栄養失調　原義 mal（悪い）

**0329 nourish** [nə́:riʃ | nʌ́r-]　動 養う、育てる

派 nourishment　名 食物、栄養を与えること

• 語源 **hos**（もてなし）

**0330 hospital** [háspitl | hɔ́s-]　名 病院　原義 もてなし

派 hospitalize [háspitəlàiz]　動 入院させる

**0331 hospitality** [hàspətǽləti | hɔ̀s-]　名 もてなし
**0332 hotel** [houtél]　名 ホテル
**0333 host** [hóust]　名 ホスト　動 ホスト役を務める

UNIT 27 病気・病院

Chapter3 Science

# UNIT 28 感染・接触  STEP 1 過去問を解く

## 1

I'll get in touch with you by telephone tomorrow.

亜細亜大学

1. confess
2. find
3. talk
4. contact

## 2 空欄にあてはまる適切な語を選んでください。

This disease is most ( ) during the summer months, and is very much worse in wet seasons.

立命館大学

1. defective
2. pretentious
3. prevalent
4. spontaneous

## 3

Health experts have warned that the continual movement of people, animals, and birds across borders has increased the risk of worldwide ( ).

英語検定準1級

1. proceedings
2. epidemics
3. ejections
4. disclosures

## 4

After three students reported symptoms of a new kind of influenza, all of the classes at the school were canceled to try to prevent an ( ) in the town.

TEAP

1. exaggration
2. evaluation
3. epidemic
4. exhibition

126

## STEP 2 正解を見抜く

### 1

I'll contact you by telephone tomorrow.　　正解 ④

訳 明日電話であなたと連絡を取りましょう。

- confess 動 白状する
- find 動 見つける
- talk 動 話す
- contact 動 接触する、連絡をとる

> get in touch with 人「連絡を取る」、keep in touch with 人「連絡を取り続ける」

### 2

This disease is most prevalent during the summer months, and is very much worse in wet seasons.　　正解 ③

訳 この病気は夏期に最も広まり、雨期にはさらにいっそう広まりやすい。

- defective 形 欠点のある
- pretentious 形 うぬぼれた
- prevalent 形 流行した
- spontaneous 形 自発的な

> prevail「流行する」の形容詞形です

### 3

Health experts have warned that the continual movement of people, animals, and birds across borders has increased the risk of worldwide epidemics.　　正解 ②

訳 医学の専門家は、人々、動物、および鳥の国境を越えた絶え間ない移動が世界的な流行病の危険を増加させたと警告しました。

- proceeding 名 進行
- ejection 名 追放
- epidemic 名 流行病、伝染病
- disclosure 名 発覚

### 4

After three students reported symptoms of a new kind of influenza, all of the classes at the school were canceled to try to prevent an epidemic in the town.　　正解 ③

訳 3人の生徒が新しい種類のインフルエンザの症状を訴えた後、町での伝染を防ぐため、全ての学校での授業が中止された。

- exaggration 名 誇張
- epidemic 名 伝染病
- evaluation 名 評価
- exhibition 名 展覧会

UNIT 28 感染・接触

Chapter3 Science

## STEP 3 連鎖式に語彙を増やす 28

● 語源 tact（触る）

**0334 touch** [tʌ́tʃ] 動 触る
- コロ get in touch with A（Aに連絡する）
- でた! If there's anything urgent, you can get in touch with me.
（急を要することがあれば、私に連絡しても大丈夫です） 早稲田大学
- コロ keep in touch with A（Aと連絡を取り続ける）

**0335 contact** [kɑ́ntækt | kɔ́n-] 動 接触する、連絡をつける 名 接触、付き合い

**0336 attach** [ətǽtʃ] 動 添付する、貼り付ける
- コロ attach A to B（BにAを貼り付ける）
- 派 **attachment** 名 添付、貼り付け
- 反 **detach** [ditǽtʃ] 動 取り外す
- 派 **detachment** 名 分離

**0337 intact** [intǽkt] 形 手つかずの、処女の
- コロ remain intact（手つかずのままである）

**0338 integrate** [íntəgrèit] 動 統合する、融合する
- 派 **integration** 名 統合、融合
- 派 **integrity** [intégrəti] 名 完全、正直さ
- 派 **integral** 形 完全の、不可欠な

**0339 tactics** [tǽktiks] 名 個人の戦略 原義 相手に接触する方法
- 類 **strategy** [strǽtədʒi] 名 （団体の）戦略
- でた! Our team's victory had much to do with our coach's aggressive strategies.
（我々のチームの勝利は、監督の攻撃的な戦略と大いに関係があった） 拓殖大学

**0340 contagious** [kəntéidʒəs] 形 伝染する
- 類 **infect** [infékt] 動 伝染する、感染させる 原義 in（中に）＋fect（作る）
- 派 **infection** 名 （水・空気による）感染
- 派 **infectious** [infékʃəs] 形 伝染性の
- でた! A yawn is like an infectious disease.
（あくびは感染症のようなものだ） 津田塾大学

| 0341 | **epidemic** [èpədémik] | 形 伝染病の　名 伝染病 |
|---|---|---|

でた！ Epidemics were spread by crowded towns and trade.
（伝染病は混雑した街と貿易によって広まった） TOEFL

| 0342 | **spread** [spréd] | 動 広がる（＋out）　活 spread-spread-spread |
|---|---|---|
| | 派 **widespread** [wáidspréd] | 形 広範囲に及ぶ |

| 0343 | **prevail** [privéil] | 動 流行する、普及する、打ち勝つ |
|---|---|---|

でた！ The prevailing winds became stronger.
（勢力のある風は次第に強くなった） TOEFL

| | 派 **prevalent** [prévələnt] | 形 流行している |
|---|---|---|
| | 派 **prevalence** | 名 普及、流行 |

| 0344 | **vaccine** [væksí:n] 発 | 名 ワクチン |
|---|---|---|
| 0345 | **virus** [váiərəs] 発 | 名 ウイルス |
| 0346 | **germ** [dʒə́:rm] | 名 病原菌、細菌 |

でた！ Germs were discovered as the leading cause of death.
（病原菌は死の原因となるものとして発見された） TOEFL

| 0347 | **parasite** [pǽrəsàit] | 名 寄生虫 |
|---|---|---|
| 0348 | **immune** [imjú:n] | 形 免疫のある |

コロ immune system（免疫システム）

| | 派 **immunity** | 名 免疫性 |
|---|---|---|

| 0349 | **chronic** [kránik \| krɔ́n-] | 形 慢性の |
|---|---|---|

でた！ People with chronic illnesses are at greater risk of contracting influenza.
（持病のある人はインフルエンザにかかる可能性が高い） 早稲田大学

| 0350 | **antibiotic** [æ̀ntibaiátik] | 名 抗生物質 |
|---|---|---|

UNIT 28　感染・接触

Chapter3 Science

# UNIT 29 傾向・流行

**STEP 1** 過去問を解く

## 1

People with religious faith ( ) to be more content than those with.

亜細亜大学

1. tend
2. spend
3. keep
4. save

## 2

The doctor warned parents that children would be ( ) to catch cold in winter.

東京理科大学

1. absorbed
2. capable
3. boring
4. liable

## 3

The more stress you are under, the more ( ) you are to get sick.

東京都市大学

1. hardly
2. likely
3. wrongly
4. seriously

## 4

Young people are especially <u>prone to</u> this disease.

青山学院大学

1. liable to
2. crucial to
3. essential to
4. related to

## STEP 2 正解を見抜く

### 1

People with religious faith <u>tend</u> to be more content than those with.

正解 ①

**訳** 宗教的信仰がある人々はそうでない人より満足する傾向がある。

- **tend** 動 傾向がある
- **spend** 動 費やす
- **keep** 動 保つ
- **save** 動 救う

> tend to A で「〜する傾向がある」、content は「満足している」という形容詞です

### 2

The doctor warned parents that children would be <u>liable</u> to catch cold in winter.

正解 ④

**訳** 医者は、子供は冬に風邪を引きやすいと両親に警告しました。

- **absorbed** 形 熱中して
- **capable** 形 有能な
- **boring** 形 たいくつな
- **liable** 形 (病気などに) かかりやすい

> be liable to A で「A にかかりやすい」となり、悪い事に用いられます

### 3

The more stress you are under, the more <u>likely</u> you are to get sick.

正解 ②

**訳** ストレスが多いほど、あなたは病気になりやすい。

- **hardly** 副 ほとんど〜ない
- **likely** 副 おそらく
- **wrongly** 副 誤って
- **seriously** 副 ひどく

> the ＋比較級, the 比較級の構文で「〜すればするほど〜なる」。be likely to A で (A しそうな) という意味になります

### 4

Young people are especially <u>liable to</u> this disease.

正解 ①

**訳** 若者は特にこの病気にかかりやすい。

- **liable** 形 (病気などに) かかりやすい
- **crucial** 形 決定的な
- **essential** 形 不可欠の
- **related** 形 関係のある

UNIT 29 傾向・流行

Chapter3 Science

## STEP 3 連鎖式に語彙を増やす 🎧29

● 語源 **tend tens tent**(伸ばす)

**0351 tent** [tént] 　　　名 テント

**0352 tension** [ténʃən] 　　　名 緊張
　派 **tense** 　　　形 緊張した、張り詰めた

**0353 tend** [ténd] 　　　動 傾向がある（+ to）
　でた！ Many pianists tend to be children of wealthy families.
　（多くのピアニストは裕福な家庭の子供の傾向がある） 〔関西外国語大学〕
　派 **tendency** 　　　名 傾向
　コロ have a tendency to A（Aする傾向がある）

**0354 tender** [téndər] 　　　形 柔らかい、優しい

**0355 attend** [əténd] 　　　動 出席する、注意する（+ to）
　でた！ We have to attend to what he tells us.
　（私たちは、彼が我々に対して言うことに注意して聞かなければならない） 〔慶應義塾大学〕

**0356 attendance** [əténdəns] 　　　名 出席
　コロ take attendance（出席をとる）

　類 **present** [préznt] 　　　形 出席して、現在の
　でた！ There were 200 people present at the meeting.
　（その会議には200名が参加した） 〔東京理科大学〕
　でた！ We do not have any more information at the present time.
　（現在、私たちにはこれ以上の情報はございません） 〔東京理科大学〕

　派 **presence** 　　　名 出席、存在

　反 **absent** [ǽbsənt] 　　　形 欠席している（+ from）

　派 **absence** 　　　名 欠席
　コロ in one's presence（〜のいるところで、直面して）

**0357 attention** [əténʃən] 　　　名 注意、注目
　でた！ Music education has received a lot of attention in recent years.
　（音楽教育が近年多くの注目を浴びている） 〔立教大学〕

**0358 pretend** [priténd] 　　　動 ふりをする（+ to）
　派 **pretense** 　　　名 見せかけ

## 0359 intend [inténd]
動 意図する

でた！ All we readers have to do is to find out what the author intended to say.
（我々読者は作者が何を言おうとしているのか探り出しさえすれば良い） 東京大学

派 **intention** 名 意図

派 **intentional** 形 意図的な
コロ intentional walk（敬遠による四球）※野球用語

派 **intentionally** 副 意図的に

## 0360 extend [iksténd]
動 拡張する、伸ばす

派 **extension** 名 拡張、髪の毛のエクステ

派 **extensive** 形 幅広い、広範囲な

## 0361 likely [láikli]
形 ありそうな、起こりそうな

でた！ Mars is the most likely place for life in our solar system.
（火星は我々の太陽系の中で最も生命の可能性がありえる場所である） TOEFL

コロ be likely to A（Aしそうな）
コロ be apt to A（Aしがちである）

でた！ People are more apt to be helped in small towns than in big cities.（大都市よりも小さな町中の方が、人はより助けてもらえる傾向が高いということがわかる） 中央大学

コロ be prone to A（Aする傾向がある）

でた！ They are prone to bone fracture.
（彼らは骨が折れやすい傾向にある） 上智大学

## 0362 liable [láiəbl]
形 しがちである、病気にかかりやすい、責任がある

コロ be liable to A（Aしがちである）

でた！ Men are liable to be at the mercy of the current of the time.
（人間は時の流れのなすがままになりがちである） 立正大学

派 **liability** 名 責任、義務

## 0363 trend [trénd]
名 傾向、風潮、流行、トレンド

類 **fashion** [fǽʃən] 名 流行

でた！ What sort of coats are in fashion this year?
（どんな種類のコートが今年流行していますか） 青山学院大学

派 **fashionable** 形 流行の、上流階級の

## 0364 lean [líːn]
動 傾く、もたれる（＋on, against） 名 傾向、傾斜

コロ lean forward（前かがみになる）

Chapter3 Science | 133

# UNIT 30 習慣・伝統

**STEP 1 過去問を解く**

## 1

I've lived near the airport so long that I'm now ( ) to the noise of the airplanes.

センター試験

1. aware
2. conscious
3. familiar
4. used

## 2

A recent survey indicates that the eating ( ) of Japanese are changing very fast, especially among young people.

大東文化大学

1. foods
2. habits
3. meals
4. performances
5. types

## 3

Getting used to a foreign culture is a ( ) that takes some time.

センター試験

1. career
2. characteristic
3. policy
4. process

## 4

They ( ) to old customs in everything.

中央大学

1. belong
2. follow
3. stay
4. stick

## STEP 2 正解を見抜く

### 1

I've lived near the airport so long that I'm now used to the noise of the airplanes.

正解 ④

**訳** 空港の近くに長く住んでいるので飛行機の騒音に慣れている。

- aware 形 気づいて
- conscious 形 気づいて
- familiar 形 親しい、精通している
- used 形 慣れて

be used to ～ ing「～することに慣れている」、used to A「かつてよくAしたものだ（過去の習慣）」の混同に注意！

### 2

A recent survey indicates that the eating habits of Japanese are changing very fast, especially among young people.

正解 ②

**訳** 最近の調査で特に若者の間で、日本人の食習慣が急激に変わっているとわかる。

- food 名 食物
- meal 名 食事
- type 名 型
- habit 名 癖
- performance 名 演技

habitは「悪い癖や習慣」でcustomは「習慣、文化的なしきたり」のイメージ

### 3

Getting used to a foreign culture is a process that takes some time.

正解 ④

**訳** 外国の文化に慣れることはある程度の時間がかかるプロセスである。

- career 名 経歴
- characteristic 名 特徴
- policy 名 政策
- process 名 過程、プロセス

### 4

They stick to old customs in everything.

正解 ④

**訳** 彼らが全てにおいて古い習慣を堅持している。

- belong 動 所属する
- follow 動 従う
- stay 動 滞在する
- stick 動 くっつく、堅持する

stick to Aで「Aに固執する」1つのことに固執して考えを曲げないイメージ

UNIT 30 習慣・伝統

Chapter3 Science

## STEP 3 連鎖式に語彙を増やす 🎧30

● 語源 hab (持つ)

### 0365 habit [hǽbit]
名 癖、（良くない）習慣

It is very difficult to persuade all smokers to give up the habit.
（すべての喫煙者を説得してその習慣をやめさせるのは非常に難しい） 立教大学

コロ be in the habit of ~ing （〜する習慣がある）

Bill is in the habit of drinking milk with all his meals.
（ビルは食事の度に牛乳を飲む習慣がある） 東海大学

コロ get rid of the habit of ~ing （癖を直す）

You should get rid of your bad habit of staying up late.
（あなたは夜更かしする悪い癖をやめた方がいいよ） 摂南大学

派 habitual [həbítʃuəl] ア 形 習慣的な

### 0366 habitat [hǽbitæt]
名 生息地

The habitat extended throughout Europe.
（生息地はヨーロッパ中に広がった） TOEFL

派 habitation 名 居住

### 0367 inhabit [inhǽbit]
動 住む

派 inhabitant 名 住民

### 0368 custom [kʌ́stəm]
名 慣習　原義 自分のもの

派 customs 名 関税

派 customize 動 カスタマイズする

派 accustom 動 慣れさせる

コロ get accustomed to A （Aに慣れる）= get used to A

People are already accustomed to ATMs and self-service gas pumps.
（人々は既にATMやセルフ給油機に慣れている） 立教大学

> customは「慣習的な習慣」。
> customの原義は「自分のもの」
> customize「カスタマイズ（自分の好みに合わせて設定）する」
> customer「顧客」
> customs「関税」
> accustom「慣れさせる」

### 0369 tradition [trədíʃən]
名 伝統　原義 先祖から引き渡されたもの

派 traditional 形 伝統的な

### 0370 conventional [kənvénʃənl]
形 型にはまった、従来の

コロ conventional theory （従来の理論）

The conventional style of school education should be thoroughly reviewed.
（昔ながらの学校教育のあり方は徹底的に見直さなければならない） 群馬大学

派 convention 名 （政治・宗教上の）大会、集会、習慣、協定

## 0371 rule [rúːl] 　　名 規則　動 支配する

- Rules are made to be broken.
  （規則は破られるためにある）
- as a rule （概して、普通は）
- As a rule, I get up at 7:00 every morning.
  （普通は毎朝7時に起床します） 〔東海大学〕
- by and large （概して）
- By and large, the Japanese economy has performed quite well.
  （概して、日本の経済は極めて順調にやってきた） 〔中央大学〕
- on the whole （全体として）
- We must take this matter into account on the whole.
  （私たちはこの件を全体として考慮に入れなければならない） 〔慶應義塾大学〕
- make it a rule to A （Aということにしている）
- Mr. Smith makes it a rule to take a walk every morning.
  （スミスさんは毎朝散歩することにしています） 〔慶應義塾大学〕
- be used to ~ ing （～に慣れている）
- used to A （よくAしたものだ）
- would often A （よくAしたものだ）※状態動詞は使えない。

## 0372 adopt [ədɑ́pt | ədɔ́pt] 　　動 （理論・技術を）採用する
- adopt a method （方法を採用する）

派 **adoption** 　名 採用、養子にすること

## 0373 familiar [fəmíljər] 　　形 親しい、精通している
- He is not familiar with the topic the professor is discussing.
  （教授が議論しているトピックに、彼は精通していない） 〔TOEFL〕

反 **unfamiliar** 　形 よく知らない、見慣れない、珍しい

## 0374 stick [stík] 　　名 杖　動 突き刺す
- stick to A （Aに固執する）　　be stuck （行き詰まっている）
- stick to the point （論点から逸れない）
- The nail that sticks out gets hit with the hammer.
  （出る杭は打たれる）

## 0375 process [prɑ́ses | próu-] 　　名 過程、プロセス　動 処理する
- When one person teaches another through speech or writing, this process is called learning by instruction.
  （人が他人に口頭や文字で教えるこの過程がいわゆる習って覚えるということだ） 〔成城大学〕

UNIT 30 習慣・伝統

Chapter3 Science

# UNIT 31 発明・達成

**STEP 1** 過去問を解く

## 1

He devised a folding toothbrush for travelers which became a bestseller.

上智大学

1. sold
2. bought
3. invented
4. described

## 2

An (　　) is a machine or process which has been made or thought of for the first time.

センター試験

1. expression
2. illustration
3. imagination
4. invention

## 3

The only way for us to (　　) this task is to get help from Mr. Smith.

立命館大学

1. accomplish
2. benefit
3. require
4. seek

## 4

Clare wants to be a doctor, but I doubt very much if she will (　　) her ambition.

上智大学

1. qualify
2. receive
3. achieve
4. construct

## STEP 2 正解を見抜く

### 1

He invented a folding toothbrush for travelers which became a bestseller.

正解 ③

**訳** 彼は旅行者用の折りたたみ歯ブラシを発明し、ベストセラーとなった。

- **sell** 動 売る
- **buy** 動 買う
- **invent** 動 発明する
- **describe** 動 描写する

### 2

An invention is a machine or process which has been made or thought of for the first time.

正解 ④

**訳** 発明とは最初に考えられ作られた機械や工程のことをいう。

- **expression** 名 表現
- **illustration** 名 実例、イラスト
- **imagination** 名 想像
- **invention** 名 発明

in（中に）+ vent（来る）
＝頭の中に良いアイデアが来る＝発明

### 3

The only way for us to accomplish this task is to get help from Mr. Smith.

正解 ①

**訳** 我々がこの仕事を成し遂げるための唯一の方法は、スミス氏に援助して頂くことだ。

- **accomplish** 動 達成する
- **benefit** 動 ためになる
- **require** 動 必要とする
- **seek** 動 求める

### 4

Clare wants to be a doctor, but I doubt very much if she will achieve her ambition.

正解 ③

**訳** クレアは医師になりたがっていますが、私は、彼女が大望を遂げるかどうか大変疑問に思っています。

- **qualify** 動 資格を与える
- **achieve** 動 達成する
- **receive** 動 受け取る
- **construct** 動 建設する

UNIT 31 発明・達成

Chapter3 Science

## STEP 3 連鎖式に語彙を増やす 31

### ● 語源 vent（来る）

**0376 invent** [invént] 　動 発明する、考案する、話をでっち上げる
原義 in（中に）＋vent（来る）

でた! Walter found it difficult to tell the truth, so he had to invent a story.
（ウォルターは真実を話しづらかったので作り話をしなければならなかった） センター試験

派 **invention** 　名 発明

**0377 event** [ivént] 　名 イベント　原義 e（外に）＋vent（来る）

でた! History is the story of the events that led to the present.
（歴史とは現在に導いた出来事についての話である） 首都大学東京

**0378 prevent** [privént] 　動 防ぐ、妨げる

でた! Researchers are developing a vaccine that will prevent AIDS.
（研究者たちはエイズを予防するワクチンを開発中である） 慶應義塾大学

コロ prevent A from ~ing（Aが~することを妨げる）

でた! Lack of time prevents me from writing to you.
（時間がなくて君に手紙が書けないんだよ） 日本大学

派 **prevention** 　名 防止
派 **preventive** 　形 予防の

> クリスマス前の約4週間を指す。その4週間は祈りと断食の時期である。

**0379 advent** [ǽdvent] 　名 出現　原義 キリストの降臨

でた! With the advent of computers, many tasks have been made easier.
（コンピュータの出現と共に、多くの仕事が容易になった） TOEFL

**0380 create** [kriéit] 　動 創造する

でた! Identity needs to be created, just like works of art are created.
（芸術作品が作り出されるのと同様、個性も作り出される必要がある） 中央大学

派 **creative** 　形 創造的な
派 **creativity** 　名 創造性
派 **creation** 　名 創造
派 **creature** [kríːtʃər] 発 　名 生き物

> tureはラテン語で過去分詞を表します。「創造されたもの」つまり神によって創造されたのが生き物なのです。

**0381 devise** [diváiz] 発 ア 　動 考案する、工夫する　原義 分割する

コロ make up（作り出す）

> 分割するには工夫が必要だったので考案するという意味になった。

派 **device** 　名 装置、工夫
コロ safety device（安全装置）

140

| 0382 | **develop** [divéləp] | 動 発展させる |
|---|---|---|
| | コロ develop a product（製品を開発する） | |
| | 派 **development** | 名 発展 |

| 0383 | **improve** [imprúːv] | 動 改善させる、よくなる |
|---|---|---|
| | でた! Science and technology have improved our lives over the past 150 years.<br>（科学技術は過去150年にわたって我々の生活を向上させてきた） | 東京大学 |
| | 派 **improvement** | 名 改善、向上 |

| 0384 | **exploit** [ikspl´ɔit] | 動 開発する、私的な目的で不当に利用する |
|---|---|---|
| | 派 **exploitation** | 名 開発、利用 |

| 0385 | **install** [instɔ́ːl] | 動 設置する、インストールする |
|---|---|---|
| | でた! You can install solar panels on your roof.<br>（屋根に太陽光パネルを設置することができます） | 関西大学 |
| | 派 **installation** | 名 設置 |

| 0386 | **exist** [igzíst] | 動 存在する |
|---|---|---|
| | 派 **existence** | 名 存在 |
| | コロ come into existence（生まれる） コロ bring A into existence（Aを生み出す） | |

| 0387 | **patent** [pǽtnt] | 名 特許 形 特許の 動 特許を取る |
|---|---|---|

| 0388 | **achieve** [ətʃíːv] | 動 達成する、成し遂げる、獲得する |
|---|---|---|
| | 派 **achievement** | 名 達成、偉業、業績 |
| | コロ sense of achievement（達成感） | |
| | でた! The press described Einstein's theories as the greatest achievement in history.<br>（報道はアインシュタインの理論は歴史上最も偉大な業績であると述べた） | 東京理科大学 |
| | 類 **attain** | 動 達成する、到達する |

| 0389 | **accomplish** [əkɑ́mpliʃ, əkʌ́m- \| əkʌ́m-, əkɔ́m-] ア | 動 達成する、成し遂げる |
|---|---|---|
| | 派 **accomplishment** | 名 達成、功績、業績 |

| 0390 | **fulfill** [fulfíl] ア | 動 果たす、実現する、満たす |
|---|---|---|
| | 派 **fulfillment** | 名 遂行、実現 |

| 0391 | **ambition** [æmbíʃən] | 名 野望、野心 |
|---|---|---|
| | 派 **ambitious** | 形 野心のある、大望を抱いた |

UNIT 31 発明・達成

# UNIT 32 生産・利益

## STEP 1 過去問を解く

### 1

A: Do you know what they (　　) at the big factory near the river?
B: I'm pretty sure that they make car parts there.

英語検定準2級

1. produce
2. reply
3. require
4. perform

### 2

Recently, manufacturing technology has increased (　　), or the amount of goods and services available.

慶応義塾大学

1. producers
2. products
3. produce
4. productivity

### 3

Because of improved technology, factory (　　) is expected to rise this year.

学習院大学

1. outbreak
2. outcome
3. outlook
4. output

### 4

Renewable sources of energy such as solar power have an important role to play in (　　) electricity in the future.

中央大学

1. dominating
2. generating
3. innovating
4. participating

142

## STEP 2 正解を見抜く

### 1

A: Do you know what they produce at the big factory near the river?
B: I'm pretty sure that they make car parts there.

正解 ①

**訳** A：あなたは、彼らが川の近くの大きい工場で何を生産しているかを知っていますか？
B：私は、彼らがそこで自動車部品を作っていることをかなり確信しています。

**produce** 動生産する　　**reply** 動返事する
**require** 動必要とする
**perform** 動演じる

工場（factory）で何をしているのか問う文章なのでproduce（生産する）が連想できます

### 2

Recently, manufacturing technology has increased productivity, or the amount of goods and services available.

正解 ④

**訳** 最近手工業技術は生産性を上げ、また商品の量やサービスを利用可能にしている。

**producer** 名プロデューサー
**product** 名商品
**produce** 動生産する
**productivity** 名生産性

### 3

Because of improved technology, factory output is expected to rise this year.

正解 ④

**訳** 技術の改善により、今年の工場の生産高が上がることが期待される。

**outbreak** 名勃発
**outcome** 名結果
**outlook** 名見解
**output** 名生産高

### 4

Renewable sources of energy such as solar power have an important role to play in generating electricity in the future.

正解 ②

**訳** ソーラーパワーなどの再生可能エネルギーは将来電気を起こす上で重要な役割を演じる。

**dominate** 動支配する
**generate** 動生み出す
**innovate** 動革新する
**participate** 動参加する

generate electricityは「発電する」です。ちなみにgeneratorは「発電機」

Chapter3 Science

## STEP 3 連鎖式に語彙を増やす 🎧32

● 語源 duce（導く）

### 0392 produce [prədjúːs | -djúːs]
動 生産する
原義 pro（前に）+ duce（導く）= 人の前に出す

でた! We will need more water to produce our food in the future.
（将来は、食糧を生産するためにより多くの水が必要になるだろう） 早稲田大学

派 **reproduce** — 動 再生する、複製する

派 **production** — 名 生産
コロ mass production（大量生産）

### 0393 productive [prədʌ́ktiv]
形 生産的な

派 **reproductive** — 形 生殖の、複写の

派 **productivity** — 名 生産性
コロ increase productivity（生産性を高める）

派 **product** — 名 商品

類 **output** — 名 （一定期間の）生産高

### 0394 introduce [ìntrədjúːs | -djúːs]
動 紹介する、導入する
原義 into（最初に）+ duc（導く）

コロ introduce A to B（BにAを紹介する）

派 **introduction** — 名 紹介、導入

でた! The introduction of farming methods during the agricultural revolution changed the status of women.
（農業革命の間の耕作方法の導入が女性の地位を変えた） TOEFL

派 **introductory** — 形 紹介の、入門的な

### 0395 conduct [kəndʌ́kt] ⚠
動 熱・光・電気を伝導する、調査・業務を行う
[kɑ́ndʌkt] 名 行為

でた! Different materials conduct heat differently.
（素材が異なると熱伝導率も異なる） センター試験

派 **conductor** — 名 案内人、指導者、添乗員

派 **semiconductor** — 名 半導体

- 語源 **gen**(生む)

0396 **genius** [dʒíːnjəs] 名 天才

0397 **generation** [dʒènəréiʃən] 名 世代
- generation gap (世代差)

派 **generate** 動 生み出す
- generate electricity (発電する)

派 **generator** 名 発電機

0398 **gene** [dʒíːn] 名 遺伝子

派 **genetic** 形 遺伝子の
- genetic modification (遺伝子組み換え)

0399 **gender** [dʒéndər] 名 ジェンダー、社会的・文化的な性
- gender stereotype (社会的性に関する固定観念)

0400 **gentle** [dʒéntl] 形 優しい、穏やかな
- in a gentle voice (優しい声で)

派 **gentleman** 名 紳士

0401 **general** [dʒénərəl] 形 一般的な
- in general (概して)

でた! In general, the weather in Scotland is very changeable.
(概して、スコットランドの天気はとても変わりやすい)  関西大学

派 **generally** 副 一般的に
- generally speaking (一般的に言って)

0402 **manufacture** [mænjufǽktʃər] 動 製造する 名 製造  原義 manu(手で) + fac(作る)

でた! In ancient Egypt, perfume was already manufactured in factories.
(古代エジプトでは既に工場で香水が製造されていた)  成城大学

類 **manual** 形 手で行う、肉体の 名 マニュアル、手引き
- manual labor (肉体労働)

0403 **yield** [jíːld] 動 産出する、生む、屈服する
名 生産高、収穫量

でた! Farmers rush to adopt higher yielding varieties of corn of mixed species.
(農家はより多くの産出ができる多様な混合種のコーンを競って採り入れた)  東京大学
- yield to A (Aに屈する)
- give in to A (Aに降参する、屈服する)

でた! My mother finally has given in to my view.
(母はついに折れて私の考えを受け入れた)  愛知工業大学

UNIT 32 生産・利益

Chapter3 Science | 145

# UNIT 33 電話・会話

## STEP 1 過去問を解く

### 1

John <u>rang up</u> Hanna and told her the news.

立命館大学

1. stopped
2. telephoned
3. visited
4. woke up

### 2

He suddenly (　　) up the phone while I was speaking.

関西学院大学

1. shut
2. hung
3. cut
4. hang

### 3

Please hold the (　　) for a moment.

青山学院大学

1. conversation
2. call
3. line
4. receiver

### 4

Daniel kept on telephoning the customer service center to complain, but the line was always (　　).

中央大学

1. full
2. busy
3. crowded
4. occupied

## STEP 2 正解を見抜く

### 1

John telephoned Hanna and told her the news. 正解 ②

**訳** ジョンはハンナに電話してその知らせを伝えた。

- stop 動 止める
- telephone 動 電話をかける、電話で伝える
- visit 動 訪問する
- wake up 目が覚める

### 2

He suddenly hung up the phone while I was speaking. 正解 ②

**訳** 彼は私が話しているとき突然電話を切った。

- shut up しまい込む
- hang up （電話を）切る
- cut up 細かく切る
- hang up （電話を）切る

### 3

Please hold the line for a moment. 正解 ③

**訳** 電話を切らずにしばらくお待ち下さい。

- conversation 名 会話
- call 名 （電話の）呼び出し
- line 名 電話線
- receiver 名 受話器

### 4

Daniel kept on telephoning the customer service center to complain, but the line was always busy. 正解 ②

**訳** ダニエルは苦情を言うためにお客様サービスセンターに電話したが、ずっと話中だった。

- full 形 いっぱいの
- busy 形 電話が話中の
- crowd 動 群がる
- occupy 動 占領する

> busyは「忙しい」以外にも「人通りが多い、電話が話し中である」という意味があります。busy streetは「繁華街」です

Chapter3 Science | 147

## STEP 3 連鎖式に語彙を増やす 🎧33

● 語源 tele（遠い）

### 0404 telephone [téləfòun]
名 （本来有線の）電話　動 電話する
原義 tele（遠い）＋phone（音声）

でた! A man named Alexander Graham Bell invented the world's first telephone.
（アレキサンダー・グラハム・ベルという男が世界で最初の電話を発明した）　早稲田大学

コロ call up（電話をかける）

派 **phone**　名 （無線の）電話

### 0405 television [téləvìʒən]
名 テレビ　原義 tele（遠い）＋pathy（感情）

でた! Television has often been accused of promoting obesity and aggression in the young.（テレビは若者たちの肥満や攻撃性を促進するとよく非難されてきた）　名古屋大学

### 0406 telegram [téligræm]
名 電報　原義 tele（遠い）＋gram（書く）

### 0407 telescope [téləskòup]
名 望遠鏡　原義 tele（遠い）＋scope（覗く）

### 0408 cellphone [sélfóun]
名 携帯電話

類 **cell** [sél]　名 細胞、独房、電池

コロ recharge cellphone（携帯電話を充電する）
コロ My cellphone is out of service now.（私の携帯電話は今圏外です）

### 0409 mobile [móubəl | -bail]
形 移動可能な

コロ mobile phone（携帯電話）

でた! Some 75 percent of all telephones in Africa are mobile.
（アフリカの全電話のおよそ75％が携帯電話である）

コロ give A a ring（Aに電話をかける）

でた! As soon as you get to San Diego, please give me a ring.
（サンディエゴに着いたらすぐに電話してください）　青山学院大学

コロ give A a shot（Aに電話をかける）

### 0410 line [láin]
名 電話線、商売

コロ The line is busy.（話中です）

でた! What line are you in?
（あなたの商売は何ですか）　早稲田大学

コロ hold on（電話を切らないで待つ）　コロ hang up（電話を切る）

### 0411 conversation [kànvərséiʃən | kɔ̀n-]
名 会話

でた! Their conversation carried on for about an hour.
（彼らの会話は約一時間続いた）　横浜市立大学

派 **converse**　動 会話をする

| 類 chat [tʃæt] | 動 雑談する、おしゃべりする |
| | 名 チャット、雑談、おしゃべり |

# UNIT 34　維持・保持

## STEP 1 過去問を解く

### 1

The principal managed to keep the students' interest until the end of her speech.

大東文化大学

1. combine
2. explain
3. contain
4. maintain

### 2

Frequent (　　) helps your bicycle last longer.

上智大学

1. equipment
2. maintenance
3. regulation
4. contact

### 3

The NPO is trying to promote (　　) agriculture which doesn't cause damage to the environment.

東京理科大学

1. audible
2. horrible
3. incapable
4. sustainable

### 4

Some companies (　　) their traditional ways of doing business despite the trend for new business style.

立命館大学

1. detached
2. emitted
3. retained
4. stranded

## STEP 2 正解を見抜く

### 1

The principal managed to maintain the students' interest until the end of her speech.

正解 ④

**訳** その校長はスピーチが終わるまで生徒の関心を何とか維持しようとした。

- **combine** 動 結合する
- **explain** 動 説明する
- **contain** 動 含む
- **maintain** 動 維持する

> maintainの語源はmain（手で）+ tain（保つ）

### 2

Frequent maintenance helps your bicycle last longer.

正解 ②

**訳** たびたび点検すれば、自転車を長く持たせることができる。

- **equipment** 名 装置
- **maintenance** 名 維持、整備
- **regulation** 名 規制
- **contact** 名 接触

> maintenance（維持）は日本語でもメンテナンスと言いますね

### 3

The NPO is trying to promote sustainable agriculture which doesn't cause damage to the environment.

正解 ④

**訳** その非営利組織は環境に害を与えない環境に優しい農業を推進しようとしています。

- **audible** 形 聞こえる
- **horrible** 形 恐ろしい
- **incapable** 形 ～することが出来ない
- **sustainable** 形 持続可能な、環境に優しい

> sustainableの語源はsus（下で）+ tain（保つ）+ able（可能）＝下で保つことができる＝持続可能な

### 4

Some companies retained their traditional ways of doing business despite the trend for new business style.

正解 ③

**訳** 最新のビジネススタイルにも関わらず、伝統的なやり方を維持する会社もある。

- **detach** 動 引き離す
- **emit** 動 （熱・匂いを）放つ
- **retain** 動 保つ、維持する
- **strand** 動 取り残される

> retainの語源はre（強調）+ tain（保つ）＝強く保つ＝維持する

UNIT 34 維持・保持

Chapter3 Science

## STEP 3 連鎖式に語彙を増やす 🎧34

● 語源 tain（保つ）

### 0412 maintain [meintéin]
動 維持する　原義 main（手で）＋tain（保つ）

でた! The Romani people maintain a strong sense of identity and culture..
（ロマニの人々は強いアイデンティティの意識と文化を維持している）　明治大学

派 **maintenance** 名 維持、メンテナンス、整備
コロ regular maintenance （定期保守）

### 0413 sustain [səstéin]
動 （建物を）支える、（家族の生命を）維持する
原義 sus（下に）＋tain（保つ）

コロ sustain economic growth （経済成長を維持する）

でた! Wetlands are indispensable to sustain water plants and animals.
（湿地は水生の動植物の生命を維持するのに不可欠である）　追手門学院大学

派 **sustainable** 形 支持できる、維持できる
でた! Bicycles are the most sustainable and efficient form of urban transportation.
（自転車は、都市交通で最も持続可能で効率のいい形式である）　同志社大学

### 0414 retain [ritéin]
動 保つ、維持する
原義 re（強調）＋tain（保つ）

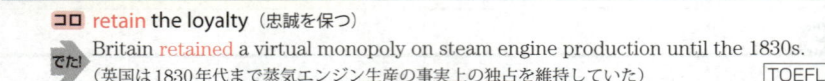

コロ retain the loyalty （忠誠を保つ）

でた! Britain retained a virtual monopoly on steam engine production until the 1830s.
（英国は1830年代まで蒸気エンジン生産の事実上の独占を維持していた）　TOEFL

派 **retention** 名 保持、記憶

### 0415 entertain [èntərtéin] ⑦
動 楽しませる

でた! Adults often use songs to entertain children.
（子供を楽しませるために大人はよく歌を使う）　東北大学

派 **entertainment** 名 娯楽
類 **pastime** [pǽstàim] 名 気晴らし、娯楽

### 0416 attain [ətéin]
動 達成する、成し遂げる

コロ attain fame （有名になる）

派 **attainment** 名 達成、実現

## 0417 obtain [əbtéin]
**動** 獲得する

How did you obtain such a precious painting?
（そんな貴重な絵をどうやって手に入れたのですか） 〔東海大学〕

**コロ** come by（手に入れる）

**派** obtainable　　**形** 獲得できる、入手可能な

## 0418 contain [kəntéin]
**動** 含む　　原義 con（共に）＋ tain（保つ）

English dictionaries contain many more words than those of other languages.
（英語の辞書は他の言語の単語よりも多くの単語を含んでいる） 〔拓殖大学〕

**派** content [kάntent] ⑦　　**名** 中身、内容、コンテンツ　**形** 満足して

Parents should check the content of video games before buying them for their children.
（親は子供にテレビゲームを買い与える前に、その内容を確認すべきだ） 〔センター試験〕

Are you content with your own business?
（あなたは自分の仕事に満足していますか）

**類** satisfy [sǽtisfài]　　**動** 満足させる

**コロ** be satisfied with A（Aに満足している）

George looked satisfied when I apologized to him for my rudeness.
（私が失礼だったと謝るとジョージは満足したようだった） 〔成城大学〕

**派** satisfaction　　**名** 満足

## 0419 detain [ditéin]
**動** 引き留める

**コロ** detain suspects（容疑者を拘留する）

**派** detention　　**名** 留置、居残り

## 0420 abstain [æbstéin, əb-]
**動** 慎む、控える　　原義 abs（分離）＋ tain（保つ）

**類** refrain [rifréin]　　**動** 控える

**コロ** refrain from ~ing（～するのを差し控える）

You are supposed to refrain from smoking in this auditorium.
（この講堂では喫煙は差し控えて下さい） 〔東北大学〕

UNIT 34　維持・保持

Chapter3 Science

# UNIT 35 動作・活動

**STEP 1** 過去問を解く

## 1

If better employment opportunities can be provided in small towns, the (　　　) of country folk to the cities can be slowed.

センター試験

1. journey
2. motion
3. movement
4. passage

## 2

The up and down (　　　) that boats make at sea causes some people to feel sick. This feeling is called "seasickness."

英語検定2級

1. mission
2. expense
3. theme
4. motion

## 3

It <u>functions</u> mechanically in the same way that an automobile engine does.

中央大学

1. works
2. builds
3. develops
4. walks

## 4

Brett has many spare-time (　　　): he swims, paints, plays the violin, and so on.

センター試験

1. actions
2. activities
3. exercises
4. habits

154

## STEP 2 正解を見抜く

### 1

If better employment opportunities can be provided in small towns, the movement of country folk to the cities can be slowed.  正解 ③

訳 もし小さな町で雇用機会が提供されれば、都市に移り住む人々の動きはゆっくりになるだろう。

- journey 名（陸上の比較的長い）旅行
- motion 名動き
- movement 名動き
- passage 名通路

> motionは「抽象的な動き」、movementは「具体的な動き」

### 2

The up and down motion that boats make at sea causes some people to feel sick. This feeling is called "seasickness."  正解 ④

訳 ボートが海で作り出す上下の動きで人々は具合が悪くなります。これを船酔いと言います。

- mission 名任務
- theme 名テーマ
- expense 名費用
- motion 名動き

### 3

It works mechanically in the same way that an automobile engine does.  正解 ①

訳 それは自動車のエンジンと同じ方式で機械的に作動する。

- work 動作動する
- build 動建てる
- develop 動発展する
- walk 動歩く

### 4

Brett has many spare-time activities: he swims, paints, plays the violin, and so on.  正解 ②

訳 ブレットは水泳、絵画、バイオリンの演奏など余暇の活動が多彩だ。

- action 名行為
- activity 名活動
- exercise 名運動
- habit 名癖

Chapter3 Science

## STEP 3 連鎖式に語彙を増やす 35

### ● 語源 mov mob mot (動く)

**0421 move** [múːv] 　動 動く、引っ越す、感動させる　名 動き
I can beat you at chess in less than five moves.
(私は、5つ未満の動きであなたをチェスで負かすことができます)　早稲田大学

派 **movement**　名 運動、動作

派 **motion**　名 動き、動作

派 **movie**　名 映画
コロ movie theater (映画館)

類 **film**　名 映画《英》

**0422 remove** [rimúːv]　動 取り除く
The scientists carefully removed all possibilities of error from their research.
(科学者達はその研究における誤りの可能性を全て注意深く取り除いた)　青山学院大学

派 **removable**　形 取り外しできる

派 **removal**　名 除去

**0423 emotion** [imóuʃən]　名 感情　原義 e (外に) + mot (動く)
Hands reveal our inward emotions.
(手は私たちの内心の感情を表します)　学習院大学

派 **emotional**　形 感情の

**0424 promote** [prəmóut]　動 促進する　原義 pro (前に) + mot (動く)
Most countries are promoting their tourist industries.
(ほとんどの国が観光産業を促進している)　法政大学

派 **promotion**　名 促進、昇進

**0425 remote** [rimóut]　形 遠い、離れた、辺鄙な
Japanese honor their more remote family ancestors.
(日本人はより遠い家系の先祖を崇拝する)　上智大学

派 **distant** [dístənt]　形 距離がある、遠い

派 **distance**　名 距離
コロ fly over long distance (長距離を飛行する)
Seen at a distance, she might have been taken for a woman of about fifty.
(少し離れてみれば、彼女は50歳くらいの女性に見間違えられたかもしれない)　早稲田大学

## 0426 motive [móutiv] 名 行動を起こさせるための動機

でた! Some students have a special motive for studying English.
（英語学習に特別な動機を持っている学生もいる） 法政大学

派 **motivate** [móutəvèit] 動 動機を与える
でた! Grades motivate most students to do well in their studies.
（学問において、成績は生徒によく勉強するような動機を与える） TOEFL

派 **motivation** 名 動機

## 0427 incentive [inséntiv] 名 やる気を起こさせるための動機

## 0428 stimulate [stímjulèit] 動 刺激する

派 **stimulus** [stímjuləs] 名 刺激 複 stimuli

## 0429 machine [məʃíːn] 名 機械

派 **mechanic** 名 機械工

派 **mechanism** 名 仕組み、メカニズム

## 0430 work [wə́ːrk] 動 動く、働く、作動する

## 0431 function [fʌ́ŋkʃən] 名 機能 動 機能する、働く

コロ brain function （脳の機能）

でた! The alarm system was not functioning when the burglars broke into the house.
（泥棒が入ったときに、その警報装置は作動していなかった） 中央大学

派 **functional** 形 機能の

## 0432 act [ǽkt] 動 行動する、演じる

でた! All you have to do is to act on his advice.
（あなたは彼のアドバイスに従いさえすれば良い） 明治大学

派 **action** 名 行動

派 **active** 形 活発な

派 **activity** 名 活動

## 0433 passive [pǽsiv] 形 受動的な

コロ passive voice （受動態）

## 0434 impulse [ímpʌls] 名 衝動

コロ on impulse （衝動的に）

派 **impulsive** 形 衝動的な

Chapter3 Science

### coffee break ☕

　OECD生徒の学習到達度調査PISAで数学的リテラシー、読解力、科学的リテラシーの世界ランキングが発表されました。

|  | 数学的リテラシー | 読解力 | 科学的リテラシー |
|---|---|---|---|
| 1位 | 上海 | 上海 | 上海 |
| 2位 | シンガポール | 韓国 | フィンランド |
| 3位 | 香港 | フィンランド | 香港 |
| 4位 | 韓国 | シンガポール | シンガポール |
| 5位 | 台湾 | カナダ | 日本 |

　2000年度の調査で日本は、数学的リテラシーで世界1位、科学的リテラシーで世界2位と世界でも教育大国として知れ渡りましたが、今は数学的リテラシーは9位、読解力は8位、科学的リテラシーは5位と段々と順位を下げています。

　私は小学校から高校までの上海の学校を訪問し、授業を見学し、先生や生徒にインタビューをしました。

　日本と違うところは「英語の授業で母語は使用しない」ということと、「教師は全員大学院卒」ということでした。教師はパワーポイントを使用し、視覚教材を取り入れ生徒を魅了する教育を行っていました。教師と生徒が互いにコミュニケーションをとるインタラクティブな授業が非常に印象的でした。

　フィンランドでは授業時間が少なく、定期テストもありません。授業は少人数制で「考える事」を中心とした教育で伸び伸びと子どもが育つ環境を提供しています。

# Chapter 4
# Society

## UNIT 36　輸送機関　STEP 1 過去問を解く

### 1

A: Excuse me. Does this train go directly to the airport?
B: No. You'll have to (　　　) to Green Line at the next station.

英語検定2級

1. overcome
2. interpret
3. transfer
4. relate

### 2

The new mayor promised to improve (　　　) in the city by adding more bus and train services.

英語検定2級

1. transportation
2. opposition
3. recognition
4. nutrition

### 3

I happened to see my old friends in the train (　　　) for London.

東京理科大学

1. binding
2. entering
3. heading
4. overtaking

### 4

We may encounter strong (　　　) during the flight, so please keep your seat belt fastened when you are seated.

英語検定準1級

1. affection
2. inspection
3. turbulence
4. interference

**STEP 2 正解を見抜く**

## 1

A: Excuse me. Does this train go directly to the airport?
B: No. You'll have to transfer to Green Line at the next station. 正解 ③

訳 A：すみません。この電車は直接空港に向かいますか。
B：いいえ。次の駅でグリーンラインに乗り換えなければなりません。

- **overcome** 動 打ち勝つ
- **interpret** 動 通訳する
- **transfer** 動 乗り換える
- **relate** 動 関連づける

transferの語源はtrans（横切る）＋fer（運ぶ）
＝別の電車に荷物を持って運ぶ＝乗り換える

## 2

The new mayor promised to improve transportation in the city by adding more bus and train services. 正解 ①

訳 新しい市長は、バスと電車のサービスをもっと増やすことにより市内輸送を改善すると約束しました。

- **transportation** 名 輸送
- **opposition** 名 反対
- **recognition** 名 認識
- **nutrition** 名 栄養

## 3

I happened to see my old friends in the train heading for London. 正解 ③

訳 ロンドンに向かう電車の中で旧友に遭遇した。

- **bind** 動 縛る
- **enter** 動 入る
- **head for A** Aに向かう
- **overtake** 動 追いつく、追い越す

head（頭）をfor
（方向に向ける）＝
目的地に向かう

## 4

We may encounter strong turbulence during the flight, so please keep your seat belt fastened when you are seated. 正解 ③

訳 飛行中は乱気流に遭遇するかもしれないので、着席しているときはシートベルトを着用しつづけてください。

- **affection** 名 愛情
- **inspection** 名 検査
- **turbulence** 名 乱気流
- **interference** 名 妨害

turbulenceの語源はturb（乱す）です。グルグル回るイメージから乱気流が連想できますね

UNIT 36 輸送機関

Chapter4 Society

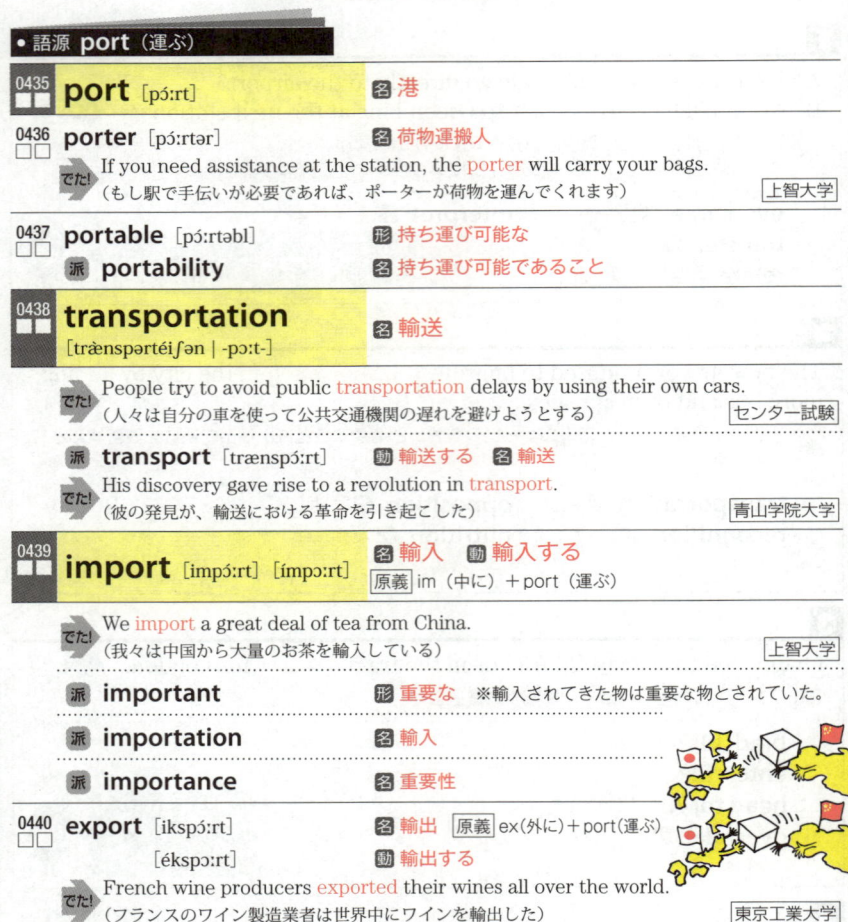

## STEP 3 連鎖式に語彙を増やす 🎧36

### ● 語源 port (運ぶ)

**0435 port** [pɔ́ːrt] 　名 港

**0436 porter** [pɔ́ːrtər] 　名 荷物運搬人
でた! If you need assistance at the station, the porter will carry your bags.
(もし駅で手伝いが必要であれば、ポーターが荷物を運んでくれます) 〔上智大学〕

**0437 portable** [pɔ́ːrtəbl] 　形 持ち運び可能な
派 **portability** 　名 持ち運び可能であること

**0438 transportation** [trænspərtéiʃən | -pɔːt-] 　名 輸送
でた! People try to avoid public transportation delays by using their own cars.
(人々は自分の車を使って公共交通機関の遅れを避けようとする) 〔センター試験〕

派 **transport** [trænspɔ́ːrt] 　動 輸送する　名 輸送
でた! His discovery gave rise to a revolution in transport.
(彼の発見が、輸送における革命を引き起こした) 〔青山学院大学〕

**0439 import** [impɔ́ːrt] [ímpɔːrt] 　名 輸入　動 輸入する
原義 im (中に) + port (運ぶ)
でた! We import a great deal of tea from China.
(我々は中国から大量のお茶を輸入している) 〔上智大学〕

派 **important** 　形 重要な　※輸入されてきた物は重要な物とされていた。
派 **importation** 　名 輸入
派 **importance** 　名 重要性

**0440 export** [ikspɔ́ːrt] 　名 輸出　原義 ex(外に) + port(運ぶ)
[ékspɔːrt] 　動 輸出する
でた! French wine producers exported their wines all over the world.
(フランスのワイン製造業者は世界中にワインを輸出した) 〔東京工業大学〕

**0441 passport** [pǽspɔːrt | páːs-] 　名 パスポート

**0442 sport** [spɔ́ːrt] 　名 スポーツ

元々sportはdisportであったが、頭音の消滅でsportになった。disportはdis (離れて) + port (運ぶ) なので、気持ちを違った場所に運ぶというニュアンスから気晴らしするという連想ができる。

## 0443 transfer [trænsfə́:r | trænsfə́:]
動 乗り換える、移す、転勤させる
名 乗り換え、移動

でた! Transferring Japanese "management techniques" directly to America won't work.
（日本式「経営術」を直接アメリカに移してもうまくいかないだろう） 福岡教育大学

でた! I don't mind being transferred as long as the job is interesting.
（仕事が面白ければ転勤になっても大丈夫です） 神奈川大学

## 0444 deliver [dilívər]
動 配達する、意見を述べる、演説をする、子を産む

でた! Articles bought here will be delivered free of charge.
（ここでお買い上げの品は無料で配達いたします） 横浜市立大学

派 delivery 名 配達、発言、出産

## 0445 commute [kəmjú:t]
動 通勤する、通学する
派 commuter 名 通勤者

## 0446 bind [báind]
動 縛る、結ぶ 活 bind-bound-bound

コロ be bound for A （A行きである）

でた! This airplane is bound for Paris.
（この飛行機はパリ行きです） センター試験

コロ be bound to A （Aする義務がある）

でた! Parents are bound to look after their children.
（両親は子供の世話をする義務がある） 東北薬科大学

コロ head for A （Aに向かう）

## 0447 convey [kənvéi]
動 運ぶ、伝える、伝達する

コロ conveyer belt （ベルトコンベアー）

でた! It is very difficult to convey the exact meaning of an idiom in a foreign language.
（外国語の熟語の正確な意味を伝達するのは非常に難しい） 関西外国語大学

## 0448 freight [fréit]
名 貨物

## 0449 carriage [kǽridʒ]
名 馬車、乗り物

類 carsick 名 車酔い

コロ jet lag （時差ぼけ）

## 0450 turbulence [tə́:rbjuləns]
名 乱気流、大荒れ

でた! The jet could fly faster and clear of storms and turbulence.
（ジェット機は速度を上げ、嵐や乱気流を逃れることができた） 早稲田大学

派 turbulent 形 荒れ狂う

UNIT 36 輸送機関

Chapter4 Society

# UNIT 37 交通・渋滞  STEP 1 過去問を解く

## 1

We took the train to Tokyo Disneyland in order to (　　) the heavy traffic.

英語検定準2級

1. avoid
2. prevent
3. keep
4. accept

## 2

There is always (　　) in the city center.

青山学院大学

1. a heavy traffic
2. heavy traffic
3. heavy traffics
4. the heavy traffics

## 3

The roads were so (　　) during Golden week that it took us almost 2 hours to drive the 10 kilometers from the highway to our house.

立命館大学

1. cautious
2. crowded
3. impressive
4. prominent

## 4

I'm sorry. I'm late. I was (　　) up by the traffic.

日本大学

1. delayed
2. congested
3. blocked
4. held

## STEP 2 正解を見抜く

### 1

We took the train to Tokyo Disneyland in order to avoid the heavy traffic.

正解 ①

訳 渋滞を避ける為に東京ディズニーランドまで電車に乗った。

- **avoid** 動 避ける
- **prevent** 動 妨げる
- **keep** 動 続ける
- **accept** 動 受け入れる

### 2

There is always heavy traffic in the city center.

正解 ②

訳 シティーセンターはいつも渋滞している。

- **heavy traffic** 交通渋滞

> trafficはuncountable noun（不可算名詞）なので冠詞のaや複数形のsが付くことはありません

### 3

The roads were so crowded during Golden week that it took us almost 2 hours to drive the 10 kilometers from the highway to our house.

正解 ②

訳 ゴールデンウィーク中で道路が非常に混雑していたので、高速道路から家までの10キロの道のりを車で2時間もかかった。

- **cautious** 形 注意深い、用心深い
- **crowded** 形 混雑している
- **impressive** 形 印象的な
- **prominent** 形 卓越した

### 4

I'm sorry. I'm late. I was held up by the traffic.

正解 ④

訳 すみません。遅れます。渋滞に巻き込まれました。

- **delay** 動 遅らせる
- **congest** 動 混雑させる
- **block up** ふさぐ
- **hold up** （車などが）停止する

> be held up by the trafficで「渋滞に巻き込まれる」という熟語です

UNIT 37 交通・渋滞

Chapter4 Society

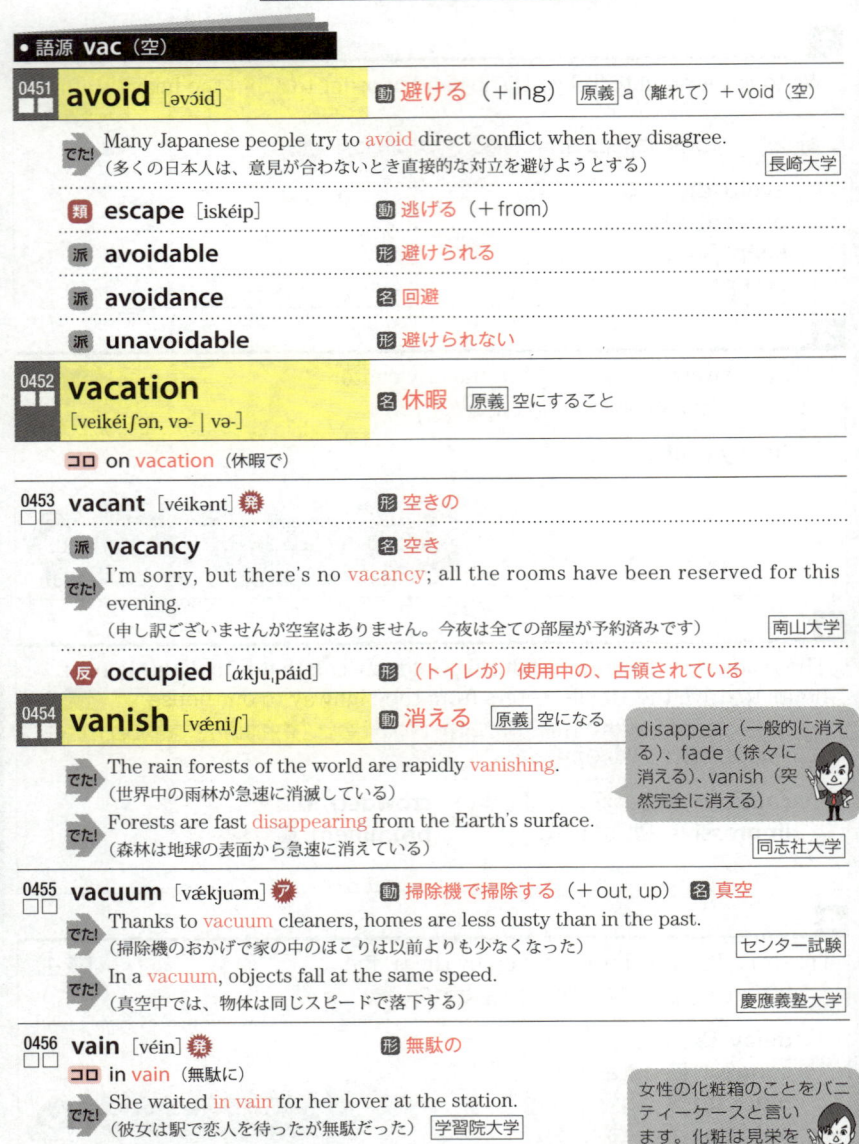

## STEP 3 連鎖式に語彙を増やす 🎧37

● 語源 vac（空）

**0451 avoid** [əvɔ́id]　動 避ける（+ing）　原義 a（離れて）+ void（空）

でた! Many Japanese people try to avoid direct conflict when they disagree.
（多くの日本人は、意見が合わないとき直接的な対立を避けようとする）　[長崎大学]

- 類 **escape** [iskéip]　動 逃げる（+from）
- 派 **avoidable**　形 避けられる
- 派 **avoidance**　名 回避
- 派 **unavoidable**　形 避けられない

**0452 vacation** [veikéiʃən, və- | və-]　名 休暇　原義 空にすること

コロ on vacation（休暇で）

**0453 vacant** [véikənt]発　形 空きの

- 派 **vacancy**　名 空き

でた! I'm sorry, but there's no vacancy; all the rooms have been reserved for this evening.
（申し訳ございませんが空室はありません。今夜は全ての部屋が予約済みです）　[南山大学]

- 反 **occupied** [ákju,páid]　形 （トイレが）使用中の、占領されている

**0454 vanish** [vǽniʃ]　動 消える　原義 空になる

> disappear（一般的に消える）、fade（徐々に消える）、vanish（突然完全に消える）

でた! The rain forests of the world are rapidly vanishing.
（世界中の雨林が急速に消滅している）

でた! Forests are fast disappearing from the Earth's surface.
（森林は地球の表面から急速に消えている）　[同志社大学]

**0455 vacuum** [vǽkjuəm]　動 掃除機で掃除する（+out, up）　名 真空

でた! Thanks to vacuum cleaners, homes are less dusty than in the past.
（掃除機のおかげで家の中のほこりは以前よりも少なくなった）　[センター試験]

でた! In a vacuum, objects fall at the same speed.
（真空中では、物体は同じスピードで落下する）　[慶應義塾大学]

**0456 vain** [véin]　形 無駄の

コロ in vain（無駄に）

> 女性の化粧箱のことをバニティーケースと言います。化粧は見栄を表します。

でた! She waited in vain for her lover at the station.
（彼女は駅で恋人を待ったが無駄だった）　[学習院大学]

- 派 **vanity**　名 虚栄心、見栄

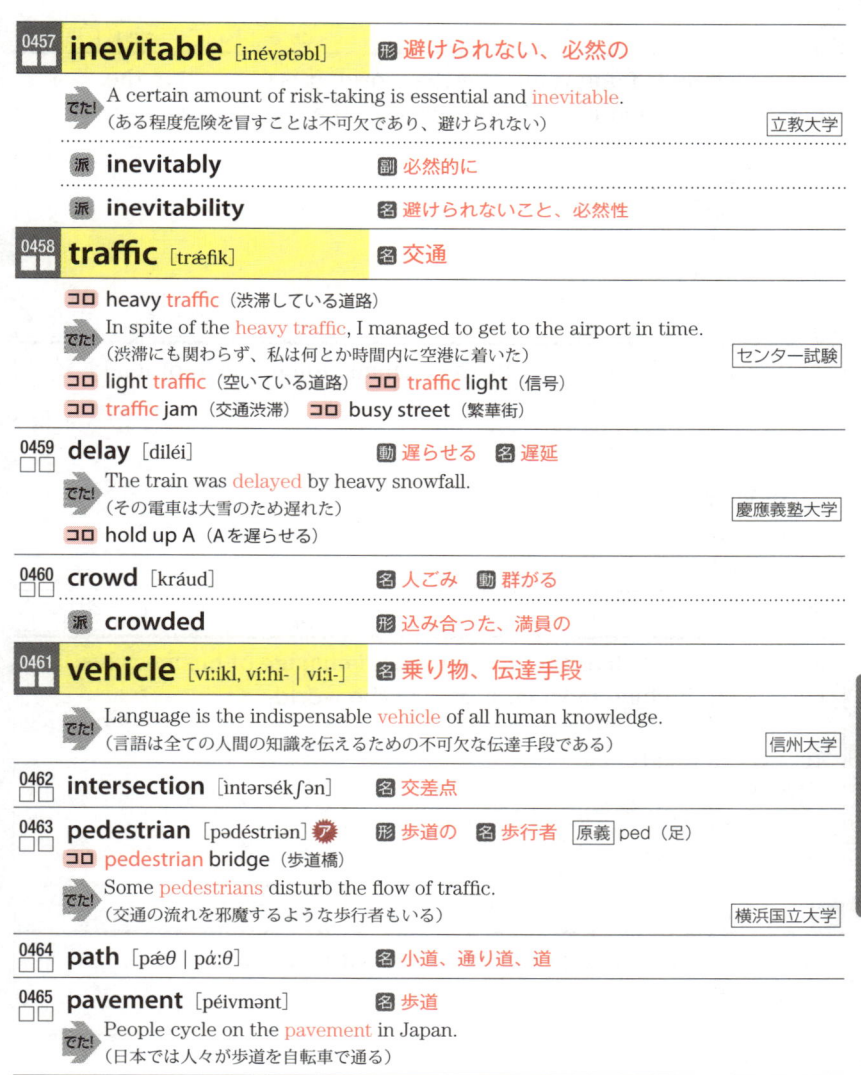

## 0457 inevitable [inévətəbl] 形 避けられない、必然の

A certain amount of risk-taking is essential and inevitable.
(ある程度危険を冒すことは不可欠であり、避けられない) 立教大学

派 inevitably 副 必然的に

派 inevitability 名 避けられないこと、必然性

## 0458 traffic [trǽfik] 名 交通

コロ heavy traffic (渋滞している道路)

In spite of the heavy traffic, I managed to get to the airport in time.
(渋滞にも関わらず、私は何とか時間内に空港に着いた) センター試験

コロ light traffic (空いている道路)　コロ traffic light (信号)
コロ traffic jam (交通渋滞)　コロ busy street (繁華街)

## 0459 delay [diléi] 動 遅らせる　名 遅延

The train was delayed by heavy snowfall.
(その電車は大雪のため遅れた) 慶應義塾大学

コロ hold up A (Aを遅らせる)

## 0460 crowd [kráud] 名 人ごみ　動 群がる

派 crowded 形 込み合った、満員の

## 0461 vehicle [víːikl, víːhi- | víːi-] 名 乗り物、伝達手段

Language is the indispensable vehicle of all human knowledge.
(言語は全ての人間の知識を伝えるための不可欠な伝達手段である) 信州大学

## 0462 intersection [ìntərsékʃən] 名 交差点

## 0463 pedestrian [pədéstriən] 形 歩道の　名 歩行者　原義 ped (足)

コロ pedestrian bridge (歩道橋)

Some pedestrians disturb the flow of traffic.
(交通の流れを邪魔するような歩行者もいる) 横浜国立大学

## 0464 path [pǽθ | pάːθ] 名 小道、通り道、道

## 0465 pavement [péivmənt] 名 歩道

People cycle on the pavement in Japan.
(日本では人々が歩道を自転車で通る)

UNIT 37 交通・渋滞

Chapter4 Society

# UNIT 38　場所・範囲　STEP 1 過去問を解く

## 1

Easter Island is famous all over the world. It is (　　) in the Pacific Ocean, about 3,700 km west of Chile.

英語検定2級

1. defined
2. established
3. located
4. constructed

## 2

Arabic script was (　　) by the Roman alphabetic in official documents.

関西外国語大学

1. replaced
2. redeemed
3. represented
4. ridiculed

## 3

The use of English as the international language of business has (　　) to include most countries in the world.

明海大学

1. experienced
2. enlarged
3. expanded
4. exaggerated

## 4

Travel outside our solar system is not within the (　　) of possibility.

上智大学

1. realms
2. reason
3. reality
4. reduction

## STEP 2 正解を見抜く

### 1

Easter Island is famous all over the world. It is located in the Pacific Ocean, about 3,700 km west of Chile.

正解 ③

> 訳 イースター島は世界中で有名です。それはチリの約3,700km西の太平洋上に位置しています。

- define 動 定義する
- locate 動 位置する
- construct 動 建設する
- establish 動 設立する

locateの語源はloc（場所）です。テレビの業界用語のロケはlocationから来ています

### 2

Arabic script was replaced by the Roman alphabetic in official documents.

正解 ①

> 訳 アラビア文字は公文書においてはローマ文字に取って代わられた。

- replace 動 取って代わる
- redeem 動 取り返す
- represent 動 代表する
- ridicule 動 ばかにする

### 3

The use of English as the international language of business has expanded to include most countries in the world.

正解 ③

> 訳 国際的なビジネス言語として英語を使用することは世界中のほとんどの国にまで広がっている。

- experience 動 経験する
- expand 動 広がる
- enlarge 動 拡大する
- exaggerate 動 誇張する

### 4

Travel outside our solar system is not within the realms of possibility.

正解 ①

> 訳 太陽系の外側を旅行することは可能な領域ではない。

- realm 名 領域
- reason 名 理由
- reality 名 現実
- reduction 名 縮小

UNIT 38　場所・範囲

Chapter4 Society

# STEP 3 連鎖式に語彙を増やす 🎧38

● 語源 **loc**（場所）

## 0466 **local** [lóukəl]
形 地元の

## 0467 **location** [loukéiʃən]
名 場所

でた! The researchers should have chosen a different location for their experiment.
（研究者らは実験のために違った場所を選択すべきだった） `TOEFL`

派 **locate**
動 位置する

## 0468 **allocate** [ǽləkèit]
動 分配する

派 **allocation**
名 分配、配置、割り当て

## 0469 **place** [pléis]
動 置く　名 場所

コロ place an order（注文する）

でた! Elephants never forget places they've already visited.
（象は一度訪れた場所を決して忘れない） `同志社大学`

派 **placement**
名 配置、置くこと

## 0470 **replace** [ripléis]
動 置き換える、入れ替える、取って代わる

コロ replace A with B（AをBと取り替える）

でた! Time viewing television is replaced by Internet time.
（テレビを見る時間はインターネットの時間に取って代わられている） `青山学院大学`

## 0471 **displace** [displéis]
動 取って代わる

コロ take the place of A（Aを取って代わる）

## 0472 **territory** [térətɔ̀ːri | -təri]
名 領土、地域、縄張り

でた! Significant discoveries of mineral deposits encouraged prospectors and settlers to move into the territories.
（ミネラル鉱床の重大な発見により、試掘者や開拓移民がその地域に移り住んだ） `TOEFL`

派 **territorial**
形 領土の

コロ territorial dispute（領土紛争）

## 0473 **province** [právins | próv-]
名 州、地方、範囲

でた! In Canada, most speakers of French live in the province of Quebec.
（カナダでは、フランス語を話す人はほとんどケベック州に住んでいる） `学習院大学`

## 0474 **prefecture** [príːfektʃər | -tjùə]
名 県、府

コロ Yamanashi prefecture（山梨県）

**0475 region** [ríːdʒən] 名 地域、分野
でた! W.Disney is taking Western entertainment to the world's most populated region.
（ウォルト・ディズニーは西洋的娯楽を世界で最も人口が多い地域に持ってきている）
東京国際大学

派 **regional** 形 地方の、地域の

**0476 range** [réindʒ] 名 範囲 動 整列させる、範囲にわたる
コロ a wide range of A（広範囲のA） コロ range from A to B（AからBにわたる）

類 **area** [ɛ́əriə] 名 地域

**0477 realm** [rélm] 発 名 領域、分野、王国
でた! What is the most profound question in the realm of philosophy?
（哲学の領域で最も難解な問いとは何ですか）
早稲田大学

**0478 extent** [ikstént] 名 範囲、程度
コロ to some extent（ある程度まで）

派 **extend** 動 （平面的、線上に）拡張する、伸ばす
でた! The department store extended the sale until Monday.
（そのデパートは月曜日までセールを延長した）
長崎外国語大学

派 **extensive** 形 広範囲な
コロ extensive knowledge（幅広い知識）
でた! The storm caused extensive damage to the old temple.
（その嵐は古い寺に広範囲の損害をもたらしました）
獨協大学

派 **extension** 名 拡張、髪の毛のエクステ

**0479 expand** [ikspǽnd] 動 空間的に広がる
コロ expand business in Asia（アジアで事業を拡大する）
でた! In Senegal, Islam has expanded to cover almost a third of the population.（セネガルでは、人口のほぼ3分の1を占めるほどにイスラム教が広がっている）

派 **expansion** 名 拡大

UNIT 38　場所・範囲

Chapter4 Society

# UNIT 39 旅行・予約

**STEP 1 過去問を解く**

## 1

Tom is planning to sail from New York to London in the boat. He is buying a lot of things to take on his long (　　).

英語検定準2級

1. network
2. climate
3. voyage
4. statement

## 2

Tom loves adventure, so he's joining an (　　) which is going to explore the Amazon.

上智大学

1. expedition
2. extension
3. exhibition
4. emergency

## 3

I have (　　) with the dentist this afternoon.

青山学院大学

1. an appointment
2. a reservation
3. a promise
4. an order

## 4

I'd like to make (　　) for the express train that leaves at 6:00.

東洋大学

1. a reservation
2. a promise
3. an appointment
4. a subscription

## STEP 2 正解を見抜く

### 1

Tom is planning to sail from New York to London in the boat. He is buying a lot of things to take on his long voyage.

正解 ③

**訳** トムは、ボートでニューヨークからロンドンまで航海するのを計画しています。彼は彼の長距離航海に持っていく多くの物を買っています。

- network 名 ネットワーク
- voyage 名 航海
- statement 名 名声
- climate 名 気候

> フランス語でBon voyageは「いってらっしゃい、良い旅を」を意味します

### 2

Tom loves adventure, so he's joining an expedition which is going to explore the Amazon.

正解 ①

**訳** トムは冒険がとても好きなので、彼はアマゾンを探検する遠征に参加しています。

- expedition 名 遠征
- extension 名 延長
- exhibition 名 展覧会
- emergency 名 非常事態

> expeditionの語源はex（外に）＋ped（足）＝外に足を運ぶ＝遠足、遠征

### 3

I have an appointment with the dentist this afternoon.

正解 ①

**訳** 私は、今日の午後に歯医者の予約があります。

- appointment 名 予約
- reservation 名 予約
- promise 名 約束
- order 名 注文

> 覚え方！面と向かってappointment。面会や病院の予約

### 4

I'd like to make a reservation for the express train that leaves at 6:00.

正解 ①

**訳** 私は、6:00発の急行列車の予約をしたいと思います。

- reservation 名 予約
- promise 名 約束
- appointment 名 指名
- subscription 名 購読

> 覚え方！席に座ってreservation。ホテルやレストランの予約

UNIT 39 旅行・予約

Chapter4 Society

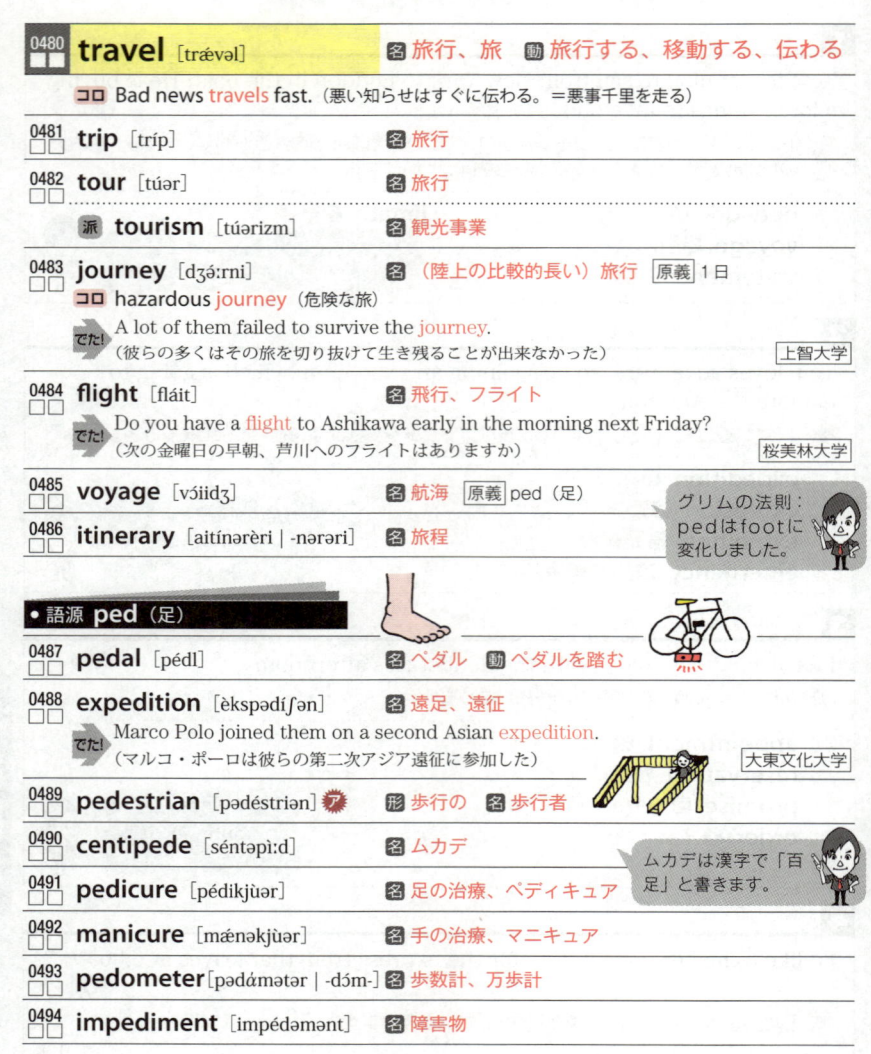

## STEP 3 連鎖式に語彙を増やす

**0480 travel** [trǽvəl] 　名 旅行、旅　動 旅行する、移動する、伝わる
- コロ Bad news travels fast.（悪い知らせはすぐに伝わる。＝悪事千里を走る）

**0481 trip** [tríp]　名 旅行

**0482 tour** [túər]　名 旅行

派 **tourism** [túərizm]　名 観光事業

**0483 journey** [dʒə́ːrni]　名 （陸上の比較的長い）旅行　原義 1日
- コロ hazardous journey（危険な旅）
- でた! A lot of them failed to survive the journey.
（彼らの多くはその旅を切り抜けて生き残ることが出来なかった）　上智大学

**0484 flight** [fláit]　名 飛行、フライト
- でた! Do you have a flight to Ashikawa early in the morning next Friday?
（次の金曜日の早朝、芦川へのフライトはありますか）　桜美林大学

**0485 voyage** [vɔ́iidʒ]　名 航海　原義 ped（足）

**0486 itinerary** [aitínərèri | -nərəri]　名 旅程

> グリムの法則: pedはfootに変化しました。

### ● 語源 ped（足）

**0487 pedal** [pédl]　名 ペダル　動 ペダルを踏む

**0488 expedition** [èkspədíʃən]　名 遠足、遠征
- でた! Marco Polo joined them on a second Asian expedition.
（マルコ・ポーロは彼らの第二次アジア遠征に参加した）　大東文化大学

**0489 pedestrian** [pədéstriən]　形 歩行の　名 歩行者

**0490 centipede** [séntəpìːd]　名 ムカデ

> ムカデは漢字で「百足」と書きます。

**0491 pedicure** [pédikjùər]　名 足の治療、ペディキュア

**0492 manicure** [mǽnəkjùər]　名 手の治療、マニキュア

**0493 pedometer** [pədɑ́mətər | -dɔ́m-]　名 歩数計、万歩計

**0494 impediment** [impédəmənt]　名 障害物

## 0495 appointment [əpɔ́intmənt]
名 (面会や病院等の) 約束、予約、任命

I can't see you tomorrow since I have an appointment to see Dr. Bean at 3:00.
(3時にビーン先生に診てもらうので明日は会えません)
〔学習院大学〕

派 **appoint** 動 指名する、任命する
The students appointed her to be their class representative.
(学生たちは、彼女を学級委員になるように任命しました)
〔立命館大学〕

## 0496 designate [dézignèit]
動 指定する

Smoking is allowed only in designated areas on campus.
(喫煙はキャンパスの指定されたエリアのみで許されています)
〔立教大学〕

派 **designation** 名 指定、指名

## 0497 reservation [rèzərvéiʃən]
名 (ホテルや乗り物等の) 予約

I asked my secretary to make a reservation for me on the 10:20 flight to New York.
(私は秘書に、10時20分発ニューヨーク行きの空の便を予約するように頼んだ)
〔中央大学〕

派 **reserve** 動 予約する
I want to reserve a room with an east view.
(東向きの部屋を予約したいです)
〔青山学院大学〕

## 0498 promise [prɑ́mis | prɔ́m-]
名 約束 動 約束する

I promise that I will return the book to you next week.
(私は必ず来週あなたにこの本を返すと約束します)
〔立教大学〕

派 **promising** 形 前途有望な
He is a promising young politician.
(彼は前途有望な若い政治家だ)
〔南山大学〕

## 0499 book [búk]
動 予約する 名 本

I would like to book a table for four at six o'clock.
(私は、6時に4名の席を予約したいと思います)
〔東海大学〕

---

UNIT 39 旅行・予約

> 覚え方を紹介します。
> 面と向かって appointment
> 席に座って reservation

Chapter4 Society

# UNIT 40 観光・景色

## STEP 1 過去問を解く

### 1

On a clear day, Mt. Fuji is (    ) from over one hundred miles away.

英語検定2級

1. visible
2. imaginable
3. flexible
4. capable

### 2

This room (    ) a fine view of the city.

南山大学

1. commences
2. commands
3. comments
4. commits

### 3

The thief ran away at the (    ) of a policeman.

センター試験

1. screen
2. scenery
3. sight
4. seeing

### 4

He came to inspect the house (    ) buying it.

慶應義塾大学

1. in the event of
2. with a view of
3. with reference to
4. on account of

## STEP 2 正解を見抜く

### 1

On a clear day, Mt. Fuji is visible from over one hundred miles away.

正解 ①

訳 天気の良い日には、富士山は100マイル離れたところから見えます。

- **visible** 形 見える
- **imaginable** 形 想像できる
- **flexible** 形 柔軟性がある
- **capable** 形 有能な

> visibleの語源はvis（見る）+ able（可能）= 目に見える。invisible manで「透明人間」

### 2

This room commands a fine view of the city.

正解 ②

訳 この部屋から都市のすばらしい眺めを一望できます。

- **commence** 動 始める
- **command** 動 見渡す
- **comment** 動 解説する
- **commit** 動 犯す

> commandは重要多義語です。P.179参照

### 3

The thief ran away at the sight of a policeman.

正解 ③

訳 泥棒は警察を一目見ると逃げ出した。

- **screen** 名 画面
- **scenery** 名 景色
- **sight** 名 光景
- **seeing** 名 見ること

> at the sight of A「Aを一目見て」

UNIT 40　観光・景色

### 4

He came to inspect the house with a view of buying it.

正解 ②

訳 彼はその家を買う目的で詳しく調べに来た。

- **in the event of**（万一）〜の場合には
- **with a view of ~ing** 〜する目的で
- **with reference to** 〜に関して
- **on acount of** 〜の理由で

Chapter4 Society

## STEP 3 連鎖式に語彙を増やす 🎧40

● 語源 vis（見る）

### 0500 view [vjúː] 名 眺め、見解、意見、見通し　原義 見る

- from my point of view （私の見解からすれば）
- from a more realistic point of view （より現実的な視点から見て）
- with a view of ~ing （～する目的で）
- He saves the greater part of his salary with a view of buying a car.
（彼は車を買うために給料の多くを貯金している）　成蹊大学
- The different experiences people have may lead to different views of things.
（人々が持つ異なった経験が異なったものの考え方へ導くだろう）　青山学院大学

### 0501 visit [vízit] 動 訪問する　原義 vis（見る）＋it（行く）

- pay a visit （訪問する）
- They paid me frequent visits last week.
（彼らは先週頻繁に私のところを訪れた）　英語検定準1級
- drop in （立ち寄る）
- Why don't you drop in and see me some time?
（いつか私に会いに家に寄ってみるのはどうですか）　西南学院大学
- call on （訪ねる）

### 0502 vision [víʒən] 名 視力、未来像

- 派 visible 形 目に見える　原義 vis（見る）＋able（可能）
- Rainbows are sometimes visible in waterfalls.
（滝の中に虹が見えるときもある）　京都大学
- 派 invisible 形 目に見えない
- 派 visual 形 視覚の
- visual image （視覚映像）
- 派 visualize 動 視覚化する

### 0503 review [rivjúː] 動 復習する、評論する　名 復習、評論

- If you plan to go to Paris next year, you had better review your French.
（もし来年パリに行く予定を立てるなら、フランス語を復習した方がいいでしょう）　上智大学

### 0504 revise [riváiz] 動 改訂する、改正する

- I will be ready to revise my views whenever one of my ideas proves to be wrong.
（私の考えが一つでも間違っていると分かれば、いつでも私は見解を修正するつもりだ）　筑波大学
- 派 revision 名 改訂、修正

### 0505 television [téləvìʒən] 名 テレビ

## 0506 provide [prəváid]
**動** 供給する　原義 pro（前を）＋ vid（見る）

- コロ provide A with B （BをAに与える）
- でた! All languages can provide us with valuable information about society.
（全ての言語は我々に社会に関する貴重な情報を供給することができる） 青山学院大学
- 派 provision　**名** 供給、用意

## 0507 sight [sáit]
**名** 光景、視覚　原義 見ること

- でた! There are a lot of people who can't stand the sight of blood.
（血を見ることに耐えられない人がたくさんいる） 慶應義塾大学
- コロ at first sight （一目で）　コロ catch sight of A （Aを見つける）
- コロ lose sight of A （Aを見失う）
- でた! People will gradually lose sight of the original purpose.
（人々は次第に本来の目的を見失うだろう） 横浜国立大学
- 派 sightseeing [sáitsì:iŋ]　**名** 観光
- 派 insight [ínsàit]　**名** 洞察力、見識
- 派 intuition [ìntju:íʃən]　**名** 洞察力、直感
- コロ by intuition （直感的に、勘で）

## 0508 interview [íntərvjù:]
**名** 面接、インタビュー　**動** 面談する

- でた! The manager interviews candidates from various cultures and backgrounds every year.
（マネージャーは毎年、様々な文化や経歴を持つ候補者と面接をしています） 立命館大学

## 0509 command [kəmǽnd | -má:nd]
**動** 命令する、見渡す
**名** 命令、見晴らし、（言葉を）自由に操る力

- でた! She has a good command of French.
（彼女はフランス語を操る能力がある） 中央大学

## 0510 spectacle [spéktəkl]
**名** 光景、眼鏡

- でた! Radio cannot bring us visual spectacles.
（ラジオは視覚的な光景を伝えることは出来ない） 同志社大学
- 派 spectacular [spektǽkjulər]　**形** 目を見張らせる

## 0511 landscape [lǽndskéip]
**名** 風景　原義 land（土地）＋ scape（景色）

- コロ rural landscape （田舎の景色）

## 0512 scenery [sí:nəri]
**名** 風景、景色

- 派 scene　**名** 場面、シーン、現場、舞台、景色、光景
- コロ behind the scenes （裏舞台で、秘密に）

UNIT 40　観光・景色

Chapter4 Society

# UNIT 41 地域・社会　STEP 1 過去問を解く

## 1

When Grace was in her third year of high school, she formed a small (　　　) for students interested in computers.

英語検定2級

1. recognition
2. application
3. formation
4. association

## 2

One of the good things about living in a small (　　　) is that everyone knows everybody else.

上智大学

1. community
2. metropolitan
3. connection
4. cosmic

## 3

The booming human population is concentrated more and more in large (　　　) areas. Many cities now have millions of inhabitants.

上智大学

1. urban
2. farming
3. forest
4. rural

## 4

I prefer (　　　) life to city life because it is much more peaceful.

学習院大学

1. district
2. countryside
3. urban
4. rural

## STEP 2 正解を見抜く

### 1

When Grace was in her third year of high school, she formed a small association for students interested in computers.　正解 ④

訳　グレースが高校三年生のとき、コンピュータに興味がある生徒のための小さな団体を作りました。

- **recognition** 名認識
- **formation** 名構成、編成
- **association** 名団体、協会
- **application** 名申し込み

associationの語源はsoc（交わる）です。人と人とが交わることがassociationです。soccer（サッカー）も同語源

### 2

One of the good things about living in a small community is that everyone knows everybody else.　正解 ①

訳　小さな地域社会での暮らしの利点の1つは、みんなお互いのことを知っているということである。

- **community** 名地域社会
- **connection** 名連結
- **cosmic** 形宇宙の
- **metropolitan** 名大都市の住民

constitutionの語源はcon（共に）＋st（立たせる）＝みんなで成り立たせるもの＝憲法。statue（像）のstと同語源

### 3

The booming human population is concentrated more and more in large urban areas. Many cities now have millions of inhabitants.　正解 ①

訳　人口の急増はますます都市部に集中している。今や多くの都市が何百万もの人を抱えている。

- **urban** 形都市の
- **forest** 名森
- **farming** 名農場
- **rural** 形田舎の

### 4

I prefer rural life to city life because it is much more peaceful.　正解 ④

訳　私は田舎暮らしの方が都会暮らしよりも好きだ。なぜなら、田舎生活の方がはるかに平穏だからだ。

- **district** 名地域
- **countryside** 名田舎
- **urban** 形都市の
- **rural** 形田舎の

UNIT 41 地域・社会

Chapter4 Society

## STEP 3 連鎖式に語彙を増やす 41

● 語源 SOC（交わる）

### 0513 society [səsáiəti]　图 社会

- コロ aging society（高齢化社会）
- でた! Doctors have duties to society, as well as to patients.
（医者は患者だけではなく社会に対しても義務がある）　慶應義塾大学

派 **social**　形 社会の
でた! We humans are social animals.
（我々人間は社会的な動物である）　明治大学

派 **sociable**　形 社交的な
でた! The Johnsons are very sociable people. They love giving parties.
（ジョンソン家の人たちはとても社交的です。彼らはパーティーを開催するのが大好きです）　上智大学

派 **sociology**　图 社会学

派 **sociologist**　图 社会学者

### 0514 associate [əsóuʃièit, -si-]　動 連想する、関連づける、交際する　图 仲間

- コロ associate A with B（AとBを関連づける）
- でた! In order to learn a word, a child must be able to associate its sound with its meaning.（単語を学習するために、子供はその音と意味を結びつけることが出来なければならない）　上智大学

派 **association**　图 連想、協会
コロ Parent-Teacher Association（PTA）

### 0515 soccer [sάkər | sɔ́kə]　图 サッカー

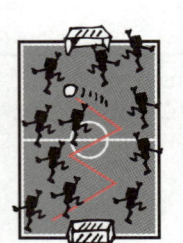

つながる、結び付くイメージ

## 0516 community [kəmjúːnəti] 名 共同社会、共同体、集団

- international community（国際社会）
- Laws are rules for people in communities.
  （法律は共同体内の人々のための規則である） 〔日本大学〕

## 0517 urban [áːrbən] 形 都市の
- urban area（都市部）

派 **suburban** 形 郊外の

## 0518 rural [rúərəl] 形 田舎の
- rural life（田舎の生活）

## 0519 countryside [kʌ́ntrisáid] 名 地方、田舎

## 0520 district [dístrikt] 名 地域、地区
- A huge snake had taken up residence in the district.
  （巨大な蛇はその地域に住み着いた） 〔早稲田大学〕

## 0521 welfare [wélfɛ̀ər] 名 福祉、幸福
- social welfare（社会福祉）
- Modern American women contribute to national and international welfare.
  （現代のアメリカ人女性達は国家および国際的な福祉に貢献している） 〔立命館大学〕

UNIT 41 地域・社会

Chapter4 Society

# UNIT 42 政治・憲法　STEP 1 過去問を解く

## 1

Democracy is a political system in which all the citizens can have a voice in (　　).

昭和女子大学

1. economy
2. corporation
3. evolution
4. government

## 2

The (　　) of Japan makes it clear that it will not make any kind of war.

駒澤大学

1. Resignation
2. Constitution
3. Subscription
4. Punctuation

## 3

A disarmament (　　) may never be signed by all the major powers of the world.

青山学院大学

1. undertaking
2. prescription
3. proposition
4. treaty

## 4

After the dictator's death, anarchy and confusion (　　) for several years.

慶應義塾大学

1. rained
2. reigned
3. reined

## STEP 2 正解を見抜く

### 1

Democracy is a political system in which all the citizens can have a voice in government.

正解 ④

訳 民主主義は全ての市民が政府に関して発言権を持つ政治的な制度である。

- **economy** 名 経済
- **corporation** 名 企業
- **evolution** 名 進化
- **government** 名 政府

### 2

The Constitution of Japan makes it clear that it will not make any kind of war.

正解 ②

訳 日本国憲法は戦争のようなことを起こさないと明確にしている。

- **resignation** 名 辞職
- **constitution** 名 憲法
- **subscription** 名 購読
- **punctuation** 名 句読点

> constitutionの語源はcon（共に）＋ st（立たせる）＝みんなで成り立たせるもの＝憲法。statue（像）のstと同語源

### 3

A disarmament treaty may never be signed by all the major powers of the world.

正解 ④

訳 世界の主要な強国すべてが、軍縮条約に調印することは永遠にないかもしれない。

- **undertaking** 名 事業
- **prescription** 名 処方箋
- **proposition** 名 提案
- **treaty** 名 条約

### 4

After the dictator's death, anarchy and confusion reigned for several years.

正解 ②

訳 独裁者の死後、数年間は無政府状態と混乱が支配した。

- **rain** 動 雨が降る
- **reign** 動 統治する、支配する
- **rein** 動 馬を操る

UNIT 42 政治・憲法

Chapter4 Society

## STEP 3 連鎖式に語彙を増やす 🎧42

### 0522 **government** [gʌ́vərnmənt]
名 政府、政治

- コロ federal government（連邦政府）
- でた! One reason for persistent poverty is the failure of government.
（貧困が続いている一つの理由は政府の失敗によるものだ）

派 **govern** — 動 治める、統治する、支配する、管理する
- コロ govern the country（国を統治する）

派 **governor** — 名 知事
- でた! The evidence indicates that the governor is involved in the scandal.
（その証拠は知事がそのスキャンダルに関与している事を示している）〔中央大学〕

派 **governance** — 名 統治、支配

類 **reign** [réin] — 名 統治、支配　動 統治する、支配する

### 0523 **president** [prézədənt]
名 大統領、社長　原義 pre（前に）＋ sid（座る）

- でた! He spoke as if he had seen the president.
（彼はまるで大統領に会ったことがあるような口ぶりだ）〔東京理科大学〕

### 0524 **minister** [mínəstər]
名 大臣
- コロ Prime Minister（総理大臣）

派 **ministry** — 名 省
- コロ Ministry of Education（文部省）

### 0525 **ambassador** [æmbǽsədər]
名 大使

派 **embassy** [émbəsi] — 名 大使館

### 0526 **politics** [pɑ́lətìks | pɔ́l-]
名 政治、政治学

派 **policy** — 名 政策
- コロ policy maker（政策立案者）

派 **political** — 形 政治の

派 **politician** — 名 政治家

### 0527 **democracy** [dimɑ́krəsi | -mɔ́k-]
名 民主主義

- でた! Democracy cannot survive without freedom of speech.
（民主主義は言論の自由なしには存続できない）〔福島大学〕

| | | |
|---|---|---|
| 派 | **democratic** | 形 民主主義の |
| 0528 | **advocate** [ǽdvəkèit] | 名 主張者　動 主張する |
| 派 | **advocacy** [ǽdvəkəsi] | 名 弁護、支持 |
| 0529 | **bureaucracy** [bjuərάkrəsi \| -rɔ́k-] | 名 官僚政治、官僚社会 |
| 派 | **bureaucratic** [bjùərəkrǽtik] | 形 官僚主義の |
| 派 | **bureau** [bjúərou] | 名 局、事務局、案内所 |
| 0530 | **treaty** [trí:ti] | 名 条約、協定 |
| 0531 | **pact** [pǽkt] | 名 条約、協定 |

### 0532 **constitution** [kὰnstətjú:ʃən \| kɔ̀nstitjú:-]
名 憲法、構成

でた! The constitution does not actually abolish the old practice.
（憲法は実際にその古い習慣を廃止しているのではない）　　上智大学

派 **constitute** 動 制定する、構成する

でた! Antarctica and the ocean that surrounds it constitute 40 percent of the planet.
（南極大陸とそれを囲む海は地球の40％を構成している）　　TOEFL

派 **constitutional** 形 憲法の、構成上の

| | | |
|---|---|---|
| 0533 | **diplomacy** [diplóuməsi] | 名 外交　原義 di（2つ）＋plo（折る） |
| 派 | **diplomat** [dípləmæt] | 名 外交官 |
| 0534 | **congress** [kάŋgris \| kɔ́ŋgres] | 名 米国議会 |
| 0535 | **parliament** [pάːrləmənt] | 名 英国議会 |
| 0536 | **the Diet** | 名 日本議会 |
| 0537 | **hierarchy** [háiərὰːrki] | 名 階級組織 |
| 0538 | **aristocracy** [ærəstάkrəsi \| -tɔ́k-] | 名 貴族階級 |

書類を二つ折りにするため

UNIT 42　政治・憲法

# UNIT 43　選挙・重要

## STEP 1 過去問を解く

### 1

The Democratic (　　) gave an inspiring speech during the election campaign.

亜細亜大学

1. party
2. branch
3. candidate
4. policy

### 2

These are two strong (　　) in the election, so it will be very interesting to see the result.

英語検定2級

1. commuters
2. correspondents
3. witnesses
4. candidates

### 3

The British public went to the polls last spring.

立命館大学

1. had a heated discussion
2. voted in an election
3. expressed their opinions
4. organized political actions

### 4

The results of the election will be (　　) for our future.

青山学院大学

1. crucial
2. exclusive
3. inclusive
4. punctual

## STEP 2 正解を見抜く

### 1

The Democratic candidate gave an inspiring speech during the election campaign.

正解 ③

訳 民主党の候補者は選挙運動の間、感動的な演説をした。

- party 名 党
- branch 名 枝、支店
- candidate 名 候補者
- policy 名 政策

candidateの語源はcand（白）。古代ローマでは候補者が白衣を着ていたことが由来です。candle（キャンドル）、chandelier（シャンデリア）も同語源

### 2

These are two strong candidates in the election, so it will be very interesting to see the result.

正解 ④

訳 その選挙には二人の有力な候補者がいるので、結果を見るのが非常に興味深い。

- commuter 名 通勤者、通学者
- correspondent 名 通信員
- witness 名 目撃者
- candidate 名 候補者

### 3

The British public voted in an election last spring.

正解 ②

訳 イギリス人は去年の春、投票に行った。

- have a heated discussion 白熱した議論をする
- vote in an election 選挙で投票する
- express their opinions 彼らの意見を述べる
- organize political actions 政治活動を組織する

### 4

The results of the election will be crucial for our future.

正解 ①

訳 選挙の結果は我々の将来において重要となる。

- crucial 形 重要な
- exclusive 形 排他的な
- inclusive 形 含めた
- punctual 形 時間に厳しい

UNIT 43 選挙・重要

Chapter4 Society

## STEP 3 連鎖式に語彙を増やす 🎧43

**0539 vote** [vóut]    名 投票    動 投票する

でた! Australian Aborigines were given the right to vote only after World War II.
（オーストラリア先住民は選挙権をようやく第二次世界大戦のあとに与えられた） 早稲田大学

**0540 elect** [ilékt]    動 選挙で選ぶ    原義 e（外に）＋ elect（選ぶ）

派 **election**    名 選挙

でた! In political elections, actual votes are cast anonymously.
（政治選挙において実際の投票は無記名で行われる） 慶應義塾大学

コロ **run for**（立候補する）

でた! My uncle is going to run for governor in the election next fall.
（私のおじは来年の秋の選挙で知事に立候補するつもりだ） 駒澤大学

**0541 ballot**    名 投票用紙

コロ absentee ballot（不在者投票用紙）

**0542 campaign**    名 選挙運動《米》、キャンペーン

コロ campaign pledge（公約）

**0543 poll** [póul]    名 世論調査

コロ conduct a poll（世論調査を行う）

でた! Unlike an opinion poll, an exit poll asks who the voter actually voted for.
（世論調査とは異なり、出口調査は投票者が実際に誰に投票したかを尋ねる） 慶應義塾大学

### ● 語源 cand（白）

**0544 candidate** [kǽndidèit, -dət]    名 候補者、志願者

**0545 candle** [kǽndl]    名 ろうそく

**0546 chandelier** [ʃændəlíər]    名 シャンデリア

## 0547 crucial [krúːʃəl]
形 重大な、重要な、決定的な

でた! Antarctica plays a crucial role in the global environmental system.
(南極大陸は地球の環境システムにおいて、重大な役割を果たしている) TOEFL

派 essence 名 本質

## 0548 essential [isénʃəl]
形 不可欠の、本質的な

でた! A positive attitude is essential for success.
(成功には積極的な態度が不可欠である) 学習院大学

## 0549 significant [signífikənt]
形 重要な

でた! Poor countries have a significant chance of falling into a poverty trap.
(貧しい国々は貧困の罠にはまる可能性が大いにある)

反 insignificant 形 無意味な

派 significantly 副 著しく、顕著に

でた! The chemical phenomenon affects the corrosion rate very significantly.
(その化学物質は腐食率に著しく影響を与える) 東京大学

派 significance 名 重要性

反 insignificance 名 無意味

派 signify 動 示す、意味する

## 0550 signature [sígnətʃər]
名 署名、サイン ※芸能人が書くサインはautograph。

## 0551 token [tóukən]
名 印、象徴
コロ as a token of A (Aのしるしとして)

## 0552 vital [váitl]
形 生命の、極めて重要な 原義 vit（生きる）

でた! Conversation is vital to our development and fulfillment as human beings.
(会話は人間としての発展や自己実現にとって極めて重要である) 慶應義塾大学

派 vitality [vaitǽləti] 名 生命力

UNIT 43 選挙・重要

Chapter4 Society | 191

## UNIT 44 要求・必要

**STEP 1 過去問を解く**

### 1

In many countries, drivers are (　　) to wear seat belts at all times.

英語検定2級

1. compared
2. exported
3. required
4. occurred

### 2

The workers (　　) that the company pay overtime.

上智大学

1. promoted
2. demanded
3. satisfied
4. conducted

### 3

His help is (　　) for the success of the plan.

立命館大学

1. cautious
2. indispensable
3. unpleasant
4. unsung

### 4

The year 1776 is a very <u>significant</u> one in American history. It is the year the country was born.

亜細亜大学

1. similar
2. superior
3. conscious
4. important

## STEP 2 正解を見抜く

### 1

In many countries, drivers are required to wear seat belts at all times.

正解 ③

訳 多くの国では、運転手はいつもシートベルトを締めなければなりません。

- **compare** 動 比較する
- **export** 動 輸出する
- **require** 動 要求する
- **occur** 動 起こる

> requireの語源はre（再び）＋quire（求める）＝繰り返し求める＝要求する

### 2

The workers demanded that the company pay overtime.

正解 ②

訳 労働者らは、残業手当を支払うよう会社に要求しました。

- **promote** 動 促進する
- **demand** 動 要求する
- **satisfy** 動 満足させる
- **conduct** 動 案内する

### 3

His help is indispensable for the success of the plan.

正解 ②

訳 彼の援助はその計画の成功に欠かせない。

- **cautious** 形 注意深い
- **indispensable** 形 必要不可欠な
- **unpleasant** 形 不愉快な
- **unsung** 形 歌われていない

### 4

The year 1776 is a very important one in American history. It is the year the country was born.

正解 ④

訳 1776年はアメリカの歴史において非常に重要な年だ。国が誕生した年である。

- **similar** 形 似ている
- **superior** 形 優れている
- **conscious** 形 意識している
- **important** 形 重要な

UNIT 44 要求・必要

Chapter4 Society

## STEP 3 連鎖式に語彙を増やす 🎧44

- 語源 quire quest（求める）

### 0553 require [rikwáiər] 動 要求する、必要とする

- コロ require A to B（AにBすることを要求する）
- でた！ New skills are required to remain feminine and also be strong.
（女性的であり、且つたくましくあるために、女性には新たな資質が求められている） 法政大学
- でた！ You are required to learn a foreign language.
（あなた達は外国語を学ぶことを求められている） 神奈川大学

- 派 requirement 名 必要条件、必需品
- コロ meet the requirement（条件を満たす）

- 派 requisite [rékwəzit] 形 必須の

- 類 demand [dimǽnd | -má:nd] 動 要求する 名 需要、要求
- コロ meet the demand（需要を満たす）
- でた！ Eventually, the supply will increase to meet the demand.
（最終的には、需要を満たすために供給が増えるだろう） 横浜国立大学

- 派 demanding 形 骨の折れる、過酷な

- 類 seek [sí:k] 動 求める

> ask → request → demand の順に強くなる。

### 0554 request [rikwést] 動 求める、頼む

- でた！ He strongly requested an increase in salary.
（彼は昇給を強く求めた） 國學院大学

- 類 beg [bég] 動 請う、求める、頼む

- 派 begger 名 こじき

### 0555 quest [kwést] 名 探究
- コロ in quest of A（Aを求めて）

### 0556 question [kwéstʃən] 名 質問

- コロ out of the question（問題外で、論外で）
- でた！ The manager's proposal was out of the question.
（そのマネージャーの提案は問題外であった） 日本大学

- 派 questionnaire 名 アンケート用紙

### 0557 conquer [káŋkər | kóŋ-] 発 動 （永続的に）征服する

- でた！ In 1066, the French conquered England.
（1066年にフランスがイギリスを征服した） 都留文科大学

- 派 conquest 名 征服

## 0558 inquire [inkwáiər] 動 尋ねる
- inquire A of B (AをBに尋ねる)
- inquire into A (Aを調査する)
  - They are inquring into the matter.
  - (その件は調査中です) 〔青山学院大学〕
- inquire after (安否を問う、病気を見舞う)
  - I called on him to inquire after his health.
  - (彼の健康を見舞いに彼を訪ねた) 〔明治大学〕

派 **inquiry** [inkwáiəri] 名 質問

## 0559 pursue [pərsúː | -sjúː] 動 追求する、従事する
- pursue the objective (目的を追求する)
  - She was determined to pursue a career in journalism.
  - (彼女はジャーナリズムの道に進むと心に決めていた) 〔慶應義塾大学〕

派 **pursuit** [pərsúːt | -sjúːt] 名 追求、従事
  - Aristotle was busily engaged in the pursuit of all wisdom.
  - (アリストテレスは全ての英知の追求を熱心に行った) 〔上智大学〕

## 0560 necessary [nésəsèri | -səri] 形 必要な

派 **necessity** 名 必要性

## 0561 indispensable [ìndispénsəbl] 形 必要不可欠な
- Childhood is recognized as an indispensable period of life.
- (子供時代は人生において欠かすことの出来ない時期として認識されている) 〔立命館大学〕

## 0562 chief [tʃíːf] 形 最高の、主要な 名 長、頭 〔原義〕頭

## 0563 elementary [èləméntəri] 形 基本の、初歩の
- elementary school (小学校)《米》

派 **element** 名 要素、元素

## 0564 basic [béisik] 形 基礎の、基本的な

派 **base** 名 基礎、土台
- be based on A (Aに基づいている)
  - Her skill as a teacher is based on her understanding of young people.
  - (彼女の教師としての技量は、若者への理解に基礎を置いている) 〔立教大学〕

UNIT 44 要求・必要

Chapter4 Society

# UNIT 45 原因・結果　STEP 1 過去問を解く

## 1

( ) and effect haven't been identified yet.

関西学院大学

1. Cause
2. Factor
3. Origin
4. Root

## 2

The new tax increase ( ) widespread demonstrations across the country.

立命館大学

1. discarded
2. intruded
3. provoked
4. subtracted

## 3

The railway collision ( ) in the deaths of three hundred and fifty passengers.

名城大学

1. took
2. gave
3. resulted
4. dealt

## 4

When thinking practically, the ultimate test for any idea is how well it works — what ist practical <u>consequences</u> are.

中京大学

1. causes
2. results
3. goals
4. purposes

## STEP 2 正解を見抜く

### 1

Cause and effect haven't been identified yet. 　　正解 ①

訳 原因と結果はまだ特定されていません。

- cause 名原因
- factor 名要因
- origin 名起源
- root 名根本

### 2

The new tax increase provoked widespread demonstrations across the country. 　　正解 ③

訳 その新たな増税は国全体に広範囲に及ぶデモを引き起こした。

- discard 動捨てる
- intrude 動押しつける
- provoke 動引き起こす
- subtract 動引く

### 3

The railway collision resulted in the deaths of three hundred and fifty passengers. 　　正解 ③

訳 鉄道衝突は、350人の乗客の死をもたらしました。

- take 動取る
- give 動与える
- result 動結果として生じる
- deal 動扱う

### 4

When thinking practically, the ultimate test for any idea is how well it works — what ist practical results are. 　　正解 ②

訳 物事を実際的に考える場合、どんな考えについても最終的に決め手となるのは、それがどれだけ上手く行くかということである。つまり、その考えは実践において、どういう結果をもたらすかということである。

- cause 名原因
- goal 名目標
- result 名結果
- purpose 名目的

Chapter4 Society

## STEP 3 連鎖式に語彙を増やす 45

### 0565 result [rizʌ́lt]
名 結果　動 結果として終わる（+in）、結果として生じる（+from）

でた! He regretted the result of the experiment.
（実験の結果に彼は悔やんでいる） TOEFL

### 0566 consequence [kánsəkwèns | kɔ́nsikwəns]
名 結果、成り行き、影響

でた! He did not consider the consequences of his decision.
（彼は自分の決断の結果を考慮していなかった） TOEFL

### 0567 outcome [áutkʌ́m]
名 結果

でた! The teacher asked us to predict the outcome of the experiment.
（教師は私たちに実験の結果を予測するように言った） 中央大学

### 0568 factor [fǽktər]
名 要因

### 0569 trigger [trígər]
動 きっかけとなる、引き金を引く、引き起こす
名 （鉄砲の）引き金

### 0570 provoke [prəvóuk]
動 怒らせる

でた! The installation of speed cameras provoked an angry response from the public.
（スピードカメラの設置は国民からの怒りの反応を引き起こした） TOEFL

派 provocation　名 怒らせること、挑発

### 0571 evoke [ivóuk]
動 記憶・行動を呼び起こす、喚起する

コロ evoke sympathy（同情を喚起する）

派 evocation　名 喚起

### 0572 cause [kɔ́ːz]
動 引き起こす
名 原因、（社会的な運動の）主義

でた! Smoking causes a lot of health problems.
（喫煙は健康問題を多数引き起こす） 法政大学

コロ give rise to A（Aを引き起こす）

でた! You behavior will give rise to misunderstanding.
（あなたの振る舞いは誤解を生むでしょう） 東洋大学

## 0573 reason [ríːzn]  名 理由

**on the ground** (〜の理由で)
The project was abandoned on the ground that it was too expensive.
(その計画は値段が高すぎるという理由で断念された) 立教大学

**due to** (〜のせいで)
Dr. Miller was unable to give his speech due to the late arrival of his plane.
(ミラー博士は、飛行機の遅延のせいで、彼のスピーチをすることができませんでした) センター試験

**on account of A** (Aの理由で)
The train was delayed on account of the accident.
(その電車は事故で遅れました) 関東学院大学

**thanks to** (〜のおかげで)
She was able to go to college thanks to the scholarship.
(彼女は奨学金のおかげで大学に行くことが出来た) 京都産業大学

**owing to** (〜のために)
He had an accident owing to careless driving.
(不注意な運転のため彼は事故を起こした) 法政大学

**bring about** (引き起こす)

**take place** (起こる)
The next Olympics will take place in Beijing.
(次のオリンピックは北京で催される) 中央大学

**lead to A** (Aに繋がる)
The genius of Einstein leads to Hiroshima.
(アインシュタインの才能が広島に繋がる) パブロ・ピカソ

UNIT 45 原因・結果

Chapter4 Society | 199

# UNIT 46 企業・労働  STEP 1 過去問を解く

## 1

Multinational (　　) engage in economic activities in more than one country.

立命館大学

1. communications
2. concentrations
3. contributions
4. corporations

## 2

The East and the West can work together for their (　　) benefit and progress.

立命館大学

1. alternative
2. dependent
3. enthusiastic
4. mutual

## 3

In South East Asia, the logging is almost always done by imported (　　).

中央大学

1. country
2. threat
3. trees
4. labor
5. statement

## 4

Successful family life requires a certain amount of give-and-take.

立命館大学

1. relief
2. caution
3. devotion
4. cooperation

## STEP 2 正解を見抜く

### 1

Multinational corporations engage in economic activities in more than one country.

正解 ④

訳 多国籍企業は2つ以上の国で経済活動に従事しています。

- communication 名伝達
- concentration 名集中
- contribution 名寄付
- corporation 名法人、会社

### 2

The East and the West can work together for their mutual benefit and progress.

正解 ④

訳 東部と南部はお互いの利益と発展のために協力しうる。

- alternative 形二者択一の
- dependent 形従属した
- enthusiastic 形熱狂的な
- mutual 形相互の

### 3

In South East Asia, the logging is almost always done by imported labor.

正解 ④

訳 東南アジアでは、木材の伐採搬出作業はほとんど外国からの労働者によってなされています。

- country 名国
- tree 名木
- statement 名陳述
- threat 名脅威
- labor 名労働力、労働者

### 4

Successful family life requires a certain amount of cooperation.

正解 ④

訳 家族生活を成功させるためには、互いに譲り合うことがある程度必要である。

- relief 名安心
- caution 名注意
- devotion 名献身
- cooperation 名協力

UNIT 46 企業・労働

Chapter4 Society

## STEP 3 連鎖式に語彙を増やす 🎧46

### 0574 business [bíznis] 名 職業、事業、ビジネス

- **コロ** on business（出張で）⇔ on vacation（休暇で）
- **でた!** He went to Paris on business.
（彼は先月出張でパリへ行った） 〔慶應義塾大学〕
- **コロ** it's none of one's business（関係がない）
- **でた!** It's none of your business how I choose to spend my money.
（私がどのようにお金を使うかはあなたに関係ない） 〔法政大学〕

### 0575 corporation [kɔ̀:rpəréiʃən] 名 法人、企業、会社

- **コロ** multinational corporation（多国籍企業）
- **でた!** The success of a corporation lies in its ability to make effective use of its assets.
（企業の成功は資産を有効に使う能力にかかっている） 〔慶應義塾大学〕

- 派 **corporate** 形 法人の

### 0576 incorporate [inkɔ́:rpərèit] 動 組み入れる、合体させる
- **コロ** incorporate A into B（AをBに取り入れる）

- 派 **incorporation** 名 合併、合体

### 0577 enterprise [éntərpràiz] ⚠ 名 事業、企業

### 0578 cooperation [kouàpəréiʃən | -ɔ̀p-] 名 協力

- **でた!** There may be nothing more important than human cooperation.
（人間の協力ほど大切な物はないかもしれない） 〔立教大学〕

- 派 **cooperate** 動 協力する
- 派 **cooperative** 形 協力的な

### 0579 mutual [mjú:tʃuəl] 形 相互の
- **コロ** mutual understanding（相互理解）

- 派 **mutually** 副 相互に

### 0580 interact [ìntərækt] 動 相互作用する（+ with）

- **でた!** Culture is how the past interacts with the future.
（文化とはいかに過去が未来と相互作用するかということだ） 〔TOEFL〕

- 派 **interactive** 形 相互に作用する
- 派 **interaction** 名 相互作用

- 語源 labor（働く）

## 0581 labor [léibər]  名 労働、骨折り、苦労

コロ labor force（労働力）

でた！ When she finally succeeded after hours of work, she felt that her labor had been worthwhile.
（彼女がやっとの想いで何時間も働いた時、自分の苦労は価値がある物だと感じた） 立命館大学

## 0582 elaborate [ilǽbərət]  形 入念な、複雑な  動 念入りに作る

でた！ Japan is famous for its elaborate wrapping of presents.
（日本はプレゼントを入念にラッピングする事で有名である） 東京国際大学

派 elaboration  名 入念さ、精密さ

## 0583 collaboration [kəlæbəréiʃən]  名 協力

でた！ Nothing new that is really interesting comes without collaboration.
（本当に面白く新鮮な物というのは、協力なくしては生まれない） 立命館大学

派 collaborate  動 共同して行う

## 0584 laboratory [lǽbərətɔ̀ːri | ləbɔ́rətəri]  名 実験室、研究所

※省略形 lab

lavatory（トイレ）と混同注意

でた！ They need to go to the lab to complete an experiment.
（彼らは実験を終わらせるために実験室に行く必要がある） TOEFL

# UNIT 47 雇用・解雇

**STEP 1** 過去問を解く

## 1

A line of ( ) men and women waited at the office door in search of work.

亜細亜大学

1. obliged
2. unemployed
3. supplied
4. pulled

## 2

If you resign from your job, you ( ).

上智大学

1. come back
2. quit it
3. stay there
4. get fired

## 3

He fears that he may be ( ) because of his poor command of English.

立命館大学

1. established
2. estimated
3. transferred
4. transported

## 4

It was nearly impossible for ( ) people to find work during the Great Depression.

慶應義塾大学

1. unemployed
2. lucid
3. lucrative
4. producing

## STEP 2 正解を見抜く

### 1

A line of unemployed men and women waited at the office door in search of work.

正解 ②

**訳** 失業している男女の列は、事務所のドアで仕事を求めて待ちました。

- **oblige** 動義務づける
- **unemployed** 形失業した
- **supply** 動供給
- **pull** 動引く

### 2

If you resign from your job, you quit it.

正解 ②

**訳** もしあなたが辞職したら、それをやめるということです。

- **come back** 戻ってくる
- **quit** 動辞職する
- **stay** 動滞在する
- **get fired** くびになる

### 3

He fears that he may be transferred because of his poor command of English.

正解 ③

**訳** 彼は彼の乏しい英語力のせいで、転勤になることを恐れています。

- **establish** 動設立する
- **estimate** 動見積もる
- **transfer** 動転勤させる
- **transport** 動輸送する

### 4

It was nearly impossible for unemployed people to find work during the Great Depression.

正解 ①

**訳** 世界恐慌の間、失業者が職を見つけるのは不可能に近かった。

- **unemployed** 形失業した
- **lucid** 形明快な
- **lucrative** 形儲かる
- **producing** 形生み出す

UNIT 47 雇用・解雇

Chapter4 Society

## STEP 3 連鎖式に語彙を増やす 47

**0585 employ** [implɔ́i] 動 雇う

派 **employment** 名 職業

派 **employer** 名 雇用者

派 **employee** [implɔ́ii:, èmplɔ́i: | èmplɔ́i:] ⑦ 名 従業員
コロ full-time employee（正社員）
でた! An employee did not follow the instruction.
（従業員は指示に従わなかった）
TOEFL

反 **unemployment** 名 失業
コロ unemployment rate（失業率）

類 **hire** [háiər] 動 雇う、一時的に借りる

**0586 career** [kəríər] ⑦ 名 経歴、（生涯を通しての）職業

でた! There are many students who are thinking of a career in tourism.
（旅行会社で仕事をしようと考えている学生がたくさんいる）
学習院大学

類 **background** [bǽkgráund] 名 生い立ち、経歴、背景
でた! In a small town where I live, the schools have children of many different cultural backgrounds.
（私が住む小さな街では、異なった文化的背景を持つ子供が学校に沢山います）
明治大学

**0587 profession** [prəféʃən] 名 専門職、職業

派 **professional** 形 プロの 名 プロ

反 **amateur** [ǽmətʃùər] ⑦ 形 アマチュアの 名 アマチュア

**0588 workforce** [wə́:rkfɔ́:rs] 名 労働力、労働人口
でた! The entry of many women into the workforce has deeply changed America's corporate culture.
（多くの女性が労働に加わることでアメリカの企業文化を一変させた）
慶應義塾大学

> job（仕事）、occupation（一般的な仕事）、career（生涯の仕事）、business（営業目的の仕事）、profession（専門知識を必要とする仕事）、vocation（原義 voc（声）神の声によって呼ばれる＝選ばれし職業。使命感を持って行う仕事）、calling（天職）

> 髪の毛のパーマは永久的にクセをつけること

### 0589 permanent [pə́ːrmənənt]
形 永久の、永続的な　名 パーマ

でた! My job is permanent, so I will not have to look for another.
（私の仕事は終身雇用なので、他の仕事を探す必要がありません）　亜細亜大学

派 **permanently**　副 永久に

### 0590 temporary [témpərèri | -rəri]
形 一時的な

派 **temporarily**　副 一時的に

### 0591 transfer [trænsfə́ːr]
動 転勤させる、乗り換える、移す
名 転勤、乗り換え、移動　※名前動後

でた! I don't mind being transferred as long as the job is interesting.
（仕事が面白ければ転勤になっても大丈夫です）　神奈川大学

### 0592 fire [fáiər]
動 クビにする、解雇する、火をつける、燃やす
名 火、火事

でた! He was fired for his imcompetence.
（彼は無能なため解雇された）　青山学院大学

類 **flame** [fléim]　名 炎
コロ eternal flame（永遠の炎）

でた! We watched the fire, fascinated by the orange flames.
（我々はオレンジ色の炎に魅せられながら、たき火を見た）　上智大学

派 **flammable**　形 可燃性の

### 0593 dismiss [dismís]
動 解雇する、考えを捨てる
原義 dis（離れて）＋miss（送る）＝離れた場所に送る＝クビにする

でた! The government should not be able to dismiss judges.
（政府が裁判官を解任できるようなことがあってはならない）　慶應義塾大学

派 **dismissal**　名 解雇
コロ lay off（一時的に解雇する）

### 0594 recruit [rikrúːt]
動 募集する、新しく入れる　名 新入社員
コロ recruit new staff（新しいスタッフを募集する）

派 **recruitment**　名 新入社員募集

### 0595 resign [rizáin]
動 辞職する、辞任する
原義 re（再び）＋sign（サインする）

派 **resignation**　名 辞職、辞任

UNIT 47　雇用・解雇

Chapter4 Society

# UNIT 48 経営・会議

**STEP 1** 過去問を解く

## 1

I have an uncle who (　　) a Japanese restaurant in Chicago.

1. arrives
2. comes
3. lies
4. runs

東京理科大学

## 2

Even the most advanced robots have to be <u>supervised</u> by humans all the time.

1. revised
2. structured
3. overseen
4. driven

獨協大学

## 3

A (　　) is a meeting, often lasting a few days, which is organized on a particular subject or to bring together people who have a common interest.

1. register
2. laboratory
3. party
4. conference

中央大学

## 4

The parts for these VCRs are manufactured in Japan, then shipped to Malaysia for (　　) into the finished product.

1. assembly
2. compiling
3. distribution
4. attachment

英語検定準1級

## STEP 2 正解を見抜く

### 1

I have an uncle who runs a Japanese restaurant in Chicago.

正解 ④

**訳** 私にはシカゴで日本料理店を経営する叔父がいます。

- arrive 動 到着する
- come 動 来る
- lie 動 嘘をつく
- run 動 経営する

> runは「走る」以外に「走らせる」という他動詞があります。そこから「経営する」という意味が生まれました

### 2

Even the most advanced robots have to be overseen by humans all the time.

正解 ③

**訳** 最先端のロボットでさえも常に人間によって管理されなければならない。

- revise 動 改訂する
- structure 動 構成する
- oversee 動 管理する
- drive 動 運転する

> superviseの語源はsuper（超えて）+ vis（見る）= 上から見る = 監督する、管理する

### 3

A conference is a meeting, often lasting a few days, which is organized on a particular subject or to bring together people who have a common interest.

正解 ④

**訳** conferenceとはしばしば数日に渡る会合であり、ある特定の題材について組織されたり、共通の関心を持つ人々を集めるために組織されるものである。

- register 名 登録
- party 名 パーティー、党
- laboratory 名 実験室
- conference 名 会議

### 4

The parts for these VCRs are manufactured in Japan, then shipped to Malaysia for assembly into the finished product.

正解 ①

**訳** これらのビデオレコーダーのための部品は、日本で製造されていて、最終工程の組み立てのためにマレーシアに出荷されています。

- assembly 名 組み立て
- distribution 名 分配
- compile 動 資料を集める
- attachment 名 添付

UNIT 48 経営・会議

## STEP 3 連鎖式に語彙を増やす 48

**0596 run** [rán]
動 走る、経営する
※他動詞的に考えて何かを持続的に走らせる=経営する

**0597 manage** [mǽnidʒ]
動 管理する [原義] man（手）※手を使って動かす
コロ manage to A（なんとかしてAする）
でた! Did you manage to find a good hotel?
（何とか良いホテルを見つけたんですか） 青山学院大学

派 **management**
名 管理、マネージメント
コロ effective management（効果的経営）
でた! The management of water required organization.
（水の管理には組織化が必要だった） TOEFL

派 **manager** [mǽnidʒər]
名 マネージャー、経営者、管理人

**0598 control** [kəntróul]
動 管理する、制御する 名 管理、制御、支配
でた! The government controlled the trade in salt.
（政府は塩の取引を管理した） 中央大学

**0599 administer** [ædmínistər | əd-]
動 行政管理する

派 **administration**
名 行政管理

**0600 supervise** [súːpərvàiz | sjúː-]
動 監督する、管理する
[原義] super（上から）+ vis（見る）

派 **supervisor**
名 監督

類 **oversee** [óuvərsíː]
動 監督する、見渡す 活 oversee-oversaw-overseen

類 **monitor** [mánətər]
動 監視する 名 モニター

**0601 conference** [kάnfərəns | kɔ́n-]
名 会議、協議会
コロ summit conference（首脳会議）
でた! Mr. Johnson will take part in the international conference next week.
（ジョンソン氏は来週国際会議に参加する予定である） 中央大学

派 **confer**
動 贈与する（+ on）、打ち合わせをする（+ with）

類 **meeting**
名 ミーティング、会議
でた! The meeting finished thirty minutes ago.
（会議は30分前に終了しました） センター試験

**0602 council** [káunsəl]
名 協議会
コロ the Security Council（安全保障協議会）

## 0603 assemble [əsémbl]
**動** 人を集める、組み立てる
原義 as（向かって）＋sem（同じ）

でた! He assembled the youngest members of his staff to design a new car.
（彼は新しい車をデザインするのに彼のスタッフの最も若いメンバーを集めた）　早稲田大学

派 **assembly**　**名** 集合、組み立て

## 0604 accumulate [əkjúːmjulèit]
**動** 徐々に集める、蓄積する

でた! Certain minerals are more likely to be accumulated in large quantities than others.
（特定の鉱石は他の物より大量に集めやすい）　TOEFL

派 **accumulation**　**名** 蓄積

## 0605 gather [gǽðər]
**動**（あちこちから）寄せ集める
コロ gather evidence（証拠を集める）

でた! Early people hunted animals and gathered wild plants.
（古代の人々は動物を狩り、野生植物を集めた）　日本大学

派 **gathering**　**名** 会合、集まり

## 0606 collect [kəlékt]
**動**（取捨選択しながら）集める
原義 co（共に）＋lect（選ぶ）

派 **collection**　**名** 収集、コレクション

## 0607 scatter [skǽtər]
**動** まき散らす、ばらまく、散在する

でた! English is more widely scattered than any other language has ever been.
（英語は他の言語がかつてない程、広範囲に散在している）　早稲田大学

## 0608 organize [ɔ́ːrgənàiz]
**動** 組織する

でた! Modern sports, organized on a nationwide basis, began in Britain around 1850.
（全国的基準で組織された近代スポーツは、1850年頃の英国で始まった）　早稲田大学

派 **organization**　**名** 組織
コロ non-profit organization（NPO＝非営利組織）

派 **organizational**　**形** 組織的な

## 0609 combine [kəmbáin]
**動** 結びつける
コロ combine A with B（AとBを結びつける）

でた! Wisdom comes when we combine creativity with experience.
（英知とは創造性と経験を結びつけた時にやってくるものだ）　神奈川大学

派 **combination**　**名** 結合

でた! Tulips in the wild bloomed in unusual color combination.
（荒野のチューリップは異常な色の組み合わせで開花した）　TOEFL

UNIT 48　経営・会議

Chapter4 Society

## UNIT 49　設立・建設　STEP 1 過去問を解く

### 1

My grandfather <u>established</u> his company in his early twenties.

中央大学

1. divided
2. employed
3. founded
4. neglected

### 2

A new organization has been (　　) to enable the government to control the content of information available to Internet users.

中央大学

1. set down
2. set on
3. set up
4. set with

### 3

One of the foremost aims of the United States during World War II was the (　　) of a lasting peace, including the formation of an economic order.

関西学院大学

1. continuation
2. exaltation
3. repetition
4. establishment

### 4

(　　) designs and oversees the construction of a building.

駒澤大学

1. A gardener
2. An architect
3. A carpenter
4. A guard

## STEP 2 正解を見抜く

### 1

My grandfather founded his company in his early twenties. 正解 ③

訳 私の祖父は20代前半で会社を設立した。

- **divide** 動 割る
- **employ** 動 雇う
- **found** 動 設立する
- **neglect** 動 無視する

> find（見つける）の過去形 found とは別の単語です

### 2

A new organization has been set up to enable the government to control the content of information available to Internet users. 正解 ③

訳 新しい組織は、インターネットユーザにとって利用可能な情報の内容を政府が制御するのを可能にするために設立されました。

- **set down** 書き留める
- **set on** けしかける
- **set up** 設立する
- **set with** （宝石などで）飾る

### 3

One of the foremost aims of the United States during World War II was the establishment of a lasting peace, including the formation of an economic order. 正解 ④

訳 第二次世界大戦中のアメリカ合衆国の主要な目標の一つは、経営秩序の形成を含む恒久な平和の確立であった。

- **continuation** 名 継続
- **exaltation** 名 昇進
- **repetition** 名 反復
- **establishment** 名 確立

> 会社や団体に est.1969 などと書いてありますが established の省略形です

UNIT 49 設立・建設

### 4

An architect designs and oversees the construction of a building. 正解 ②

訳 建築家は建物を設計し、その建築を監督する。

- **gardener** 名 庭師
- **architect** 名 建築家
- **carpenter** 名 大工
- **guard** 名 守衛

Chapter4 Society

## STEP 3 連鎖式に語彙を増やす 🎧49

### 0610 establish [istǽbliʃ]
**動** 設立する、確立する　[原義] 強固なものにする

- **コロ** establish a school （学校を設立する）
- **でた!** The Japanese government has been making efforts to establish a system to promote volunteer activities.
（日本政府はボランティア活動を推進する制度を確立しようと努力を続けている）　[センター試験]

**類** set up　設立する、立ち上げる
- **コロ** set up an organization　（組織を設立する）

**派** establishment　**名** 設立、確立

### 0611 institute [ínstətjùːt | -tjùːt]
**動** (制度・習慣を) 制定する、設立する
**名** 学会、協会、研究所　[原義] in (中に) + st (立てる)

- **コロ** institute of education　（教育研究所）

**派** institution　**名** 設立、制定、施設
- **コロ** educational institution　（教育施設）

### 0612 construct [kənstrʌ́kt]
**動** 建設する、組み立てる
[原義] con (共に) + st (立てる)

- **でた!** Canals were constructed to transport goods by boat.
（運河は商品を船で輸送するために建設された）　[南山大学]

**派** construction　**名** 建築、工事、構成
- **コロ** under construction　（工事中）
- **でた!** The Opera House had been under construction for 17 years.
（オペラハウスは17年間ずっと工事中だった）　[TOEFL]

### 0613 structure [strʌ́ktʃər]
**名** 構造、建造物
- **コロ** internal structure　（内部構造）

### 0614 build [bíld]
**動** 建てる　**活** build-built-built
- **コロ** build up　（築き上げる、身体を鍛える）

**派** building　**名** 建物

日本のビルの概念とは違いhouse, school, factoryなど全体を表します。日本語のビルはoffice building。

### 0615 found [fáund]
**動** (寄付金で) 設立する、創設する

- **コロ** found a hospital for children in Africa　（アフリカの子供たちのために病院を設立する）
- **でた!** After four years of planning, the university was founded in 1995.
（4年間の計画立案の後、大学は1995年に設立されました）　[麗澤大学]

**派** foundation　**名** 創設、設立、基礎、(化粧品の) ファンデーション

| 派 | **fund** [fʌ́nd] | 名 基金、資金 |

| 派 | **fundamental** | 形 根本的な、基本的な、重要な　原義 基礎 |

コロ make a fundamental mistake（基本的な間違いを犯す）

でた！ Teaching how to think is a fundamental part of the educational system.
（ものの考え方を教えることが教育制度の重要な要素なのである）　高知大学

---

**0616 erect** [irékt]　　　動 像を建てる　形 直立した

コロ erect a monument（記念碑を建てる）

でた！ After the tower was erected, the workers began to paint it.
（塔が建てられた後、作業員達は塗装を始めた）　青山学院大学

| 派 | **erection** | 名 建設、直立 |

---

**0617 architecture** [ɑ́ːrkətèktʃər] 発　　名 建築

でた！ The architecture was popular during the Roman occupation.
（建築はローマの占領期間に人気であった）　TOEFL

| 派 | **architectural** | 形 建築上の |

| 派 | **architect** [ɑ́ːrkətèkt] | 名 建築家 |

でた！ Shigeru Ban is a great Japanese architect who utilizes paper in his modern buildings.
（坂茂は紙を現代建築に利用する日本の素晴らしい建築家である）

UNIT 49　設立・建設

---

## coffee break ☕ 建築家　坂茂

　私が最も尊敬する人は坂茂さんという建築家（architect）です。高校時代、教科書で彼の独創的なアイデアと世界のために何ができるかという信念に魅了されてから、追い続けています。坂茂さんは高校卒業後、渡米しアメリカの大学を卒業、ハーバード大学の客員教授を務め、世界中で必要とされています。英語で建築（architecture）という専門を磨き、世界で必要とされるという理想的な道を歩いています。高校時代に「自分もこうなりたい！」や「あの人はすごい！」と思えるような存在に出会えることは努力するための原動力となります。皆さんもロールモデルを見つけてみましょう。

Chapter4 Society

# UNIT 50 観客・顧客 STEP 1 過去問を解く

## 1

The people who watch a sporting event without taking part are called (　　).

センター試験

1. clients
2. customers
3. guests
4. spectators

## 2

During Golden Week, airplanes and trains are usually full of (　　).

南山大学

1. audiences
2. customers
3. guests
4. passengers

## 3

The department store is always packed with (　　).

近畿大学

1. guests
2. clients
3. customers
4. passengers

## 4

The able attorney has large number of (　　).

青山学院大学

1. patients
2. buyers
3. clients
4. patrons

## STEP 2 正解を見抜く

### 1

The people who watch a sporting event without taking part are called spectators.

正解 ④

訳 スポーツ競技に参加するのではなく、観戦する人々のことを観客と言います。

- client 名依頼人
- customer 名お店の客
- guest 名ゲスト
- spectator 名観客

spectatorの語源はspect（見る）＋or（人）＝見る人＝観客

### 2

During Golden Week, airplanes and trains are usually full of passengers.

正解 ④

訳 ゴールデンウィークの間、通常、飛行機と列車は乗客でいっぱいです。

- audience 名観衆、聴衆
- customer 名顧客
- guest 名客
- passenger 名乗客

### 3

The department store is always packed with customers.

正解 ③

訳 そのデパートはいつも客でいっぱいである。

- guest 名客
- client 名顧客、（弁護士などの）依頼人
- customer 名顧客
- passenger 名乗客

### 4

The able attorney has large number of clients.

正解 ③

訳 有能な弁護士には、多くのクライアントがいます。

- patient 名患者
- buyer 名買い手
- client 名顧客、（弁護士などの）依頼人
- patron 名保護者、後援者

UNIT 50　観客・顧客

Chapter4 Society

## STEP 3 連鎖式に語彙を増やす 50

**0618 customer** [kʌ́stəmər] 名 顧客、買い物する客
でた! Most department stores are crowded with customers on Sundays.
(日曜日はほとんどのデパートが買い物客で込み合っている) 〔青山学院大学〕

**0619 client** [kláiənt] 名 顧客、(弁護士などの) 依頼人

**0620 guest** [gést] 発 名 ゲスト、(招待された) 客

**0621 passenger** [pǽsəndʒər] 名 乗客

**0622 spectator** [spékteitər] 名 観客、見物人 原義 見る人
でた! The spectators got all the more excited on account of the unexpected result of the game.
(観客は予想外の試合結果のためにますます興奮した) 〔京都外国語大学〕

● 語源 aud (聞く)

**0623 audio** [ɔ́ːdiòu] 形 耳の

**0624 audience** [ɔ́ːdiəns] 名 聴衆 原義 聞く人
コロ large audience (多くの聴衆)
でた! The soccer game was shown on a big screen in front of a large audience.
(そのサッカーの試合は、大観衆の前の巨大なスクリーンに映し出された) 〔センター試験〕

**0625 audition** [ɔːdíʃən] 名 オーディション

**0626 auditorium** [ɔ̀ːditɔ́ːriəm] 名 講堂、観客席

> audは「聞く」という語源なのでオーディションは「聞いて行うもの」

**0627 obey** [oubéi | əb-] 動 従う
コロ obey a command (命令に従う)
でた! Most people obey the unwritten rules of their society instinctively.
(ほとんどの人は本能的に社会の暗黙のルールに従っている) 〔東京外国語大学〕

派 **obedience** 名 服従

派 **obedient** 形 従順な

反 **disobey** 動 反抗する

**0628 conform** [kənfɔ́ːrm] 動 順応する、一致する
コロ conform to the rule (規則に従う)

派 **conformity** 名 服従、一致

### coffee break ☕ 海外進学という選択

　海外の大学に進学するということを考えたことはありますか？
　中国や韓国では海外進学という選択が当たり前になってきている中、日本人は未だに内向きな考えを持っています。
　私が中国、上海の学校で高校生にインタビューをしてみると多くの学生が海外進学を目指して勉強しているとのことでした。上海には海外進学塾やアメリカの大学入試SATに対応する塾がたくさんあります。
　日本の大学入試では文法重視の形式的な英語力が求められます。外国人が読んでも分からない英文読解力が求められます。それに加え、1度のチャンスで人生が左右されてしまうセンター試験で「英語ができない」と評価されてしまいます。ネイティブでさえもセンター試験で満点を取れません。センター試験に失敗したとしても、世界基準で考えれば気にすることはないのです。
　世界にはもっと自分に合った環境があるはずです。私の予想ですが、これからは海外進学塾が増え、東京大学よりハーバード大学という時代が来ると確信しています。
　今の日本では東大を卒業しても就職が困難な時代です。センター試験や大学入試の結果が全てではありません。世界に目を向けて、自分に合った環境を見つけ出してください。

# UNIT 51　給料・税金

## STEP 1 過去問を解く

### 1

My salary is too (　　). Would you raise it a little bit?

大阪電通大学

1. cheap
2. few
3. little
4. small

### 2

Mika works part-time as a school counselor at some elementary schools, and she (　　) 1,500 dollars a month.

神戸学院大学

1. pays
2. catches
3. loses
4. earns

### 3

A (　　) is an amount of money that you have to pay to the government so that it can pay for public services.

明治大学

1. fare
2. tip
3. deposit
4. tax

### 4

The price on the tag (　　) the 5% consumption tax.

センター試験

1. charges
2. consists
3. describes
4. includes

## STEP 2 正解を見抜く

### 1

My salary is too small. Would you raise it a little bit?  　　正解 ④

訳　私の給料はわずか過ぎます。それをほんの少し上げてもらえませんか？

- cheap 形 安い
- few 形 少数の
- little 形 少量の
- small 形 少ない

> salaryは1つの固まりとして考えるためsmallを使います。salaryの語源は「塩」です。salad（サラダ）と同じ語源

### 2

Mika works part-time as a school counselor at some elementary schools, and she earns 1,500 dollars a month.　　正解 ④

訳　ミカはスクールカウンセラーとしていくつかの小学校でアルバイトしています。そして、彼女は1カ月に1,500ドルの収入を得ています。

- pay 動 支払う
- lose 動 失う
- catch 動 捕える
- earn 動 稼ぐ

### 3

A tax is an amount of money that you have to pay to the government so that it can pay for public services.　　正解 ④

訳　税金は、公共事業に支払うためにあなたが政府に支払わなければならないお金の額です。

- fare 名 料金
- tip 名 チップ
- deposit 名 預金
- tax 名 税金

### 4

The price on the tag includes the 5% consumption tax.　　正解 ④

訳　値札の価格は、5％の消費税を含んでいます。

- charge 動 請求する
- consist 動 ～から成る
- describe 動 記述する
- include 動 含む

> includeの語源はin（中に）+clud（閉める）=含む。反意語はexclude（省く）です

UNIT 51　給料・税金

Chapter4 Society

## STEP 3 連鎖式に語彙を増やす 51

**0629 salary** [sǽləri] 名 給料  原義 塩（salt）を買うためのお金
※塩は当時貴重であったため。

でた! She began to work harder, because her salary was raised.
（給料が上がったので彼女はより一生懸命働き始めた） 〔関西学院大学〕

**0630 wage** [wéidʒ] 名 賃金
コロ minimum wage（最低賃金）

**0631 earn** [ə́:rn] 動 稼ぐ
コロ earn money（お金を稼ぐ）
コロ make a living（生計を立てる）

でた! She makes a living by teaching English to some children.
（彼女は、何人かの子供に英語を教えることによって、生計を立てています） 〔立命館大学〕

**0632 income** [ínkʌm] 名 収入

でた! The family lives on her small income.
（その家族は彼女のわずかな収入で暮らしている） 〔東京理科大学〕

**0633 revenue** [révənjù:] 名 歳入、収入

でた! The development of nuclear energy will mean increased revenue for the government.
（核エネルギーの開発は、政府の歳入の増加に繋がるであろう） 〔上智大学〕

**0634 tax** [tǽks] 名 税金  動 課税する
コロ income tax（所得税）　コロ residential tax（住民税）

でた! The word "tax" means money to be paid by people or business for public purposes.
（「税金」とは公的目的のために、国民や企業から支払われるべき金を意味する） 〔センター試験〕

**0635 interest** [íntərəst] 名 利子

**0636 duty** [djú:ti] 名 義務、税金
コロ on duty（勤務時間内で）　コロ off duty（勤務時間外で）
コロ duty-free shop（免税店）

でた! Whatever the circumstances, it is the duty of adults to protect children.
（いかなる状況でも、子供を守るのは大人の義務だ） 〔高崎経済大学〕

## 0637 impose [impóuz]

**動** 課す
原義 im（上に）＋ pose（置く）

impose tax
（税を課す）

- コロ impose obligation（義務を課す）
- コロ impose A on B（BにAを課す）
- でた! Costa Rica imposed a water tax on major water users.
（コスタリカは大部分の水の使用者に水道税を課した） 法政大学

派 imposition **名** 課税

## 0638 include [inklú:d]

**動** 含む 原義 in（中に）＋ clud（閉める）

でた! The price includes everything except your evening meals.
（価格には夕食代を除く全てを含みます） 同志社大学

派 inclusive **形** 包括した、包括的な

派 inclusion **名** 包括、包含

## 0639 benefit [bénəfit]

**名** （人間的な）利益、恩恵
**動** ためになる、利益になる

- コロ for the benefit of A（Aのために）
- でた! Use of solar power will benefit all mankind.
（太陽光発電の使用は全人類のためになるだろう） TOEFL

派 beneficial [bènəfíʃəl] **形** 有益な
- コロ do A good（Aに利益を与える）

## 0640 profit [práfit | prɔ́f-]

**名** （金銭的な）利益

でた! It remains to be seen whether the business will bring a profit to us.
（その事業が我々に利益をもたらすかどうかは分からないままである） 中央大学

派 profitable **形** 有益な、儲かる、ためになる

でた! Higher education has become a profitable market in the rich countries.
（高等教育は裕福な国で有益な市場となっている） 同志社大学

UNIT 51 給料・税金

Chapter4 Society

# UNIT 52 料金・費用　STEP 1 過去問を解く

## 1

The train (　　) from here to Fifth Avenue is 2 dollars.

立教大学

1. charge
2. cost
3. fare
4. fee

## 2

If both of us join the fitness club at the same time, the membership (　　) will be lower.

東京経済大学

1. fare
2. fee
3. toll
4. tax

## 3

A : I'd like to take a cooking class at your school. How much do you (　　)?
B : The fee is 10,000 yen for three lessons.

青山学院大学

1. charge
2. cost
3. deposit
4. take

## 4

At first, the school had a very small (　　) for its summer festival, but it managed to collect a lot of money from families in the area.

英語検定2級

1. remark
2. surface
3. budget
4. thrill

## STEP 2 正解を見抜く

### 1

The train fare from here to Fifth Avenue is 2 dollars.

正解 ③

訳 ここからFifth Avenueまでの鉄道運賃は、2ドルです。

- **charge** 動 請求する
- **cost** 動 (費用が) かかる
- **fare** 名 料金、運賃
- **fee** 名 謝礼、手数料

> fareの原義は「行く」。旅行に行くことから「運賃」という意味が生まれました。farewellは「ごきげんよう」を意味し、お別れの時に使います。そのためfarewell partyは「送別式」となりました

### 2

If both of us join the fitness club at the same time, the membership fee will be lower.

正解 ②

訳 もし私たちの二人ともが同時にフィットネスクラブに入会したら、メンバー料金が安くなります。

- **fare** 名 料金、運賃
- **toll** 名 使用料金
- **fee** 名 謝礼、手数料
- **tax** 名 税

### 3

A : I'd like to take a cooking class at your school. How much do you charge?
B : The fee is 10,000 yen for three lessons.

正解 ①

訳 A：貴校にてお料理の授業を受講したいのですが。費用はいくらでしょうか。
B：料金は3回の授業につき10000円です。

- **charge** 動 請求する
- **deposit** 動 預ける
- **cost** 動 (費用が) かかる
- **take** 動 取る

### 4

At first, the school had a very small budget for its summer festival, but it managed to collect a lot of money from families in the area.

正解 ③

訳 当初その学校は夏祭りの為の予算が少なかったが、その地域の家庭から何とかお金を集めることができた。

- **remark** 名 批評
- **budget** 名 予算、経費
- **surface** 名 表面
- **thrill** 名 スリル

UNIT 52 料金・費用

Chapter4 Society

## STEP 3 連鎖式に語彙を増やす 52

- 語源 pend pens (費やす)

**0641 spend** [spénd]　　動 時・金を費やす (+ing)

でた！ We spend our lives thinking about aging.
（私たちは年をとることについて考えながら生きている） ［センター試験］

**0642 expensive** [ikspénsiv]　　形 値段が高い、高価な
派 expense　　名 費用
コロ household expense （家計費）
でた！ This amount of money is not enough to cover both tuition and living expenses.
（この金額では学費と生活費を賄うには十分ではない） ［青山学院大学］
コロ at any expense （どんなに犠牲をはらっても、どんなに費用がかかっても）

**0643 expenditure** [ikspénditʃər]　　名 支出、出費
でた！ We can avoid unnecessary expenditure by introducing a new system.
（我々は新たなシステムを導入することにより不要な出費を避けることが出来る） ［学習院大学］

**0644 pension** [pénʃən]　　名 年金
コロ pension system （年金制度）
でた！ The pension needs of old people vary greatly.
（老人の年金の必要性は大きく変わる） ［専修大学］

**0645 compensate** [kámpənsèit] ⑦　　動 補償する、補う (+for)
コロ make up for A （Aを埋め合わせる）
でた！ Nothing can make up for the loss of nature.
（何事も自然の損失を埋め合わせることはできない） ［駒澤大学］

派 compensation　　名 補償

**0646 indispensable** [ìndispénsəbl]　　形 必要不可欠な (+for)
でた！ Childhood is recognized as an indispensable period of life.
（子供時代は人生において欠かすことの出来ない時期として認識されている） ［立命館大学］

派 dispense　　動 なしで済ます (+with)
でた！ In doing this, we cannot dispense with his help.
（これをやる上で、彼の援助なしではやっていけない） ［慶應義塾大学］
コロ do without A （Aなしで済ます）
でた！ We had to do without petrol during the fuel crisis.
（燃料危機の間はガソリンなしで済まさなければならなかった） ［明治大学］

**0647 cost** [kɔ́:st | kɔ́st]　　名 費用、犠牲　動 費用がかかる、犠牲にさせる
活 cost-cost-cost
コロ at any cost, at all costs （どんなに犠牲をはらっても、どんなに費用がかかっても）

でた! We must prevent that kind of disaster at all costs.
（我々はどんな犠牲をはらってもこのような災害を防がなければならない） 京都外国語大学

**0648 budget** [bʌ́dʒit] 　名 予算　動 予算を立てる

でた! Due to budget cuts, we have to cut overtime pay.
（予算の削減のせいで、残業代を減らさなければならない） 青山学院大学

**0649 means** [míːnz] 　名 収入、方法、手段

**0650 subsidize** [sʌ́bsədàiz] 　動 助成金を与える

派 **subsidy** [sʌ́bsədi] 　名 補助金、助成金

**0651 fare** [féər] 　名 乗り物の運賃

**0652 fee** [fíː] 　名 手数料

でた! Some people climbed over the fence to avoid paying the entrance fee.
（入場料の支払いから免れるためにフェンスを乗り越えた人もいた） 京都外国語大学

**0653 charge** [tʃɑːrdʒ] 　名 サービスに対する料金、責任
　動 請求する、充電する

コロ in charge of A（Aの担当である）

**0654 bill** [bíl] 　名 請求書

**0655 purchase** [pə́ːrtʃəs] 発 　動 購入する　名 購入

**0656 finance** [fáinæns] 　名 財政

派 **financial** 　形 財政上の、経済的な
コロ financial support（財政援助）

**0657 afford** [əfɔ́ːrd] 　動 余裕がある
コロ cannot afford to A（Aする余裕がない）

派 **affordable** 　形 手頃な、入手可能な

**0658 economical** [èkənámikəl] ア 　形 経済的な

でた! I've come to think that buying in bulk is more economical than shopping for small quantities.
（少量での買い物よりも大量購入の方がより経済的だと私は考えるようになった） 青山学院大学

**0659 estimate** [éstəmèit] 　動 見積もる

でた! It is worth considering the estimated cost of the project.
（その企画の見積額は考慮する価値がある） 法政大学

派 **estimation** 　名 見積もり

UNIT 52　料金・費用

Chapter4 Society　227

# UNIT 53 通貨・銀行  STEP 1 過去問を解く

## 1

The exchange rates for foreign (　　) change daily.

関西外国語大学

1. currency
2. policies
3. languages
4. atmosphere

## 2

Robert had no money in his bank (　　).

南山大学

1. account
2. interest
3. deposit
4. loan

## 3

Banks in Japan tend to offer much lower (　　) rates than in America or Britain.

学習院大学

1. benefit
2. interest
3. cost
4. profit

## 4

I'm short of cash at the moment. I need to go to a bank and (　　) some money.

東京理科大学

1. deposit
2. dump
3. raise
4. withdraw

## STEP 2 正解を見抜く

### 1

The exchange rates for foreign currency change daily.  　　正解 ①

**訳** 外貨の為替レートは毎日変わります。

- **currency** 名 通貨
- **policy** 名 政策
- **language** 名 言語
- **atmosphere** 名 雰囲気

> currencyの語源はcur（走る）＝現在世の中を走っているもの＝通貨

### 2

Robert had no money in his bank account.  　　正解 ①

**訳** ロバートは銀行口座にお金が全くなかった。

- **account** 名 口座
- **interest** 名 利子
- **deposit** 名 預金
- **loan** 名 ローン、融資

> bank account（銀行口座）

### 3

Banks in Japan tend to offer much lower interest rates than in America or Britain.  　　正解 ②

**訳** 日本の銀行はアメリカやイギリスの銀行よりはるかに低い金利をつける傾向がある。

- **benefit** 名 利益
- **interest** 名 利子
- **cost** 名 費用
- **profit** 名 利益

> interestは重要多義語で「興味」の他に「利子」という意味があります

### 4

I'm short of cash at the moment. I need to go to a bank and withdraw some money.  　　正解 ④

**訳** 私は現在、現金が不足しています。私は、銀行に行って預金を下ろす必要があります。

- **deposit** 動 預ける
- **dump** 動 ドシンと落とす
- **raise** 動 上げる
- **withdraw** 動 （預金を）引き出す

UNIT 53　通貨・銀行

Chapter4 Society

## STEP 3 連鎖式に語彙を増やす 53

● 語源 cur course（走る）

### 0660 currency [kə́:rənsi]　名 通貨

- コロ foreign currency（外貨）
- でた! The Japanese currency is gaining strength against the dollar.
（日本の通貨はドルに対して力を付けている）　TOEFL

### 0661 currently [kə́:rəntli]　副 現在では

- でた! There are estimated to be about 5,000 languages currently spoken in the world today.
（世界中で現在話されている言語は、約5,000語であると推定されている）　東京大学

### 0662 current [kə́:rənt]　形 現在の　名 流れ　原義 流れ

- コロ electric current（電流）
- でた! There are deep currents in this kind of river.
（この種の川には深い流れがある）　慶應義塾大学

### 0663 occur [əkə́:r]　動 起こる、生じる

原義 oc（〜に向かって）＋cur（走る）

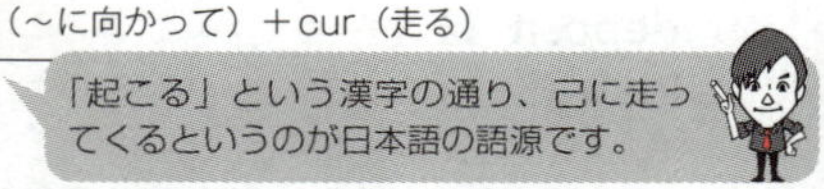

「起こる」という漢字の通り、己に走ってくるというのが日本語の語源です。

- でた! It is when you are short of sleep that sleepwalking is most likely to occur.
（夢遊病が最も起こりやすいのは睡眠不足の時である）　中央大学

- 派 occurrence [əkə́:rəns]　名 発生、事件
- でた! His failure to show up for the nine o'clock class was a rather frequent occurrence.
（彼が9時の授業に姿を見せないのはかなり頻繁に起こることだった）　早稲田大学

### 0664 convert　動 変える、転換する、外貨に両替する、改宗させる

- コロ convert one's religion to Christianity（キリスト教に改宗する）
- でた! When boiled, liquids convert into gases.
（液体が沸騰すると気体になります）　TOEFL
- コロ foreign exchange（外国為替）　コロ exchange converter（為替換算機）

- 派 conversion　名 転換、改宗

## 0665 invest [invést] 動 投資する

- invest A in B (AをBに投資する)
- Our company has invested a lot of money in the new project.
(我々の会社はその新しい事業に多くのお金を投資した) 〔立命館大学〕

**派 investment** 名 投資
- foreign investment (海外投資)

**派 investor** 名 投資家

## 0666 safe [séif] 名 金庫 形 安全な

- This safe is for keeping valuables in.
(この金庫は貴重品を入れておくためのものだ) 〔慶應義塾大学〕

**派 safety** 名 安全性、無事

## 0667 security [sikjúərəti] 名 安全、警備

- A franchise offers more security than starting an independent business.
(フランチャイズは独立して事業を始めるよりも、より安全性を提供する) 〔TOEFL〕

**派 secure** 形 安全な 動 安全にする、確保する、守る

## 0668 account [əkáunt] 名 計算、口座 動 説明する（+ for）

- take A into account (Aを考慮する)   bank account (銀行口座)
- on account of A (Aのため)

## 0669 deposit [dipázit] 動 置く、預ける 名 預金

- put aside A (Aを貯金する)
- ordinary deposit (普通預金)

## 0670 withdraw [wiðdrɔ́ː] 動 引き出す、退かせる
（活）withdraw-withdrew-withdrawn

- withdraw money from a bank (銀行からお金を引き出す)
- About half of these children have been withdrawn from school.
(これらの子供の約半数が退学している) 〔同志社大学〕

**派 withdrawal** 名 預金の引き出し、払い戻し、退学
- Gloria had to make a withdrawal from her savings to pay tuition.
(グロリアは学費を支払うために彼女の預金から引き出さなければならなかった) 〔TOEFL〕

UNIT 53 通貨・銀行

Chapter4 Society | 231

# UNIT 54　破産・借金

**STEP 1** 過去問を解く

## 1

The man was once wealthy, but is now (　　). 　　上智大学

1. broke
2. fallen
3. spoiled
4. failed

## 2

I'd like to go with you but I can't (　　) the plane fare. 　　拓殖大学

1. use
2. lend
3. afford
4. allow

## 3

The economist, a Nobel-prize winner, (　　) bankrupt when he put his theory into practice. 　　学習院大学

1. came
2. went
3. fell
4. failed

## 4

Louis XIV gave the exclusive right to sell coffee to one supplier. Unfortunately this raised the price of coffee so much that consumption declined and the merchant faced <u>bankruptcy</u>. 　　同志社大学

1. imprisonment
2. legal responsibility
3. profit
4. financial failure

## STEP 2 正解を見抜く

### 1

The man was once wealthy, but is now broke.

正解 ①

**訳** その男はかつて裕福でしたが、今は一文無しです。

- **break** 動 破壊させる
- **fall** 動 落ちる
- **spoil** 動 台無しにする
- **fail** 動 失敗する

> brokeは形容詞形で「お金がない」という意味になります

### 2

I'd like to go with you but I can't afford the plane fare.

正解 ③

**訳** 私はあなたと一緒に行きたいのですが、飛行機料金を都合することができません。

- **use** 動 使う
- **lend** 動 貸す
- **afford** 動 余裕（金、暇など）がある
- **allow** 動 許す

### 3

The economist, a Nobel-prize winner, went bankrupt when he put his theory into practice.

正解 ②

**訳** その経済学者はノーベル賞受賞者であったが、自分の理論を実行に移したところ、破産した。

- **go bankrupt** 破産する

> bankruptの語源はbank（銀行）＋rupt（壊れる）＝破産

### 4

Louis XIV gave the exclusive right to sell coffee to one supplier. Unfortunately this raised the price of coffee so much that consumption declined and the merchant faced financial failure.

正解 ④

**訳** ルイ14世がコーヒー販売の独占権を一人の供給元に与えた。しかし不幸にも、このことでコーヒーの価格が上昇して消費が低下したため、その商人は財政破綻に直面することになってしまった。

- **imprisonment** 名 投獄
- **profit** 名 利益
- **legal responsibility** 法的責任
- **financial failure** 財政破綻

UNIT 54 破産・借金

Chapter4 Society

## STEP 3 連鎖式に語彙を増やす 54

• 語源 rupt（壊れる）

**0671 bankrupt** [bǽŋkrʌpt] 形 破産した  原義 bank（銀行）＋rupt（壊れる）
- コロ go bankrupt（破産する）
- 派 **bankruptcy** 名 破産

**0672 erupt** [irʌ́pt] 動 噴火する  原義 e（外に）＋rupt（壊れる）
- でた! The volcano erupts.（火山は噴火する）
- 派 **eruption** 名 噴火

**0673 corrupt** [kərʌ́pt] 形 墜落した　動 墜落させる、買収する
- 派 **corruption** 名 墜落、違法行為、買収
- でた! The corruption or loss of friendship is the hell on earth every person dreads.
  （友情が腐敗したり友情を失ったりすることは誰もが恐れるこの世の地獄である）  明治学院大学

**0674 interrupt** [ìntərʌ́pt] 動 邪魔する、中断する  原義 inter（2つの間）
- 派 **interruption** 名 妨害、中断

**0675 disrupt** [disrʌ́pt] 動 分裂させる、崩壊させる、混乱させる
- でた! Many people experience globalization as a force to disrupt culture.
  （多くの人は文化を崩壊させる力として国際化を体験する）  早稲田大学
- 派 **disruption** 名 分裂、崩壊、混乱
- でた! Heavy snow caused widespread disruption to the city's rail system.
  （大雪のせいで街の電車に広範囲な混乱を引き起こした）  英語検定準1級

**0676 abrupt** [əbrʌ́pt] 形 突然の  原義 急に壊れる
- でた! There was an abrupt change in the weather.
  （天候に突然の変化がありました）  TOEFL

**0677 debt** [dét] 発 名 債務、借金
- コロ be in debt（借金している）　コロ debt hell（借金地獄）
- 派 **indebted** 形 借金がある、借りがある、恩恵がある（＋to）
- でた! Japan is heavily indebted to China for the development of its written language.
  （日本は書き言葉の発展において、中国に非常に恩恵を受けている）  慶應義塾大学

**0678 owe** [óu] 発 動 借りがある、恩がある
- コロ owe A to B（AはBのおかげである）
- でた! I owe my success to your help.
  （私の成功はあなたの援助のおかげだ）  茨城大学

でた！ As he is a man of his word, he will surely pay what he owes you.
(彼は約束を守る人なので、彼が君に借りているものは必ず返すだろう) 学習院大学

> a man of 抽象名詞＝a 形容詞 manの例です。a man of promise=a promising man（前途有望な人）、a man of letters（文学者）、a man of sense=a sensible man（良識のある人）

| 0679 | **surplus** [sə́:rplʌs] | 名 黒字、余り、剰余金　形 余った |

| 0680 | **deficit** [défəsit] | 名 不足、赤字 |

コロ trade deficit（貿易赤字）

でた！ Both parents work to cover the deficit in the family budget.
(両親は家計の赤字を埋めるために働いている) 慶應義塾大学

| 0681 | **prosperity** [prɑspérəti] | 名 繁栄 |

でた！ After India's independence from Britain, Bombay's prosperity continued.
(インドのイギリスからの独立後、ボンベイの繁栄は続いた) 中央大学

派 **prosper** 動 繁栄する

派 **prosperous** 形 繁栄している

でた！ In the early 1900s, San Francisco was a prosperous city.
(19世紀初頭、サンフランシスコは繁栄した街であった) TOEFL

| 0682 | **thrive** [θráiv] | 動 繁栄する、成長する |

派 **thriving** 形 繁栄する、繁盛する

| 0683 | **flourish** [flə́:riʃ] | 動 繁栄する、繁殖する |

派 **flourishing** 形 繁栄する、繁盛する

| 0684 | **wealth** [wélθ] | 名 富、財産 |

派 **wealthy** 形 裕福な

コロ well off（裕福な）

| 0685 | **luxury** [lʌ́kʃəri] | 名 ぜいたく品 |

コロ live in luxury（ぜいたくに生活する）

派 **luxurious** 形 ぜいたくな

UNIT 54 破産・借金

Chapter4 Society

# UNIT 55 価値・感謝

**STEP 1** 過去問を解く

## 1

After Grand Motors went bankrupt, the ( ) of its stock fell eighty percent.

東京理科大学

1. valuable
2. valuate
3. valued
4. value

## 2

A: Samantha, why do you always wear that necklace?
B: It's very ( ) to me. My father gave it to me just before he died.

英語検定2級

1. mature
2. precious
3. expensive
4. acceptable

## 3

The Mona Lisa is a ( ) work of art, so it is displayed behind a thick pane of glass in the museum.

獨協大学

1. valueless
2. worthless
3. priceless
4. penniless

## 4

To ( ) something means to know its value or good qualities.

センター試験

1. appreciate
2. predict
3. advertise
4. provide

236

## STEP 2 正解を見抜く

### 1

After Grand Motors went bankrupt, the value of its stock fell eighty percent.

正解 ④

**訳** Grand Motorsが破産した後に、株価が80パーセント下落しました。

- valuable 形 高価な
- valuate 動 評価する、査定する
- value 名 価値

### 2

A: Samantha, why do you always wear that necklace?
B: It's very precious to me. My father gave it to me just before he died.

正解 ②

**訳** A：サマンサ、なんでいつもそのネックレスを付けてるの。
B：これは私にとってとても貴重なんです。父が亡くなる直前に私にくれたのです。

- mature 形 成熟した
- expensive 形 高価な
- precious 形 貴重な
- acceptable 形 容認できる

preciousの原義は「価値」です。価値があるため「貴重な」という意味になります

### 3

The Mona Lisa is a priceless work of art, so it is displayed behind a thick pane of glass in the museum.

正解 ③

**訳** モナリザは貴重な美術品であるので、博物館では厚いガラスの後ろに展示されています。

- valueless 形 価値のない
- worthless 形 価値のない
- priceless 形 きわめて貴重な
- penniless 形 無一文の

pricelessは値段が付けられない程、価値があるので「極めて貴重な」となります

### 4

To appreciate something means to know its value or good qualities.

正解 ①

**訳** 正しく価値を理解するということは、その価値と良い質を分かっているということである。

- appreciate 動 正しく価値を理解する
- advertise 動 広告する
- predict 動 予言する
- provide 動 供給する

UNIT 55 価値・感謝

Chapter4 Society

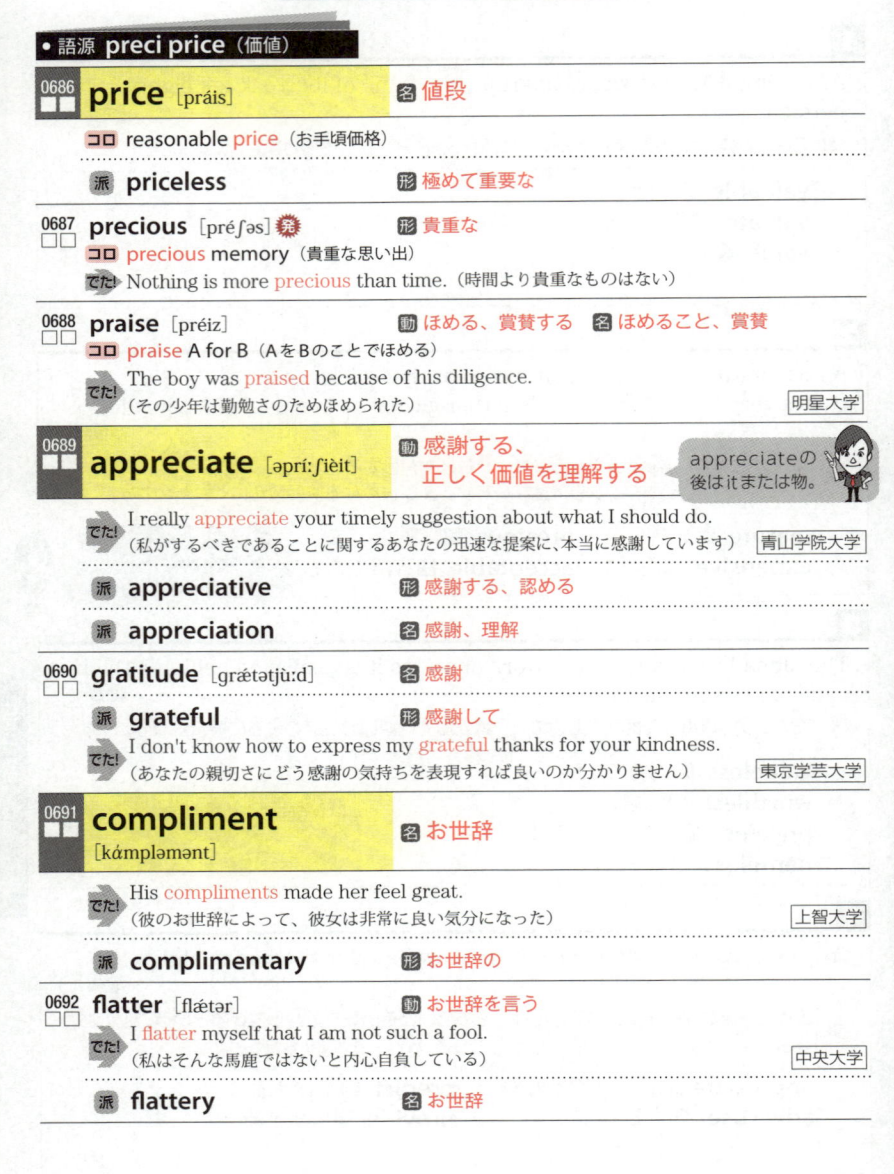

## STEP 3 連鎖式に語彙を増やす 55

- 語源 preci price（価値）

**0686 price** [práis] 名 値段
- reasonable price（お手頃価格）
- 派 priceless 形 極めて重要な

**0687 precious** [préʃəs] 形 貴重な
- precious memory（貴重な思い出）
- でた! Nothing is more precious than time.（時間より貴重なものはない）

**0688 praise** [préiz] 動 ほめる、賞賛する 名 ほめること、賞賛
- praise A for B（AをBのことでほめる）
- でた! The boy was praised because of his diligence.
（その少年は勤勉さのためほめられた） 明星大学

**0689 appreciate** [əpríːʃièit] 動 感謝する、正しく価値を理解する
> appreciateの後はitまたは物。
- でた! I really appreciate your timely suggestion about what I should do.
（私がするべきであることに関するあなたの迅速な提案に、本当に感謝しています） 青山学院大学
- 派 appreciative 形 感謝する、認める
- 派 appreciation 名 感謝、理解

**0690 gratitude** [grǽtətjùːd] 名 感謝
- 派 grateful 形 感謝して
- でた! I don't know how to express my grateful thanks for your kindness.
（あなたの親切さにどう感謝の気持ちを表現すれば良いのか分かりません） 東京学芸大学

**0691 compliment** [kámpləmənt] 名 お世辞
- でた! His compliments made her feel great.
（彼のお世辞によって、彼女は非常に良い気分になった） 上智大学
- 派 complimentary 形 お世辞の

**0692 flatter** [flǽtər] 動 お世辞を言う
- でた! I flatter myself that I am not such a fool.
（私はそんな馬鹿ではないと内心自負している） 中央大学
- 派 flattery 名 お世辞

## 0693 reward [riwɔ́ːrd]  名 報酬  動 報いる

でた! Her success is just reward for all her hard work.
（彼女の成功は彼女の全ての努力に対する正当な報酬だ） 上智大学

派 **rewarding**  形 価値のある
コロ challenging and rewarding job （やりがいがあって価値ある仕事）

## 0694 worth [wə́ːrθ]  形 価値がある（+ ing）  名 価値

でた! However hard it may be, it is worth trying.
（どんなに難しくても、それはやってみる価値がある） 津田塾大学

派 **worthy** 発  形 値する（+ of）、ふさわしい

派 **worthless**  形 価値がない

## 0695 deserve [dizə́ːrv]  動 受けるに値する

でた! He deserves to be the Prime Minister of Japan.
（彼は日本の総理大臣になるに値する）

## 0696 value [vǽljuː]  名 価値  動 高く評価する

でた! Copies of great paintings have little commercial value.
（偉大な絵画の複製にはほとんど商業的価値はない） 早稲田大学
コロ make much of A （Aを重んじる）
でた! I didn't make much of her opinion.
（私は彼女の意見を重要視しなかった） 立命館大学

派 **valuable**  形 価値の高い  名 貴重品 上智大学

派 **invaluable**  形 評価できない程価値がある

## 0697 congratulate [kəngrǽtʃulèit]  動 祝う

コロ congratulate A on B （AをBのことで祝う）
でた! My friends congratulated me on my success.
（私の友達が私の成功をお祝いしてくれた） 早稲田大学

派 **congratulation**  名 祝うこと、（間投詞的に）おめでとう（-s）

## 0698 celebrate [séləbrèit]  動 祝う

派 **celebrated**  形 名高い、有名な
コロ celebrated people （著名人）

派 **celebration**  名 お祝い

派 **celebrity**  名 有名人、著名人

UNIT 55 価値・感謝

Chapter4 Society | 239

# UNIT 56 合法・違法　STEP 1 過去問を解く

## 1

For their safety and the safety of others, drivers must (　　) the traffic rules.

センター試験

1. observe
2. overlook
3. test
4. violate

## 2

Smoking in a hospital is a (　　) of the city law and you will be fined if you do it.

青山学院大学

1. prevention
2. limitation
3. violation
4. integration

## 3

In many countries, it is (　　) to sell alcoholic drinks to the young who are under 18.

東京理科大学

1. illegal
2. immune
3. innate
4. irrational

## 4

He had a (　　) reason for being late to class. The trains were delayed due to the snowstorm.

立命館大学

1. ferocious
2. legitimate
3. progressive
4. respected

240

## STEP 2 正解を見抜く

### 1

For their safety and the safety of others, drivers must observe the traffic rules.

正解 ①

**訳** 運転手自身の安全と他の人の安全のために、彼らは交通規則を守らなければならない。

- **observe** 動 法律を守る
- **overlook** 動 大目に見る
- **test** 動 試験する
- **violate** 動 法律を破る

> observeは重要多義語です。「法律を守る」の他に「観察する」があります

### 2

Smoking in a hospital is a violation of the city law and you will be fined if you do it.

正解 ③

**訳** 病院内での喫煙は市条例違反であるため、もしタバコを吸った場合は罰金を科せられます。

- **prevention** 名 防止
- **violation** 名 違法行為
- **limitation** 名 制限
- **integration** 名 統合

### 3

In many countries, it is illegal to sell alcoholic drinks to the young who are under 18.

正解 ①

**訳** 多くの国では、18未満の若者にアルコール飲料を販売することは違法です。

- **illegal** 形 不法の
- **immune** 形 免疫のある
- **innate** 形 生まれつきの
- **irrational** 形 不合理な

> illegalの語源はi（否定）＋leg（法律）

### 4

He had a legitimate reason for being late to class. The trains were delayed due to the snowstorm.

正解 ②

**訳** 彼は授業に遅刻したことに対する正当な理由があった。吹雪のせいで電車が遅れたのだった。

- **ferocious** 形 どうもうな
- **progressive** 形 進歩的な
- **legitimate** 形 合法の
- **respected** 形 評判の高い

UNIT 56 合法・違法

Chapter4 Society

## STEP 3 連鎖式に語彙を増やす 56

● 語源 leg（法律）

**0699 law** [lɔ́ː]  名 法律

- コロ law firm（弁護士事務所）　コロ break the law（法律を破る）
- 派 **lawful**　形 合法的な
- 派 **lawyer**　名 弁護士
- 類 **attorney** [ətə́ːrni]　名 弁護士

**0700 legal** [líːɡəl]　形 合法の、法律の

でた！ Based on various legal systems and cultural values, the document is an agreed set of standards.
（様々な法律制度や文化的価値に基づき、その文書は合意された一連の基準となっている）
立命館大学

- 反 **illegal** [ilíːɡəl]　形 違法の

でた！ Illegal acts are acts forbidden by law.
（違法行為とは法律によって禁じられている行為のことである）
上智大学

**0701 legitimate** [lidʒítəmət]　形 適法の、正当な

でた！ The engineer had a legitimate reason for changing the design of the building.
（その技師には建物の設計を変えるための正当な理由があった）
TOEFL

- 派 **legitimacy** [lidʒítəməsi]　名 正当性、合法性
- 派 **legislate** [lédʒislèit]　動 法律を定める
- 派 **legislation** [lèdʒisléiʃən]　名 立法
- コロ enact legislation（法を施行する）

**0702 loyal** [lɔ́iəl]　形 忠実な、誠実な

> royal「王国の」と混同注意

- コロ be loyal to A（Aに対して忠実である）
- 派 **loyalty** [lɔ́iəlti]　名 忠実

**0703 privilege** [prívəlidʒ]　名 特権　原義 priv（個人の）＋ leg（法律）

でた！ Use our credit card and get the privilege of a five percent discount at selected stores.
（我々のクレジットカードを使って指定された店で5パーセントの割り引きの特権をもらってください）
英語検定準1級

## 0704 valid [vǽlid] 形 有効な、妥当な

The students had a valid reason for missing class.
(その生徒には授業を欠席した正当な理由があった) TOEFL

**反** invalid  形 無効な

**派** validate [vǽlədèit]  動 有効にする

**派** validity  名 妥当性、法的有効性

Tests are useful when validity has been established.
(妥当性が確立されれば、テストは役に立つものである) 慶應義塾大学

## 0705 violence [váiələns]  名 暴力、違法

0706 People attended the meeting to discuss domestic violence.
(家庭内暴力について議論するため人々はその集会に参加した) 早稲田大学

**派** violent  形 激しい、暴力的な
**コロ** violent storm (激しい嵐)

The rate of violent crime has risen over the last ten years.
(暴力犯罪の発生率はこの10年間で上昇した) 早稲田大学

**派** violate  動 違反する、侵害する

No one should be allowed to violate the human rights of others.
(他人の人権を侵害することは誰も許されるべきではない) 慶應義塾大学

**派** violation  名 違反行為

## 0707 obey [oubéi | əb-]  動 従う

**コロ** obey the rule (規則に従う)

There is nothing for it but to obey the order.
(その命令に従うほか仕方がありません) 大阪市立大学

**派** obedience  名 従うこと、服従

**派** obedient  形 従順な

## 0708 observe [əbzə́ːrv]  動 (法律を)守る、遵守する、観察する
**コロ** observe the law (法律を守る)

**派** observance  名 遵守

**派** observation  名 観察

Dolphins quickly learn by observation and spontaneously imitate human activities.
(イルカは観察することで物事をすぐに学び、自発的に人間の活動を模倣します) TOEFL

UNIT 56 合法・違法

Chapter4 Society

# UNIT 57 裁判・訴訟

**STEP 1 過去問を解く**

## 1

The judge (　　) the defendant to 3 months in jail for his dangerous driving

青山学院大学

1. sentenced
2. tested
3. threw
4. warned

## 2

The store clerk was upset by the manager's (　　) that she had stolen money from the cash register. She said she would never do such a thing.

英語検定2級

1. temptation
2. accusation
3. designation
4. activation

## 3

When I first came to live here in Japan, there was a lot of (　　) against me, but now everyone accepts me.

東京理科大学

1. preference
2. prejudice
3. prevention
4. prospect

## 4

In the U.S., whenever there is a problem with a company's products, people hire a lawyer and (　　) the company.

英語検定準1級

1. owe
2. sue
3. claim
4. fine

## STEP 2 正解を見抜く

### 1

The judge sentenced the defendant to 3 months in jail for his dangerous driving.

正解 ①

**訳** その裁判官は被告人の危険運転に対して禁固3ヶ月の刑を言い渡しました。

- **sentence** 動 判決を下す
- **test** 動 試験する
- **throw** 動 投げる
- **warn** 動 警告する

sentenceは「文章」という意味の他に「判決を下す」という意味があります

### 2

The store clerk was upset by the manager's accusation that she had stolen money from the cash register. She said she would never do such a thing.

正解 ②

**訳** 彼女がレジからお金を盗んだというマネージャの非難でその店員は動揺しました。 彼女はそのようなことを決してしないと言いました。

- **temptation** 名 誘惑
- **designation** 名 指名
- **accusation** 名 告発
- **activation** 名 活性化

### 3

When I first came to live here in Japan, there was a lot of prejudice against me, but now everyone accepts me.

正解 ②

**訳** 私が初めて日本に滞在しに来たとき、私に対して多くの偏見があったが、今は皆私を受け入れている。

- **preference** 名 好み
- **prevention** 名 防止
- **prejudice** 名 偏見
- **prospect** 名 見込み

prejudiceの語源はpre（前に）＋judge（判断する）＝前に判断する＝偏見

### 4

In the U.S., whenever there is a problem with a company's products, people hire a lawyer and sue the company.

正解 ②

**訳** アメリカでは、ある会社の製品に関する問題があるときはいつも、人々は弁護士を雇って、その会社を訴えます。

- **owe** 動 借りがある
- **claim** 動 要求する
- **sue** 動 訴える
- **fine** 動 罰金を科す

UNIT 57 裁判・訴訟

Chapter4 Society

## STEP 3 連鎖式に語彙を増やす

● 語源 jut（正しい）

### 0709 court [kɔ́ːrt]
名 裁判、公判、テニスのコート

- 類 **trial** [tráiəl] 名 試み、裁判
- コロ trial and error（試行錯誤）
- でた! He succeeded on his third trial.
（彼は三回目の挑戦で成功した） 〔中央大学〕

### 0710 sentence [séntəns]
名 判決、文 動 判決を下す

- でた! At the end of his trial he was sentenced for murder.
（彼の最後の判決で、殺人罪と判決を下されました） 〔学習院大学〕

### 0711 judge [dʒʌ́dʒ]
動 判断する 名 裁判官、審判

- コロ judging from A（Aから判断すると）
- 派 **judgment** 名 判断

### 0712 justify [dʒʌ́stəfài]
動 正当化する 原義 just（正しい）

- でた! The end justifies the means.
（結果は手段を正当化する） 〔一橋大学〕
- 派 **justification** 名 正当化
- 派 **justice** 名 正義

### 0713 prejudice [prédʒudis]
名 偏見（＋ against）
原義 pre（前に）＋ judice（判断する）

- コロ have prejudice against A（Aに偏見を持つ）
- でた! Prejudice means disliking a particular group of people without reason.
（偏見とは理由もなく特定の集団の人々を嫌うことである） 〔中央大学〕

### 0714 stereotype [stériətàip]
名 ステレオタイプ、固定観念 動 型にはめる

- コロ gender stereotype（性に関する固定観念）

### 0715 jury [dʒúəri]
名 陪審

- でた! In Britain, only 1% of criminal cases end up before a jury.
（イギリスでは、刑事事件の1％のみが陪審の前に終わる） 〔早稲田大学〕

### 0716 verdict [vɜ́ːrdikt]
名 評決

- コロ guilty verdict（有罪判決）

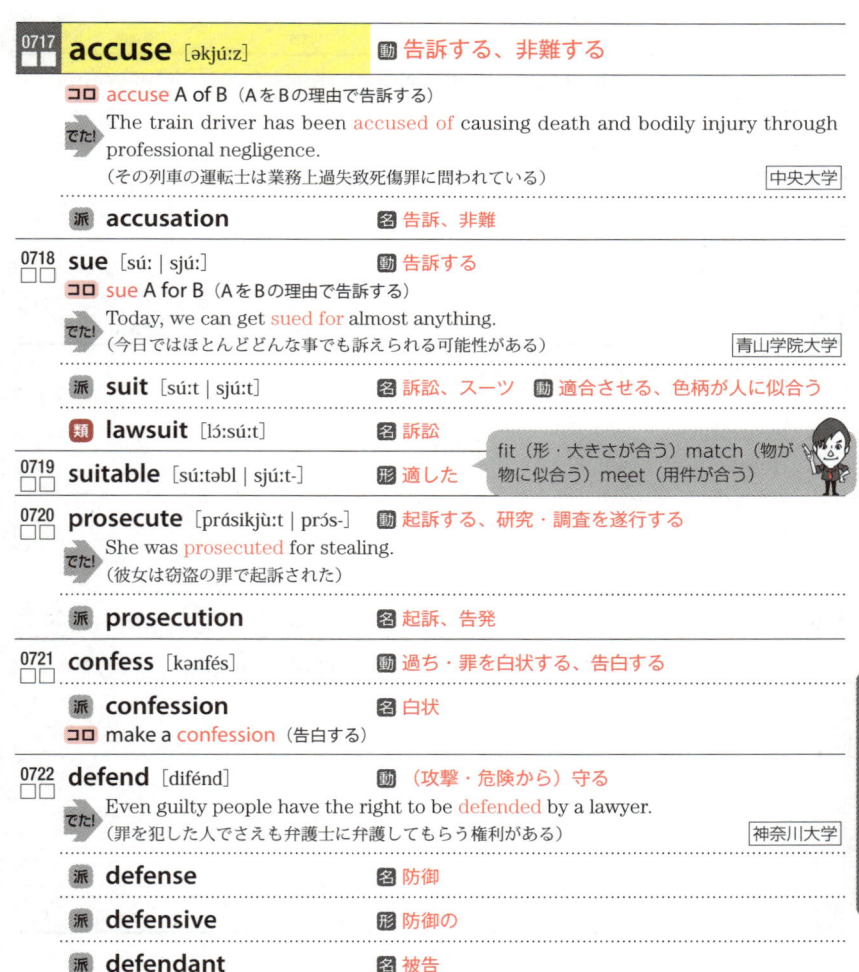

## 0717 accuse [əkjúːz] 動 告訴する、非難する

コロ accuse A of B（AをBの理由で告訴する）

でた! The train driver has been accused of causing death and bodily injury through professional negligence.
（その列車の運転士は業務上過失致死傷罪に問われている）　中央大学

派 accusation　名 告訴、非難

## 0718 sue [súː | sjúː] 動 告訴する

コロ sue A for B（AをBの理由で告訴する）

でた! Today, we can get sued for almost anything.
（今日ではほとんどどんな事でも訴えられる可能性がある）　青山学院大学

派 suit [súːt | sjúːt]　名 訴訟、スーツ　動 適合させる、色柄が人に似合う

類 lawsuit [lɔ́ːsùːt]　名 訴訟

## 0719 suitable [súːtəbl | sjúːt-] 形 適した

fit（形・大きさが合う）match（物が物に似合う）meet（用件が合う）

## 0720 prosecute [prásikjùːt | prɔ́s-] 動 起訴する、研究・調査を遂行する

でた! She was prosecuted for stealing.
（彼女は窃盗の罪で起訴された）

派 prosecution　名 起訴、告発

## 0721 confess [kənfés] 動 過ち・罪を白状する、告白する

派 confession　名 白状

コロ make a confession（告白する）

## 0722 defend [difénd] 動 （攻撃・危険から）守る

でた! Even guilty people have the right to be defended by a lawyer.
（罪を犯した人でさえも弁護士に弁護してもらう権利がある）　神奈川大学

派 defense　名 防御

派 defensive　形 防御の

派 defendant　名 被告

UNIT 57　裁判・訴訟

Chapter4 Society

# UNIT 58 犯罪・処罰

## STEP 1 過去問を解く

### 1
The recent survey indicates that serious crimes (　　　) by young adults are increasing.

立命館大学

1. accused
2. committed
3. pursued
4. released

### 2
He has been at large since last week.

立命館大学

1. available
2. dead
3. on a diet
4. out of prison

### 3
Slow down a bit. Otherwise, you'll have to pay a huge (　　　) for speeding.

立教大学

1. admission
2. charge
3. fine
4. tuition

### 4
The boy took great (　　　) to solve the problem.

中央大学

1. effects
2. struggles
3. senses
4. pains

## STEP 2 正解を見抜く

### 1

The recent survey indicates that serious crimes committed by young adults are increasing.

正解 ②

訳 最近の調査で青少年による犯罪が増えていることが分かった。

- accuse 動 告訴する
- commit 動 犯す
- pursue 動 追求する
- release 動 放つ

commit a crime は「罪を犯す」です

### 2

He has been out of prison since last week.

正解 ④

訳 彼は先週から自由の身だ。

- available 形 利用可能である
- dead 形 死んでいる
- on a diet 減量している
- out of prison 脱獄する

at large には「逃走中で」という意味があります

### 3

Slow down a bit. Otherwise, you'll have to pay a huge fine for speeding.

正解 ③

訳 少しスピードを落として。そうしないとスピード違反で多額の罰金を払うことになるよ。

- admission 名 入場料
- charge 名 料金
- fine 名 罰金
- tuition 名 授業料

fine は重要多義語です

### 4

The boy took great pains to solve the problem.

正解 ④

訳 少年はその問題を解くのにとても苦労した。

- take pains 苦労する

## STEP 3 連鎖式に語彙を増やす 🎧58

### 0723 crime [kráim] 名 犯罪
- コロ commit a crime（罪を犯す）
- でた! The rate of serious crime has increased 10 percent this year.（今年は重大犯罪の割合が10パーセント増えた） 〔学習院大学〕
- 派 **criminal** [krímənl] 名 犯罪者 形 犯罪の
- コロ criminal act（犯罪行為） コロ criminal investigation（犯罪捜査）

### 0724 sin [sín] 名 宗教的・道徳的の罪

### 0725 murder [mə́:rdər] 名 殺人
- コロ attempted murder（殺人未遂）
- 派 **murderer** 名 殺人犯
- コロ behind bars（服役中） コロ at large（逃走中で、自由で）

### 0726 arrest [ərést] 動 逮捕する
- コロ under arrest（逮捕されて）
- 類 **apprehend** [æprihénd] 動 逮捕する

### 0727 rob [ráb | rɔ́b] 動 引ったくる、奪う（＋ of）
- コロ rob A of B（AからBを奪う）
- でた! TV has robbed us of our enjoyment of conversation at dinner at home.（テレビは家庭から、夕食時の家族団欒を奪ってしまった） 〔日本大学〕
- 派 **robbery** [rábəri | rɔ́b-] 名 引ったくり、強盗

### 0728 deprive [dipráiv] 動 権利を奪う（＋ of）
- コロ deprive A of B（AからBを奪う）
- 派 **deprivation** 名 剥奪、損失、欠如

### 0729 convict [kənvíkt] 動 有罪を宣告する 名 囚人
- 派 **conviction** 名 確信、有罪判決

### 0730 detect [ditékt] 動 見抜く、見つけ出す
- 派 **detective** 名 探偵 形 探偵の
- 派 **detection** 名 探知、発覚

### 0731 jail [dʒéil] 名 刑務所
- 類 **prison** [prízn] 名 刑務所

## 0732 suspect [sʌ́spekt] [səspékt] 名 容疑者 動 疑う

でた！ The suspect is a six-foot-tall male, wearing a black sweater with a white logo.
（その容疑者は身長6フィートの男性で白いロゴ入りの黒いセーターを着ている） 中京大学

でた！ The policeman suspected the boy of shoplifting.
（警官はその少年に万引きの疑いを抱いていた） 東京都市大学

派 **suspicious** 形 疑い深い

派 **suspicion** 名 疑い

## 0733 doubt [dáut] 動 疑う 名 疑い

派 **doubtful** 形 確信がない、疑わしい

派 **dubious** [djúːbiəs | djúː-] 形 疑わしい

## 0734 guilty [gílti] 形 罪の意識がある

コロ feel guilty about A （Aに対して罪悪感を抱く）

派 **guilt** 名 法律違反

## 0735 innocent [ínəsənt] 形 無罪の、無邪気な

派 **innocence** 名 無罪

## 0736 fine [fáin] 名 罰金 動 罰金を課す 形 元気な、晴れた、細い

## 0737 pain [péin] 名 痛み

コロ pain killer（痛み止め） コロ take pains（苦労する）

派 **painful** 形 痛い

## 0738 penalty [pénəlti] 名 刑罰、罰金
コロ death penalty（死刑）

でた！ They insist strongly that the death penalty should be abolished.
（彼らは死刑は廃止されるべきだと強く主張している） 慶應義塾大学

派 **penalize** [pénəlti] 動 罰する

## 0739 punish [pʌ́niʃ] 動 罰する、処罰する
コロ punish A for B（AをBに関して罰する）

でた！ Bars can be severely punished if they serve alcohol to minors.
（バーは未成年者にアルコールを提供すると、厳しく罰せられる可能性がある） 早稲田大学

派 **punishment** 名 罰、処罰
コロ capital punishment（死刑）

UNIT 58 犯罪・処罰

Chapter4 Society

# UNIT 59 証拠・保証

**STEP 1 過去問を解く**

## 1

This computer is (　　) for two years.

桜美林大学

1. promised
2. defended
3. guarded
4. guaranteed

## 2

We need to promote economic growth while (　　) the protection of the environment.

立命館大学

1. distinguishing
2. ensuring
3. frightening
4. transporting

## 3

I was interviewed as a (　　) to the traffic accident.

立命館大学

1. guest
2. host
3. passenger
4. witness

## 4

There is no (　　) that any member of the current government was involved in the scandal.

慶應義塾大学

1. insight
2. obstacle
3. recognition
4. evidence

## STEP 2 正解を見抜く

### 1

This computer is guaranteed for two years. 正解 ④

訳 そのコンピュータは2年間保証されている。

- **promise** 動約束する
- **defend** 動防御する
- **guard** 動守る
- **guarantee** 動保証する

> 芸能人のギャラはguarantee「契約出演料、保証金」のことです

### 2

We need to promote economic growth while ensuring the protection of the environment. 正解 ②

訳 我々は環境保護を確実にしながら、経済成長を促進する必要がある。

- **distinguish** 動区別する
- **ensure** 動確実にする
- **frighten** 動怖がらせる
- **transport** 動輸送する

### 3

I was interviewed as a witness to the traffic accident. 正解 ④

訳 私は目撃者として交通事故について聞かれました。

- **guest** 名客
- **host** 名主人
- **passenger** 名乗客
- **witness** 名証人

> witnessは「目撃する」という動詞でも使えます

### 4

There is no evidence that any member of the current government was involved in the scandal. 正解 ④

訳 現在の政府の構成員のうち誰かがスキャンダルに巻き込まれたという証拠はない。

- **insight** 名洞察
- **obstacle** 名障害物
- **recognition** 名認識
- **evidence** 名証拠

UNIT 59 証拠・保証

Chapter4 Society

## STEP 3 連鎖式に語彙を増やす 59

- 語源 **sure**（確かな）

### 0740 insure [inʃúər] 動 保険をかける

- 派 **insurance** 名 保険
- コロ social insurance（社会保険）
- コロ take the entrance exams at three private universities as insurance
  （滑り止めとして3つの私立大学の入学試験を受ける）
- でた! Many part-timers are now entitled to health insurance.
  （多くのパートの従業員は、現在健康保険に加入する資格がある） 〔北海道大学〕

### 0741 guarantee [gæ̀rəntíː] 名 保証 動 保証する

芸能人のテレビ出演のギャラ（保証金）

- でた! In an ideal world, just one language would guarantee mutual understanding and peace.
  （理想的な世界では、ただ一つの言語が相互理解と平和を保証するものだろう） 〔法政大学〕

### 0742 ensure [inʃúər | -ʃɔ́ː] 動 確実にする

- でた! The government should ensure that the project meets the citizens' needs.
  （政府はその計画が、市民の要求を満たしているかどうか確実にすべきだ） 〔学習院大学〕

### 0743 assure [əʃúər] 動 保証する、確信する

- 派 **assurance** 名 保証、確信
- 派 **reassure** 動 安心させる
- 派 **reassurance** 名 安心

- 語源 **cert**（確かな）

### 0744 certain [sə́ːrtn] 形 確かな、ある

- コロ for certain（確かに）
- でた! Certain things are better left unsaid.
  （ある事は言わないでいた方がよい） 〔中央大学〕
- でた! As the old saying goes, nothing in life is certain but death and taxes.
  （古い諺にあるように、死と税金以上に確かな物はない） 〔慶應義塾大学〕

- 派 **certainly** 副 確かに、もちろん
- 派 **ascertain** [æ̀sərtéin] 動 確かめる
- 派 **certainty** [sə́ːrtnti] 名 確信、確実性
- 反 **uncertain** 形 不確かな

254

## 0745 certify [sə́:rtəfài] 動 文書で証明する

- certified public accountant (公認会計士)
- 派 **certificate** [sərtífikət] 名 証書 動 証明書を与える
- teaching (teacher's) certificate (教員免許書)
- でた! The death of family member must be verified by a death certificate.
  (家族がなくなった場合は死亡診断書によって証明されなければならない) [TOEFL]
- 派 **certification** 名 証明

## 0746 qualify [kwáləfài | kwɔ́l-] 動 資格を与える

- qualify A for B (AにBの資格を与える)
- でた! The man is well qualified for the position in our department.
  (その男は、私たちの部署ではその地位に非常に適任である) [立命館大学]
- 派 **qualification** 名 資格、適性
- 反 **disqualify** 動 失格させる

## 0747 entitle [intáitl] 動 資格を与える、権利を与える(＋to)

- でた! Only members of the company are entitled to use the facilities.
  (会社の会員のみが、施設を使用する資格がある) [上智大学]

## 0748 prove [prú:v] 動 証明する

- prove to be A (Aだとわかる)
- でた! The new machine will prove to be of great use.
  (その新しい機械は非常に役立つと分かるでしょう) [関西学院大学]
- turn out to be A (Aだとわかる)
- でた! Unfortunately the murderer turned out to be my neighbor.
  (不幸にもその殺人犯はうちの近隣だとわかった) [日本大学]
- 派 **proof** 名 証拠
- 反 **disprove** [disprú:v] 動 誤りを立証する

## 0749 evidence [évədəns] 名 証拠

- scientific evidence (科学的証拠)
- でた! There is a lot of evidence that smoking is bad for your health.
  (喫煙が人体に有害という証拠がたくさんあります) [学習院大学]
- 派 **evident** 形 明らかな

## 0750 witness [wítnis] 名 目撃者 動 目撃する

- でた! I was interviewed as a witness.
  (私は目撃者としてインタビューを受けた) [立命館大学]

UNIT 59 証拠・保証

Chapter4 Society | 255

# UNIT 60 主張・基準  STEP 1 過去問を解く

## 1

Even after he had been convicted of the crime, he (　　) that he was innocent.

立命館大学

1. insisted
2. permitted
3. requested
4. required

## 2

Theresa : How could the captain miss seeing it and hit something that huge?
Tim : (　　) it was because of the thick fog.

上智大学

1. He excuses
2. He claims
3. He blamed
4. He exclaimed

## 3

What should be the (　　) for deciding what qualifies as an Olympic sport?

立命館大学

1. comparison
2. criticism
3. standard
4. substance

## 4

Jimmy is like an alien to me. He and I have nothing in (　　).

武蔵大学

1. common
2. conversation
3. general
4. order

## STEP 2 正解を見抜く

### 1

Even after he had been convicted of the crime, he insisted that he was innocent.

正解 ①

訳 犯罪によって有罪と宣告された後にさえ、彼は潔白であると主張しました。

- **insist** 動 主張する
- **permit** 動 許す
- **request** 動 要請する
- **require** 動 必要とする

insistの語源はin(中に)+sist(立つ)=中にしっかり立って譲らないイメージです

### 2

Theresa : How could the captain miss seeing it and hit something that huge?
Tim : He claims it was because of the thick fog.

正解 ②

訳 テレサ：一体どうして船長さんはそんな巨大なものを見のがしてぶつかってしまったのかしら。
ティム：濃霧のせいだと彼は主張しているよ。

- **excuse** 動 許す
- **claim** 動 主張する
- **blame** 動 非難する
- **exclaim** 動 叫ぶ

日本語でクレームは苦情を意味しますが、英語では「主張する」という意味。苦情の場合のクレームはcomplainを使います

### 3

What should be the standard for deciding what qualifies as an Olympic sport?

正解 ③

訳 オリンピックの種目を決めるのに規格は何であるべきですか。

- **comparison** 名 比較
- **criticism** 名 批評
- **standard** 名 基準
- **substance** 名 物質

### 4

Jimmy is like an alien to me. He and I have nothing in common.

正解 ①

訳 ジミーは私にとって異星人のようです。彼と私は共通点がありません。

- **common** 形 共通の
- **conversation** 名 会話
- **general** 形 一般の
- **order** 名 順序

UNIT 60 主張・基準

Chapter4 Society

## STEP 3 連鎖式に語彙を増やす 60

**0751 insist** [insíst] 動 主張する（+ on, that SV）

でた! Some people insist that a little alcohol is good for your health.
（少量のアルコールは健康に良いと主張する人もいる） 大分大学

派 **insistent** 形 しつこい

派 **insistence** 名 主張

**0752 claim** [kléim] 動 主張する

でた! The author claims that disabled people are socially excluded.
（著者は障害者は社会的に排除されていると主張する） 早稲田大学

**0753 persist** [pərsíst] 動 固執する（+ in）、主張する
原義 per（完全に）+ sist（立つ）

派 **persistent** 形 粘り強い、しつこい

派 **persistence** 名 固執、しつこさ

● 語源 just（正しい）

**0754 injure** [índʒər] 動 肉体的に傷つける

でた! The sailor was found injured, but alive.
（その船員は負傷していたが生きている状態で見つかった） 東京理科大学

派 **injury** 名 怪我
コロ suffer injury（負傷する）

〔傷に関連する単語〕

| wound | 動 武器を使って傷つける |
| hurt | 動 精神的に傷つける |
| damage | 動 修復可能な程度に破壊する |
| harm | 動 物理的に傷つける |
| bruise 発 | 名 打撲傷 |

**0755 rational** [ræʃənl] 発 形 合理的な
コロ rational explanation（合理的な説明）

**0756 logical** [ládʒikəl | lɔ́dʒ-] 形 論理的な

派 **logic** 名 論理

258

## 0757 consist [kənsíst]
動 成り立つ（＋of）、ある（＋in）
でた！ The meeting consists mainly of women.
（その会議は主に女性で成り立っている） 慶應義塾大学

## 0758 comprise [kəmpráiz]
動 構成する
でた！ The research team comprises dozens of psychologists.
（その研究チームは数十人の心理学者から成りたっている） 同志社大学

## 0759 consistent [kənsístənt]
形 首尾一貫した
反 inconsistent 形 矛盾する
派 consistence 名 首尾一貫

## 0760 misunderstand [mìsʌndərstǽnd] 動 誤解する
派 misunderstanding 名 誤解
コロ get A wrong （Aのことを誤解する）
でた！ Don't get me wrong. I'm not complaining.
（誤解するな。文句を言っているわけじゃないんだ） 上智大学

類 misleading [mìslíːdiŋ] 形 誤解を招きやすい
類 misconception [mìskənsépʃən] 名 誤解

## 0761 norm [nɔ́ːrm]
名 標準　原義 基準
派 normal 形 標準の
反 abnormal 形 異常な

## 0762 criterion [kraitíəriən] 発
名 基準　複 criteria

## 0763 ordinary [ɔ́ːrdənèri | ɔ́ːrdənəri] 形 普通の
コロ ordinary people （一般人）
反 extraordinary 形 並外れた

## 0764 standard [stǽndərd]
名 基準
コロ living standards （生活水準）

## 0765 common [kámən | kɔ́m-]
形 共通の
コロ have A in common （Aを共通して持っている）
でた！ English and Latin had many vocabulary words in common.
（英語とラテン語は共通した多くの語彙があった） TOEFL

UNIT 60 主張・基準

Chapter4 Society

# UNIT 61　時間・世代

**STEP 1　過去問を解く**

## 1

This watch needs repairing: it (　　) 20 minutes a day.

関東学院大学

1. accelerates
2. gains
3. increases
4. progresses

## 2

In traditional American Indian culture, the family is not only strong, it spans many (　　).

上智大学

1. facts
2. children
3. generations
4. means
5. places

## 3

It has been almost a decade since I married my husband.

桜美林大学

1. at the same time
2. ten years
3. two weeks
4. contemporary

## 4

An annual meeting is held once a year.

昭和大学

1. daily
2. weekly
3. monthly
4. yearly

## STEP 2 正解を見抜く

### 1

This watch needs repairing: it gains 20 minutes a day.   正解 ②

**訳** この時計は修理が必要です。一日に20分進みます。

- **accelerate** 動 加速させる
- **gain** 動 時間が進む
- **increase** 動 増す
- **progress** 動 進歩する

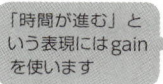

「時間が進む」という表現にはgainを使います

### 2

In traditional American Indian culture, the family is not only strong, it spans many generations.   正解 ③

**訳** 伝統的なアメリカ・インディアン文化では、家族は強いだけでなく、それは何世代にもわたるのである。

- **fact** 名 事実
- **generation** 名 世代
- **place** 名 場所
- **children** 名 子供たち
- **means** 名 手段

### 3

It has been almost ten years since I married my husband.   正解 ②

**訳** 夫と結婚してから約10年になります。

- **at the same time** それと同時に
- **ten years** 10年間
- **two weeks** 2週間
- **contemporary** 形 現代の、同世代の

decadeのdecの語源は「10」です。December（12月）は元々10月でした

### 4

A yearly meeting is held once a year.   正解 ④

**訳** 年次総会は年に一回開催される。

- **daily** 形 毎日の
- **weekly** 形 毎週の
- **monthly** 形 毎月の
- **yearly** 形 毎年の

annualのannuの語源は「1年」です。anniversaryは「1年に1回の記念日」です

Chapter4 Society

## STEP 3 連鎖式に語彙を増やす 61

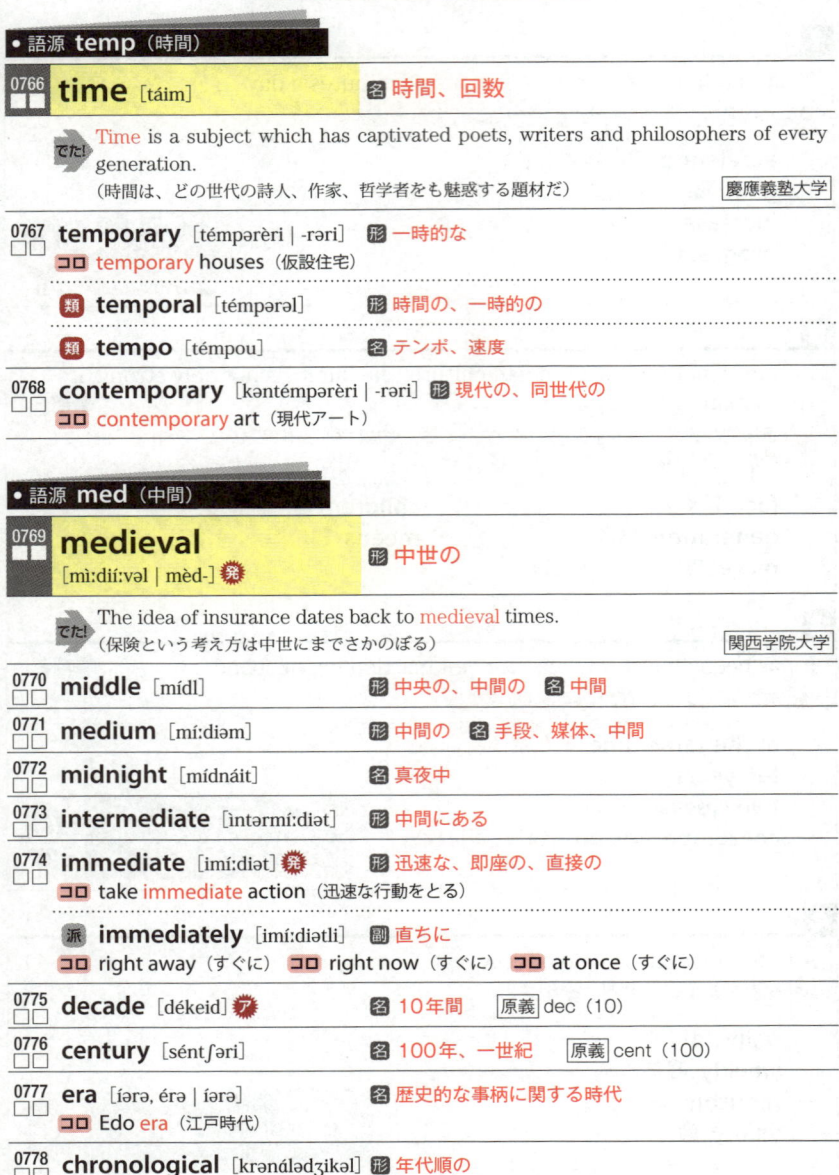

### ● 語源 temp（時間）

**0766 time** [táim] 名 時間、回数

でた! Time is a subject which has captivated poets, writers and philosophers of every generation.
（時間は、どの世代の詩人、作家、哲学者をも魅惑する題材だ）　慶應義塾大学

**0767 temporary** [témpərèri | -rəri] 形 一時的な
コロ temporary houses（仮設住宅）

類 **temporal** [témpərəl] 形 時間の、一時的の

類 **tempo** [témpou] 名 テンポ、速度

**0768 contemporary** [kəntémpərèri | -rəri] 形 現代の、同世代の
コロ contemporary art（現代アート）

### ● 語源 med（中間）

**0769 medieval** [mì:dií:vəl | mèd-] 発 形 中世の

でた! The idea of insurance dates back to medieval times.
（保険という考え方は中世にまでさかのぼる）　関西学院大学

**0770 middle** [mídl] 形 中央の、中間の 名 中間

**0771 medium** [mí:diəm] 形 中間の 名 手段、媒体、中間

**0772 midnight** [mídnáit] 名 真夜中

**0773 intermediate** [ìntərmí:diət] 形 中間にある

**0774 immediate** [imí:diət] 発 形 迅速な、即座の、直接の
コロ take immediate action（迅速な行動をとる）

派 **immediately** [imí:diətli] 副 直ちに
コロ right away（すぐに）　コロ right now（すぐに）　コロ at once（すぐに）

**0775 decade** [dékeid] 7 名 10年間　原義 dec (10)

**0776 century** [séntʃəri] 名 100年、一世紀　原義 cent (100)

**0777 era** [íərə, érə | íərə] 名 歴史的な事柄に関する時代
コロ Edo era（江戸時代）

**0778 chronological** [krənálədʒikəl] 形 年代順の

| 0779 | **epoch** [épək \| íːpɔk] | 名 時期、時代、新時代を開く出来事 |

| 0780 | **term** [tə́ːrm] | 名 期間、学期、専門用語、間柄、条件（-es） |

| 0781 | **span** [spǽn] | 名 期間 |

コロ life span（寿命）＝ life expectancy

| 0782 | **ancient** [éinʃənt] | 形 古代の |

コロ in ancient times（古代に）

でた！ The ancient Egyptians knew about the human body.
（古代エジプト人は人間の肉体についてよく知っていた） センター試験

| 0783 | **modern** [mádərn \| mɔ́d-] | 形 現代の |

でた！ Taipei may not be widely known for its modern architecture.
（台北は近代建築物ではそれほど広く知られていないかもしれない） センター試験

| 0784 | **previous** [príːviəs] | 形 時間・順序が以前の、前の |

派 **previously** | 副 以前は、前もって

| 0785 | **former** [fɔ́ːrmər] | 形 前の、前者の |

コロ former president（前大統領）

| 0786 | **latter** [lǽtər] | 形 後ろの、後者の |

| 0787 | **annual** [ǽnjuəl] | 形 一年の、毎年の |

コロ annual income（年収）

派 **annually** | 副 毎年

| 0788 | **anniversary** [æ̀nəvə́ːrsəri] | 名 記念日 |

コロ wedding anniversary（結婚記念日）

| 0789 | **recent** [ríːsnt] | 形 最近の |

コロ recent years（近年）

派 **recently** | 副 最近

類 **lately** [léitli] | 副 最近

| 0790 | **nowadays** [náuədèiz] | 副 今日では |

コロ these days（最近では）

| 0791 | **gain** [géin] | 動 時間が進む、得る |

コロ gain weight（体重が増える）

| 0792 | **generation** [dʒènəréiʃən] | 名 世代 | 原義 gen（生む）

コロ generation gap（世代差）

UNIT 61 時間・世代

Chapter4 Society 263

# UNIT 62 期限・厳守

## STEP 1 過去問を解く

### 1

I was sick over the weekend and couldn't finish my homework in time to ( ) the teacher's deadline.

英語検定2級

1. touch
2. jump
3. carry
4. meet

### 2

Her first baby is ( ) in June.

駒澤大学

1. carry
2. planning
3. due
4. brought

### 3

I should have returned this DVD last Friday. It is now four days ( ).

青山学院大学

1. excessive
2. long
3. overdue
4. postponed

### 4

Robin Robins is an excellent student and is always ( ) for class.

青山学院大学

1. puncture
2. punctuation
3. punctual
4. punctured

## STEP 2 正解を見抜く

### 1

I was sick over the weekend and couldn't finish my homework in time to meet the teacher's deadline.

正解 ④

**訳** 私は、週末の間、病気だったので、教師の締め切りに間に合うように時間内に宿題を終えることができませんでした。

- **touch** 動触る
- **jump** 動跳ぶ
- **carry** 動運ぶ
- **meet** 動会う、(要求などを) 満たす

> meetは「人に会う」以外に「要求や期待を満たす」という意味があります

### 2

Her first baby is due in June.

正解 ③

**訳** 彼女の初めての赤ん坊は、6月が予定日です。

- **carry** 動運ぶ
- **planning** 名立案
- **due** 形期日になって
- **brought** 動bring (持って来る) の過去形

> dueは重要多義語です。ここでは「誕生予定」を表します

### 3

I should have returned this DVD last Friday. It is now four days overdue.

正解 ③

**訳** 私は、先週の金曜日にこのDVDを返さなければいけませんでした。現在、4日間期限が過ぎています。

- **excessive** 形度を超した
- **long** 形長い
- **overdue** 形延滞の
- **postpone** 動延期する

### 4

Robin Robins is an excellent student and is always punctual for class.

正解 ③

**訳** ロビン・ロビンズは素晴らしい学生でいつも授業の時間を守っています。

- **puncture** 動パンクする
- **punctuation** 名句読点
- **punctual** 形時間を厳守する

> 時間を守らない人に対してBe punctual. (時間を守れ) という表現が使えます

Chapter4 Society

## STEP 3 連鎖式に語彙を増やす 62

**0793 deadline** [dédláin]　　名 締め切り
- meet the deadline（締め切りに間に合わせる）

**0794 due** [djú: | djú:]　　形 支払期限のきた、誕生予定の、相応の、尊敬を当然受けるべき
- でた! Sam didn't know that the mathematics assignment was due next Friday.
  （サムは数学の課題が次の金曜日だったことを知らなかった）〔学習院大学〕
- due to A（Aのせいで、原因で）
- でた! He failed the examination three times due to his laziness.
  （彼は怠惰さのせいで3回試験に落ちた）〔亜細亜大学〕

類 **overdue** [òuvərdjú:]　　形 期限の過ぎた

**0795 postpone** [poustpóun]　　動 延期する　原義 post（後で）＋pone（置く）
- put off A（Aを延期する）
- でた! The game has been put off due to the bad weather.
  （悪天候のためその試合は延期された）〔関西外国語大学〕

**0796 cancel** [kǽnsəl]　　動 中止する
- call off A（Aを中止する）
- でた! The lecture was called off because the speaker was ill.
  （講演者が病気のため講義は中止された）〔慶應義塾大学〕

**0797 schedule** [skédʒu:l | ʃédju:l]　　名 スケジュール
- on schedule（予定通り）

---

**入試問題にチャレンジ**　（　）には同じ語が入ります。何でしょうか？

- The opera singer had to give up the title role in Carmen (　) to a bad cold.
- The report is (　) on Wednesday, but I haven't even started to write it.
- The matter will be settled in (　) course of time.
- The professor was satisfied because he was treated with (　) respect.
- Her first baby is (　) in June.

〔明治大学〕

答 due

• 語源 point punct（点）

**0798 point** [pɔ́int] 　名 点、段階、程度　動 指摘する（+ out）

The teacher pointed out to me why my answer was wrong.
（先生はなぜ私の解答が間違っているのかを指摘した）　〔千葉大学〕

コロ to the point（適切な、要領を得る）

His remarks on the subject are much to the point.
（その議題に関する彼の意見は、当を得ている）　〔慶應義塾大学〕

**0799 appoint** [əpɔ́int]　動 任命する、指名する
派 appointment　名 任命、約束

**0800 disappoint** [dìsəpɔ́int]　動 落胆させる、がっかりさせる

The teacher was disappointed when most of her students did badly on the test.
（自分の生徒のほとんどがテストで悪い点をとったとき先生はがっかりした）　〔津田塾大学〕

コロ let down A（Aを失望させる）

派 disappointment　名 落胆、失望

**0801 punctual** [pʌ́ŋktʃuəl]　形 時間に厳しい

Our teacher told our class to be punctual next morning.
（私たちの先生はクラスのみんなに明日の朝は時間を守るように伝えた）　〔上智大学〕

派 punctuality　名 時間厳守

---

**入試問題にチャレンジ** 　( ) には同じ語が入ります。何でしょうか？

・Critics ( ) out that the prince, on his income, should be paying tax.
・The supports beneath the iron bridge have decayed to the ( ) where they are hazardous.
・Let's stick to discussing whether the road should be built at all. The exact cost is beside the ( ).

〔慶應義塾大学〕

答 point

UNIT 62　期限・厳守

Chapter4 Society | 267

# UNIT 63 連続・継続

**STEP 1** 過去問を解く

## 1

It has been raining for five days in (　　　).

1. a line
2. a row
3. a while
4. meantime

青山学院大学

## 2

What came next in the (　　　) of events?

1. debt
2. loaf
3. sequence
4. twin

立命館大学

## 3

She often worked for twenty-four hours (　　　).

1. end on
2. on end
3. at an end
4. end for end

國學院大学

## 4

His new novel has been at the top of the best-seller list for five (　　　) weeks.

1. consecutive
2. continued
3. following
4. proceeding

東京理科大学

## STEP 2 正解を見抜く

### 1

It has been raining for five days in a row. 　　正解 ②

訳 5日間連続で雨が降っています。

**in a row** 連続で

> in a row「連続で」「一列に」。law「法律」、low「低い」、raw「生の」、row「列」

### 2

What came next in the sequence of events? 　　正解 ③

訳 そのイベントの次に何が来ましたか。

**debt** 名債務
**loaf** 名パン一個
**sequence** 名連続するもの
**twin** 名双子

### 3

She often worked for twenty-four hours on end. 　　正解 ②

訳 彼女はしばしば24時間続けて働いた。

**on end** 続けて

> on end「続けて」「直立して」

### 4

His new novel has been at the top of the best-seller list for five consecutive weeks. 　　正解 ①

訳 彼の新しい小説は連続5週間ベストセラーリストの上位に位置しています。

**consecutive** 形連続した
**continue** 動続く
**following** 形次の
**proceed** 動進む

UNIT 63 連続・継続

Chapter4 Society

## STEP 3 連鎖式に語彙を増やす 63

### 0802 continue [kəntínjuː] 動 続く、続ける

- コロ continue drinking（飲み続ける）
- でた! She agrees that research should continue in spite of problems.
（彼女は問題があっても実験を続けることに同意している） TOEFL
- 派 continuity 名 連続

### 0803 continent [kántənənt | kɔ́nti-] 名 大陸 原義 続いている土地

- コロ the continent of Eurasia（ユーラシア大陸）
- でた! The continents were located close to the equator.
（その大陸は赤道の近くに位置していた） TOEFL
- 派 continental 形 大陸の
- でた! In many continental European countries, children learn two languages at school.
（多くのヨーロッパ大陸の国では子供は学校で2カ国語を学ぶ） 同志社大学

### 0804 row [róu] 名 列

raw（生の）と混同注意

- コロ in a row（連続して）
- 類 endless [éndlis] 形 終わりがない
- コロ on end（ある一定期間続けて）
- でた! It rained three days on end.
（3日続きの雨だった） 慶應義塾大学

---

● 語源 sequ secut su（従う）

### 0805 consequence [kánsəkwèns | kɔ́nsikwəns] ア 名 結果、影響、重大性

### 0806
- コロ in consequence of A（Aの結果として）
- でた! A change in temperature might have serious consequences.
（気温の変化は深刻な結果を招くかもしれない） 早稲田大学
- 派 consequently 副 その結果
- 派 consequent 形 結果として起こる

### 0807 sequel [síːkwəl] 名 続き
- コロ the sequel to the comic（その漫画の続き）

| 派 **sequence** [síːkwəns] | 名 連続するもの |

コロ in sequence（順々に）

でた！ Music is nothing more than a sequence of sound waves.
（音楽とは音波の連続にすぎない） 慶應義塾大学

| 派 **sequential** | 形 連続的な |

---

0808 **subsequent** [sʌ́bsikwənt] ア 形 その後の結果

| 派 **subsequence** [sʌ́bsikwəns] | 名 続いて起こること |

| 派 **subsequently** | 副 その後、続いて |

でた！ Subsequently, All Hallows Eve became Halloween.
（その後、万聖節前夜祭はハローウィーンになった） 東北大学

---

0809 **consecutive** [kənsékjutiv] 形 連続する

コロ three consecutive wins（三連勝）

0810 **succeed** [səksíːd] 動 続く（+to）、続ける（+in）

| 派 **success** [səksés] ア | 名 成功 |

| 派 **successful** | 形 成功した |

| 派 **succession** | 名 連続 |

コロ in succession（連続して）

でた！ Mysterious thing happened in succession.
（不思議なことが連続で起こった） 青山学院大学

| 派 **successive** [səksésiv] | 形 連続した |

UNIT 63 連続・継続

Chapter4 Society

# UNIT 64 永遠・遺産　STEP 1 過去問を解く

## 1

He has gone back to Arizona for good.

1. successfully
2. happliy
3. fortunately
4. forever
5. soon

中央大学

## 2

Small children have teeth which usually fall out between the ages of five and twelve, after which they get their (　　) teeth.

センター試験

1. false
2. forever
3. general
4. permanent

## 3

After the car hit the boy, he (　　) unconscious for two days.

センター試験

1. remained
2. remembered
3. removed
4. rescued

## 4

A: What did you do on your trip?
B: We visited the (　　) of a very ancient castle.

英語検定2級

1. destinations
2. elements
3. conditions
4. remains

## STEP 2 正解を見抜く

### 1

He has gone back to Arizona <u>forever</u>.

正解 ④

訳 彼は永久にアリゾナ州に帰ってしまった。

- successfully 副 成功して
- happily 副 幸いにも
- fortunately 副 幸運にも
- forever 副 永遠に
- soon 副 すぐに

for good「永久に」

### 2

Small children have teeth which usually fall out between the ages of five and twelve, after which they get their <u>permanent</u> teeth.

正解 ④

訳 小さな子供の歯は、永久歯が生えると、通常5歳から12歳の間に抜け落ちます。

- false 形 誤った
- forever 副 永遠に
- general 形 一般的な
- permanent 形 永久的な

permanentの語源はper（完全に）+man（留まる）＝完全にそこに留まっている＝永久の

### 3

After the car hit the boy, he <u>remained</u> unconscious for two days.

正解 ①

訳 車が少年にぶつかった後に、彼は、2日間無意識のままでした。

- remain 動 ～のままである
- remember 動 覚えている
- remove 動 移す
- rescue 動 救う

remainのmainも（留まる）という語源で、mansion（マンション、大豪邸）も同語源です

### 4

A: What did you do on your trip?
B: We visited the <u>remains</u> of a very ancient castle.

正解 ④

訳 A：旅行で何をしたの。
B：古代のお城の遺産を訪ねました。

- destination 名 目的地
- condition 名 状態
- element 名 要素
- remains 名 遺跡

UNIT 64　永遠・遺産

Chapter4 Society

## STEP 3 連鎖式に語彙を増やす 64

● 語源 main man（留まる）

### 0811 remain [riméin]
動 ままである　名 残り、遺産、遺体

- コロ remain to be seen（不明のままである）
- でた! Large quantities of coal remain in the Asian-Pacific region.
（アジアの太平洋地域では大量の石炭がある）　〔センター試験〕

- 派 remainder　名 残り物
- 類 leftover [léftóuvər]　名 残り物

### 0812 mansion [mǽnʃən]
名 大豪邸

### 0813 permanent [pə́:rmənənt]
形 永久の

- コロ permanent teeth（永久歯）
- 派 permanently　副 永久に
- 類 forever [fɔ́:révər]　副 永遠に
- コロ for good（永遠に）
- でた! He decided to leave his hometown for good.
（彼は故郷を永久に去ることを決めた）　〔青山学院大学〕

### 0814 inherit [inhérit]
動 相続する、遺伝で受け継ぐ

- コロ inherit property（財産を相続する）　コロ take over A（Aを引き継ぐ）
- 派 inheritance [inhérətəns]　名 相続、遺産
- でた! The upper class tends to acquire wealth through inheritance.
（上流階級の人々は遺産相続を通して富を獲得する）　〔TOEFL〕

### 0815 heritage [héritidʒ]
名 遺産

- コロ world heritage site（世界遺産）
- でた! Museums should show both new pop art and old national heritage.
（美術館は新しいポップアートと古い国家遺産の両方を展示すべきです）　〔慶應義塾大学〕

## 0816 eventually [ivéntʃuəli] 副 結局、最終的に

でた! Eventually the couple will pay off their mortgage and own their house.
（結局そのカップルは抵当を清算し、一軒家を所有するでしょう）  TOEFL

## 0817 eternal [itə́:rnl] 形 永遠の、永久の

でた! Christians believe that after death, there is eternal life.
（キリスト教徒は死後に永遠の命があると信じている）  別府大学

派 **eternity** [itə́:rnəti] 名 永遠

UNIT 64 永遠・遺産

Chapter4 Society

# UNIT 65　最新・最初　STEP 1 過去問を解く

## 1

The <u>initial</u> step is often the most difficult.

上智大学

1. quickest
2. last
3. longest
4. first

## 2

He bought the dictionary but he was soon disappointed to find that it didn't have <u>up-to-date</u> words.

学習院大学

1. day-to-day
2. the latest
3. the oldest
4. technical

## 3

The young scientists were at first thrilled about living in the Arctic for a year, but after a month in the freezing climate, the (　　) wore off.

英語検定準1級

1. parallel
2. tedium
3. commodity
4. novelty

## 4

A: Hi, Gabriel, I heard that you started taking judo classes.
B: Yeah, that's right. Of course, I'm still a (　　), but my instructor says I have the potential to be pretty good.

英語検定1級

1. mentor
2. novice
3. bigot
4. warden

## STEP 2 正解を見抜く

### 1

The first step is often the most difficult.

正解 ④

訳 最初の段階はいつも困難なものである。

- quickest 形 quick（速い）の最上級
- last 形 最後の
- longest 形 long（長い）の最上級
- first 形 第一の、最初の

initialは「最初の」「頭文字」という意味があります

### 2

He bought the dictionary but he was soon disappointed to find that it didn't have the latest words.

正解 ②

訳 彼は辞書を買ったが、すぐにそれが最新の単語を載せていないことがわかってがっかりした。

- day-to-day 形 日々の
- old 形 古い
- latest 形 最新の
- technical 形 技術の

up-to-date「最新の」⇔out-of-date「時代遅れの」

### 3

The young scientists were at first thrilled about living in the Arctic for a year, but after a month in the freezing climate, the novelty wore off.

正解 ④

訳 その若い科学者たちは、最初は1年間北極に暮らすことに関してぞくぞくしましたが、凍てつくように寒い気候での1カ月後には、目新しさは消え去りました。

- parallel 形 平行の
- tedium 名 退屈
- commodity 名 日用品
- novelty 名 目新しさ

noveltyの語源はnov（新しい）です。novelty goods（ノベルティーグッズ）

### 4

A: Hi, Gabriel, I heard that you started taking judo classes.
B: Yeah, that's right. Of course, I'm still a novice, but my instructor says I have the potential to be pretty good.

正解 ②

訳 A：こんにちは、ガブリエル、私はあなたが柔道のクラスを受け始めると聞きました。
B：うん、そうです。もちろん、それでも私は初心者ですが、私のインストラクターは、私にはかなり良くなる可能性があると言ってくれています。

- mentor 名 良い指導者
- novice 名 初心者
- bigot 名 排他主義者
- warden 名 管理人

novの語源が（新しい）から「初心者」が連想できます

UNIT 65 最新・最初

Chapter4 Society

## STEP 3 連鎖式に語彙を増やす 65

**0818 latest** [léitist] 形 最新の
- latest novel（最新版の小説）　brand new（真新しい）
- up-to-date（最新の）

**0819 old-fashioned** [óuld-fǽʃənd] 形 時代遅れの
- out of date（時代遅れの）
- Professor Smith's fashion sense is hopelessly out of date.
（スミス教授のファッションセンスは絶望的に時代遅れである） 明海大学
- behind the times（時代遅れの）
- Grandfather's ideas are really behind the times.
（祖父の考えは非常に時代遅れである） 立命館大学

### ● 語源 nov（新しい）

**0820 novel** [nάvəl | nɔ́v-] 名 小説　形 目新しい　原義 新しいこと
- You cannot understand this difficult novel without the exercise of imagination.
（この難しい小説は想像力を働かせることなしには理解出来ない） 上智大学

派 **novelty** [nάvəlti | nɔ́v-] 名 目新しさ

**0821 innovation** [ìnəvéiʃən] 名 革新
- technological innovation（技術革新）
- The pace of technological innovation slows down.
（技術革新のペースがゆっくりになっている） TOEFL

派 **innovate** [ínəvèit] 動 革新する

派 **innovative** 形 革新的な

### ● 語源 sol（孤独）

**0822 obsolete** [ὰbsəlíːt | ɔ́bsəlìːt] 形 時代遅れの、廃れた
- Some people believe that writing instruments, such as pencils and pens, will soon be obsolete.
（鉛筆やペン等の筆記用具はすぐに廃れるだろうと信じている人もいる） TOEFL

**0823 isolate** [áisəlèit] 動 孤立させる
- isolate A from B（AをBから切り離す）
- Many koalas now live in isolated patches of poor quality forest.
（多くのコアラは今や孤立した地域の質の悪い森に住んでいる） 北海道大学

| | | | |
|---|---|---|---|
| | 派 **isolation** | 名 孤立 | |
| 0824 | **solitary** [sálətèri \| sɔ́litəri] | 形 孤独な | |
| でた! | Young children first of all engage in solitary independent play.<br>(幼児は最初に孤独な独立した遊びに没頭する) | | 慶應義塾大学 |
| 0825 | **solitude** [sálətjùːd \| sɔ́litjùːd] | 名 孤独 | |
| | 派 **loneliness** [lóunlinəs] | 名 孤独 | |
| | 派 **lonely** [lóunli] | 形 孤独な | |
| | コロ feel lonely (孤独を感じる) | | |
| 0826 | **solo** [sóulou] | 名 ソロ、独唱 | |
| 0827 | **solitaire** [sálətèər \| sɔ̀litéə] | 名 ソリティア | ソリティアとは1人で遊ぶトランプのことです |
| 0828 | **first** [fə́ːrst] | 形 最初の | |
| | 派 **initial** [iníʃəl] | 形 最初の　名 頭文字 | |
| | コロ initial stage (初期段階) | | |
| | 派 **initiate** [iníʃièit] | 動 始める、着手する | |
| | 派 **initiative** [iníʃiətiv] | 名 主導権 | |
| | 類 **beginning** | 名 初め | |
| 0829 | **final** [fáinl] | 形 最終の　原義 終わり | |
| でた! | The final evaluation has not yet been made.<br>(最終評価はまだ下されていない) | | 大阪大学 |
| | 派 **finalize** | 動 終了させる、完成させる | |
| | 派 **finale** [finǽli \| -náːli] | 名 終楽章 | |
| | 派 **finish** | 動 終える | |
| 0830 | **over** [óuvər] | 副 終わって　前 ～の上に | |
| | コロ Game over. (ゲーム終了) | | |
| 0831 | **commence** [kəméns] | 動 始める、始まる | |
| | 派 **commencement** | 名 開始、卒業式 | |
| 0832 | **launch** [lɔ́ːntʃ] 発 | 動 発射する、始める | |
| | コロ launch a blog (ブログを立ち上げる) | | |
| でた! | Thailand launched a national health-care program in 2001.<br>(タイは2001年に国家保健医療計画を始めた) | | 慶應義塾大学 |

UNIT 65 最新・最初

Chapter4 Society

# UNIT 66 尊敬・軽蔑　STEP 1 過去問を解く

## 1

He is a great statesman. Everybody <u>looks up to</u> him.

成蹊大学

1. honors
2. believes in
3. depends upon
4. respects

## 2

He did not <u>look down upon</u> even those children.

駒澤大学

1. understand
2. despise
3. like
4. forgive

## 3

If you are not (　　) toward your elders in Japanese society, you will often get into trouble.

慶応義塾大学

1. respective
2. respectable
3. respectful
4. respecting

## 4

(　　) activities are those approved of by society because they are considered to be fair and honest.

センター試験

1. Respect
2. Respectable
3. Respecting
4. Respective

## STEP 2 正解を見抜く

### 1

He is a great statesman. Everybody respects him.

正解 ④

訳 彼は偉大な政治家である。皆が彼を尊敬している。

- honor 動 名誉を与える
- believe in を信じる
- depend upon 依存する
- respect 動 尊敬する

### 2

He did not despise even those children.

正解 ②

訳 彼はその子供達さえ軽蔑しませんでした。

- understand 動 理解する
- despise 動 軽蔑する
- like 動 好む
- forgive 動 許す

### 3

If you are not respectful toward your elders in Japanese society, you will often get into trouble.

正解 ③

訳 日本社会において年長者に向かって礼儀正しくしないと、よく問題に巻き込まれます。

- respective 形 それぞれの
- respectable 形 堅実な
- respectful 形 丁重な
- respecting 前 〜に関して

### 4

Respectable activities are those approved of by society because they are considered to be fair and honest.

正解 ②

訳 堅実な活動は公平で誠実であると考えられているため、社会に認められたものである。

- respect 動 尊敬する
- respectable 形 堅実な
- respecting 前 〜に関して
- respective 形 それぞれの

UNIT 66 尊敬・軽蔑

Chapter4 Society

## STEP 3 連鎖式に語彙を増やす 66

### 0833 respect [rispékt]　動 尊敬する　名 尊敬、点

- コロ in every respect（あらゆる点で）
- でた! In Poland, musicians are highly respected.
  （ポーランドでは音楽家は非常に尊敬されている） ［センター試験］
- コロ look up to A（Aを尊敬する）
- でた! His father is looked up to by all.
  （彼の父は皆から尊敬されています） ［早稲田大学］

### 0834 respective [rispéktiv]　形 それぞれの
派 respectively　副 それぞれに

### 0835 respectful [rispéktfəl]　形 敬意を表する
派 respectable　形 尊敬すべき、立派な

### 0836 honor [ánər | ɔ́n-]　動 敬意を示す、名誉を与える　名 敬意、名誉、光栄

- コロ honor student（特待生）　コロ in honor of A（Aに敬意を表して）
- でた! A welcome meeting was held in honor of Mr. Smith.
  （スミス氏に敬意を表して歓迎会が開催された） ［早稲田大学］

派 honorable　形 敬意のある、名誉な

### 0837 honest [ánist | ɔ́n-]　形 正直な
派 honesty　名 正直
でた! Some day you will realize that honesty pays.
（正直が割にあうということにいつか気づくでしょう） ［中央大学］

### 0838 worship [wə́ːrʃip]　動 崇拝する、礼拝する　名 崇拝、礼拝
でた! Stonehenge has worship of the sun as its probable purpose.
（ストーンヘンジは太陽崇拝がたぶんその目的である） ［早稲田大学］

### 0839 esteem [istíːm]　動 尊敬する、高く評価する
- コロ self-esteem（自尊心）

### 0840 dignity [dígnəti]　名 威厳、尊厳
- コロ die with dignity（尊厳死する）

反 indignity [indígnəti]　名 自分に対する侮辱

● 語源 mir（驚く）

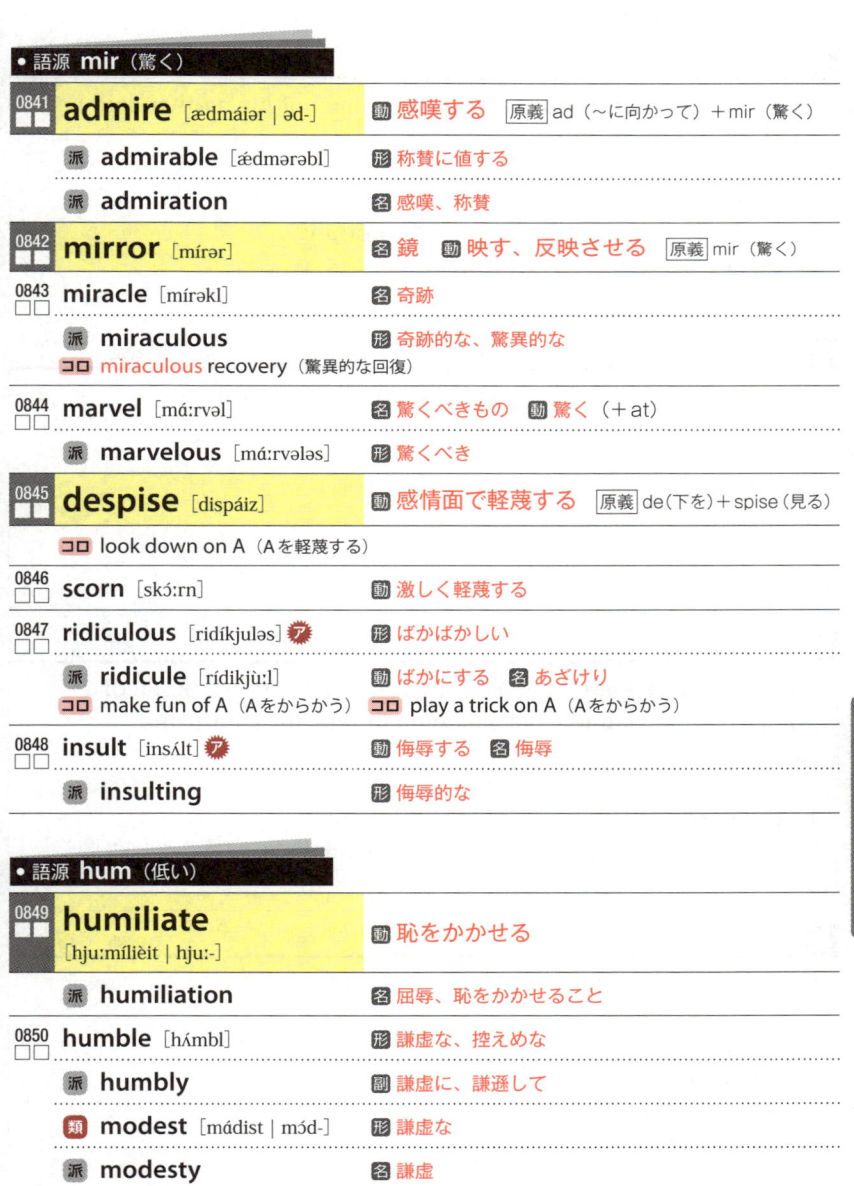

| 0841 | **admire** [ædmáiər \| əd-] | 動 感嘆する　原義 ad（〜に向かって）＋mir（驚く） |

派 **admirable** [ǽdmərəbl]　形 称賛に値する

派 **admiration**　名 感嘆、称賛

| 0842 | **mirror** [mírər] | 名 鏡　動 映す、反映させる　原義 mir（驚く） |

0843 **miracle** [mírəkl]　名 奇跡

派 **miraculous**　形 奇跡的な、驚異的な
コロ miraculous recovery（驚異的な回復）

0844 **marvel** [má:rvəl]　名 驚くべきもの　動 驚く（＋at）

派 **marvelous** [má:rvələs]　形 驚くべき

| 0845 | **despise** [dispáiz] | 動 感情面で軽蔑する　原義 de（下を）＋spise（見る） |

コロ look down on A（Aを軽蔑する）

0846 **scorn** [skɔ́:rn]　動 激しく軽蔑する

0847 **ridiculous** [ridíkjuləs]　形 ばかばかしい

派 **ridicule** [rídikjù:l]　動 ばかにする　名 あざけり
コロ make fun of A（Aをからかう）　コロ play a trick on A（Aをからかう）

0848 **insult** [insʌ́lt]　動 侮辱する　名 侮辱

派 **insulting**　形 侮辱的な

● 語源 hum（低い）

| 0849 | **humiliate** [hju:mílièit \| hju:-] | 動 恥をかかせる |

派 **humiliation**　名 屈辱、恥をかかせること

0850 **humble** [hʌ́mbl]　形 謙虚な、控えめな

派 **humbly**　副 謙虚に、謙遜して

類 **modest** [mádist \| mɔ́d-]　形 謙虚な

派 **modesty**　名 謙虚

UNIT 66　尊敬・軽蔑

Chapter4 Society

# UNIT 67　関係・関連

**STEP 1** 過去問を解く

## 1

The policeman asked him about the crime but his mother said he had (　　) to do with it.

中央大学

1. nobody
2. anything
3. anybody
4. nothing
5. somebody

## 2

It's none of your (　　) who I want to go out with.

立教大学

1. care
2. concern
3. interest
4. knowledge
5. regard

## 3

Yumi and Mark got married in London last Saturday. Some of Yumi's (　　) came from Japan including her aunt from Hokkaido.

英語検定2級

1. relatives
2. owners
3. candidates
4. specialists

## 4

He lives in a dream world, (　　) reality.

慶應義塾大学

1. equal to
2. conform to
3. indifferent to
4. according to

## STEP 2 正解を見抜く

### 1

The policeman asked him about the crime but his mother said he had nothing to do with it.

正解 ④

**訳** 警察は彼にその罪について尋ねたが、彼の母は彼はそれに関係がないと言った。

- **nobody** 代 だれも〜ない
- **anybody** 代 だれか
- **nothing** 代 何も〜ない
- **somebody** 代 だれか、ある人
- **anything** 代 何か

have nothing to do with A (Aに関係がない)

### 2

It's none of your concern who I want to go out with.

正解 ②

**訳** 俺が誰と付き合おうとお前には関係がない。

- **care** 名 注意、用心
- **concern** 名 関心事
- **interest** 名 興味
- **knowledge** 名 知識
- **regard** 名 注意、配慮

It's none of your concern (business). (あなたには関係がない)

### 3

Yumi and Mark got married in London last Saturday. Some of Yumi's relatives came from Japan including her aunt from Hokkaido.

正解 ①

**訳** 由美とマークは先週の土曜日ロンドンで結婚した。北海道に住む叔母を含む由美の親戚の何人かが日本から来た。

- **relative** 名 親戚
- **candidate** 名 候補者
- **owner** 名 所有者
- **specialist** 名 専門家

### 4

He lives in a dream world, indifferent to reality.

正解 ③

**訳** 彼は空想の世界に生きていて、現実には無関心である。

- **equal to** 〜と同一の
- **conform to** 〜に従う
- **indifferent to** 〜に無関心な
- **according to** 〜によれば

UNIT 67 関係・関連

Chapter4 Society

## STEP 3 連鎖式に語彙を増やす 67

### 0851 relate [riléit] 動 関連付ける

**コロ** be related to A (Aに関連している)
**でた!** All living things are related to one another.
（全ての生物はお互いに関連している） 〔中央大学〕

**派** relation 名 関係

**派** relative [rélətiv] 形 相対的な、関係がある、比較的な 名 親類
**でた!** All knowledge in the social sciences is relative.
（社会科学における全ての知識は相対的なものだ） 〔立命館大学〕

**派** relatively 副 比較的に
**でた!** Old English, incomprehensible to modern ears, was spoken by relatively few people.
（現代人の耳には理解できない古英語は、比較的少数の人々に話されていた） 〔早稲田大学〕

**派** relationship [riléiʃənʃip] 名 関係、関連
**でた!** What is the relationship between supply and demand?
（需要と供給の関係は何ですか） 〔TOEFL〕

### 0852 relevant [réləvənt] 形 関係がある
**でた!** He thinks the topic is not relevant for linguistics class.
（彼は言語学の授業にそのトピックは関係ないと思っている） 〔TOEFL〕

**反** irrelevant 形 無関係の

### 0853 concern [kənsə́:rn] 動 関係がある、心配させる 名 懸念

**コロ** be concerned with A (Aに関係している)
**でた!** She established an organization concerned with child adoption.
（彼女は子供の養子に関する組織を設立した） 〔関西学院大学〕

**コロ** be concerned about A (Aについて心配している)
**でた!** He is concerned about his parents' health.
（彼は両親の健康について心配している） 〔東京国際大学〕

**派** concerning 前 〜に関して
**コロ** have something to do with A (Aに関係がある)
**コロ** have nothing to do with A (Aに関係がない)

### 0854 indifferent [indífərənt] 形 無関心な（+ to）

**派** indifference 名 無関心

### 0855 affair 名 事件、事情、浮気
**コロ** foreign affair (外交問題) **コロ** have an affair with A (Aと浮気する)

## 0856 engage [ingéidʒ]
動 従事させる（＋in）

でた! He has been engaged in this study for nearly ten years.
（彼はこの研究に10年近く従事している） 日本大学

派 **engagement** 名 婚約、約束
コロ engagement ring（婚約指輪）

• 語源 **guard gard**（見守る）

## 0857 regard [rigá:rd]
動 みなす、見る、評価する
名 関心、注意、挨拶（-es）

でた! Please give my regards to your father.
（お父さんに宜しくお伝え下さい） 東洋大学
コロ regard A as B（AをBとみなす）　コロ with regard to A（Aに関して）

派 **regarding** 前 ～に関して

派 **regardless** 副 関わらず（＋of）

でた! Regardless of size, all adult insects have a similar body structure.
（大きさに関わらず、全ての成熟した昆虫は同類のボディー構造をしている） TOEFL

## 0858 guard [gá:rd]
動（注意深く見張って攻撃・危険から）守る、護衛する

派 **guardian** 名 保護者

## 0859 guarantee [gærəntí:]
名 保証　動 保証する

芸能人のテレビ出演のギャラ（保証金）

UNIT 67 関係・関連

Chapter4 Society

# UNIT 68 表現・印象　STEP 1 過去問を解く

## 1

A: Why does Robert have such a sad (　　) on his face?
B: His cat died last night.

英語検定2級

1. expression
2. statement
3. pressure
4. delivery

## 2

There are many different ways of (　　) one's opinion.

立命館大学

1. compressing
2. depressing
3. expressing
4. oppressing

## 3

I have the (　　) that your sister doesn't like me.

南山大学

1. impression
2. insurance
3. intention
4. intersection

## 4

I'm very (　　) by your work so I'm going to promote you.

同志社大学

1. impressed
2. emotional
3. disappointed
4. felt

## STEP 2 正解を見抜く

### 1

A: Why does Robert have such a sad expression on his face?
B: His cat died last night.

正解 ①

**訳** A:ロバートはなぜあんな悲しい表情をしているのですか。
B:昨夜、彼の猫が死んだんです。

**expression** 名表現　　**statement** 名声明
**pressure** 名圧力　　**delivery** 名配達

expressの語源はex（外に）+press（押す）=体の中から外に押し出す=表現する

### 2

There are many different ways of expressing one's opinion.

正解 ③

**訳** 個人の意見を述べるのには、たくさんの異なった方法があります。

**compress** 動圧縮する
**depress** 動下へ押す
**express** 動表現する
**oppress** 動圧迫する

### 3

I have the impression that your sister doesn't like me.

正解 ①

**訳** あなたの姉妹は私のことを好きではないという印象があります。

**impression** 名印象
**insurance** 名保険
**intention** 名意図
**intersection** 名交差点

impressの語源はim（中に）+press（押す）。first impression（第一印象）

### 4

I'm very impressed by your work so I'm going to promote you.

正解 ①

**訳** あなたの仕事ぶりに感銘を受けましたので、あなたを昇進します。

**impressed** 形感銘を受けた
**emotional** 形感情的な
**disappointed** 形失望した
**feel** 動感じる

UNIT 68　表現・印象

Chapter4 Society

## STEP 3 連鎖式に語彙を増やす 🎧68

### ● 語源 press（押す）

**0860 press** [prés] 　動 押す　名 押すこと、印刷、雑誌

- コロ pressing problem（差し迫った問題）
- 派 **pressure**　名 圧力、プレッシャー
- でた! The boiling point of water is 100 degrees centigrade at standard pressure.
（水の沸点は標準気圧では摂氏100℃である）　〔慶應義塾大学〕

**0861 express** [iksprés]　動 表現する　原義 ex（外に）＋ press（押す）

- コロ Thoughts are expressed by means of words.（思想は言葉によって表現される）
- でた! The concept of zero was not clearly expressed in most ancient number systems.
（ゼロの概念は、古代の数の体系ではほとんどの場合ははっきり示されていなかった）　〔センター試験〕
- 派 **expressive**　形 表現する
- 派 **expression**　名 表現

**0862 impress** [imprés]　動 感銘を与える　原義 im（中に）＋ press（押す）

- 派 **impressive**　形 印象的な
- 派 **impression**　名 印象
- コロ first impression（第一印象）
- でた! What's your impression of her?
（彼女の印象はどうですか）　〔学習院大学〕
- でた! His lecture left a deep impression on the minds of those present.
（彼の講義は出席していた人々に深い印象を残した）　〔センター試験〕

**0863 depress** [diprés]　動 憂鬱にさせる　原義 de（下に）＋ press（押す）

- 派 **depressed**　形 落胆した
- 派 **depression**　名 憂鬱、鬱病、不景気、意気消沈
- コロ the Great Depression（世界恐慌）
- でた! More than 30 million American women suffer from depression.
（3,000万人以上のアメリカ人女性が鬱病に苦しんでいる）　〔青山学院大学〕

**0864 suppress** [səprés]　動 鎮圧する　原義 sup（下に）＋ press（押す）

- でた! Is it healthy for boys to learn to suppress their sorrow?
（少年たちが悲しみに堪えるようになるのは健全なことなのだろうか）　〔北海道大学〕
- 派 **suppression**　名 鎮圧

## 0865 oppress [əprés]
動 (残酷に) 圧迫する

でた! History is filled with terrible tales of men oppressing other men.
(歴史は、人間が人間を虐げる悲惨な話で満ちている) 立教大学

## 0866 compress [kəmprés]
動 圧縮する、短縮する
原義 com (共に) + press (押す)

派 compression  名 圧縮、要約

• 語源 imag imit (写す、映す)

## 0867 imagine [imædʒin]
動 想像する

でた! Can you imagine the speed at which the earth goes around the sun?
(地球が太陽の周りを回る速さを想像できますか) 青山学院大学

派 image [ímidʒ] 発  名 イメージ、よく似た人

でた! Tom is the very image of his father thirty years ago.
(トムは30年前の父親にそっくりだ) 青山学院大学

類 fancy [fænsi]  名 空想、思いつき  動 好む、想像する  形 高級な

派 imagination  名 想像

派 imaginative  形 想像の、想像力に富んだ

でた! Our leaders are imaginative and often come up with new ideas.
(我々のリーダーは創造力に富んでいて新しい考えをよく思いつく) センター試験

派 imaginary  形 想像上の、架空の

でた! King Arthur of England was an imaginary person.
(イギリスのアーサー王は架空の人物だった) 甲南大学

派 imaginable  形 想像できる

## 0868 imitate [ímətèit]
動 まねする、見習う、手本にする

派 imitation  名 模倣、まね

UNIT 68 表現・印象

Chapter4 Society  291

## UNIT 69 許可・容認　STEP 1 過去問を解く

### 1

Students are (　　) to choose courses from among a large selection.

明治大学

1. wondering
2. interesting
3. examined
4. allowed

### 2

Although I was going to be rather busy on that day, I decided to (　　) the invitation to the party.

センター試験

1. accept
2. agree
3. catch
4. gain

### 3

It goes without saying that chewing gum is not (　　) in this class.

学習院大学

1. agreed
2. concerned
3. performed
4. permitted

### 4

The professor didn't (　　) of the new experiment that Kate and her friends wanted to try.

学習院大学

1. adopt
2. agree
3. approve
4. permit

## STEP 2 正解を見抜く

### 1

Students are allowed to choose courses from among a large selection.

正解 ④

訳 学生は幅広い選択肢からコースを選ぶことが出来る。

- wonder 動 不思議に思う
- interest 動 興味を持たせる
- examine 動 調査する
- allow 動 許す

### 2

Although I was going to be rather busy on that day, I decided to accept the invitation to the party.

正解 ①

訳 その日は忙しかったけど、そのパーティーの招待を受け入れることを決めた。

- accept 動 受け入れる
- agree 動 同意する
- catch 動 取る
- gain 動 得る

### 3

It goes without saying that chewing gum is not permitted in this class.

正解 ④

訳 このクラス内でチューインガムが許されていないのは言うまでもない。

- agree 動 同意する
- concern 動 関係する
- perform 動 実行する
- permit 動 許す

UNIT 69 許可・容認

### 4

The professor didn't approve of the new experiment that Kate and her friends wanted to try.

正解 ③

訳 教授は、ケイトと彼女の友人が試みたがっていた新しい実験を認めませんでした。

- adopt 動 採用する
- agree 動 同意する
- approve 動 認める
- permit 動 許可する

ofが後に続くのはapprove「認める」のみです

Chapter4 Society

## STEP 3 連鎖式に語彙を増やす 🎧69

### ● 語源 cap cip ceive cept（取る）

**0869 accept** [æksépt, ək-]
動 贈り物や申し出を受け入れる
原義 ac（〜に向かって）＋ cept（取る）

でた! The theory is now widely accepted.
（その理論は今や広く受け入れられている） 早稲田大学

派 **acceptance** 名 受諾、受け入れ

**0870 receive** [rɪsíːv] 動 提供や配達されたものを受け取る
コロ receive a letter of acceptance from Harvard University（ハーバード大学から合格通知を受け取る）

派 **reception** [rɪsépʃən] 名 受付、歓迎会

派 **receipt** [rɪsíːt] 発 名 レシート、領収書

**0871 capture** [kǽptʃər] 動 捕獲する
コロ capture the murderer（殺人犯を捕まえる）

派 **captive** 形 捕獲された

派 **captivity** 名 捕獲された状態

**0872 except** [iksépt] 接 除いて 動 除く 原義 ex（外に）＋ cept（取る）
コロ except for A（Aを除いて）

派 **exception** 名 除外

派 **exceptional** 形 例外の

> 日本語では例外というとマイナスのイメージがありますが、exceptionalは優秀なニュアンスがあります。

**0873 perceive** [pərsíːv] 動 （五感で）知覚する 原義 per（完全に）＋ ceive（取る）

派 **perception** 名 知覚、認識

**0874 conceive** [kənsíːv] 動 思いつく

派 **concept** 名 コンセプト、発想、概念

でた! In the year 1000, there was no concept of antiseptic at all.
（西暦1000年には消毒剤という概念は全くなかった） 東京大学

派 **conception** 名 心に抱くこと

派 **conceivable** 形 思いつきやすい

> idea→conception→conceptの順に抽象的になる。

### ● 語源 mit mis（送る）

**0875 admit** [ædmít | əd-] 動 （入場を）許す、（自分の行為を）認める

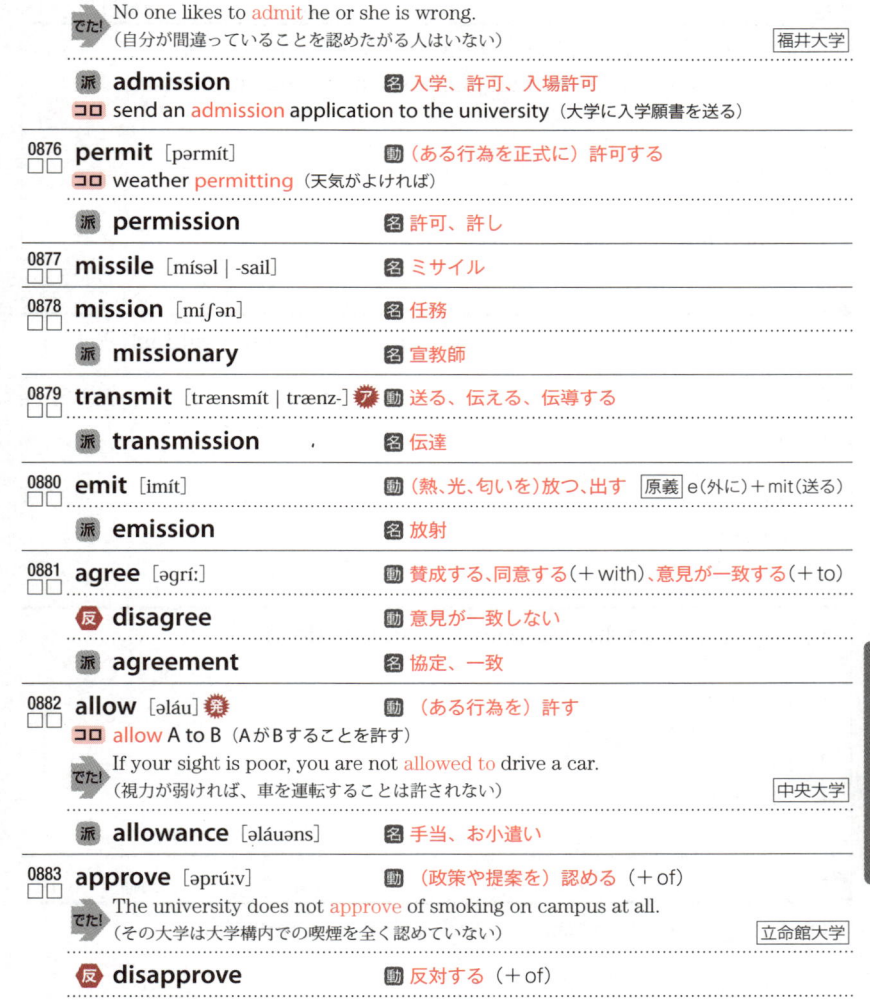

| | | |
|---|---|---|
| でた! | No one likes to admit he or she is wrong.<br>(自分が間違っていることを認めたがる人はいない) | 福井大学 |

**派 admission** 　名 入学、許可、入場許可
コロ send an admission application to the university（大学に入学願書を送る）

---

**0876 permit** [pərmít] 　動（ある行為を正式に）許可する
コロ weather permitting（天気がよければ）

**派 permission** 　名 許可、許し

---

**0877 missile** [mísəl | -sail] 　名 ミサイル

---

**0878 mission** [míʃən] 　名 任務

**派 missionary** 　名 宣教師

---

**0879 transmit** [trænsmít | trænz-] ⑦ 　動 送る、伝える、伝導する

**派 transmission** 　名 伝達

---

**0880 emit** [imít] 　動（熱、光、匂いを）放つ、出す　原義 e(外に)+mit(送る)

**派 emission** 　名 放射

---

**0881 agree** [əgríː] 　動 賛成する、同意する(+with)、意見が一致する(+to)

**反 disagree** 　動 意見が一致しない

**派 agreement** 　名 協定、一致

---

**0882 allow** [əláu] 発 　動（ある行為を）許す
コロ allow A to B（AがBすることを許す）

でた! If your sight is poor, you are not allowed to drive a car.
（視力が弱ければ、車を運転することは許されない）　中央大学

**派 allowance** [əláuəns] 　名 手当、お小遣い

---

**0883 approve** [əprúːv] 　動（政策や提案を）認める（+of）

でた! The university does not approve of smoking on campus at all.
（その大学は大学構内での喫煙を全く認めていない）　立命館大学

**反 disapprove** 　動 反対する（+of）

**派 approval** 　名 賛成、認可

---

**0884 concede** [kənsíːd] 　動 しぶしぶ認める
コロ concede defeat（敗北を認める）

**派 concession** 　名 譲歩、容認

UNIT 69　許可・容認

Chapter4 Society

# UNIT 70 拒否・否定

**STEP 1** 過去問を解く

## 1

Julie's company asked her to move to San Francisco, but she ( ) because she had just bought a house in Boston.

英語検定準2級

1. replied
2. refused
3. developed
4. depended

## 2

John <u>turned down</u> the invitation because he had to visit his parents.

東海大学

1. remembered
2. declined
3. forgot
4. accepted

## 3

My application to the company was <u>turned down</u>.

神戸学院大学

1. refused
2. admitted
3. received
4. accepted

## 4

That suspect ( ) that he had assaulted a policeman.

法政大学

1. refused
2. denied
3. contradicted
4. declined

## STEP 2 正解を見抜く

### 1

Julie's company asked her to move to San Francisco, but she refused because she had just bought a house in Boston.

正解 ②

**訳** ジュリーの会社は、サンフランシスコに転勤するように彼女に頼みましたが、ちょうどボストンに家を買ったところだったので、彼女は拒否しました。

- reply 動 答える
- develop 動 発展する
- refuse 動 断る
- depend 動 頼る

> refuseの語源はre（再び）+fuse（注ぐ）=お願いされたものを注ぎ返すイメージ

### 2

John declined the invitation because he had to visit his parents.

正解 ②

**訳** ジョンは両親を訪問しなければならなかったので、その招待を辞退しました。

- remember 動 覚えている
- decline 動 辞退する
- forget 動 忘れる
- accept 動 承諾する

> declineの語源はde（下に）+cline（傾く）=頭を下に傾けるイメージ=頭を下げて断る

### 3

My application to the company was refused.

正解 ①

**訳** 会社へ提出した私のアプリケーションは、却下されました。

- refuse 動 断る
- admit 動 認める
- receive 動 容認する
- accept 動 受け入れる

### 4

That suspect denied that he had assaulted a policeman.

正解 ②

**訳** その容疑者は、彼が警察官に暴行を加えたことを否認しました。

- refuse 動 断る
- deny 動 否定する、否認する
- contradict 動 否定する、矛盾する
- decline 動 辞退する

UNIT 70 拒否・否定

Chapter4 Society

## STEP 3 連鎖式に語彙を増やす 70

- 語源 fuse(注ぐ)

### 0885 refuse [rifjú:z]
**動** (申し出・要求等を) 断る
原義 re (再び) + fuse (注ぐ)

受け入れたものを注ぎ返す

でた！ He refused to accept such an absurb proposal.
(彼はそのようなばかげた提案を受け入れることを拒んだ) 横浜市立大学

**派 refusal** **名** 拒否

**コロ** turn down (断る)

でた！ The committee has turned down his application.
(委員会は彼の申し出を断った) 慶應義塾大学

**類 decline** **動** (丁寧に)断る、減少する
原義 de (下に) + cline (傾く)
頭を下に傾けてお辞儀するイメージ

### 0886 confuse [kənfjú:z]
**動** 混乱させる
原義 con (共に) + fuse (注ぐ)
同時にいろんなことをお願いされて混乱するイメージ

**コロ** confuse A with B (AとBを混合させる)

でた！ Do not confuse being close to power with actually having power.
(権力の近くにいることと実際に権力を持っていることを混同してはいけない) 明治大学

**派 confusion** **名** 混乱

でた！ Confusion arises about what it means to be "a good parent."
(「良い親」であるとは何を意味するかに関して混乱が生じる) センター試験

### 0887 fusion [fjú:ʒən]
**名** 融合
**コロ** nuclear fusion (核融合)

### 0888 infuse [infjú:z]
**動** 注ぐ 原義 in (中に) + fuse (注ぐ)

• 語源 ject（投げる）

### 0889 reject [ridʒékt]
動 (申し出・提案等をきっぱり) 断る、拒絶する  [原義] re (再び) ＋ ject (投げる)

きっぱり投げ返す

派 rejection　名 拒否

### 0890 inject [indʒékt]
動 注射する　[原義] in (中に) ＋ ject (投げる)

派 injection　名 注射

### 0891 project [prádʒekt | prədʒékt]
名 プロジェクト、計画　動 計画する

0892 でた！ The project involved 60 people, aged 60 to 83.
（そのプロジェクトには60歳から83歳までの60人が参加してきた）　　早稲田大学

派 projection　名 投影

派 projector　名 プロジェクター

### 0893 deject [didʒékt]
動 落胆する　[原義] de (下に) ＋ ject (投げる)

派 dejected　形 意気消沈した

派 dejection　名 意気消沈

UNIT 70 拒否・否定

Chapter4 Society

## UNIT 71 問題・迷惑　STEP 1 過去問を解く

### 1

If your parents see you doing that, you'll get into (　　　).

同志社大学

1. anxiety
2. trouble
3. struggle
4. problem

### 2

You should be (　　　) of yourself for doing such a silly thing.

駒澤大学

1. afraid
2. angry
3. ashamed
4. delighted

### 3

When you make a mistake in public, you feel (　　　).

名古屋女子大学

1. affection
2. embarrassed
3. frightened
4. irritated

### 4

The law also prohibits sexual harassment in the workplace.

早稲田大学

1. annoyance
2. attendance
3. enjoyment
4. treatment

## STEP 2 正解を見抜く

### 1

If your parents see you doing that, you'll get into trouble. 　正解 ②

訳 もしあなたがそうしているところを両親が見たら、面倒なことになるでしょう。

- **anxiety** 名 心配
- **trouble** 名 困ったこと
- **struggle** 名 苦闘
- **problem** 名 問題

get into trouble
（問題を起こす）

### 2

You should be ashamed of yourself for doing such a silly thing. 　正解 ③

訳 あなたはそんな愚かなことをした自分を恥じるべきだ。

- **afraid** 形 恐れている
- **angry** 形 怒っている
- **ashamed** 形 恥じている
- **delighted** 形 喜んでいる

### 3

When you make a mistake in public, you feel embarrassed. 　正解 ②

訳 人前で間違えると、恥ずかしい思いをする。

- **affection** 名 愛情
- **embarrassed** 形 恥ずかしい
- **frightened** 形 恐れている
- **irritated** 形 イライラしている

### 4

The law also prohibits sexual annoyance in the workplace. 　正解 ①

訳 その法律はまた職場における性的嫌がらせも禁止している。

- **annoyance** 名 うざがらせること
- **attendance** 名 出席
- **enjoyment** 名 楽しみ
- **treatment** 名 扱い

UNIT 71　問題・迷惑

Chapter4 Society

## STEP 3 連鎖式に語彙を増やす 🎧71

**0894 trouble** [trʌ́bl] 名 問題、心配
- コロ be in trouble (困った状態である)  コロ get into trouble (問題を起こす)
- 派 **troublesome** [trʌ́blsəm] 形 面倒くさい、厄介な

**0895 matter** [mǽtər] 名 問題
- でた! What's the matter with you? (あなたどうかしたの)

**0896 problem** [prάbləm | prɔ́b-] 名 問題

**0897 issue** [íʃuː] 名 問題、出版物 動 発行する、公布する
- コロ political issue (政治的問題)  コロ at issue (論争中で)
- でた! Sexual harassment is a serious issue and should be treated as such.
(セクハラは深刻な問題であり、そういうものとして扱われるべきである) 〔近畿大学〕

**0898 perplex** [pərpléks] 動 混乱させる
- 派 **perplexing** 形 面倒な

**0899 puzzle** [pʌ́zl] 動 困惑させる 名 パズル、難問
- 派 **puzzling** 形 困惑させるような

**0900 embarrass** [imbǽrəs] 動 恥ずかしがらせる
- 派 **embarrassment** 名 困惑、決まり悪さ

**0901 irritate** [írətèit] 動 いらいらさせる
- 派 **irritable** [írətəbl] 形 怒りっぽい、過敏な
- でた! An unpleasant sensation of fatigue makes us bad-tempered and irritable.
(疲労の不快感は私たちを気難しくし、怒りっぽくする) 〔早稲田大学〕
- 派 **irritation** 名 いら立ち

**0902 annoy** [ənɔ́i] 動 いらいらさせる、悩ます
- 派 **annoyance** 名 いら立ち、うざがらせること
- 類 **harassment** [hərǽsmənt] 名 嫌がらせ
- コロ sexual harassment (セクハラ)

**0903 nuisance** [njúːsns | njúː-] 名 迷惑

**0904 bother** [bάðər | bɔ́ð-] 動 悩ます

## 0905 upset [ʌpsét]
動 動揺させる、ひっくり返す　形 動揺した
活 upset-upset-upset

でた！ Your father will be very upset when he hears about it.
（それを聞いたらあなたのお父さんはとても動揺するでしょう）　中央大学

コロ beside oneself（我を忘れて、気が動転して）

でた！ He failed the exam and is beside himself.
（彼は試験に落ちて、気が動転している）　立命館大学

## 0906 regret [rigrét]
動 後悔する（＋ing）　名 後悔、残念

でた！ I regret saying such terrible things to my brother.
（私は、兄にそんなひどいことを言った事を後悔している）　立命館大学

派 regrettable　形 遺憾な

## 0907 pity [píti]
名 哀れみ、同情

コロ It's a pity that S V（SVで残念である）

でた！ It is a pity that nobody was saved in the accident, isn't it?
（その事故で誰も助からなかったのは残念ですよね）　センター試験

## 0908 shame [ʃéim]
名 恥

でた！ It's a shame your wife couldn't come. I really wanted to meet her.
（あなたの奥さんが来られなかったのは残念です。本当に会いたかったです）　センター試験

派 ashamed　形 恥じている（＋of）

派 shameful　形 恥ずかしい

## 0909 anxious [ǽŋkʃəs]
形 心配している（＋about）、切望している（＋to）

でた！ I am anxious about your health.
（私はあなたの健康を心配しています）　横浜国立大学

でた！ Everybody was anxious to know what had happened.
（誰でも何が起こったか知りたがっていた）　横浜国立大学

派 anxiety [æŋzáiəti]　名 心配

類 worry [wə́ːri | wʌ́ri]　動 心配する　名 心配

コロ be worried about A（Aを心配する）

UNIT 71　問題・迷惑

Chapter4 Society

# UNIT 72　誘惑・障害　STEP 1 過去問を解く

## 1

The news of his retirement (　　) public attention.

青山学院大学

1. gathered
2. charmed
3. collected
4. attracted

## 2

A: Turn down that music! You're going to (　　) the neighbors.
B: OK, I'm sorry. I'll use the headphones.

英語検定2級

1. entertain
2. impress
3. tempt
4. disturb

## 3

Don't (　　) me while I am studying.

上智大学

1. contract
2. retract
3. extract
4. distract

## 4

People prefer to pay more money for safer food. But still, the high price of organic food is an (　　) for a majority of people.

中央大学

1. object
2. obligation
3. obscurity
4. obstacle

## STEP 2 正解を見抜く

### 1

The news of his retirement attracted public attention. 正解 ④

訳 彼が引退するというニュースは世間の関心を集めた。

- gather 動 集める
- charm 動 魅了する
- collect 動 集める
- attract 動 魅惑する

> attractの語源はat（〜に向かって）＋tract（引く）＝何かに向かって引きつける＝魅了する

### 2

A: Turn down that music! You're going to disturb the neighbors.
B: OK, I'm sorry. I'll use the headphones. 正解 ④

訳 A：音楽の音量を下げなさい。あなたは近所の人に迷惑をかけることになりますよ。
B：はい、すみません。ヘッドフォンを使うことにします。

- entertain 動 楽しませる
- tempt 動 誘惑する
- impress 動 印象を与える
- disturb 動 妨害する

### 3

Don't distract me while I am studying. 正解 ④

訳 私が勉強している間は、邪魔しないでください。

- contract 動 契約する
- retract 動 取り消す
- extract 動 引き出す
- distract 動 そらす

> distractの語源はdis（分離）＋tract（引く）＝違う方向に引きつける＝そらす

### 4

People prefer to pay more money for safer food. But still, the high price of organic food is an obstacle for a majority of people. 正解 ④

訳 人々はより安全な食べ物のためにより高いお金を払いたがる。しかしそれでも有機食品の高値は多くの人々にとって障害となっている。

- object 名 目的
- obscurity 名 不明瞭さ
- obstacle 名 障害物
- obligation 名 義務

> obstacleの語源はob（近くに）＋st（立つ）＝近くに立って邪魔するもの＝障害物

UNIT 72 誘惑・障害

Chapter4 Society

## STEP 3 連鎖式に語彙を増やす 72

**0910 disturb** [distə́:rb] 動 かき乱す、騒いで邪魔する
- 派 **disturbance** 名 妨害、騒動

**0911 interfere** [ìntərfíər] 動 口出し・手出し・邪魔する、干渉する（＋with）
- 派 **interference** 名 邪魔、妨害、干渉

**0912 interrupt** [ìntərʌ́pt] 動 邪魔する、中断する
- 原義 inter（2つの間）＋rupt（壊れる）
- でた! Stop interrupting each other and listen carefully.
（お互いの口を挟むのはやめてしっかり聞け）〔明治大学〕
- 派 **interruption** 名 妨害、中断

**0913 hinder** [híndər] 動 妨げる
- コロ hinder A from ~ing（Aが～するのを妨げる）

**0914 invade** [invéid] 動 侵略する、侵害する
- 派 **invasion** 名 侵略、侵害
- コロ invasion of privacy（プライバシーの侵害）

**0915 intervene** [ìntərví:n] 動 干渉する、仲介する
- 原義 inter（2つの間）＋ven（来る）
- 派 **intervention** 名 干渉、介在

**0916 obstacle** [ɑ́bstəkl | ɔ́b-] 名 障害物 原義 ob（前に）＋st（立つ）

### ● 語源 treat, tract（引く）

**0917 distract** [distrǽkt] 動 注意をそらす
- コロ distract A from B（Aの気をBからそらす）
- 派 **distraction** 名 放心状態

**0918 extract** [ikstrǽkt] 動 抽出する、取り出す 原義 ex（外に）＋tract（引く）
- でた! A biologist extracted sequence information from DNA in museum specimens.
（ある生物学者は博物館の標本のDNAから配列情報を抽出した）〔早稲田大学〕
- 派 **extraction** 名 抽出
- でた! Petroleum extraction can have a negative impact on the environment.
（石油抽出は環境に対してマイナスの影響を与えうる）〔TOEFL〕

**0919 attract** [ətrǽkt] 動 魅了する
- でた! Discount stores attract customers by offering high-quality goods at low prices.
（ディスカウントストアは高品質の商品を低価格で提供することで顧客を引きつける）〔茨城大学〕

| 派 | **attractive** | 形 魅力的な |

| 派 | **attraction** | 名 魅力、引きつけること |

でた! Dubai has preserved some of the most interesting historical attractions.
（ドバイは最も面白い歴史的な名所のいくつかを保存してきた） 立命館大学

0920 **contract** [kάntrækt | kɔ́n-]　名 契約　動 契約する
コロ make a contract with A （Aと契約を結ぶ）

0921 **appeal** [əpíːl]　動 訴える、アピールする　名 訴え、上訴

| 派 | **appealing** | 形 魅力的な |

でた! Working abroad is appealing to many people.
（外国で働くことは多くの人にとって魅力的である） TOEFL

0922 **fascinate** [fǽsənèit]　動 魅了する

| 派 | **fascinating** | 形 魅惑的な |
| 派 | **fascination** | 名 魅力 |

0923 **charm** [tʃáːrm]　名 魅力　動 魅了する

でた! The charm of travel lies in its new experiences.
（旅行の魅力はその新しい経験にある） 立教大学

| 派 | **charming** | 形 魅力的な |
| 類 | **moving** | 形 感動的な |
| 類 | **touching** | 形 感情的な |

0924 **curious** [kjúəriəs]　形 好奇心の強い、珍しい

| 派 | **curiosity** [kjùəriásəti | -ɔ́s-] | 名 好奇心 |

0925 **excite** [iksáit]　動 興奮させる

でた! Feeling nervous is a little bit like feeling excited.
（緊張していると感じることは興奮していると感じることと少し似ている） 慶應義塾大学

| 派 | **exciting** | 形 興奮させる |

0926 **tempt** [témpt]　動 誘惑する

| 派 | **temptation** | 名 誘惑 |

でた! He never gave way to temptation.
（彼は決して誘惑にのらなかった） 慶應義塾大学

| 派 | **tempting** | 形 魅力的な |

UNIT 72　誘惑・障害

Chapter4 Society

# UNIT 73 謝罪・責任

**STEP 1 過去問を解く**

## 1

You should ( ) to Mrs. Smith for your rude behavior the other night. She was very hurt by it.

英語検定準2級

1. permit
2. express
3. apologize
4. explain

## 2

Your allegations are completely untrue, and I demand an immediate ( ).

上智大学

1. appreciation
2. approval
3. apology
4. appraisal

## 3

We regret to announce that Lionair flight LA028 to Washington has been canceled due to heavy snow. We apologize for the ( ) it may cause.

中央大学

1. inconvenience
2. perseverance
3. significance
4. conscious

## 4

It was the teacher's ( ) to close the windows in all the classrooms at the end of each school day.

英語検定2級

1. demonstration
2. responsibility
3. involvement
4. possession

## STEP 2 正解を見抜く

### 1

You should apologize to Mrs. Smith for your rude behavior the other night. She was very hurt by it.

正解 ③

訳 あなたは先日の夜の失礼な振る舞いについて、スミスさんに謝るべきです。彼女はそれによって非常に傷ついたのです。

permit 動許す
apologize 動謝罪する
express 動表現する
explain 動説明する

apologizeの使い方は apologize to 人 for 事

### 2

Your allegations are completely untrue, and I demand an immediate apology.

正解 ③

訳 あなたの主張は完全に虚偽です、そして、私は直ちに謝罪を要求します。

appreciation 名理解力
approval 名賛成
apology 名謝罪
appraisal 名評価

### 3

We regret to announce that Lionair flight LA028 to Washington has been canceled due to heavy snow. We apologize for the inconvenience it may cause.

正解 ①

訳 残念ながら、ワシントンへのLionair航空 LA028便が大雪のため欠航になったことを発表します。私たちはそれが引き起こすかもしれないご迷惑をお詫びします。

inconvenience 名不便
significance 名重要性
perseverance 名忍耐力
conscious 形意識している

### 4

It was the teacher's responsibility to close the windows in all the classrooms at the end of each school day.

正解 ②

訳 それぞれの授業日の最後に、全ての教室の窓を閉めるのは教師の責任であった。

demonstration 名論証
responsibility 名責任
involvement 名関与
possession 名所有

responsibilityの語源はre（再び）＋spond（答える）＋able（可能）＝再び答えることができること＝何を聞いても対応できること＝責任

UNIT 73 謝罪・責任

Chapter4 Society

## STEP 3 連鎖式に語彙を増やす 🎧73

### 0927 apologize [əpálədʒàiz | əpɔ́l-]
動 謝罪する

でた! Any boy who breaks a window while playing baseball should apologize to his teacher.
(野球をしていて窓を割った男の子は誰でも先生に謝ったほうがよい) 〔東洋大学〕

派 **apology** 名 謝罪

でた! We understand how important apologies and forgiveness are in relationships.
(我々は関係を築く上でどれだけ謝罪と許しが重要か理解している) 〔法政大学〕

### 0928 sorry [sári, sɔ́ːri | sɔ́ri]
形 気の毒で

類 **sorrow** [sárou, sɔ́ːr- | sɔ́r-] 名 悲しみ

### 0929 grieve [gríːv]
動 悲しむ

派 **grief** [gríːf] 名 深い悲しみ、悲嘆

類 **lament** [ləmént] 動 嘆き悲しむ 名 悲嘆

### 0930 despair [dispéər]
名 絶望

コロ in despair (絶望して)

でた! Poverty leads to despair, a sense of injustice and alienation.
(貧困は絶望、不公平感、疎外感を生む) 〔早稲田大学〕

派 **desperate** [déspərət] 形 絶望的な

派 **desperation** 名 絶望

### 0931 misery [mízəri]
名 惨めさ、悲惨、苦悩

派 **miserable** [mízərəbl] 形 惨めな

コロ feel miserable (情けない思いをする)

### 0932 mercy [mə́ːrsi]
名 慈悲、情け

コロ at the mercy of A (Aのなすがままに)

でた! Farmers are always at the mercy of the weather.
(農民はいつも天候のなすがままである) 〔慶應義塾大学〕

派 **merciful** 形 慈悲深い

### 0933 convenient [kənvíːnjənt]
形 便利な ※人を主語にとらない

でた! I would like to see you tomorrow. What time is convenient for you?
(明日お会いしたいのですがいつ都合が宜しいでしょうか) 〔南山大学〕

**派 convenience** 名 便利
コロ at one's convenience（自分の都合が良い時に）

**反 inconvenient** 形 不便な
でた! Lunar years were inconvenient for agricultural purposes.
（太陰暦は農業目的には不便であった） TOEFL

**派 inconvenience** 名 不便

---

• 語源 **spond**（答える）

**0934 sponge** [spʌ́ndʒ] 名 スポンジ

**0935 respond** [rispánd | -spɔ́nd] 動 反応する　原義 re（再び）+ pond（答える）

**派 response** 名 反応
でた! Parental response to media violence varies.
（メディアの暴力に対する親の反応は様々である） 早稲田大学
コロ in response to A（Aに応じて）
でた! Money poured in response to the appeal for help for the earthquake.
（地震に対する援助の求めに応じて、資金がつぎ込まれた） 上智大学

re（再び）+ spons（答える）
= able（可能）= どんなことを聞いても答えることができる = 責任がある

**0936 responsible** [rispánsəbl | -spɔ́n-] 形 責任がある（+ for）
でた! We are responsible for our own choices.
（我々は自分自身の選択に対して責任がある） 上智大学

**派 responsibility** [rispànsəbíləti | -spɔ̀n-] ⑦ 名 責任
コロ assume responsibility（責任を負う）
でた! Human beings have to think seriously about their responsibility to the planet.
（人類は地球に対する自分の責任について真剣に考えなくてはならない） センター試験

**0937 correspond** [kɔ̀:rəspánd | kɔ̀rəspɔ́nd]
動 一致・相当する（+ to, with）、文通する（+ with）
原義 co（共に）+ re（再び）+ spond（答える）

でた! The broad line on the map corresponds to roads.
（地図上の太い線は道路に相当します） 武蔵大学

**派 correspondence** 名 一致、文通

**派 correspondent** 名 文通する人、通信員

UNIT 73　謝罪・責任

Chapter4 Society　311

# UNIT 74 危険・恐怖

**STEP 1** 過去問を解く

## 1

It is very (　　) for small children to play with fire.

1. dangerous
2. equivalent
3. exclusive
4. rural

立命館大学

## 2

A diet that includes a large amount of junk food increases the (　　) of having a heart attack.

1. level
2. rate
3. reason
4. risk

学習院大学

## 3

"(　　)! There's a car coming," the mother shouted to her young daughter.

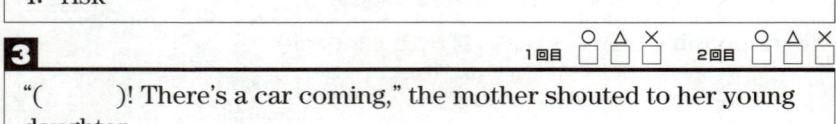

1. Danger
2. Watch out
3. Caution
4. Attention

明治大学

## 4

The guide always (　　) tourists about the dangers of crossing the street in Rome.

1. speaks
2. recommends
3. remembers
4. warns

学習院大学

## STEP 2 正解を見抜く

### 1

It is very dangerous for small children to play with fire. 　正解 ①

訳 小さい子供の火遊びは、非常に危険です。

- **dangerous** 形 危険な
- **equivalent** 形 等しい
- **exclusive** 形 排他的な
- **rural** 形 田舎の

### 2

A diet that includes a large amount of junk food increases the risk of having a heart attack. 　正解 ④

訳 多量のジャンクフードを含んでいる食事は、心臓発作の危険性を増加させます。

- **level** 名 標準
- **rate** 名 割合
- **reason** 名 理由
- **risk** 名 危険

> 一般的な危険 danger と異なり、「予測できる危険」を表します

### 3

"Watch out! There's a car coming," the mother shouted to her young daughter. 　正解 ②

訳 母親は「注意しなさい。車が来てる。」と彼女の若い娘に叫びました。

- **danger** 名 危険
- **watch out** 気をつける
- **caution** 名 用心
- **attention** 名 注意

> Watch out!「危ない！」「気をつけて！」は Be careful!「気をつけて！」より緊急性があります

### 4

The guide always warns tourists about the dangers of crossing the street in Rome. 　正解 ④

訳 そのガイドは、ローマで通りを渡るときの危険に関して、いつも旅行者に警告します。

- **speak** 動 話す
- **recommend** 動 推薦する
- **remember** 動 覚えている
- **warn** 動 警告する

UNIT 74 危険・恐怖

Chapter4 Society | 313

## STEP 3 連鎖式に語彙を増やす 74

### 0938 dangerous [déindʒərəs] 形 危険な

**派 danger** 名 危険
コロ be in danger of A（Aの危険がある）
でた! The beautiful bird is said to be in danger of dying out.
（その美しい鳥は絶滅の恐れがあると言われている） 早稲田大学

**派 endanger** [indéindʒər] 動 危険にさらす

**派 endangered** 形 絶滅危惧種の
コロ endangered species（絶滅危惧種）

**派 endangerment** 名 危険にさらすこと、危機的状況

### 0939 crisis [kráisis] 名 危機 （複）crises
コロ financial crisis（金融危機）

**派 critical** [krítikəl] 形 危機的な、批評の、重大な

### 0940 hazard [hǽzərd] 名 危険

> 自動車のハザードランプは危険を表すランプです。

**派 hazardous** 形 危険な

**類 risk** 名 危険、恐れ
コロ take a risk（リスクを負う） コロ at any risk（どんな危険を冒しても＝ぜひとも）

**派 risky** 形 危険な

**類 peril** [pérəl] 名 危険

**派 perilous** 形 危険な

### 0941 caution [kɔ́ːʃən] 名 用心、警告

**派 cautious** 形 用心深い

**派 precaution** 名 用心、警戒 原義 pre（前に）＋caution（用心する）

### 0942 warn [wɔ́ːrn] 動 警告する
コロ warn A of B（AにBを警告する） コロ warn A to B（AにBするように警告する）

**派 warning** 名 警告

### 0943 harm [háːrm] 名 害 動 害する、物理的に傷つける
コロ do A harm（Aに害を与える）

**派 harmful** 形 有害な

| 0944 | **scare** [skɛ́ər] | 動 怖がらせる、怯えさせる |
|---|---|---|
| | 派 scary | 形 怖い、恐ろしい |
| 0945 | **frighten** [fráitn] | 動 怯えさせる |
| | 派 frightening | 形 恐ろしい |
| | 派 fright | 名 恐怖 |
| 0946 | **threaten** [θrétn] | 動 脅す、脅迫する |
| | でた! Crop failures threatened the entire population.<br>（不作が全人口を脅かした） | TOEFL |
| | 派 threat [θrét] 発 | 名 脅威、脅し |
| | でた! Due to a bomb threat, they cleared the stadium of spectators.<br>（爆弾の恐れがあったため、彼らはスタジアムから観客を避難させた） | 青山学院大学 |
| 0947 | **awful** [ɔ́:fəl] | 形 恐ろしい、ひどい |
| | コロ awful weather（ひどい天気） | |
| 0948 | **terrify** [térəfài] | 動 怖がらせる |
| | 派 terrifying | 形 恐ろしい |
| | 派 terror | 名 恐怖 |
| 0949 | **terrible** [térəbl] | 形 恐ろしい、ひどい |
| | 派 terribly | 副 ひどく、非常に |
| 0950 | **horrible** [hɔ́:rəbl, hár- \| hɔ́r-] | 形 恐ろしい |
| | 派 horror | 名 恐怖 |
| 0951 | **tragic** [trǽdʒik] | 形 悲劇の |
| | 派 tragedy | 名 悲劇 |
| | でた! The tragedy of the Titanic is well known.<br>（タイタニックの悲劇はよく知られている） | 中央大学 |
| | 反 comic [kámik \| kɔ́m-] | 形 喜劇の |
| | 派 comedy | 名 喜劇 |
| 0952 | **fear** [fíər] | 名 恐れ |
| | コロ for fear of A（Aを恐れて、Aしないように） | |

UNIT 74 危険・恐怖

Chapter4 Society

## UNIT 75　遠慮・失礼　STEP 1 過去問を解く

**1**

If you need more details, please do not (　　) to contact us at 123-4567.

学習院大学

1. stop
2. try
3. hesitate
4. turn

**2**

Please (　　) from talking on the phone.

駒澤大学

1. refrain
2. remain
3. quit
4. refuse

**3**

I know that Mike has been very busy recently, but I think it was very (　　) of him to ignore your invitation.

英語検定2級

1. impolite
2. impossible
3. indescribable
4. respectful

**4**

It isn't (　　) of you to call me up at this hour of the night.

慶応義塾大学

1. discreet
2. possible
3. sufficient
4. satisfactory

## STEP 2 正解を見抜く

### 1

If you need more details, please do not **hesitate** to contact us at 123-4567.

正解 ③

訳 より詳細をお知りになりたければ、ご遠慮なく123-4567に電話して私たちに連絡してください。

- **stop** 動 止める
- **hesitate** 動 ためらう
- **try** 動 試みる
- **turn** 動 回す

hesitate to A
(Aすることをためらう)

### 2

Please **refrain** from talking on the phone.

正解 ①

訳 電話での通話は差し控えてください。

- **refrain** 動 差し控える
- **remain** 動 居残る
- **quit** 動 やめる
- **refuse** 動 断る

refrain from ~ing
(~することを控える)

### 3

I know that Mike has been very busy recently, but I think it was very **impolite** of him to ignore your invitation.

正解 ①

訳 マイクが最近ずっと忙しいのは分かっているが、あなたの招待を無視するのは失礼だったと思う。

- **impolite** 形 無礼な
- **indescribable** 形 言い表せない
- **respectful** 形 丁寧な
- **impossible** 形 不可能な

### 4

It isn't **discreet** of you to call me up at this hour of the night.

正解 ①

訳 夜こんな時間に私に電話をかけてくるなんて君は分別がないね。

- **discreet** 形 分別のある
- **possible** 形 可能な
- **sufficient** 形 十分な
- **satisfactory** 形 満足な

性格・性質を表す形容詞の後にはofが付きます。

UNIT 75 遠慮・失礼

Chapter4 Society

## STEP 3 連鎖式に語彙を増やす 75

### 0953 hesitate [hézətèit] 動 ためらう（+ to）

でた! Many Japanese students hesitate to stand out among their classroom.
（多くの日本人の生徒はクラスメイトの中で目立つのをためらう） 早稲田大学

派 **hesitant** 形 躊躇して

でた! He was hesitant to move because he could not get a good price for his old house.
（彼は前の家に良い価格が付かなかったので、引っ越すことをためらっていた） 駒澤大学

派 **hesitation** 名 躊躇

コロ feel free to A （ご自由にAして）

でた! If you have any questions, please feel free to ask me any time.
（もし何か質問があれば、いつでも遠慮なく私に聞いてください） 青山学院大学

### 0954 reluctant [rilʌ́ktənt] 形 嫌々ながらの、気の進まない

コロ be reluctant to A （Aするのを嫌がる）

でた! Mary was reluctant to go to the party at first, but she found that it was fun.
（メアリーは最初そのパーティーに行く気がしなかったが、行ってみると楽しかった） 中央大学

派 **reluctance** 名 気が進まない事

### 0955 will [wíl] 名 意志、遺言書

コロ at will （自由に）　コロ against one's will （意に反して）

派 **willing** 形 本当はやりたくないことを進んでする

コロ be willing to A （AするのをAするのを構わない）

でた! Betty didn't seem willing to join our project.
（ベティーは我々の計画に参加する気がなかったように思える） 南山大学

反 **unwilling** 形 したがらない

### 0956 lazy [léizi] 形 怠惰な

派 **laziness** 名 怠惰

類 **idle** [áidl] 形 怠惰な　動 怠ける

派 **idleness** 名 愚かさ

idol（偶像・アイドル）と同じ発音

でた! She blamed John for his idleness.
（彼女はジョンの怠惰さを非難した） 専修大学

### 0957 polite [pəláit] 形 礼儀正しい

でた! They must always be polite toward their opponents.
（彼らは相手に対していつも礼儀正しくしなければならない） 獨協大学

反 **impolite** 形 失礼な

| | | |
|---|---|---|
| 派 | **politeness** | 名 丁寧さ |
| 派 | **politely** | 副 丁寧に |

でた! I try to speak politely to my teachers.
（私は先生に対して礼儀正しく話すように心がけています） 慶應義塾大学

0958 **courtesy** [kə́:rtəsi | kə́:rtsi] 発　名 礼儀正しさ
コロ common courtesy （当たり前の礼儀）

派 **courteous** [kə́:rtiəs]　形 礼儀正しい

0959 **decency** [dí:snsi]　名 礼儀正しさ

派 **decent** [dí:snt] 発　形 ちゃんとした、社会規範をわきまえている
コロ decent clothes （ちゃんとした服装）

派 **decently**　副 ちゃんと

0960 **rude** [rú:d]　形 無礼な

派 **rudeness**　名 無礼

0961 **absurd** [æbsə́:rd | -zə́:rd | əbsə́:d]　形 馬鹿げた、不合理な

でた! Everyone thought his suggestion was absurd.
（皆彼の提案はばかげていると思った） 拓殖大学

派 **absurdity**　名 不合理

0962 **stupid** [stjú:pid | stjú:-]　形 馬鹿な

派 **stupidity**　名 愚かさ

0963 **fool** [fú:l]　名 馬鹿者

派 **foolish**　形 馬鹿な

でた! He could not account for his foolish mistake.
（彼は愚かな過ちについて説明出来なかった） 上智大学

派 **silly** [síli]　形 馬鹿な

0964 **naughty** [nɔ́:ti] 発　形 いたずらな、行儀の悪い

類 **mischief** [místʃif] 発　名 いたずら、いたずらっ子

派 **mischievous** [místʃəvəs] ア　形 いたずら好きな

UNIT 75　遠慮・失礼

Chapter4 Society

## UNIT 76 強制・義務　STEP 1 過去問を解く

### 1
There is a very (　　) rule forbidding smoking in bed.  　慶応義塾大学

1. severe
2. strong
3. hard
4. strict

### 2
Human rights groups have called for tighter (　　) on the use of television cameras to record people in public places without their knowledge.  　中央大学

1. connections
2. instructions
3. reflections
4. restrictions

### 3
Two Californian towns, Davis and Palo Alto, have <u>banned</u> smoking in public spaces.  　上智大学

1. admitted
2. kept
3. prohibited
4. required

### 4
Researchers are developing a vaccine that will (　　) AIDS.  　慶應義塾大学

1. prevent
2. describe
3. deny
4. examine

320

## STEP 2 正解を見抜く

### 1

There is a very strict rule forbidding smoking in bed.  正解 ④

訳 ベッドでの喫煙を禁じる非常に厳しい規則があります。

- severe 形 厳しい
- strong 形 力が強い
- hard 形 激しい
- strict 形 厳しい

strictの語源はstr（締める）＝キツいイメージ＝厳しい

### 2

Human rights groups have called for tighter restrictions on the use of television cameras to record people in public places without their knowledge.  正解 ④

訳 人権団体は公共の場で何も知らない人々を録画するテレビカメラの使用に対するより厳重な規制を要求した。

- connection 名 連結
- reflection 名 反射
- instruction 名 説明書
- restriction 名 制限

restrictionの語源はre（強調）＋str（締める）＝強く締める＝制限する

### 3

Two Californian towns, Davis and Palo Alto, have prohibited smoking in public spaces.  正解 ③

訳 デービスとパロアルトという2つのカリフォルニアの町が公共の場での喫煙を禁止した。

- admit 動 認める
- keep 動 保つ
- prohibit 動 禁止する
- require 動 必要とする

banは「規制的な禁止」、prohibitは「法律的な禁止」

### 4

Researchers are developing a vaccine that will prevent AIDS.  正解 ①

訳 研究者たちはエイズを予防するワクチンを開発中である。

- prevent 動 妨げる
- describe 動 記述する
- deny 動 否定する
- examine 動 調査する

UNIT 76 強制・義務

Chapter4 Society

## STEP 3 連鎖式に語彙を増やす 76

● 語源 **str**（締める）

### 0965 **strong** [strɔ́ːŋ | strɔ́ŋ] 形 強い

派 **strength** 名 強さ
でた! All tools have their strengths and weaknesses.
（全ての道具には強さと弱さがある） 明治大学

派 **strengthen** 動 強化する
コロ strengthen the muscles（筋肉を強化する）

### 0966 **strict** [stríkt] 形 厳しい

でた! Fathers and mothers tend to be strict with their first child.
（父親と母親は最初の子供には厳しくする傾向にある） 福島大学

派 **strictly** 副 厳しく

### 0967 **constrict** [kənstríkt] 動 圧縮する

### 0968 **harsh** [háːrʃ] 形 厳しい

でた! Because of the harsh weather conditions, the family decided to cancel their picnic.
（厳しい天気の状態のため、その家族はピクニックを中止する判断をした） 立命館大学

### 0969 **severe** [səvíər] ア 形 厳しい

コロ severe cold（厳しい寒さ）
でた! All states impose severe penalties on drunken drivers.
（全ての州が飲酒運転に厳しい罰を課す） 立教大学

### 0970 **restrict** [ristríkt] 動 制限する

でた! The bill to restrict juries was approved by the government.
（陪審を制限する法案が政府により可決された） 早稲田大学

派 **restriction** 名 制限

### 0971 **stress** [strés] 名 ストレス、強調 動 強調する

コロ stress the importance（重要性を強調する）
でた! Drinking is one way to relieve business stress.
（お酒を飲むことは仕事上のストレスを和らげる1つの方法だ）

派 **stressful** 形 緊張の多い

類 **distress** [distrés] 名 苦悩 動 悩ます

### 0972 **stretch** [strétʃ] 動 伸ばす 名 ストレッチ

322

## 0973 strain [stréin]
動 張る、引き締める　名 緊張

でた！ If no conversation takes place the atmosphere can become rather strained.
（会話が全く行われなければ、その場の雰囲気がいささか緊張したものになりかねない）
鹿児島大学

派 restrain [ristréin]　動 抑える

派 constraint [kənstréint]　名 強制、束縛、圧迫　動 圧迫する

## 0974 prohibit [prouhíbit, prə-]
動 規則で禁じる

コロ prohibit A from ~ing（Aが~するのを禁じる）

でた！ The law prohibits minors from smoking.
（法律は未成年者の喫煙を禁じている）
明治大学

派 prohibition　名 禁止

## 0975 ban [bǽn]
動 法的に禁じる　名 禁止

でた！ Talking on cell phones is often banned.
（携帯電話の通話は、禁止される）
早稲田大学

## 0976 forbid [fərbíd]
動 道徳的・倫理的に禁じる
活 forbid-forbade-forbidden

コロ forbid A to B（AがBするのを禁じる）

でた！ Taking photographs inside the building is strictly forbidden.
（ビルの中で写真を撮ることは、厳密に禁じられます）
法政大学

## 0977 limit [límit]
動 制限する　名 限度

派 limitation　名 制限

でた！ There needs to be some limitation to what students can wear to school.
（学生が学校で何を着ていけるのかいくらかの制限が必要である）
センター試験

派 limited　形 限られた、制限された

---

**思考の時間**　実際に入試で問われた内容です。あなたはどう答えますか？

高校における携帯電話持ち込み禁止。賛成？反対？
早稲田大学

UNIT 76　強制・義務

Chapter4 Society

# UNIT 77 制限・禁止

**STEP 1 過去問を解く**

## 1

Mathematics is a (　　　) subject at our university.

東京理科大学

1. compelling
2. compressive
3. compulsive
4. compulsory

## 2

The students were (　　　) to cancel their travel plans owing to the accident.

立命館大学

1. compelled
2. engaged
3. enrolled
4. stranded

## 3

Even though Bill didn't want to go to school this morning, his mother (　　　) him to go.

英語検定準2級

1. forced
2. overcame
3. refused
4. saved

## 4

Before our old house could be remodeled, we had to (　　　) the walls so the first story could support more weight.

英語検定準1級

1. reinforce
2. reassure
3. suspend
4. confirm

## STEP 2 正解を見抜く

### 1

Mathematics is a compulsory subject at our university.

正解 ④

訳 私たちの大学では、数学は必須科目です。

- **compelling** 形 強制的な
- **compressive** 形 圧縮の
- **compulsive** 形 強制的な
- **compulsory** 形 必修の、強制的な

> compulsory subjectは「必須科目」optional subjectは「選択科目」

### 2

The students were compelled to cancel their travel plans owing to the accident.

正解 ①

訳 事故のせいで生徒らは旅行の計画を中止せざるを得なかった。

- **compel** 動 無理やり~させる
- **engage** 動 従事させる
- **enroll** 動 入会する
- **strand** 動 座礁する

> compel A to B (Aに強制的にBさせる)

### 3

Even though Bill didn't want to go to school this morning, his mother forced him to go.

正解 ①

訳 今朝ビルは学校に行きたくなかったが、彼の母親は強制的に行かせた。

- **force** 動 ~することを強制する
- **overcome** 動 打ち勝つ
- **refuse** 動 断る
- **save** 動 救う

> force A to B (Aに強制的にBさせる)

### 4

Before our old house could be remodeled, we had to reinforce the walls so the first story could support more weight.

正解 ①

訳 私たちの古い家は改装される前に、一階がより重さを支えられるようにするため、壁を強化しなければならなかった。

- **reinforce** 動 強化する
- **suspend** 動 一時停止する
- **confirm** 動 確認する
- **reassure** 動 安心させる

> reinforceの語源はre（強調）+ in（中に）+ force（力）=中に力を入れて強くする=強化する

UNIT 77 制限・禁止

Chapter4 Society

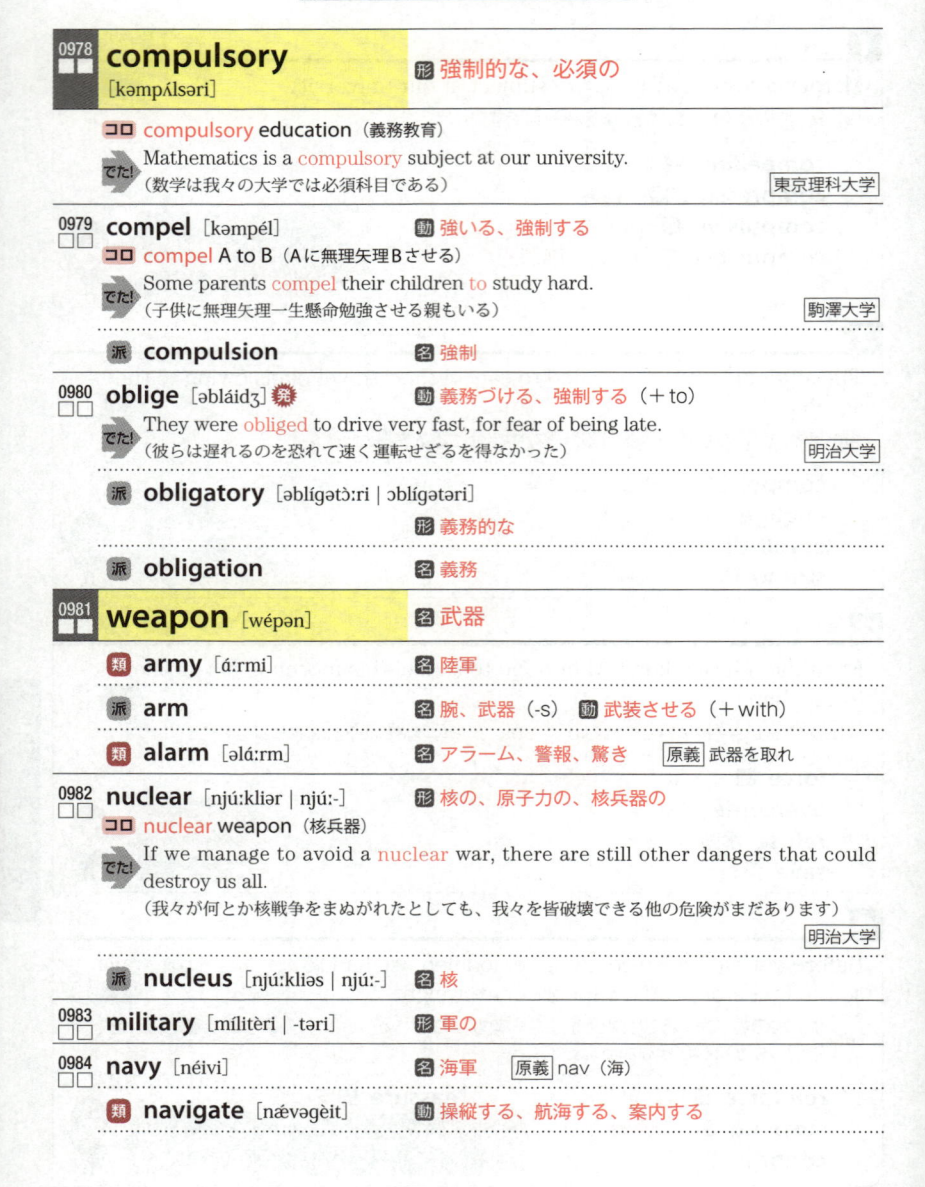

## STEP 3 連鎖式に語彙を増やす 🎧77

### 0978 compulsory [kəmpʌ́lsəri] 形 強制的な、必須の
- コロ compulsory education（義務教育）
- でた! Mathematics is a compulsory subject at our university.
（数学は我々の大学では必須科目である） 〔東京理科大学〕

### 0979 compel [kəmpél] 動 強いる、強制する
- コロ compel A to B（Aに無理矢理Bさせる）
- でた! Some parents compel their children to study hard.
（子供に無理矢理一生懸命勉強させる親もいる） 〔駒澤大学〕

派 **compulsion** 名 強制

### 0980 oblige [əbláidʒ] 動 義務づける、強制する（+ to）
- でた! They were obliged to drive very fast, for fear of being late.
（彼らは遅れるのを恐れて速く運転せざるを得なかった） 〔明治大学〕

派 **obligatory** [əblígətɔ̀:ri | ɔblígətəri] 形 義務的な

派 **obligation** 名 義務

### 0981 weapon [wépən] 名 武器

類 **army** [ɑ́:rmi] 名 陸軍

派 **arm** 名 腕、武器（-s） 動 武装させる（+ with）

類 **alarm** [əlɑ́:rm] 名 アラーム、警報、驚き 〔原義〕武器を取れ

### 0982 nuclear [njú:kliər | njú:-] 形 核の、原子力の、核兵器の
- コロ nuclear weapon（核兵器）
- でた! If we manage to avoid a nuclear war, there are still other dangers that could destroy us all.
（我々が何とか核戦争をまぬがれたとしても、我々を皆破壊できる他の危険がまだあります） 〔明治大学〕

派 **nucleus** [njú:kliəs | njú:-] 名 核

### 0983 military [mílitèri | -təri] 形 軍の

### 0984 navy [néivi] 名 海軍 〔原義〕nav（海）

類 **navigate** [nǽvəgèit] 動 操縦する、航海する、案内する

| 派 **navigation** | 名 航海、車の誘導 |

0985 **soldier** [sóuldʒər] 　　名 軍人

---

• 語源 fort, force（力）

0986 **force** [fɔ́:rs] 　　名 力　動 強制的にさせる

でた! Students were bored because the teacher just forced them to learn grammar and vocabulary.
（ただ単に文法と語彙を学ぶ事を強制させられたので、生徒はうんざりしていた）　上智大学

コロ force A to B（Aに強制的にBさせる）　コロ air force（空軍）

| 派 **forces** | 名 軍事力 |

コロ armed forces（軍隊）

| 派 **forcible** | 形 強制的な |

0987 **enforce** [infɔ́:rs] 　　動 法律を施行する、強要する

でた! The Romans had conquered England and enforced using Latin.
（古代ローマ人はイギリスを征服し、ラテン語の使用を強要した）　TOEFL

| 派 **enforcement** | 名 法律の施行 |

0988 **reinforce** [rì:infɔ́:rs] 　　動 強化する

| 派 **reinforcement** | 名 強化、補強 |

0989 **effort** [éfərt] 　　名 努力

コロ make an effort（努力する）

でた! They will not give up their efforts until they have solved the problem.
（彼らは問題を解決するまでずっと努力することを諦めない）　立教大学

| 類 **endeavor** [indévər] | 動 努力する　名 努力 |

0990 **comfort** [kʌ́mfərt] 　　名 快適さ、慰め　動 慰める

| 派 **comfortable** [kʌ́mfərtəbl] ア | 形 心地よい |

コロ feel comfortable（気持ちがいい）

| 反 **uncomfortable** | 形 居心地が悪い |

UNIT 77　制限・禁止

Chapter4 Society

# UNIT 78 廃止・停止

**STEP 1** 過去問を解く

## 1

Because of the new anti smoking law, cigarette companies must (　　) all of their advertisements from sports stadiums.

英語検定2級

1. return
2. release
3. remove
4. reveal

## 2

These ridiculous rules should have been <u>done away with</u> years ago.

中央大学

1. abolished
2. improved
3. organized
4. reformed

## 3

To a large extent slavery was (　　) in the last century.

慶應義塾大学

1. diminished
2. destroyed
3. expired
4. abolished

## 4

The best player in our rugby team was (　　) for three games for fighting.

上智大学

1. accused
2. postponed
3. suspected
4. suspended

## STEP 2 正解を見抜く

### 1

Because of the new anti smoking law, cigarette companies must remove all of their advertisements from sports stadiums. 正解 ③

訳 新しい喫煙反対の法律のせいで、タバコ会社はスポーツのスタジアムから全ての広告を取り除かなければならない。

- **return** 動 戻る
- **remove** 動 取り除く
- **reveal** 動 明らかにする
- **release** 動 解放する

removeの語源はre（再び）+ move（動かす）＝一度置いた物を再び動かす＝取り除く

### 2

These ridiculous rules should have been abolished years ago. 正解 ①

訳 これらのバカげた規則は何年も前に廃止されるべきだった。

- **abolish** 動 廃止する
- **improve** 動 改善する
- **organize** 動 組織する
- **reform** 動 改革する

do away with A（Aを廃止する）

### 3

To a large extent slavery was abolished in the last century. 正解 ④

訳 奴隷制度は前世紀にある程度まで廃止された。

- **diminish** 動 減らす
- **destroy** 動 壊す
- **expire** 動 （期限が）切れる
- **abolish** 動 廃止する

do away with A（Aを廃止する）という表現も同時に覚えておきましょう

### 4

The best player in our rugby team was suspended for three games for fighting. 正解 ④

訳 我々のチームで最高の選手が乱闘により3試合の出場停止処分となった。

- **accuse** 動 責める
- **postpone** 動 延期する
- **suspect** 動 疑う
- **suspend** 動 一時停止する

UNIT 78 廃止・停止

Chapter4 Society

## STEP 3 連鎖式に語彙を増やす 78

### 0991 remove [rimú:v] 動 取り除く
- remove a stain (しみを取る)
- 派 removal 名 除去

### 0992 exclude [iksklú:d] 動 除外する　原義 ex (外に) + clud (閉める)
でた! We cannot exclude the possibility that civil war will break out in that country.
(我々はその国で内戦が起こる可能性を排除できない) 学習院大学

- 派 exclusive 形 排他的な、独占的な
- leave out (除外する)
- rule out (除外する、否定する)

でた! The politician ruled out the possibility of war.
(その政治家は戦争の可能性を否定した) 青山学院大学

- 派 exclusion 名 除外

### 0993 abolish [əbáliʃ | əbɔ́l-] 動 廃止する
でた! They abolished the interview test last year.
(彼らは面接試験を去年廃止した) 立命館大学

- 派 abolition 名 廃止
- abolition of the death penalty (死刑の廃止)
- do away with (廃止する)

でた! The government finally did away with the law.
(政府は最終的にその法律を廃止した) 名城大学

### 0994 suspend [səspénd] 動 一時停止する
原義 sus (下に) + pend (ぶら下がる)

でた! The hospital did not accept the patient's desire to suspend all medical treatment.
(全ての治療を一時中止したいという患者の要望を病院側は受け入れなかった) 東京大学

- 派 suspension 名 一時停止

### 0995 cease [sí:s] 動 止める
でた! If not kept to oneself, a secret will cease to be one.
(誰にも言わないようにしなければ、秘密は秘密でなくなる) 明治学院大学

- 類 ceaseless 形 絶え間ない

### 0996 halt [hɔ́:lt] 動 停止する
- bring A to a halt (Aを中止させる)

でた! Today the train service was halted due to a strike.
(ストライキのせいで、今日の電車の運行は停止した) 中央大学

## coffee break ☕ センター試験廃止？ TOEFL導入？

　6年間毎日のように英語の教科書を開いて、辞書を引いたのに全く英語が話せない。難しい単語をたくさん知っているけど使えない。皆さんはこのようなことを考えた事はありますか？

　これまでの英語教育は「文法訳読式」という英語を日本語に訳す作業が目的でした。センター試験ではListeningとReadingの2技能、つまり受動的技能のみが求められていました。先生が一方的に話し、生徒は黙って聞くというスタイルは500年前から変わっていません。

　そこで文部科学省はTOEFL導入を検討するという提言をしました。TOEFLはアメリカで作られた世界で通用する英語能力試験でListening、Reading、Speaking、Writingの4技能が求められます。2技能のみを測る英語検定やTOEICは世界では認識されていません。このTOEFLというテストが日本の大学入試に代替するものになると、日本の教育全体が変わらなければなりません。

　これからの国際社会では「英語での自己表現力」が必要とされます。この単語帳を活用してインプットだけではなくアウトプットに繋がる学習を心掛けましょう。

# UNIT 79 国境・区別

## STEP 1 過去問を解く

### 1

National ( ) between countries are becoming less and less meaningful in this global economy.

拓殖大学

1. arguments
2. boundaries
3. exports
4. relations

### 2

Tim really respects his parents because they always try to make a clear ( ) between right and wrong.

英語検定2級

1. hesitation
2. evolution
3. distinction
4. extinction

### 3

Many people find it difficult to ( ) a Canadian accent from an American one.

立命館大学

1. absorb
2. define
3. distinguish
4. predict

### 4

The problem is that the American Indian culture is in danger of becoming ( ).

上智大学

1. distinct
2. distinguished
3. definite
4. infinite
5. extinct

## STEP 2 正解を見抜く

### 1

National boundaries between countries are becoming less and less meaningful in this global economy.  **正解 ②**

訳 国家間の国境は、この世界経済においてますます重要ではなくなっています。

- **argument** 名議論
- **boundary** 名国境線
- **export** 名輸出
- **relation** 名関係

### 2

Tim really respects his parents because they always try to make a clear distinction between right and wrong.  **正解 ③**

訳 トムの両親はいつも良い悪いの明瞭な区別をしようとするので、トムは両親を尊敬しています。

- **hesitation** 名ためらい
- **distinction** 名区別
- **evolution** 名進化
- **extinction** 名消滅

### 3

Many people find it difficult to distinguish a Canadian accent from an American one.  **正解 ③**

訳 多くの人々はカナダのアクセントとアメリカのアクセントを区別するのが難しいとわかる。

- **absorb** 動吸収する
- **distinguish** 動区別する
- **define** 動定義する
- **predict** 動予言する

distinguish A from B (AとBを区別する) = tell A from B

### 4

The problem is that the American Indian culture is in danger of becoming extinct.  **正解 ⑤**

訳 問題はアメリカンインディアンの文化が絶滅の危機に瀕しているということだ。

- **distinct** 形異なった
- **definite** 形明確な
- **infinite** 形無限の
- **extinct** 形絶滅した
- **distinguished** 形顕著な

extinct (消えた、絶滅した)
extinct species (絶滅危惧種)

Chapter4 Society

## STEP 3 連鎖式に語彙を増やす 79

### 0997 border [bɔ́ːrdər]
名 線

- 派 **boundary** [báundəri] 名 境界線
- コロ cross a boundary(境界を越える)
- 類 **line** [láin] 名 線、境界線
- 類 **queue** [kjúː] 発 名 線、順番待ちの列《英》

### 0998 separate [sépərèit]
動 結びついているものを分ける、分かれる、切り離す、別居する

- コロ separate A from B(BをAから引き離す)
- 派 **separately** 副 別々に

### 0999 divide [diváid]
動 集合体を分ける、割り算する

- コロ divide A into B(AをBにわける)
- 派 **division** 名 分割、区分、部門
- 類 **individual** [ìndəvídʒuəl] 名 個人 形 個々の

### 1000 share [ʃéər]
動 共有する 名 分け前

- コロ share A with B(AをBと共有する)

### 1001 discriminate [diskrímənèit]
動 差別する

- 派 **discrimination** 名 差別
- コロ racial discrimination(人種差別)
- でた! Many women claim that there is a lot of discrimination against women.
(多くの女性が女性に対する差別があると主張している) 学習院大学

### 1002 discern [disə́ːrn | -zə́ːrn]
動 見極める、識別する

- でた! Customers who can discern wine select better vintages.
(ワインを見極められる消費者は良いヴィンテージものを選ぶ) 上智大学
- 派 **discerning** 形 識別力のある

334

- 語源 stinct sting（刺す）

## 1003 stick [stík]
名 杖　動 突き刺す　活 stick-stuck-stuck

- stick to A（Aに固執する）　be stuck（行き詰まっている）
- stick to the point（論点から逸れない）
- The nail that sticks out gets hit with the hammer.（出る杭は打たれる）

派 **sticky**　形 くっつく、粘着性の

## 1004 distinguish [distíŋgwiʃ]
動 区別する

- distinguish A from B（AとBを区別する）＝ tell A from B
- Historians must distinguish facts and fictions.
（歴史家は事実と虚構を区別しなければならない）　東京外国語大学

派 **distinguished**　形 顕著な、著名な
- distinguished scholar（著名な学者）

派 **distinct**　形 別の、明瞭な

派 **distinctive**　形 独特の

派 **distinction**　名 区別
- make a clear distinction（明瞭な区別をする）
- There is a strong distinction made between friends and acquaintances.
（友達と知り合いの間には明確な区別がある）　立命館大学

## 1005 extinguish [ikstíŋgwiʃ]
動 消す、消滅させる

- put out A（Aを消す）

派 **extinction**　名 消滅、廃止
- Nearly 20,000 species of animals and plants are considered high risks for extinction in the wild.
（約20,000種もの動物と植物は、野生で高い消滅の危険性があると考えられている）　早稲田大学

派 **extinct** [ikstíŋkt]　形 消滅した、絶滅した
- extinct species（絶滅危惧種）
- Well over half of all these languages will become extinct.
（これら全ての言語の半分を遥かに超えるものが消滅するだろう）　東京大学

派 **extinguisher**　名 消火器

UNIT 79　国境・区別

Chapter4 Society

# UNIT 80 所有・占領

**STEP 1 過去問を解く**

## 1

The building was (     ) by its owners.

1. depressed
2. impressed
3. occupied
4. prevented

立命館大学

## 2

Greg (     ) all the qualities needed to be a good salesman. He has a great memory for names and loves talking to people.

英語検定2級

1. doubts
2. introduces
3. possesses
4. describes

## 3

An (     ) is a large area of land which is owned by one person, family, or organization.

上智大学

1. evidence
2. expense
3. estate
4. explosion

## 4

English ranks as the second most (     ) language in the entire world.

関西外国語大学

1. suspicious
2. colloquial
3. dominant
4. vulgar

## STEP 2 正解を見抜く

### 1

The building was occupied by its owners. 　　正解 ③

**訳** その建物は所有者によって使用されている。

- **depress** 動 意気消沈させる
- **impress** 動 印象付ける
- **occupy** 動 占領する
- **prevent** 動 妨げる

### 2

Greg possesses all the qualities needed to be a good salesman. He has a great memory for names and loves talking to people. 　　正解 ③

**訳** グレッグは優秀なセールスマンになるために必要な全ての資格を持っている。彼は人の名前の記憶力に優れ、人と話すのが好きです。

- **doubt** 動 疑う
- **possess** 動 所有する
- **introduce** 動 紹介する、導入する
- **describe** 動 描写する

### 3

An estate is a large area of land which is owned by one person, family, or organization. 　　正解 ③

**訳** 所有地とは、1人、家族、または組織によって所有されている土地の広い地域です。

- **evidence** 名 証拠
- **expense** 名 経費
- **estate** 名 所有地
- **explosion** 名 爆発

real estateは「不動産」

### 4

English ranks as the second most dominant language in the entire world. 　　正解 ③

**訳** 英語は全世界で2番目に優勢な言語である。

- **suspicious** 形 疑い深い
- **colloquial** 形 口語の
- **dominant** 形 優勢な
- **vulgar** 形 卑しい

dominantのdomの語源は「家」「主人」「支配」の3つがあります

UNIT 80　所有・占領

Chapter4 Society

## STEP 3 連鎖式に語彙を増やす 🎧80

**1006 occupy** [ákjupài | ɔ́k-] 動 占領する

**1007 派 occupied** 形 占領されている、使用中の　※空室はvacant
でた! That restroom is occupied.（あのトイレは使用中です）
コロ take up（場所を取る、問題を取り上げる）
でた! We bought a grand piano which took up half of our living room.
（我々は居間の半分の場所を取るグランドピアノを買った） 中央大学

派 **occupation** 名 占領、職業

**1008 possess** [pəzés] 動 所有する
コロ be possessed of A（Aを所有している）　コロ be possessed by A（Aにとりつかれている）

派 **possession** 名 所有
でた! The word "bilingual" primarily descries someone with the possession of two languages.
（バイリンガルという単語は主に２つの言語を操る人のことを言います） 同志社大学

**1009 own** [óun] 動 所有する

**1010** でた! A possession is an object that you own.
（所有とはあなたが持っている物のことをいいます） TOEFL

派 **owner** 名 所有者

**1011 belong** [bilɔ́ːŋ, -láŋ | -lɔ́ŋ] 動 所有する、所属する（＋to）
Does this book belong to you?
（この本はあなたの物ですか） 早稲田大学

派 **belongings** 名 所有物、身の回り品
でた! Her grandmother's silver bracelet was one of her most precious belongings.
（彼女のおばあちゃんのシルバーのブレスレットは彼女の最も貴重な所有物の一つである） 立命館大学

**1012 estate** [istéit] 名 財産、地所
コロ real estate（不動産）

**1013 property** [prápərti | prɔ́p-] 名 財産、所有地、特性
コロ private property（私有地）　コロ obtain property（物件を手に入れる）

**1014 monopoly** [mənápəli | -nɔ́p-] 名 独占

派 **monopolize** 動 独占する

• 語源 dom（家）

## 1015 dominate
[dámənèit | dɔ́m-]

動 支配する

でた! The world will be dominated by just two languages.
（世界はたった2つの言語によって支配されるだろう） 東京大学

派 **dominant** 形 支配的な、優勢な
でた! Each player has a dominant strategy.
（各プレイヤーに卓越した戦略がある） 東京外語大学

派 **domination** 名 支配、君臨、優位

派 **dominance** 名 優越、優勢

## 1016 domestic [dəméstik]

形 家庭内の、国内の

コロ domestic violence（家庭内暴力、DV）
でた! The law forbids people to smoke on domestic air flights.
（その法律は国内便での喫煙を禁じている） 成蹊大学

派 **domesticate** 動 飼いならす

反 **foreign** [fɔ́:rən, fɑ́r- | fɔ́r-] 形 外国の
でた! He compares domestic and foreign products.
（彼は国産と外国産の商品を比べている） TOEFL

類 **overseas** [óuvərsí:z] 形 外国の 副 外国に

類 **alien** [éiljən | -liən] 名 外国人、宇宙人、エイリアン 形 外国の

## 1017 dormitory
[dɔ́:rmətɔ̀:ri | -təri]

名 寄宿舎、寮《米》

1018 でた! In a dormitory, you usually have to share a room, while off-campus housing can be more private and less noisy.
（寄宿舎では通常部屋をシェアしなければならないが、一方校外の住宅ではより私的で閑静です） 明治大学

UNIT 80 所有・占領

Chapter4 Society

## coffee break ☕ 人生の転機をもたらしたオーストラリア留学

　高校2年の夏、私は胸を躍らせながら西オーストラリアのパースに留学しました。ホームステイ先はごく一般的なオーストラリアの一軒家。新婚の夫婦と2歳の娘が暮らしていて、私は机とベッドが備え付けられた6畳程のシンプルな部屋に案内されました。そして家のルールを一通り説明された時から、予想外の悲劇が始まりました。

　家にあるトイレットペーパーは使ってはいけない、つまり自分で用意するということ。シャワーは5分以内、冷蔵庫は使用禁止、18時以降は自分の部屋からの外出禁止。そんな過酷なルールでした。近くのスーパーに生活用品を買いに行き、机の下にペットボトルの水を蓄えて生活しました。親しくなるために色々なことを尋ねるように心掛けました。庭にゴルフクラブがあったのでDo you play golf?と聞くと、返事はたったひとことNo.。Have you been to Japan? の質問にもNo.というだけ。私はしだいに英語を使うことに恐怖心すら抱くようになりました。

　夕方になるとホストマザーが一人掛けのキッチンカウンターに夕食を用意してくれます。しかし、それは茹でただけの味がないマカロニだったり、湿気たポテトチップスにマヨネーズといったものでした。立ったまま食べさせられ、我慢して飲み込むしかなかった私を見たホストファミリーが、どこか嬉しそうな顔だったのを覚えています。食事を終え、Thank you.と言ってシンクに戻し食器を洗い部屋に帰ろうとすると、You are naughty.と言われました。naughtyという単語を知らなかった私はどう対応すればいいのか分かりません。ただ、それが良い言葉ではないことは分かりました。タオルを貸していただけますかと尋ねると、床から足ふきマットを拾い上げ渡される始末。逃げ出したい気持ちでいっぱいになりました。しかし多額の留学費を支払ってくれた両親には本当のことを伝えられず、3週間が過ぎていきます。

　帰国3日前となった夜のこと。このまま帰国するわけにはいかない、という気持ちで私は勇気を奮い起こしました。自分が感じてきた思いを全てホストファミリーにぶつけたのです。そして生い立ちや留学への思い、自分の家族のことや今までの人生について。笑顔で話せる関係を作るために朝までかかりました。すると彼らも日本人に対して偏見を持っていたと、青ざめた顔で打ち明かしてくれました。

　残りの3日間は別世界へと一変しました。車に乗ってゴルフに連れて行ってもらったり、レストランで外食したり。パースの観光名所にも連れていってもらいました。夜はホストファミリーと席を囲んで食事するようになりました。

　帰国の前日、両親から驚いた様子で1本の電話がありました。ホストファーザーが私の両親に対し謝罪のメールを送っていたのです。海外での楽しい生活を満喫していると思い込んでいた両親はそれを見て驚いたに違いありません。

　日本人として違った文化、価値観をもった人と異なる言語を使ったコミュニケーションの重要性を伝えていかなければ。成田空港に着いた瞬間に私がまず感じたことでした。海外に出れば、誰もが日本代表、日の丸を背負います。言語の重要性を教えてくれたこの貴重な体験に感謝しています。

※naughtyは「言うことを聞かない、いたずらっ子」という意味です

# Chapter 5
# Intention

# UNIT 81 選択・優先

**STEP 1** 過去問を解く

## 1

When I missed the last bus, I had no (　　) but to take a taxi.

センター試験

1. chance
2. choice
3. method
4. possibility

## 2

A: Were you chosen as a member of the basketball team, Alice?
B: I'm not sure yet. The final (　　) is tomorrow.

英語検定2級

1. selection
2. variety
3. absence
4. creation

## 3

He can never hide his strong (　　) for sweets.

中央大学

1. conference
2. interference
3. preference
4. reference

## 4

Our program always places the highest (　　) on the health, safety and security of our students.

立教大学

1. premier
2. premise
3. primary
4. priority

## STEP 2 正解を見抜く

### 1

When I missed the last bus, I had no choice but to take a taxi. 　正解 ②

訳　最終バスを逃したとき、タクシーに乗るしかなかった。

- **chance** 名 機会
- **choice** 名 選択
- **method** 名 方法
- **possibility** 名 可能性

> have no choice but to A（Aするしかない）

### 2

A: Were you chosen as a member of the basketball team, Alice?
B: I'm not sure yet. The final selection is tomorrow. 　正解 ①

訳　A：アリス、君はバスケットボールチームのメンバーに選ばれたんですか。
B：まだわかりません。最終選考は明日です。

- **selection** 名 選択
- **variety** 名 多様性
- **absence** 名 欠席
- **creation** 名 創造

> selectionは適切なものを慎重に考えて選ぶ

### 3

He can never hide his strong preference for sweets. 　正解 ③

訳　彼は甘いものが大好きだということを隠す事ができない。

- **conference** 名 会議
- **interference** 名 邪魔
- **preference** 名 好み
- **reference** 名 参照

> preferの語源はpre（前に）+ fer（運ぶ）=先にやりたい=好む

### 4

Our program always places the highest priority on the health, safety and security of our students. 　正解 ④

訳　私たちのプログラムはいつも私たちの学生の健康、安全、およびセキュリティに最も高い優先を置きます。

- **premier** 名 首相
- **premise** 名 前提
- **primary** 名 第一の事
- **priority** 名 優先

> priority seat（優先席）で覚えましょう

UNIT 81　選択・優先

Chapter5 Intention

## STEP 3 連鎖式に語彙を増やす 81

● 語源 lect（選ぶ）

**1019 select** [silékt]　動（適切なものを慎重に考えて）選ぶ
原義 se（分離）＋ lect（選ぶ）

派 **selection**　名 選択
コロ natural selection（自然淘汰）

**1020 choose** [tʃúːz]　動（複数の中から意志によって）選ぶ

派 **choice**　名 選択
コロ have no choice but to A（Aするしかない）
でた! The president had no choice but to resign.
（大統領は辞任するより仕方なかった）　中央大学

**1021 option** [ápʃən | ɔ́p-]　名 選択

派 **opt**　動 選ぶ

派 **optional**　形 選択の、任意の

**1022 collect** [kəlékt]　動（目的に沿って取捨選択しながら）集める
原義 co（共に）＋ lect（選ぶ）

派 **collection**　名 収集、集積
でた! Science is far more than a collection of facts and methods.
（科学とは単に事実と方法の集積では決してない）　センター試験

派 **collective**　形 集合的な、集団の
コロ collective noun（集合名詞）

**1023 elect** [ilékt]　動 投票によって選び出す

でた! A system in which the people elect their own representatives or lawmakers is called a "democracy."
（民衆が代議士や議員を選出する制度は「民主主義」と呼ばれる）　香川大学

派 **election**　名 選挙

**1024 neglect** [niglékt]　動 やるべきことを無視する、怠る
原義 neg（否定）＋ lect（選ぶ）

でた! The significance of these agricultural developments cannot be neglected.
（このような農業の発展の意義は無視できない）　東京大学

派 **negligent**　形 怠慢な

派 **negligence**　名 怠慢

## 1025 lecture [léktʃər]　名 講義、レクチャー　動 講義する、説教する

- host a series of lectures （一連の講義を主催する）
- でた! What is the main purpose of the lecture?
  （講義の主な目的は何ですか） TOEFL

> 大学のlecture（講義）は自ら選択して受講するもの。高校までのclass（クラス）の語源は「分類」なので振り分けられて作られる物です。

## 1026 legend [lédʒənd]　名 伝説

- でた! The Beauty and Beast legend is one of the classic examples.
  （美女と野獣の伝説は典型的な例の一つです） 横浜市立大学

- 派 legendary　形 伝説の、伝説的な

## 1027 designate [dézignèit]　動 指定する、指名する、任命する

- 派 designation　名 指定、指名、任命

## 1028 priority [praiɔ́ːrəti | -ɔ́r-]　名 優先

- priority seat （優先席）
- でた! The company gives high priority to improved production methods.
  （会社は生産方法の改善を最も優先している） 中央大学

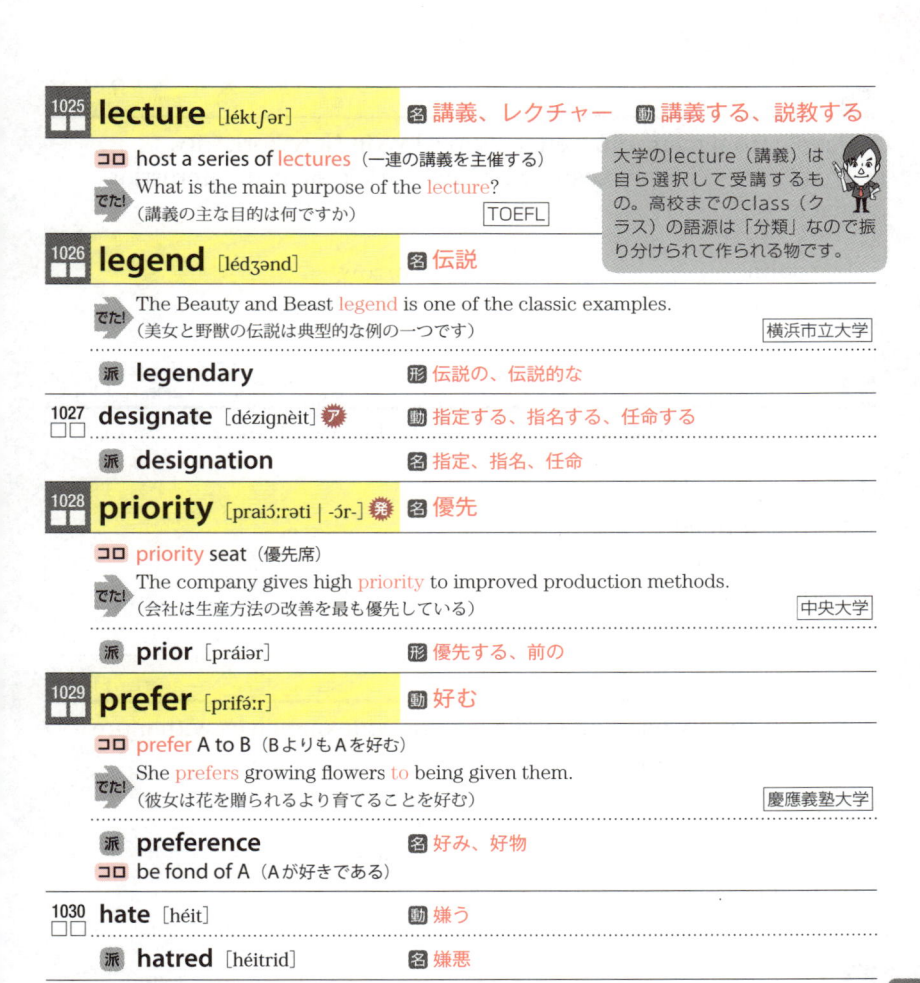

- 派 prior [práiər]　形 優先する、前の

## 1029 prefer [prifə́ːr]　動 好む

- prefer A to B （BよりもAを好む）
- でた! She prefers growing flowers to being given them.
  （彼女は花を贈られるより育てることを好む） 慶應義塾大学

- 派 preference　名 好み、好物
- be fond of A （Aが好きである）

## 1030 hate [héit]　動 嫌う

- 派 hatred [héitrid]　名 嫌悪

---

**思考の時間**　実際に入試で問われた内容です。あなたはどう答えますか？

孤島に持って行きたい３つのもの。　青山学院大学

UNIT 81　選択・優先

Chapter5 Intention　345

# UNIT 82 変化・変形

**STEP 1 過去問を解く**

## 1

People from many different cultures live in New York City. This ( ) is one reason why New York is such an interesting place.

英語検定2級

1. routine
2. sorrow
3. diversity
4. forecast

## 2

After it was cleaned and painted, the little cabin looked ( ).

南山大学

1. transported
2. transformed
3. transferred
4. translated

## 3

We also <u>modify</u> our surroundings to provide ourselves with more space and more food.

日本大学

1. accept
2. change
3. select
4. move
5. describe

## 4

The new foods discovered by Columbus <u>altered</u> the fates of nations and strengthened a growing sense of national identity.

上智大学

1. decided
2. increased
3. enriched
4. changed

## STEP 2 正解を見抜く

### 1

People from many different cultures live in New York City. This diversity is one reason why New York is such an interesting place.

正解 ③

**訳** 多くの異なった文化からの人々がニューヨークには住んでいる。この多様性はニューヨークがそのようにおもしろい場所である一つの理由である。

- **routine** 名日課
- **diversity** 名多様性
- **sorrow** 名悲しみ
- **forecast** 名予報

### 2

After it was cleaned and painted, the little cabin looked transformed.

正解 ②

**訳** 掃除してペンキを塗り替えたら、その小屋は一変した。

- **transport** 動輸送する
- **transform** 動変形させる
- **transfer** 動移す
- **translate** 動翻訳する

transformの語源はtrans（横切る）＋form（形作る）＝変形させる

### 3

We also change our surroundings to provide ourselves with more space and more food.

正解 ②

**訳** 我々はより多くの空間や食料を得るために身の回りの環境も変えている。

- **accept** 動受け入れる
- **select** 動選択する
- **describe** 動描写する
- **change** 動変える
- **move** 動動く

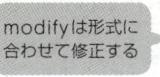

modifyは形式に合わせて修正する

### 4

The new foods discovered by Columbus changed the fates of nations and strengthened a growing sense of national identity.

正解 ④

**訳** コロンブスが発見した新しい食物は、諸国の運命を変え、増大しつつあった国家のアイデンティティという意識を強化した。

- **decide** 動決める
- **enrich** 動豊かにする
- **increase** 動増える
- **change** 動変える

alterは部分的に変化させる

UNIT 82 変化・変形

Chapter5 Intention

## STEP 3 連鎖式に語彙を増やす 82

● 語源 verse（回転）

### 1031 diversity [divə́ːrsəti | dai-] 名 多様性

コロ a diversity of A（様々なA）

でた! It is part of the reason for the diversity within the family of relationships called friendship.
（それは友情と呼ばれる関係の集団内における多様性の理由の一部である） 一橋大学

派 diversify — 動 多様化させる

派 diverse — 形 多様化した

派 biodiversity — 名 生物多様性

でた! The earth supports biodiversity ranging from microbes to huge animals and plants.
（地球は微生物から巨大な動物、そして植物に至る幅広い生物多様性を支えている） 法政大学

### 1032 conversation [kànvərséiʃən | kɔ̀n-] 名 会話

con（共に）+ verse（回転）

でた! Their conversation carried on for about an hour.
（彼らの会話は約一時間続いた） 横浜市立大学

派 converse — 動 会話をする

### 1033 reverse [rivə́ːrs] 名 逆　形 逆の　動 逆にさせる

コロ reverse the decision（判決を覆す）

派 reversible — 形 逆にできる

### 1034 advertise [ǽdvərtàiz] 動 広告する、宣伝する

でた! It is no longer permitted to advertise cigarettes on television.
（テレビでタバコの宣伝をすることはもはや許されていない） 中央大学

派 advertisement — 名 広告、宣伝　※省略ads

### 1035 revolution [rèvəlúːʃən] 名 革命、回転、公転

でた! In one year, Earth makes one revolution around the sun.
（1年で地球は太陽のまわりを一周する） 早稲田大学

派 revolve — 動 回転する

派 revolutionary — 形 革命の、画期的な

でた! The roof is the most revolutionary part of the design.
（屋根はデザインの最も画期的な部分である） TOEFL

## 1036 rotation [routéiʃən] 　名 自転

派 rotate 　動 自転する

## 1037 variety [vəráiəti] 　名 多様性

コロ a variety of A（様々なA）

でた! Children need a variety of toys to play with.
（子供は多種多様なおもちゃが必要である） 　明治大学

派 vary [véəri] 発 　動 段階的に変化する、異なる

派 various 　形 様々な

でた! There are various ways to solve problems.
（問題を解くためには様々な方法がある） 　TOEFL

## 1038 transform [trænsfɔ́:rm] 　動 根本的に変える

コロ transform A into B（AをBに変形させる）

でた! Designers transform raw material into a visually appealing product.
（デザイナーは素材を視覚的に訴える製品に変える） 　早稲田大学

派 transformation 　名 変形

## 1039 alter [ɔ́:ltər] 発 　動 部分的に変化する

でた! Industrialization altered the pace of people's lives.
（工業化が人々の生活ペースを変えた） 　慶應義塾大学

派 alternative [ɔ:ltə́:rnətiv, æl- | ɔ:l-] 発 　形 二者択一の、代わりとなる（＋to）　名 二者択一

コロ an alternative plan（代案）

でた! In India, English is a vital alternative language.
（インドでは、英語は不可欠な代替言語である） 　早稲田大学

派 alternate [ɔ́:ltərnèit, æl- | ɔ́:l-] 　形 交互の

派 alternately 　副 交互に

類 exchange [ikstʃéindʒ] 　動 全く別のものと交換する

## 1040 modify [mάdəfài | mɔ́d-] 　動 組み替える、部分修正する

派 modification 　名 組み替え、修正

コロ genetic modification（遺伝子組み換え）

## 1041 substitute [sʌ́bstətjù:t | -tjù:t] ア 　動 代わりに用いる、代理をする　名 代理　形 代理の

コロ substitute A for B（AをBの代わりに用いる）

派 substitution 　名 代理

# UNIT 83 説得・援助　STEP 1 過去問を解く

## 1

To "(　　)" means to cause someone to do something by reasoning, arguing, or begging.

センター試験

1. command
2. direct
3. order
4. persuade

## 2

The doctor (　　) that the patient be released.

関西外国語大学

1. declined
2. described
3. urged
4. complicated

## 3

To (　　) rock-loving youngsters to great music, some classical music maeketers are creating innovative music videos.

慶應義塾大学

1. avoid
2. lure
3. let
4. make

## 4

The United Nations (　　) many coutries damaged by the war.

関西学院大学

1. assisted
2. formed
3. held
4. secured

## STEP 2 正解を見抜く

### 1

To "persuade" means to cause someone to do something by reasoning, arguing, or begging. 正解 ④

**訳** 説得するということは理由付けし、議論し、お願いして誰かに何かをさせることを意味する。

- **command** 動 命じる
- **order** 動 命じる
- **direct** 動 指導する
- **persuade** 動 説得する

### 2

The doctor urged that the patient be released. 正解 ③

**訳** 医者は患者が退院するように促した。

- **decline** 動 断る
- **describe** 動 記述する
- **urge** 動 促す
- **complicate** 動 複雑にする

### 3

To lure rock-loving youngsters to great music, some classical music marketers are creating innovative music videos. 正解 ②

**訳** ロックを好む若者を偉大な音楽に誘惑するために、クラシック音楽のマーケティングを行う人の中には革新的なミュージック・ビデオを作っている人もいる。

- **avoid** 動 避ける
- **let** 動 させる
- **lure** 動 誘惑する
- **make** 動 作る

### 4

The United Nations assisted many coutries damaged by the war. 正解 ①

**訳** 国際連合は、戦争の被害を受けた多くの国を援助した。

- **assist** 動 援助する
- **form** 動 形成する
- **hold** 動 保つ
- **secure** 動 安全にする

> assistの語源はas（近くに）＋sist（立つ）＝近くに立って助ける＝援助する

UNIT 83　説得・援助

Chapter5 Intention

## STEP 3 連鎖式に語彙を増やす 83

### 1042 **persuade** [pərswéid] 発 動 説得する
- コロ persuade A into B（Aに説得してBさせる）
- でた! I tried to persuade her to quit smoking.
（私は彼女を説得して喫煙を止めさせようとした） 近畿大学
- 派 **persuasion** 名 説得

### 1043 **convince** [kənvíns] 動 納得させる、確信させる
- コロ convince A of B（AにBを確信させる）
- でた! He tried to convince them of his innocence in vain.
（彼は彼らに自分の無実を信じさせようとしたが、無駄に終わった） 立命館大学
- 派 **convincing** 形 説得力のある、納得のいく

### 1044 **urge** [ə́ːrdʒ] 発 動 促す
- コロ urge A to B（AにBするように促す）
- でた! The government is urging people to be economical with water.
（政府は人々に水に対して節約するように促している） 法政大学
- 派 **urgent** [ə́ːrdʒənt] 形 緊急の
  - コロ urgent business（緊急の仕事）
  - でた! Global warming is an urgent issue for us to tackle.
（地球温暖化は我々が取り組むべき緊急の問題である） 早稲田大学
- 派 **urgency** 名 緊急

### 1045 **lure** [lúər | ljúə] 動 誘惑する、そそのかす 名 魅力、魚釣りのルアー
- でた! Many nations promote tourism to lure foreign currency.
（多くの国家は外貨を引き寄せるために旅行事業を促進している） TOEFL

### 1046 **induce** [indjúːs | -djúːs] 動 説得する 原義 in（中に）＋duce（導く）
- コロ induce A to B（BするようにAを説得する）
- 派 **inducement** 名 誘惑、犯罪の動機
- 派 **induction** 名 誘導

### 1047 **prompt** [prámpt | prɔ́mpt] 動 誘発する 形 応答・行動が機敏な
- コロ prompt reply（即答）
- 派 **promptly** 副 迅速に、即座に
- コロ talk A into B（Aを説得してBさせる）
- コロ ask A to B（AにBするように頼む）

## 1048 emerge [ímɚ́ːrdʒ]
**動** 出てくる、現れる

でた! The very first electric computer emerged in the 1940s.
（一番初めの電気式コンピュータは1940年代に現れた） 明治大学

**派** emergency **名** 緊急
コロ in case of emergency（緊急時には）

でた! In America, you dial 911 in the case of an emergency.
（アメリカでは、非常時の場合911にダイヤルします） 上智大学

**派** emergent **形** 緊急の

**派** emergence **名** 出現

## 1049 merge [mɚ́ːrdʒ]
**動** 合併する、融合する

**派** merger **名** 合併
コロ merger and acquisition（M＆A＝合併吸収）

## 1050 compromise（ア）
**名** 妥協 **動** 妥協する（＋with）
原義 com（共に）＋promise（約束する）
コロ make a compromise（妥協する）

## 1051 assist [əsíst]
**動** 助ける、手伝う、援助する
原義 as（近くに）＋sist（立つ）

でた! Developed countries need to assist the developing world to progress.
（先進国は発展途上国の発展のために援助する必要がある） 慶應義塾大学

**派** assistant **名** 助手、アシスタント

**派** assistance **名** 援助

## 1052 support [səpɔ́ːrt]
**動** 支える、立証する、援助する **名** 支援、援助

でた! Today, rice supports more than half the world's population.
（今日、米は世界人口の半分以上を支えている） 青山学院大学

コロ stand by A（Aを援助する、待機する）

でた! I'll stand by you whatever happens.
（何が起きても私はあなたの援助を致します） 慶應義塾大学

**派** supporter **名** 支援者、サポーター
コロ give A a hand（Aに手を貸す）

## 1053 aid [éid]
**動** 助ける **名** 援助、補助器具
コロ visual aid（視覚援助） コロ band aid（ばんそうこう）

# UNIT 84　影響・評価　STEP 1 過去問を解く

## 1

Young people are often easily (　　) by their friends.

中央大学

1. inclined
2. influenced
3. inquired
4. insisted

## 2

Although he has a (　　) for being intelligent, he sometimes makes a remark altogether lacking in common sense.

東京理科大学

1. reputation
2. response
3. reward
4. skill

## 3

The <u>renowned</u> singer performed in the small town.

関西外国語大学

1. unknown
2. famous
3. talented
4. qualified

## 4

Both the children and their parents were asked to <u>assess</u> which toys were "boys" toys and which were suitable for girls.

法政大学

1. assemble
2. evaluate
3. inflate
4. simulate

## STEP 2 正解を見抜く

### 1

Young people are often easily influenced by their friends. 　正解 ②

訳 若年層は、しばしば彼らの友人の影響を容易に受けます。

- **incline** 動傾ける
- **influence** 動影響を与える
- **inquire** 動尋ねる
- **insist** 動主張する

> influenceの語源はin（中に）＋flu（流れ）＝中に流れ込む＝影響する

### 2

Although he has a reputation for being intelligent, he sometimes makes a remark altogether lacking in common sense. 　正解 ①

訳 彼は、知的であるという評判がありますが、時々、常識に欠けた意見を述べます。

- **reputation** 名評価
- **response** 名反応
- **reward** 名報酬
- **skill** 名技能

### 3

The famous singer performed in the small town. 　正解 ②

訳 その有名な歌手は小さな町で歌った。

- **unknown** 形知られていない
- **famous** 形有名な
- **talented** 形才能がある
- **qualified** 形資格がある

> famousのfamの語源は「話す」です。世間で話されている＝有名な

### 4

Both the children and their parents were asked to evaluate which toys were "boys" toys and which were suitable for girls. 　正解 ②

訳 子供と親の双方が、どのおもちゃが「男の子のおもちゃ」であり、どれが女の子に適しているか判断するように求められていた。

- **assemble** 動集める
- **inflate** 動膨らます
- **simulate** 動刺激する
- **evaluate** 動評価する

> assessは本質や価値を客観的に評価する。evaluateは有用性の観点に主眼を置いて評価する

UNIT 84 影響・評価

Chapter5 Intention

## STEP 3 連鎖式に語彙を増やす 84

### ● 語源 fan, fam（話す）

**1054 fame** [féim] 　名 名声　[原義] fam（話す）
- 派 **famous** — 形 有名な
- 反 **infamous** [ínfəməs] 発 — 形 不名誉な

**1055 renown** [rináun] 　名 名声
- 派 **renowned** [rináund] — 形 有名な

**1056 prestige** [prestíːʒ | -tíːdʒ] 　名 名声、威信、評判
- 派 **prestigious** [prestídʒiəs] 　形 名声のある、一流の
- コロ **prestigious** university（一流大学）

**1057 infant** [ínfənt] 　名 幼児　[原義] in（否定）+ fant（話す）= 話せない = 幼児
- コロ newborn **infant**（新生児）
- 派 **infancy** — 名 幼少期

**1058 reputation** [rèpjutéiʃən] 　名 評判
- コロ establish **reputation**（評判を得る）
- でた！ The novel added to his **reputation**.
  （その小説は彼の名声を増した）　東京外国語大学
- 類 **gossip** [gásəp | gɔ́s-] 　名 噂話、ゴシップ
- 類 **rumor** [rúːmər] 　名 噂
- コロ The **rumor** can't be true.（その噂は本当のはずがない）

**1059 evaluate** [ivǽljuèit] 　動 評価する
- でた！ Environmentalists are still in the process of **evaluating** how to think about nature again.
  （環境保護論者はまだ自然についてどう考えるかと再評価の最中である）　東京外国語大学
- 派 **evaluation** — 名 評価

**1060 assess** [əsés] 　動 評価する、査定する
- 派 **assessment** — 名 評価、査定

### ● 語源 flu（流れ）

**1061 flow** [flóu] 　名 流れ

## 1062 flu [flúː]
名 インフルエンザ
- bird flu（鳥インフルエンザ）

## 1063 influence [ínfluəns] ⑦
名 影響　動 影響を与える
- have an influence on A（Aに影響を与える）

派 **influential**　形 有力な、影響がある

## 1064 fluency [flúːənsi]
名 流暢さ

派 **fluent**　形 流暢な

派 **fluently**　副 流暢に

## 1065 inflation [infléiʃən]
名 膨張、インフレーション

## 1066 affluent [ǽfluənt]
形 裕福な、豊富な
- affluent society（豊かな社会）

派 **affluence**　名 裕福さ、富

## 1067 effect [ifékt]
名 間接的な影響、効果、趣旨
- the Butterfly Effect（バタフライ効果）
- come into effect（法律が施行される）

でた! The law will come into effect soon.
（その法律はすぐに施行されるでしょう）　中央大学

- to the effect that SV（SVという趣旨で）

でた! The doctor wrote a letter to the effect that his daughter would soon get better.
（医者は彼の娘はすぐ良くなるであろうという趣旨の手紙を書いた）　慶應義塾大学

派 **effective**　形 効果的な

## 1068 efficient [ifíʃənt]
形 効率的な、有能な

反 **inefficient**　形 無能な

派 **efficiency**　名 効率、有能

でた! Rising demand will produce higher efficiency for computer manufacturers.
（需要の伸びによってコンピュータの製造の効率が良くなるだろう）　慶應義塾大学

## 1069 affect [əfékt]
動 直接的に影響する

でた! Diet affects not only our physical but our mental health.
（食事は私たちの精神的健康ばかりでなく身体的健康にも影響する）　明治大学

派 **affection**　名 愛情

派 **affectionate**　形 愛情のこもった

Chapter5 Intention

# UNIT 85 決意・解決

## STEP 1 過去問を解く

### 1

Bill <u>made up his mind</u> to go to the party.

大阪電気通信大学

1. decided
2. gave up
3. refused

### 2

John won the school chess tournament last year, and he is (　　) to win it again this year.

英語検定2級

1. determined
2. designed
3. established
4. controlled

### 3

We have to find (　　) to the world's environmental problems.

センター試験

1. results
2. causes
3. solutions
4. benefits

### 4

After the fight, George (　　) Edward.

慶應義塾大学

1. resulted in
2. failed in
3. stayed at
4. reconciled with

358

## STEP 2 正解を見抜く

### 1

Bill decided to go to the party. 正解 ①

訳 ビルはパーティーに行くことを決めた。

- **decide** 動 決める
- **give up** 動 諦める
- **refuse** 動 断る

> make up one's mind
> （決心する）

### 2

John won the school chess tournament last year, and he is determined to win it again this year. 正解 ①

訳 ジョンは去年のチェスの大会で優勝し、今年もまた勝つであろうと決まっている。

- **determine** 動 決定する
- **design** 動 デザインする
- **establish** 動 設立する
- **control** 動 管理する

> be determined to A
> （Aすることに決めている）
> 通常受動態で使う

### 3

We have to find solutions to the world's environmental problems. 正解 ③

訳 私たちは世界の環境問題に解決策を見つけなければなりません。

- **result** 名 結果
- **cause** 名 原因
- **solution** 名 解決
- **benefit** 名 利益

### 4

After the fight, George reconciled with Edward. 正解 ④

訳 喧嘩の後、ジョージはエドワードと仲直りした。

- **resulted in** ～という結果に終わる
- **failed in** ～し損なう
- **stayed at** ～に滞在する
- **reconciled with** ～と仲直りする、和解する

Chapter5 Intention

## STEP 3 連鎖式に語彙を増やす 85

● 語源 cise cide（切る）

### 1070 decide [disáid]
動 決める（+to）、決定する（+on）

派 **decision** 名 決心
- make a decision（決心する）
- final decision（最終決定）
- でた! Discussion is required before a decision is made.
  （決定される前に討論が必要となる） TOEFL
- make up one's mind（決心する）
- でた! He has to make up his mind which university is better for him.
  （どの大学が彼にとって良いか決めなければならない） 関東学院大学

### 1071 determine [ditə́ːrmin]
動 決定する、決心する、決意する

- でた! She is very determined to own a store of her own.
  （彼女は自分の店を持つことを決意している） 早稲田大学

派 **determination** 名 決意、決定

### 1072 suicide [súːəsàid | sjúː-]
名 自殺  原義 sui（自分を）+ cid（切る）

- commit suicide（自殺をする）
- でた! The number of suicides increases as unemployment and bankruptcies rise.
  （自殺の数は失業と破産が増えるにつれ増加する） 成蹊大学

### 1073 scissors [sízərz]
名 はさみ

### 1074 concise [kənsáis]
形 簡潔な
- concise summary（簡潔な要約）

### 1075 precise [prisáis]
形 正確な、精密な
- precise measurement（正確な寸法）
- でた! Borders are precise lines drawn on a map, which designate the territory of a nation.
  （国境とは地図に引かれた正確な線であり、それは国の領土を示す） 千葉大学

派 **precision** 名 正確、精度

派 **precisely** 副 正確に
- でた! Though we cannot predict earthquakes precisely yet, we can prepare for them.
  （我々は地震を未だ正確に予測出来ないが、それに備える事は出来る） 上智大学

### 1076 exact [igzǽkt]
形 正確な

派 **exactly** 副 正確に、まさに、その通りです《口語》
- exactly the same（全く同じ）

## 1077 accurate [ǽkjurət] 形 正確な
**コロ** accurate information (正確な情報)

でた! The station clock is not as accurate as it should be.
(駅の時計はそれほど正確ではない) 〔慶應義塾大学〕

派 accuracy [ǽkjurəsi] 名 正確さ

でた! Experiments must be conducted with accuracy.
(実験は正確に行わなければならない) 〔TOEFL〕

反 inaccuracy [inǽkjurəsi] 名 不正確さ

## 1078 pesticide [péstəsàid] 名 農薬、殺虫剤

## 1079 insecticide [inséktəsàid] 名 殺虫剤

## 1080 homicide [hάməsàid | hɔ́m-] 名 殺人 原義 hom(同じ)+ cid(切る)

## 1081 solve [sάlv | sɔ́lv] 動 解く

派 solution 名 解決

でた! This booklet contains helpful information and solutions for problems you may have with your computer.
(この小冊子はあなたのコンピュータに発生するかもしれない問題のための役立つ情報と解決策を含んでいます) 〔学習院大学〕

派 resolve [rizάlv | -zɔ́lv] 動 決心する(+ to)、解決する

派 resolution 名 決心、抱負
**コロ** new year's resolution (新年の抱負)

## 1082 reconcile [rékənsàil] 動 和解させる

でた! The judge attemped to reconcile the parties in the dispute.
(判事は係争の当事者を和解させようと試みた) 〔慶應義塾大学〕

## 1083 settle [sétl] 動 解決する、定住する
**コロ** settle in Thailand (タイに定住する)  **コロ** settle down (落ち着く)
**コロ** settle one's difference (和解する)

でた! Both sides are looking for ways to settle their differences.
(双方とも和解する方法を探している) 〔上智大学〕

派 settlement 名 解決、定住

**思考の時間** 実際に入試で問われた内容です。あなたはどう答えますか？

これまでに選択を迫られた時にどのように決断したか。具体的に述べなさい。 〔中央大学〕

Chapter5 Intention

# UNIT 86　成功・機会

**STEP 1** 過去問を解く

## 1

A: I got tickets for next Sunday's baseball game.
B: Oh, really? Thanks. It's going to be a great (　　) for me to see real Major League players.

1. promise
2. importance
3. interest
4. opportunity

英語検定準2級

## 2

In his shirt-sleeves he felt he wasn't properly dressed for the (　　).

1. opportunity
2. chance
3. occasion
4. possibility

慶応義塾大学

## 3

His attempt to enter the university was (　　) and he celebrated with his friends.

1. succeeded
2. success
3. successful
4. successive

センター試験

## 4

It's (　　) that you have such a good friend.

1. contented
2. fortunate
3. glad
4. happy
5. satisfied

関西学院大学

## STEP 2 正解を見抜く

### 1

A : I got tickets for next Sunday's baseball game.
B : Oh, really? Thanks. It's going to be a great opportunity for me to see real Major League players.

正解 ④

**訳** A：次の日曜日の野球の試合のチケットを手に入れたよ。
B：本当に。ありがとう。本物のメジャーリーグ選手に会えることは私にとってすごい機会となるよ。

- **promise** 名約束
- **importance** 名重要性
- **interest** 名興味
- **opportunity** 名機会

### 2

In his shirt-sleeves he felt he wasn't properly dressed for the occasion.

正解 ③

**訳** 彼は半袖を着ていたので、場にふさわしい服装でないと感じた。

- **opportunity** 名機会
- **chance** 名機会
- **occasion** 名機会
- **possibility** 名可能性

> occasionはある行動をとるのに適した特定の機会、場合

### 3

His attempt to enter the university was successful and he celebrated with his friends.

正解 ③

**訳** 彼が大学に入ろうとする試みは成功し、彼は友達とお祝いした。

- **succeed** 動成功する
- **success** 名成功
- **successful** 形成功した
- **successive** 形連続した

### 4

It's fortunate that you have such a good friend.

正解 ②

**訳** そんなに良い友達がいるなんて君は幸せだね。

- **content** 形満足した
- **fortunate** 形幸運の
- **glad** 形嬉しい
- **happy** 形幸せな
- **satisfied** 形満足した

UNIT 86 成功・機会

Chapter5 Intention

## STEP 3 連鎖式に語彙を増やす 🎧86

### 1084 chance [tʃǽns | tʃάːns] 名 機会
- by chance（偶然に）
- take chances（一か八かやってみる）

### 1085 opportunity [ὰpərtjúːnəti | ɔ̀pətjúː-] 7 名 機会
でた! Job opportunities for women are increasing steadily.
（女性の仕事の機会は着実に増えている）

### 1086 occasion [əkéiʒən] 名 機会、場合、時
- on occasion（時々）
- 派 occasional 形 時々の
- 派 occasionally 副 時々
- every now and then（時々）

でた! Every now and then means occasionally.
（every now and then というのは時々という意味である）　［慶應義塾大学］

### 1087 sometimes [sʌ́mtàimz] 副 時々
- once in a while（時々）
- from time to time（時々）

---

• 語源 ceed cest（進む）

### 1088 succeed [səksíːd] 動 成功する（+in）、続く（+to）
でた! He succeeded in solving the question.
（彼はその問題を解くことに成功した）　［早稲田大学］
- make good（成功する）

でた! He is a hard worker, and I'm sure that he will make good in the new job.
（彼は一生懸命働くので彼は絶対に新しい仕事で成功すると思うよ）　［駒澤大学］

- 派 success [səksés] 7 名 成功
- 派 successful 形 成功した
- successful businessman（成功したビジネスマン）

でた! Were you successful in seeing your friend yesterday?
（昨日は友達と会えましたか）　［青山学院大学］

- 派 successive 形 連続した
- 派 succession 名 連続

### 1089 proceed [prəsíːd] 動 進む（+to）

でた！ He has to define a large number of terms before proceeding.
（彼は次に進む前に数多くの専門用語を定義しなければならない） TOEFL

派 **procedure** [prəsíːdʒər]  名 手続き、手順、措置  立命館大学

派 **proceeding**  名 進行

派 **procession**  名 行列

派 **process** [práses | próu-]  名 過程、プロセス  動 処理する

でた！ When one person teaches another through speech or writing, this process is called learning by instruction.
（人が他人に口頭や文字で教えるこの過程がいわゆる習って覚えるということだ） 成城大学

## 1090 **exceed** [iksíːd]  動 超える、勝る

コロ exceed the speed limit（制限速度を超える）

派 **excessive**  形 過度の、極端な

コロ excessive drinking（過度の飲酒）

派 **excess**  名 超過

## 1091 **ancestor** [ǽnsestər] ア  名 （個人としての）祖先

原義 an（反対に）＋cest（進む）

派 **ancestry**  名 （集団としての）祖先

## 1092 **descendant** [diséndənt]  名 子孫

派 **descend**  動 降りる、下る

派 **descent**  名 降下

類 **posterity** [pɑstérəti | pɔs-]  名 子孫

## 1093 **fortune** [fɔ́ːrtʃən]  名 運、財産

コロ fortune teller（占い師）

派 **fortunate**  形 幸運な

でた！ It's fortunate that you have found a lovely apartment.
（素敵なアパートを見つけられてあなたは幸運ですね） 関西学院大学

派 **unfortunate**  形 不幸な

派 **unfortunately**  副 不幸にも、残念ながら

でた！ Unfortunately, we are fully booked during that period.
（残念ですが、その期間は予約でいっぱいです） 東京理科大学

UNIT 86 成功・機会

Chapter5 Intention

# UNIT 87 偶然・事故

## STEP 1 過去問を解く

### 1

Yesterday I met her <u>by chance</u> at the station.

中央大学

1. accidentally
2. actually
3. purposefully
4. unfortunately

### 2

Bob happened to <u>run into</u> the same lady that he saw on the plane.

中央大学

1. chase
2. encounter
3. escape
4. cheat
5. like

### 3

A: My birthday is February 6th.
B: What a (　　)! That's my birthday, too.

英語検定2級

1. promise
2. technique
3. guarantee
4. coincidence

### 4

The most surprising thing about the (　　) was the fact that historians didn't really begin to investigate it for over thirty years.

上智大学

1. sense
2. incident
3. moment
4. people

## STEP 2 正解を見抜く

### 1

Yesterday I met her accidentally at the station.

正解 ①

訳 昨日私は駅で偶然彼女に会った。

**accidentally** 副 偶然に
**actually** 副 実際は
**purposefully** 副 意図的に
**unfortunately** 副 不幸にも

> by chance, by accident は「偶然に」

### 2

Bob happened to encounter the same lady that he saw on the plane.

正解 ②

訳 ボブは飛行機で見かけたのと同じ女性に偶然会った。

**chase** 動 追跡する
**escape** 動 逃げる
**like** 動 好む
**encounter** 動 遭遇する
**cheat** 動 騙す

### 3

A: My birthday is February 6th.
B: What a coincidence! That's my birthday, too.

正解 ④

訳 A:私の誕生日は2月6日です。
B:なんて偶然でしょう。私の誕生日も同じです。

**promise** 名 約束
**guarantee** 名 保証
**coincidence** 名 偶然の一致
**technique** 名 技術

> coincidentの語源は co（共に）+ in（中に）+ cid（落ちる）= 同時発生

### 4

The most surprising thing about the incident was the fact that historians didn't really begin to investigate it for over thirty years.

正解 ②

訳 その出来事で最も驚くべきことは30年以上歴史家たちはそれを調査しなかったという事実だ。

**sense** 名 感覚
**moment** 名 瞬間
**incident** 名 出来事
**people** 名 人々

> incidentの語源はin（中に）+ cid（落ちる）= 突然中に落ちてくるもの = 事故、出来事

UNIT 87 偶然・事故

Chapter5 Intention

## STEP 3 連鎖式に語彙を増やす 87

● 語源 cad cid cas（落ちる）

### 1094 accident [ǽksədənt] 名 事故

でた! This is nothing but an accident.
（これは全くの偶然だ） 学習院大学

派 **accidental** 形 偶然の

派 **accidentally** 副 偶然に
コロ by accident（偶然に）　コロ by chance（偶然に）

### 1095 incident [ínsədənt] 名 出来事、事件

でた! The incident occurred when their marriage was already on the rocks.
（この出来事は彼らの結婚がすでに崩壊寸前のときに起こった） 中央大学

派 **incidental** 形 偶然の、付随的な

派 **incidentally** 副 付随的に、ついでに言えば

### 1096 coincide [kòuinsáid] 動 同時発生する、一致する

でた! An increase in the coffee harvest coincided with the coming of honeybees.
（コーヒーの収穫高の増加はミツバチの到来と同時に起こった） 東京大学

派 **coincident** 形 同時に起こる

派 **coincidence** 名 同時発生、偶然の一致

原義 co（共に）＋ in（中に）＋ cid（落ちる）
＝2人とも2月9日生まれ

### 1097 casual [kǽʒuəl] 形 何気ない、カジュアルな、偶然の
原義 落ちる

派 **casualty** 名 死傷者数

### 1098 case [kéis] 名 場合、ケース

コロ in case of fire（火事の場合）

でた! Don't expect me in case it should be rainy.
（万が一雨の場合は、私が来ると思わないでください） 慶応義塾大学

## 1099 encounter [inkáuntər] 動 遭遇する 名 遭遇

- make an encounter with A（Aに遭遇する）
- meet A by chance（A(人)に偶然出くわす）
- run into A（Aに遭遇する、困難にあう）
- bump into A（Aに遭遇する）
- come across（遭遇する、出くわす）

でた！ I came across an old classmate on my way here.
（私はここへ来る途中昔のクラスメイトに偶然会った）　関西学院大学

## 1100 serendipity [sèrəndípəti] 名 思わぬ物を偶然発見する能力

## 1101 destiny [déstəni] 名 運命

でた！ Do the stars or our blood types determine our behavior and destiny?
（星座や血液型は私たちの行動や運命を決定するのですか）　慶應義塾大学

派 **destination** 名 目的地

でた！ Late as it was, they set out for the destination.
（遅かったけれど、彼らは目的地に向けて出発した）　中央大学

## 1102 doom [dúːm] 名 運命

でた！ Those who ignore culture are doomed to failure in Africa.
（アフリカでは文化を無視するものは失敗する運命にある）

## 1103 fate [féit] 名 運命、宿命

派 **fatal** 形 致命的な、運命の

でた！ One of the most fatal giveaways is what is called a "slip of the tongue."
（最も致命的な機密漏洩の一つは「失言」と呼ばれるものである）　同志社大学

派 **fatality** [feitǽləti | fə-] 名 死亡率

UNIT 87　偶然・事故

Chapter5 Intention

# UNIT 88 献身・貢献

**STEP 1** 過去問を解く

## 1

Have you made a (　　) to meet the company manager while you are in Tokyo?

立命館大学

1. commitment
2. purchase
3. release
4. thrill

## 2

Jack was so determined to succeed in his company that he (　　) most of his free time to his work.

英語検定2級

1. revealed
2. sacrificed
3. instructed
4. implied

## 3

He (　　) his life to serving the people of the nation.

立命館大学

1. concluded
2. contradicted
3. dedicated
4. defined

## 4

His (　　) to the fund was by no means miserly.

上智大学

1. contribution
2. attribution
3. retribution
4. substitution

## STEP 2 正解を見抜く

### 1

Have you made a commitment to meet the company manager while you are in Tokyo?

正解 1

**訳** あなたが東京にいる間、会社のマネージャーに会う約束をしましたか。

- **commitment** 名約束
- **purchase** 名購入
- **release** 名解放
- **thrill** 名スリル

### 2

Jack was so determined to succeed in his company that he sacrificed most of his free time to his work.

正解 2

**訳** ジャックは彼の会社で成功すると決意したので、彼の暇な時間を仕事に捧げた。

- **reveal** 動明らかにする
- **sacrifice** 動犠牲にする
- **instruct** 動教える
- **imply** 動ほのめかす

> sacrificeの語源はsacri（神に）+ fic（作る）＝神様のために捧げる＝犠牲にする

### 3

He dedicated his life to serving the people of the nation.

正解 3

**訳** 彼はその国の国民に仕えることに自分の人生を捧げた。

- **conclude** 動結論付ける
- **contradict** 動矛盾する
- **dedicate** 動捧げる
- **define** 動定義する

### 4

His contribution to the fund was by no means miserly.

正解 1

**訳** 彼のその基金に対する貢献は決して欲深いものではなかった。

- **contribution** 名寄付
- **attribution** 名帰属
- **retribution** 名天罰
- **substitution** 名代理

> contributionの語源はcon（共に）+ tribute（授ける）＝共に授けること＝貢献

UNIT 88 献身・貢献

Chapter5 Intention

## STEP 3 連鎖式に語彙を増やす 88

**1104 religion** [rilídʒən] 名 宗教
- freedom of religion（宗教の自由）
- でた! Some religions have insisted on the idea that our planet was given to us by God.
（いくつかの宗教は地球は神によって与えられたという考えを主張している） 慶應義塾大学

派 **religious** 形 宗教の
- でた! Myths are usually tied to religious beliefs.
（神話は通常、宗教的信仰と結びついている） TOEFL

類 **sacred** [séikrid] 発 形 神聖な

類 **holy** [hóuli] 形 神の、信心深い

**1105 myth** [míθ] 名 神話
- でた! Myths are stories that explain the origin of events from the distant past.
（神話は遠い過去の出来事の語源を説明する話である） TOEFL

**1106 sacrifice** [sǽkrəfàis] 名 生贄 動 犠牲にする、生贄に捧げる
原義 sacri（神に）＋ fic（作る）
- でた! The family made a great sacrifice to build their own house.
（その家族は自分たちの家を建てるために大きな犠牲を払った） 立命館大学

**1107 dedicate** [dédikèit] 動 捧げる
- dedicate A to B（AをBに捧げる）

派 **dedication** 名 献身、専念

**1108 commit** [kəmít] 動 犯す、献身する
- commit oneself to A（Aに献身する）
- でた! He urged his son to commit himself to righting social wrongs.
（彼は息子に社会の不正を糾すことに献身するように促した） 明治大学

派 **commitment** 名 献身、約束

**1109 devote** [divóut] 動 捧げる
- devote A to B（AをBに捧げる）
- でた! It is about ten years since I devoted myself to this research.
（私がこの研究に専念してから約10年になる） 中央大学

派 **devotion** 名 献身

**1110 league** [líːg] 名 同盟、リーグ 原義 結ぶ
- Major League Baseball（野球のメジャーリーグ）

## 1111 faith [féiθ]
**名** 信仰、信頼、信用

コロ have faith in A (Aを信用する)

でた! I used to believe in science and have faith in technology.
(私はかつて科学を信奉し、科学技術を信用していた) 〔明治大学〕

派 **faithful** **形** 忠実な

## 1112 ritual [rítʃuəl]
**名** 儀式、習慣的行為  **形** 儀式の

コロ religious ritual (宗教儀式)

でた! The cave paintings were part of a hunting ritual.
(洞窟壁画は狩猟の儀式の一つであった) 〔TOEFL〕

---

● 語源 tribute (授ける)

## 1113 tribute [tríbju:t]
**名** 貢ぎ物

派 **contribute** [kəntríbju:t] **動** 貢献する、寄付する、一因となる

でた! Genes certainly contribute to a long life.
(遺伝子は確かに長寿の一因を担っている) 〔センター試験〕

派 **contribution** **名** 貢献、寄付

## 1114 distribute [distríbju:t]
**動** 分配する

コロ hand out (配布する)

派 **distribution** **名** 分配、配布

## 1115 retribution [rètrəbjú:ʃən]
**名** 報い

## 1116 attribute [ətríbju:t]
**動** 帰する  **名** 特質、属性

コロ attribute A to B (AはBのおかげである)

でた! Some scholars attributed the miraculous Asian growth to Confucian values.
(一部の学者は、アジアの奇跡的な成長は儒教的価値観のおかげだと考えた) 〔成蹊大学〕

派 **attribution** **名** 帰属、属性

## 1117 ascribe [əskráib]
**動** 帰する  ※良い時にも悪い時にも使える。

コロ ascribe A to B (AをBのせいにする)

でた! We can't simply ascribe everything to their culture.
(我々はただ単に全てが文化に帰するとは言えない) 〔上智大学〕

UNIT 88 献身・貢献

Chapter5 Intention

# UNIT 89 目的・期待

**STEP 1 過去問を解く**

## 1

Joe's mother was waiting with (　　) at the airport to meet Joe and her new grandson.

英語検定2級

1. persuasion
2. representation
3. anticipation
4. illustration

## 2

My reward was well beyond my (　　).

立命館大学

1. consideration
2. expectations
3. history
4. payments

## 3

Do you have a particular <u>end</u> in mind? What are you trying to achieve?

亜細亜大学

1. plan
2. limit
3. course
4. purpose

## 4

She left the letter there (　　) so that you'd see it.

中央大学

1. accidentally
2. deliberately
3. scarcely
4. wrongly

## STEP 2 正解を見抜く

### 1

Joe's mother was waiting with anticipation at the airport to meet Joe and her new grandson.

正解 ③

訳 ジョーの母親はジョーと彼女の新しい孫に会うのを空港で期待して待っていた。

- **persuasion** 名説得
- **representation** 名代表
- **anticipation** 名期待
- **illustration** 名描写

anticipateの語源はanti（前に）+ cip（取る）＝前もって事態を想定して予測する、予期する

### 2

My reward was well beyond my expectations.

正解 ②

訳 私の報酬は、かなり私の期待を超えていました。

- **consideration** 名熟考
- **expectation** 名期待
- **history** 名歴史
- **payment** 名支払い

beyond expectation（予想以上に）

### 3

Do you have a particular purpose in mind? What are you trying to achieve?

正解 ④

訳 何か特定の目的が念頭にありますか。何を達成しようとしているのですか。

- **plan** 名計画
- **limit** 名制限
- **course** 名コース
- **purpose** 名目的

### 4

She left the letter there deliberately so that you'd see it.

正解 ②

訳 あなたがそれを見るように、彼女は故意にそこに手紙を残しました。

- **accidentally** 副偶然に
- **deliberately** 副故意に
- **scarcely** 副やっと、かろうじて
- **wrongly** 副間違って

Chapter5 Intention

## STEP 3 連鎖式に語彙を増やす 89

• 語源 pect (見る)

### 1118 expect [ikspékt]
**動** 期待する、予期する
原義 ex (外を) + pect (見る)

> でた! I was not in the least surprised, for I had fully expected.
> (私は全然驚かなかった。というのはこのくらいのことは十分予期していたからだ) 立命館大学

| 派 | expecting | **形** 妊娠している |
| 派 | expectant | **形** 期待を示す、妊娠中の |
| 派 | expectation | **名** 期待 |

コロ beyond expectation (予想外)

| 派 | expectancy | **名** 予期されるもの |

コロ life expectancy (寿命)

### 1119 pregnant [prégnənt]
**形** 妊娠している　原義 pre (前) + nan (生まれる)

コロ become pregnant (妊娠する)

| 派 | pregnancy | **名** 妊娠 |
| 類 | abortion [əbɔ́ːrʃən] | **名** 妊娠中絶 |

### 1120 prospect [práspekt | prɔ́s-]
**名** 見込み、展望、有望な人
原義 pro (前を) + spect (見る)

コロ economic prospects (経済見通し)

| 類 | outlook | **名** 見込み、展望、態度 |

### 1121 perspective [pərspéktiv]
**名** 観点、視野、見通し、遠近法
**形** 見込みがある、有望な

コロ from this perspective (この観点から)　コロ unique perspective (ユニークな視点)

| 派 | viewpoint | **名** 観点、見地 |

### 1122 retrospect [rétrəspèkt]
**名** 回想

コロ in retrospect (回想してみると)

| 派 | retrospective | **形** 回想の、レトロな |

### 1123 speculate [spékjulèit]
**動** 熟考する、思いめぐらす、推測する

コロ speculate on the outcome (結果を推測する)

| 派 | speculation | **名** 投機、思索、考察、やま |

コロ on speculation (思惑で)

## 1124 anticipate [æntísəpèit]
動 期待する、予測する
原義 anti（先に）＋cip（取る）

でた! No one can anticipate the results of the games.
（誰も試合の結果を予測できない） TOEFL

派 anticipation　名 期待、予測
コロ look forward to ～ ing（～を楽しみに待つ）

## 1125 foresee [fɔ́ːrsíː]
動 予知する、予見する

でた! People have a limited ability to foresee future technology.
（人間が将来の科学技術を予知する能力は限られている） 早稲田大学

派 foresight [fɔ́ːrsáit]　名 先見の明

## 1126 purpose [pə́ːrpəs]
名（理由、目標があっての）目的
原義 pur（前に）＋pose（置く）

でた! All readers have their own personal tastes and purposes for reading.
（全ての読者は書物に対して自分なりの好みや目的がある） 東京大学
コロ on purpose（意図的に、故意に）　コロ for the purpose of ~ing（～する目的で）

## 1127 goal [góul]
名（自分のための）目的、ゴール
コロ ultimate goal（最終目標）

## 1128 aim [éim]
名（努力して達成するための）目的、狙い　動 狙う
コロ aim at（～を狙う）

でた! The book was aimed at the young.
（その本は子供向けだった） 明治大学

## 1129 end [énd]
名（究極の）目的

でた! He'll never fail to realize his end.
（彼は必ず目的を実現するだろう） 中央大学

## 1130 intention [inténʃən]
名 意図
派 intentional　形 意図的な
派 intentionally　副 意図的に
コロ for the sake of A（Aのために）

でた! Society exists for the sake of the individual.
（社会は個人のためにあるものだ） 高知大学

## 1131 deliberate [dilíbərət]
形 故意の、慎重な
派 deliberately　副 故意に、慎重に

UNIT 89 目的・期待

Chapter5 Intention

# UNIT 90　自信・勇気　STEP 1 過去問を解く

## 1

Despite her lack of preparation, she was (　　) that she would pass the entrance examination.

立命館大学

1. annoyed
2. confident
3. doubtful
4. warned

## 2

Secret documents are often stamped "(　　)."

青山学院大学

1. Conditional
2. Confessional
3. Confidential
4. Congenital

## 3

It must have taken a lot of (　　) for him to invade the privacy of her life.

東京都市大学

1. courage
2. chances
3. permit
4. promises

## 4

The English teacher (　　) his students to watch American movies in order to practice listening to English.

英語検定2級

1. recognized
2. provided
3. encouraged
4. disturbed

## STEP 2 正解を見抜く

### 1

Despite her lack of preparation, she was confident that she would pass the entrance examination.　　正解 ②

訳　彼女は準備不足にもかかわらず、入学試験に合格すると確信していました。

- annoy　動 うざがらせる
- confident　形 自信がある
- doubtful　形 疑わしい
- warn　動 警告する

### 2

Secret documents are often stamped "Confidential."　　正解 ③

訳　秘密書類は、しばしば "Confidential" の印が押されます。

- conditional　形 条件付きの
- confessional　形 告白の
- confidential　形 秘密の
- congenital　形 生まれつきの

### 3

It must have taken a lot of courage for him to invade the privacy of her life.　　正解 ①

訳　彼女の私生活に入り込むなんて彼はとても勇気があったに違いない。

- courage　名 勇気
- chance　名 機会
- permit　名 許可
- promise　名 約束

> courageの原義は「心」です

### 4

The English teacher encouraged his students to watch American movies in order to practice listening to English.　　正解 ③

訳　英語の先生は、英語のリスニングの練習するために彼の学生がアメリカ映画を見るよう奨励しました。

- recognize　動 認識する
- encourage　動 励ます
- disturb　動 邪魔する
- provide　動 提供する

> encourageの語源はen（動詞化）＋courage（勇気）＝励ます

UNIT 90　自信・勇気

Chapter5 Intention

## STEP 3 連鎖式に語彙を増やす 🎧90

### 1132 confidence [kάnfədəns | kɔ́n-] 🗣
名 自信、秘密

- コロ in confidence（秘密で） コロ have confidence in A（Aを信頼する）
- でた! It is very important to have confidence when talking in public.
（人前で話すときに自信を持つことはとても重要である） 〔上智大学〕
- でた! I can recommend her to you with great confidence.
（私は、自信たっぷりに彼女をあなたに推薦できます） 〔立命館大学〕

派 **confident** 形 確信している、自信がある
- でた! He is not confident that he will find the materials he needs.
（彼は必要としている資料を見つけ出す自信がない） 〔TOEFL〕

派 **confidential** [kὰnfədénʃəl | kɔ̀n-] 形 秘密の
- でた! We were told that the information is strictly confidential.
（我々はその情報は極秘であると伝えられた） 〔TOEFL〕

派 **confide** [kənfáid] 動 打ち明ける、信頼する

---

### ● 語源 cred（信じる）

### 1133 credit [krédit]
名 履修単位、信用　動 信じる、信用する
原義 cred（信じる）

### 1134 credible [krédəbl] 形 信頼できる、信用できる
- でた! I think that's a very credible story.
（私は、それが非常に信頼できる話であると思います） 〔上智大学〕

反 **incredible** 形 信じられない
- でた! No one would listen to such an incredible tale.
（誰もそんな信じがたい話に耳を傾けないだろう） 〔上智大学〕

類 **unbelievable** [ʌ̀nbilí:vəbl] 形 信じられない

派 **credulous** [krédʒuləs | -dju-] 形 騙されやすい

### 1135 trust [trʌ́st] 動 信じる

派 **trustworthy** [trʌ́stwə́:rði] 形 信頼できる　原義 trust（信頼）＋worthy（値する）
- でた! He is a man of his word. He is trustworthy.
（彼は約束を守る男だ。彼は信頼できる） 〔芝浦工業大学〕

- 語源 **cour**（信じる）

| 1136 | **accord** | 名 調和、一致 |

**1137 courage** [kə́:ridʒ | kʌ́r-]　名 勇気

- 派 **courageous** [kəréidʒəs]　形 勇敢な
- 類 **brave** [bréiv]　形 勇敢な
- 派 **bravery** [bréivəri]　名 勇敢さ

**1138 encourage** [inkə́:ridʒ | -kʌ́r-]　動 励ます、促進する、やる気をもたせる
- コロ encourage A to B（AにBするように励ます）
- 派 **encouragement**　名 奨励

**1139 discourage** [diskə́:ridʒ | -kʌ́r-]　動 落胆させる、やる気をなくさせる

でた! My parents are trying to discourage me from moving to London, but I'm planning to go anyway.
（両親は私にロンドンに引っ越すのを思いとどまらせようとしているが、私はとりあえず行く計画をしています）　　［獨協大学］

でた! The teacher discourages the students from speaking Japanese in class.
（教師は生徒がクラス内で日本語を話すことをやめさせた）　　［専修大学］

- 派 **discouragement**　名 落胆

**1140 attempt** [ətémpt]　名 試み　動 試みる

- コロ attempt to climb Everest（エベレスト登頂を試みる）

でた! Mario passed his driving test on his first attempt.
（マリオは最初の挑戦で運転免許試験に合格した）　　［南山大学］

UNIT 90　自信・勇気

Chapter5 Intention | 381

# UNIT 91 使用・消費　STEP 1 過去問を解く

## 1

You should make (　　) of this opportunity.

1. emphasis
2. glimpse
3. impact
4. use

中央大学

## 2

She gives practical gifts, such as clothes.

1. expensive
2. precious
3. economical
4. useful

東海大学

## 3

When employees pay for their client's meals, they can get their money back from the company. But some people (　　) the system and get the company to pay for meals they have with friends.

1. abuse
2. preserve
3. resolve
4. obtain

英語検定2級

## 4

Some of the refrigerators (　　) 60 percent less electricity than older models.

1. pay
2. consume
3. spend
4. exhaust

英語検定2級

## STEP 2 正解を見抜く

### 1

You should make use of this opportunity. 　正解 ④

訳 あなたはこの機会を利用すべきです。

- emphasis 名強調
- glimpse 名一見
- impact 名衝撃
- use 名使用

make use of A（Aを利用する）＝use（使う）よりある目的に向かって効果的に利用する

### 2

She gives useful gifts, such as clothes. 　正解 ④

訳 彼女は、衣服などの実用的な贈り物を与えます。

- expensive 形高価な
- precious 形貴重な
- economical 形経済的な
- useful 形役に立つ

practicalはpractice（練習、実行）の形容詞で（実用的な）という意味なので「実行する上で役立つ」という意味になります

### 3

When employees pay for their client's meals, they can get their money back from the company. But some people abuse the system and get the company to pay for meals they have with friends. 　正解 ①

訳 従業員は彼らの顧客に食事代を支払うとき、彼らは会社から返金できる。しかしそのシステムを悪用し友達と食べた食事代を会社に払わせる人もいる。

- abuse 動悪用する
- preserve 動保存する
- resolve 動解決する
- obtain 動得る

abuseの語源はab（分離）＋use（使用）＝通常の使用とは離れて使用する＝乱用する

### 4

Some of the refrigerators consume 60 percent less electricity than older models. 　正解 ②

訳 旧モデルの冷蔵庫より60％少ない電気しか消費しない冷蔵庫もある。

- pay 動支払う
- consume 動消費する
- spend 動費やす
- exhaust 動疲れ果てさせる

UNIT 91 使用・消費

Chapter5 Intention | 383

## STEP 3 連鎖式に語彙を増やす 91

**1141 use** [ju:z]　　動 使う　名 使用
- コロ make use of A（Aを利用する）
- コロ make the best(most) of A（Aを最大限に利用する）
- コロ take advantage of A（Aを利用する）

**1142 abuse** [əbjú:z] 🔴　　動 虐待する、悪用する、乱用する
　　　　　　　　　　　　名 虐待、悪用、乱用
- コロ drug abuse（薬物乱用）

**1143 utilize** [jú:təlàiz]　　動 利用する
- でた! Economic analysis is currently utilized in many fields.
（経済分析は現在多くの分野で使われている）　　［慶應義塾大学］

- 派 **utility** [ju:tíləti]　　名 有用性、実用性
- 派 **utilization**　　名 利用すること

**1144 available** [əvéiləbl]　　形 利用できる
- でた! A lot of information is available in English on the Net.
（ネット上には多くの情報が英語で提供されている）　　［亜細亜大学］
- コロ avail oneself of A（Aを利用する）
- でた! Guests are free to avail themselves of our hotel facilities.
（お客様は当ホテルの設備をご自由にお使い頂けます）　　［青山学院大学］

- 派 **availability**　　名 利用できること、入手可能であること、有効性

**1145 consume** [kənsú:m | -sjú:m]　　動 消費する
- でた! American teens now spend more than 10 hours each day consuming media of some kind.
（現在アメリカ人の10代は、メディアの様な物に毎日10時間以上の時間を費やしている）　　［明治大学］

- 派 **consumption**　　名 消費
- でた! Consumption plays a crucial role in our social lives.
（消費は我々の社会生活において重大な役割を果たしている）　　［関西学院大学］

- 派 **consumer**　　名 消費者

## 1146 deal [díːl]
**名** 取引、量
**動** 扱う、処理する（+with）、分配する

- でた! He spent a great deal of time on it.
（彼はそれにたくさんの時間を費やした） 早稲田大学
- でた! The international community is ready to deal with serious issues.
（国際社会は深刻な問題を対処する準備が出来ている） 日本大学

## 1147 cope [kóup]
**動** 処理する、対処する（+with）

- でた! Can I cope with the poverty and culture shock?
（私は貧しさとカルチャーショックにうまく対処できるだろうか）
- コロ handle with A（Aを扱う） 玉川大学

## 1148 practice [præktis]
**名** 実践、練習

- コロ put A into practice（Aを実行する）
- コロ carry out A（Aを実行する）
- でた! It is often easier to make plans than to carry them out.
（実行するより計画するほうが簡単だと言われている） 東京外国語大学

**派** practical　**形** 実践的な、実用的な
- コロ practical English（実用英語）

## 1149 theory [θíːəri | θíəri]
**形** 理論、学説
- コロ in theory（理論上は）
- でた! The theory of evolution is the most convincing one so far.
（進化論はこれまでで最も説得力のあるものである） 慶應義塾大学

**派** theoretical　**形** 理論的な

---

**入試問題にチャレンジ**　（　）には同じ語が入ります。何でしょうか？

- He was given a great (　) of work to do.
- I made a (　) with him to teach me Spanish in exchange for my teaching him guitar.
- As manager of the office, I have to (　) with all sorts of problems every day.

長崎大学

答　deal

# UNIT 92　調査・実験　STEP 1 過去問を解く

## 1

The recent (　　) showed that concern about health was the most common reason for giving up smoking.

立命館大学

1. bargain
2. civilization
3. frontier
4. survey

## 2

There was a bank robbery this morning. Now the police are (　　) the crime scene for clues.

立命館大学

1. acknowledging
2. emphasizing
3. investigating
4. manifesting

## 3

If we carefully (　　) the data from our customer survey, I'm sure we'll get some ideas for new products.

英語検定2級

1. establish
2. determine
3. analyze
4. exclude

## 4

Carlos won the school science prize for a well-planned (　　) that tested the effect of electric light on flowers.

英語検定2級

1. statement
2. experiment
3. replacement
4. entertainment

## STEP 2 正解を見抜く

### 1

The recent survey showed that concern about health was the most common reason for giving up smoking. 　正解 ④

訳　最近の調査によると、禁煙の最も主要な理由は健康に対する懸念であるとわかった。

- bargain 名 売買契約
- civilization 名 文明
- frontier 名 先駆者
- survey 名 調査

> surveyは広範囲にわたる全体像を見るための調査

### 2

There was a bank robbery this morning. Now the police are investigating the crime scene for clues. 　正解 ③

訳　今朝銀行強盗があった。いま警察が手掛かりを求めて現場を調査している。

- acknowledge 動 認める
- emphasize 動 強調する
- investigate 動 調査する
- manifest 動 証明する

> investigateは真相究明するための組織的で詳細な調査や捜査

### 3

If we carefully analyze the data from our customer survey, I'm sure we'll get some ideas for new products. 　正解 ③

訳　顧客調査のデータを慎重に分析すれば、新商品のための新しいアイデアが浮かぶと確信している。

- establish 動 設立する
- analyze 動 分析する
- determine 動 決定する
- exclude 動 除外する

### 4

Carlos won the school science prize for a well-planned experiment that tested the effect of electric light on flowers. 　正解 ②

訳　カルロスは花への電灯の効果を実証するよく計画された実験により学校科学賞を勝ち取りました。

- statement 名 名声
- replacement 名 置き換え
- entertainment 名 娯楽
- experiment 名 実験

> experimentの語源はexperi（やってみる）＋ ment（名詞化語尾）＝実験

UNIT 92　調査・実験

Chapter5 Intention　387

## STEP 3 連鎖式に語彙を増やす 🎧92

**1150 survey** [sərvéi] 　　名 調査、概観　動 調査する、見渡す
- conduct a survey（調査を行う）

**1151 explore** [iksplɔ́:r] 　　動 探索する、探求する
- explore the possibilities（可能性を探る）

派 **exploration** 　名 探索

派 **explorer** 　名 探検家

**1152 investigate** [invéstəgèit] 　動 調査する
- investigate the cause（原因を調査する）
- でた！ The police are still investigating the accident.
  （警察はまだその事件について調査している） 〔東京大学〕

派 **investigation** 　名 調査
- investigation headquarters（捜査本部）
- look into（調べる）

**1153 inspect** [inspékt] 　動 詳しく調べる、点検する

派 **inspection** 　名 精査、点検、検査
- under inspection（検査中）　 fire inspection（火災検査）

**1154 examine** [igzǽmin] 　動 検査する、考察する
- examine the effects of A（Aの効果を考察する）
- look over（目を通す、調べる）

派 **examination** 　名 試験　※examは省略形
- でた！ Mary is sure to pass the examination.
  （メアリーはきっと試験に合格する） 〔中央大学〕

派 **examiner** 　名 試験官
- TOEFL examiner（TOEFLの試験官）

派 **examinee** [igzæməní:] 　名 受験者

**1155 glimpse** [glímps] 　動 ちらりと見る　名 一見
- catch a glimpse of A（Aをちらりと見る）

**1156 stare** [stéər] 　動 じっと見る（＋at）
- sit and stare（座ってじっと見る）

**1157 glance** [glǽns | glá:ns] 　動 ちらりと見る（＋at）　名 一見
- at a glance（一目見て）

| 1158 | clue [klúː] | 名 手がかり、糸口 |

コロ search for (〜を探す)

| 1159 | **analyze** [ǽnəlàiz] | 動 分析する |

派 analyst 名 分析家、アナリスト

派 analysis [ənǽləsis] ア 名 分析 (複) analyses

でた! Analysis of the substance confirms the presence of nitrogen.
（物質の分析は窒素の存在を確認する） [TOEFL]

| 1160 | synthesize [sínθəsàiz] | 動 統合する |

派 synthesis [sínθəsis] 名 統合 (複) syntheses

| 1161 | hypothesis [haipάθəsis | -pɔ́θ-] 発 名 仮説 (複) hypotheses |

でた! The use of the hypothesis is common in scientific investigation.
（科学的調査において仮説を使用することは当たり前のことである） [慶應義塾大学]

派 hypothetical [hàipəθétikəl] 形 仮説の

| 1162 | research [risə́ːrtʃ, ríːsəːrtʃ] | 名 研究、調査 |

コロ research proposal (研究計画)

● 語源 peri (試みる)

| 1163 | experience [ikspíəriəns] | 名 経験 動 経験する |

でた! He has experienced failure after failure through his life.
（彼は生涯を通して失敗に失敗を重ねてきた） [青山学院大学]

コロ go through (経験する、通り抜ける)

でた! The widowed mother had to go through a lot of hardships.
（夫を亡くした母は多くの困難を経験しなければならなかった） [早稲田大学]

類 undergo [ʌ̀ndərgóu] 動 経験する、受ける
活 undergo-underwent-undergone

でた! England was the first country to undergo an industrial revolution.
（イギリスは産業革命を経験した最初の国である） [関西学院大学]

| 1164 | experiment [ikspérəmənt] | 名 実験 |

コロ carry out experiments on animals (動物実験をする)

| 1165 | expert [ékspəːrt] | 名 専門家、名人、エキスパート |

原義 何度も試みて得た知識を持った

派 expertise [èkspərtíːz] ア 名 専門的知識

UNIT 92 調査・実験

Chapter5 Intention | 389

# UNIT 93 反対・苦情　STEP 1 過去問を解く

## 1

Charles and Sue (　　) on everything. If he likes something, she usually hates it.

英語検定2級

1. connect
2. disagree
3. conclude
4. depend

## 2

If you want to carry out the project, you may. I have no (　　) to your advancing it.

東京理科大学

1. idea
2. objection
3. mention
4. upset

## 3

Mr. Davis wrote a letter of (　　) to the company about the washing machine he bought from them.

学習院大学

1. complaint
2. conference
3. consequence
4. contribution

## 4

Betty likes to hear favorable comments, but she can't stand (　　).

慶應義塾大学

1. appreciation
2. compliments
3. metaphors
4. criticism

## STEP 2 正解を見抜く

### 1

Charles and Sue disagree on everything. If he likes something, she usually hates it.

正解 ②

**訳** チャールズとスーはすべてについて意見が異なります。彼が何かが好きなら、通常、彼女はそれが嫌いです。

- **connect** 動 結ぶ
- **conclude** 動 結論付ける
- **disagree** 動 意見が一致しない
- **depend** 動 頼る

### 2

If you want to carry out the project, you may. I have no objection to your advancing it.

正解 ②

**訳** もしあなたがプロジェクトを行いたいなら、行ってかまいません。私はあなたがそれを進めるのに異論を全く持っていません。

- **idea** 名 考え
- **mention** 名 陳述
- **objection** 名 反対
- **upset** 名 転覆

> objectionの語源はob（反対に）+ject（投げる）＝反論、異議

### 3

Mr. Davis wrote a letter of complaint to the company about the washing machine he bought from them.

正解 ①

**訳** デーヴィス氏は彼が購入した洗濯機についてその会社に苦情の手紙を書いた。

- **complaint** 名 苦情
- **conference** 名 会議
- **consequence** 名 結果
- **contribution** 名 貢献

### 4

Betty likes to hear favorable comments, but she can't stand criticism.

正解 ④

**訳** ベティーは好意的な意見を聞くのは好きだが、批判には耐えられない。

- **appreciation** 名 感謝
- **compliment** 名 お世辞
- **metaphor** 名 隠喩
- **criticism** 名 批判

## STEP 3 連鎖式に語彙を増やす 93

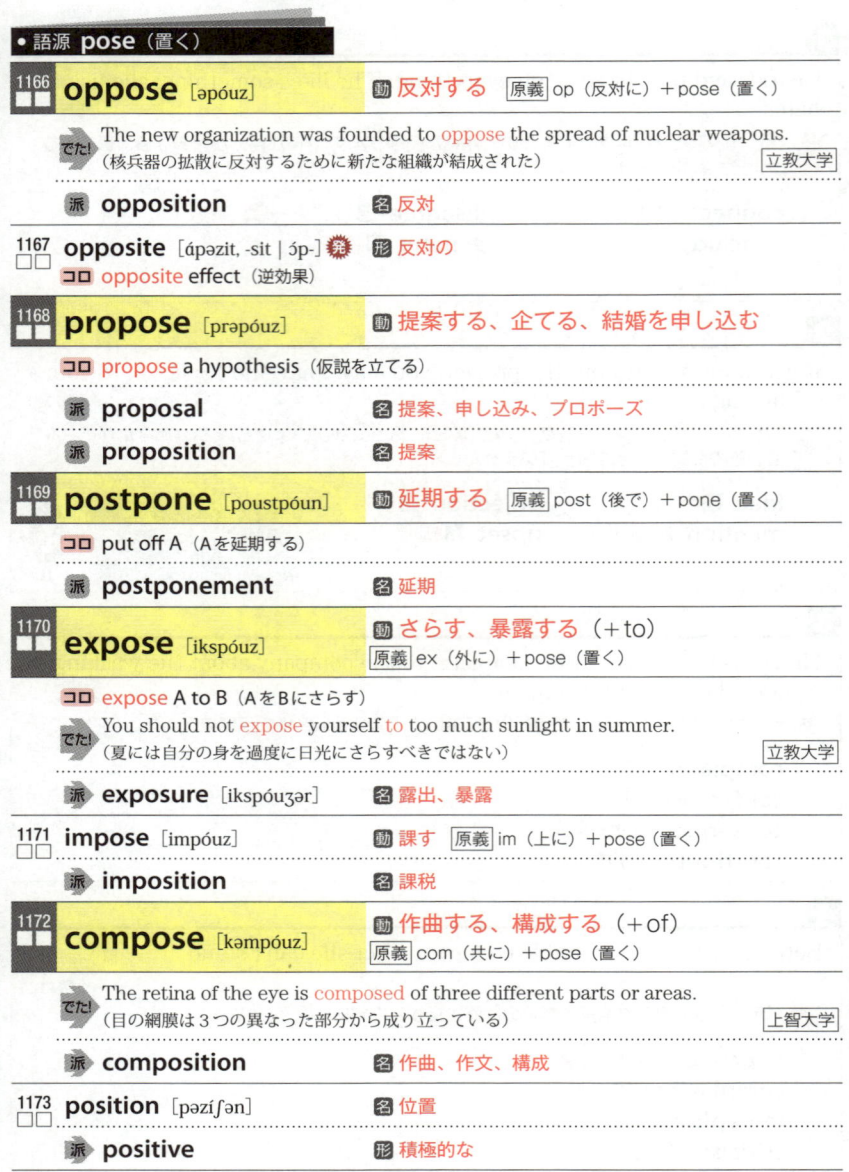

• 語源 pose（置く）

**1166 oppose** [əpóuz] 動 反対する 原義 op（反対に）+ pose（置く）

でた! The new organization was founded to oppose the spread of nuclear weapons.
（核兵器の拡散に反対するために新たな組織が結成された） 立教大学

派 opposition 名 反対

**1167 opposite** [ápəzit, -sit | ɔ́p-] 発 形 反対の
コロ opposite effect（逆効果）

**1168 propose** [prəpóuz] 動 提案する、企てる、結婚を申し込む

コロ propose a hypothesis（仮説を立てる）

派 proposal 名 提案、申し込み、プロポーズ

派 proposition 名 提案

**1169 postpone** [poustpóun] 動 延期する 原義 post（後で）+ pone（置く）

コロ put off A（Aを延期する）

派 postponement 名 延期

**1170 expose** [ikspóuz] 動 さらす、暴露する（+to）
原義 ex（外に）+ pose（置く）

コロ expose A to B（AをBにさらす）

でた! You should not expose yourself to too much sunlight in summer.
（夏には自分の身を過度に日光にさらすべきではない） 立教大学

派 exposure [ikspóuʒər] 名 露出、暴露

**1171 impose** [impóuz] 動 課す 原義 im（上に）+ pose（置く）

派 imposition 名 課税

**1172 compose** [kəmpóuz] 動 作曲する、構成する（+of）
原義 com（共に）+ pose（置く）

でた! The retina of the eye is composed of three different parts or areas.
（目の網膜は3つの異なった部分から成り立っている） 上智大学

派 composition 名 作曲、作文、構成

**1173 position** [pəzíʃən] 名 位置

派 positive 形 積極的な

392

**1174 compound** [kámpaund] [kəmpáund] 名 混合物、化合物、合成物 動 合成する

派 **composite** [kəmpázit] [kómpəzit] 名 合成物 形 混合の、合成の

派 **component** [kəmpóunənt] 名 構成要素

**1175 posture** [pástʃər | pós-] 名 姿勢

でた! A common posture for racing cyclists is to lean forward over the front wheel.
（競輪選手によくある姿勢は、前輪に覆うような前傾姿勢である） 立命館大学

**1176 object** [ábdʒikt | ɔ́b-] 動 反対する 名（個人的な願望としての）目的、物体、目的語

コロ object to A（Aに反対する）

派 **objective** 名 目標、目的格 形 目的の、客観的な

反 **subjective** [səbdʒéktiv] 形 主観的な

派 **objection** 名 反対、異論

コロ raise an objection to A（Aに異論を唱える）

**1177 protest** [próutest] 動 抗議する、反対する（+ against）

でた! Some people have protested against the new immigration law.
（新しい入国の法律に抗議した人もいる） 中央大学

派 **protestant** 名 プロテスタント

**1178 complain** [kəmpléin] 動 文句を言う（+ about, of）

でた! My mother complains of my being too lazy.
（私の母は私が怠け過ぎであることに文句を言っている） 中央大学

派 **complaint** 名 不平

**1179 criticize** [krítəsàiz] 動 批判する
コロ criticize A for B（AをBのことで批判する） コロ find fault with A（Aを非難する）

派 **critical** [krítikəl] 形 批評の、重大な、危機的な
コロ critical period hypothesis（臨界期仮説）

> ある一定の年齢を過ぎると言語習得が難しくなるという仮説

派 **critic** [krítik] 名 批評家、評論家

派 **criticism** [krítəsìzm] 名 批判、批評

**1180 deny** [dinái] 動 否定する（+ ing）

派 **denial** [dináiəl] 名 否定

UNIT 93 反対・苦情

Chapter5 Intention

# UNIT 94 明確・曖昧

**STEP 1** 過去問を解く

## 1

She didn't look at the painting for very long. It was (　　) that she didn't like it.

立命館大学

1. essential
2. obvious
3. crucial
4. substantial

## 2

I'm afraid I don't understand exactly what you mean. Could you be more (　　)?

学習院大学

1. peculiar
2. public
3. specific
4. vague

## 3

Nancy described the incident so (　　) I couldn't form any clear idea of what had happened.

明海大学

1. vaguely
2. valuably
3. changeably
4. variably

## 4

His <u>ambiguous</u> directions misled us; we did not know which road to take.

上智大学

1. doubtful
2. obscure
3. questionable
4. unequivocal
5. unreliable

## STEP 2 正解を見抜く

### 1

She didn't look at the painting for very long. It was obvious that she didn't like it.

正解 ②

**訳** 彼女は長い間その絵画を見なかった。彼女がそれを好んでいないことは明らかだ。

- **essential** 形 本質的な
- **obvious** 形 明白な
- **crucial** 形 重大な
- **substantial** 形 実在する

> obviousは見れば分かるという明白さ

### 2

I'm afraid I don't understand exactly what you mean. Could you be more specific?

正解 ③

**訳** 残念ながら、私はあなたが何を言っているかを理解していません。もっとはっきりしてもらえませんか。

- **peculiar** 形 独特の
- **specific** 形 明確な
- **public** 形 公共の
- **vague** 形 明確でない

> specificは具体的な明確さ

### 3

Nancy described the incident so vaguely I couldn't form any clear idea of what had happened.

正解 ①

**訳** ナンシーはその出来事をとても曖昧に説明したので、私は何が起きたのかはっきりと分からなかった。

- **vaguely** 副 曖昧に
- **changeably** 副 変わりやすく
- **variably** 副 変わりやすく
- **valuably** 副 高価に

> 霞んではっきりしない曖昧さ

### 4

His obscure directions misled us; we did not know which road to take.

正解 ②

**訳** 彼の曖昧な指示のため我々は迷ってしまった。どちらの道を選べばいいのか分からなかった。

- **doubtful** 形 疑わしい
- **questionable** 形 問題となる
- **unequivocal** 形 明瞭な
- **unreliable** 形 信頼できない
- **obscure** 形 曖昧な

> ambiguousは色んな意味で解釈できてしまう曖昧さ、obscureは複雑で難しく理解できない不明瞭さ

UNIT 94 明確・曖昧

Chapter5 Intention

## STEP 3 連鎖式に語彙を増やす 94

**1181 abstract** [ǽbstrækt] ア　形 抽象的な　動 抽出する
- abstract concept（抽象概念）
- 派 **abstraction**　名 抽象化

**1182 concrete** [kánkriːt | kɔ́ŋkriːt] ア　形 具体的な

**1183 define** [difáin]　動 定義する、限定する
- define A as B（AをBと定義する）
- 派 **definition** [dèfəníʃən]　名 定義、明確にすること
- definition of the word（単語の定義）
- 派 **definite**　形 明確な
- the definite article（定冠詞）
- 派 **definitely**　副 確かに（口語）、明確に
- 反 **indefinitely**　副 漠然と、不明確に、無期限に

**1184 absolute** [ǽbsəluːt] ア　形 絶対的な
- 派 **absolutely**　副 完全に、（否定の前で）全く
- absolutely necessary（絶対必要な）

**1185 specific** [spisífik] ア　形 明確な、特定の
- specific reason（明確な理由）
- 派 **specify**　動 明確に述べる、詳しく述べる

**1186 appear** [əpíər]　動 現れる、見える（+ to）
- show up（現れる）
- 派 **apparent**　形 明白な
- 派 **apparently**　副 明らかに、聞いたところでは
- 派 **appearance**　名 出現、外見
- judge by appearance（外見で判断する）

**1187 obvious** [ábviəs | ɔ́b-]　形 明白な
- obvious lies（明らかな嘘）
- 派 **obviously**　副 明らかに

**1188 explicit** [iksplísit]　形 明白な

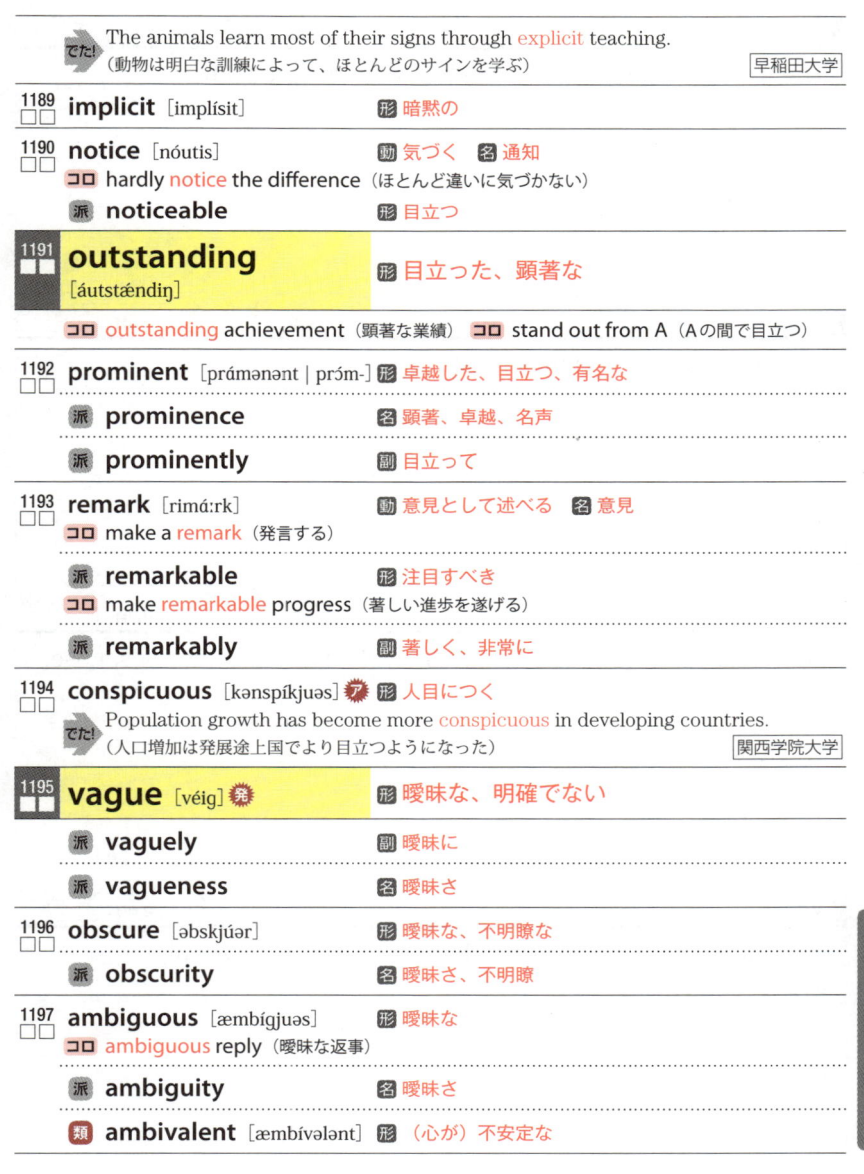

でた! The animals learn most of their signs through explicit teaching.
（動物は明白な訓練によって、ほとんどのサインを学ぶ）　早稲田大学

**1189 implicit** [implísit]　形 暗黙の

**1190 notice** [nóutis]　動 気づく　名 通知
- コロ hardly notice the difference（ほとんど違いに気づかない）
- 派 **noticeable**　形 目立つ

**1191 outstanding** [áutstǽndiŋ]　形 目立った、顕著な
- コロ outstanding achievement（顕著な業績）　コロ stand out from A（Aの間で目立つ）

**1192 prominent** [prάmənənt | prɔ́m-]　形 卓越した、目立つ、有名な
- 派 **prominence**　名 顕著、卓越、名声
- 派 **prominently**　副 目立って

**1193 remark** [rimάːrk]　動 意見として述べる　名 意見
- コロ make a remark（発言する）
- 派 **remarkable**　形 注目すべき
- コロ make remarkable progress（著しい進歩を遂げる）
- 派 **remarkably**　副 著しく、非常に

**1194 conspicuous** [kənspíkjuəs]　形 人目につく
でた! Population growth has become more conspicuous in developing countries.
（人口増加は発展途上国でより目立つようになった）　関西学院大学

**1195 vague** [véig]　形 曖昧な、明確でない
- 派 **vaguely**　副 曖昧に
- 派 **vagueness**　名 曖昧さ

**1196 obscure** [əbskjúər]　形 曖昧な、不明瞭な
- 派 **obscurity**　名 曖昧さ、不明瞭

**1197 ambiguous** [æmbígjuəs]　形 曖昧な
- コロ ambiguous reply（曖昧な返事）
- 派 **ambiguity**　名 曖昧さ
- 類 **ambivalent** [æmbívələnt]　形 （心が）不安定な

UNIT 94　明確・曖昧

Chapter5 Intention

# UNIT 95 類似・相違　STEP 1 過去問を解く

## 1

The work of a nurse is (　　) to the work of a doctor.

駒澤大学

1. regular
2. same
3. resemble
4. similar

## 2

They look so (　　) they must be twins.

日本大学

1. friendly
2. alike
3. near
4. double

## 3

Mary really (　　) after her mother; she has the same eyes, nose, and hair.

関西学院大学

1. gives
2. looks
3. keeps
4. takes

## 4

Both of them (　　) their father very much in physical appearance.

愛知大学

1. resemble
2. resemble for
3. resemble like
4. resemble to

## STEP 2 正解を見抜く

### 1

The work of a nurse is similar to the work of a doctor.

正解 ④

**訳** 看護師の仕事は医者の仕事と似ている。

- **regular** 形 通常の
- **same** 形 同じ
- **resemble** 動 似る
- **similar** 形 似ている

> similarの語源はsim（同じ）です。
> similar to A（Aに似ている）

### 2

They look so alike they must be twins.

正解 ②

**訳** 彼らはよく似ているので、双子に違いありません。

- **friendly** 形 親しい
- **alike** 形 似た
- **near** 形 近い
- **double** 形 2倍の

### 3

Mary really takes after her mother; she has the same eyes, nose, and hair.

正解 ④

**訳** メアリーは母親に本当に似ている。同じ目、鼻、髪をしているのだ。

- **take after** （直系親族に）似る

> take afterは（血縁関係がある人、直系親族に似る）

### 4

Both of them resemble their father very much in physical appearance.

正解 ①

**訳** 肉体的外観において、彼らはどちらも父親にとても似ている。

- **resemble** 動 似ている

> resembleは他動詞なので前置詞が付きません

UNIT 95 類似・相違

Chapter5 Intention | 399

## STEP 3 連鎖式に語彙を増やす 95

● 語源 sim sem (同じ)

**1198 resemble** [rizémbl]　動 似る

でた! He resembles his father in appearance.
（彼は外見が父親に似ている） 〔関西外国語大学〕

派 **resemblance**　名 類似

**1199 similar** [símələr]　形 似ている（+ to）

派 **similarity**　名 類似

**1200 simulation** [sìmjuléiʃən]　名 シミュレーション

派 **simulate**　動 真似る、模擬実験する

**1201 assemble** [əsémbl]　動 集める、組み立てる

派 **assembly**　名 集会、組み立て
コロ assembly line（流れ作業）

**1202 assimilate** [əsíməlèit]　動 同化する、吸収する

派 **assimilation**　名 同化

でた! Assimilation of a new cultural environment can be difficult.
（新しい文化的環境の同化は困難なものである） 〔TOEFL〕

**1203 simultaneous** [sàiməltéiniəs | sìm-]　形 同時の

派 **simultaneously**　副 同時に

でた! All of us live simultaneously in our own communities and in the world at large.
（我々は皆、自分自身の地域と全体として世界に同時に住んでいる） 〔早稲田大学〕

**1204 compare** [kəmpéər]　動 比較する、例える

コロ compare A with B（AとBを比較する）
でた! No laboratory is to be compared with ours in equipment.
（設備の点では我々の研究所に比べられるものはない） 〔横浜国立大学〕
コロ compare A to B（AをBに例える）
People sometimes compare death to sleep.
（死を睡眠と例えることがある） 〔成蹊大学〕

派 **comparison** [kəmpǽrisn]　名 比較

でた! The earth is small in comparison with the sun.
（太陽と比べて地球は小さい） 〔中央大学〕

派 **comparative**　形 比較による

| 派 | **comparatively** | 副 比較的に |

コロ comparatively easy（比較的に簡単な）

| 派 | **comparable** | 形 匹敵する |

## 1205 contrast [kɑ́ntræst | -trɑ́ːst]　名 対照、差異　動 比較対照する

でた! He contrasts older theories of agriculture with newer ones.
（彼は農業の旧説と新説を比較対照している）　　　　　　　　　TOEFL

## 1206 contrary [kɑ́ntreri]　名 反対、矛盾　形 反対の、矛盾した

コロ contrary to A（Aに反して）

でた! Contrary to his expectations, Peter ran out of money halfway through his vacation.
（予想に反して、ピーターは休暇の途中で金欠になった）　　　　上智大学

コロ on the contrary（それどころか、それとは逆に）
コロ to the contrary（それとは反対の）

でた! We have heard nothing to the contrary.
（私たちはそれに反する事は何も聞いていない）　　　　　　　西南学院大学

## 1207 alike [əláik]　形 同様で　副 同様に

コロ take after A（A（直系親族）に似る）

でた! Jane takes after her mother in voice and manner.
（ジェーンは声と仕草が母親に似ている）　　　　　　　　　慶應義塾大学

## 1208 difference [dífərəns]　名 違い、相違

コロ differences between Japan and China（日中間の相違）
コロ make no difference（重要でない）

でた! It makes no difference to me whether he comes or not.
（彼が来るかどうかは私にとって重要ではない）　　　　　　センター試験

| 派 | **differ** | 動 異なる（＋from） |

でた! Dogs differ from wolves in shape.
（犬はオオカミと形という点で異なる）　　　　　　　　　　慶應義塾大学

| 派 | **different** | 形 異なった（＋from） |

UNIT 95　類似・相違

Chapter5 Intention　401

# UNIT 96 適切・調整　STEP 1 過去問を解く

## 1

This is a (　　) place for a picnic.

1. likable
2. suitable
3. probably
4. careful

上智大学

## 2

If the seat is too high or too low, you can always (　　) it to a more comfortable height.

1. adopt
2. adjust
3. manage
4. focus

英語検定2級

## 3

A person whose working habits are flexible is easily able to (　　) to new job situations.

1. alight
2. adopt
3. adjust
4. arrest

上智大学

## 4

Since you know the family well, it would be <u>suitable</u> for you to send a card.

1. prestigious
2. appropriate
3. careless
4. outrageous

上智大学

## STEP 2 正解を見抜く

### 1

This is a suitable place for a picnic.

正解 ②

**訳** ここは、ピクニックに適した場所です。

- likable 形 好ましい
- suitable 形 ふさわしい
- probably 副 おそらく
- careful 形 注意深い

suitには（合う）という動詞があり、その派生語が形容詞のsuitable（ふさわしい）

### 2

If the seat is too high or too low, you can always adjust it to a more comfortable height.

正解 ②

**訳** 席が高すぎたり低すぎたりしたら、より快適な高さに調整可能です。

- adopt 動 採用する
- adjust 動 調節する
- manage 動 管理する
- focus 動 集中させる

adjustの語源はad（〜に向かって）＋just（正しい）＝正しくする＝調整する

### 3

A person whose working habits are flexible is easily able to adjust to new job situations.

正解 ③

**訳** 働く習慣がフレキシブルである人は、容易に新しい雇用状況に適応できます。

- alight 動 降りる
- adopt 動 採用する
- adjust 動 調節する
- arrest 動 逮捕する

### 4

Since you know the family well, it would be appropriate for you to send a card.

正解 ②

**訳** あなたはその家族をよく知っているので、あなたがカードを送るのが適切でしょう。

- prestigious 形 世評の高い
- appropriate 形 適切な
- careless 形 不注意な
- outrageous 形 ふらちな

UNIT 96 適切・調整

Chapter5 Intention

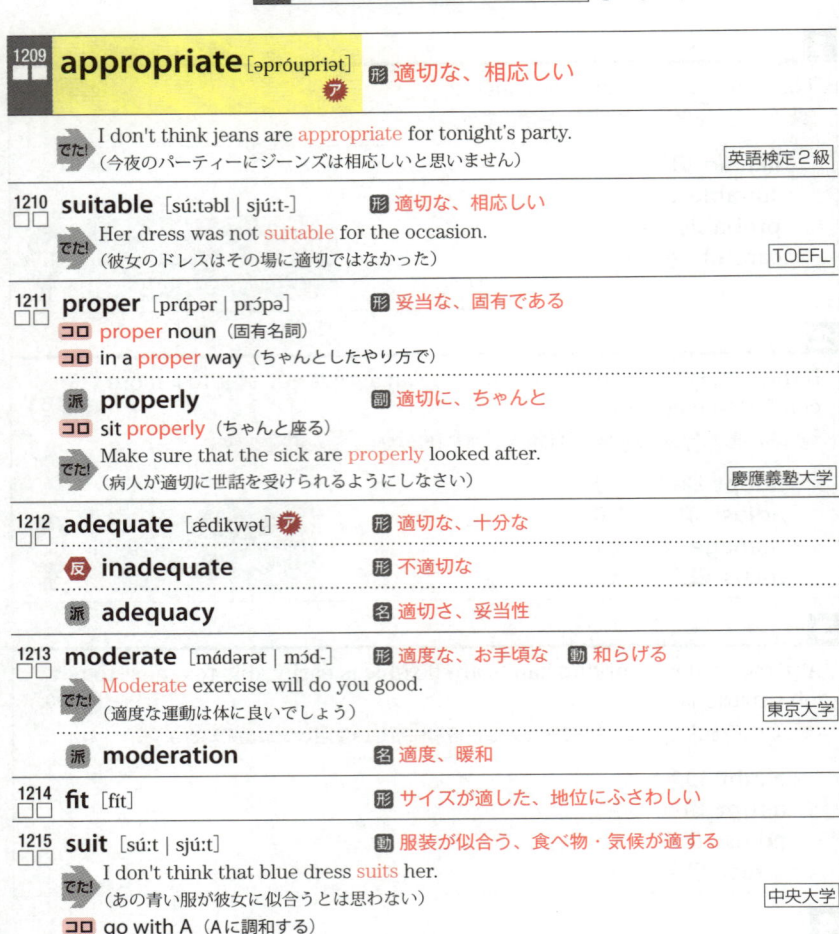

## STEP 3 連鎖式に語彙を増やす 96

**1209 appropriate** [əpróupriət] 形 適切な、相応しい
I don't think jeans are appropriate for tonight's party.
(今夜のパーティーにジーンズは相応しいと思いません) 英語検定2級

**1210 suitable** [súːtəbl | sjúːt-] 形 適切な、相応しい
Her dress was not suitable for the occasion.
(彼女のドレスはその場に適切ではなかった) TOEFL

**1211 proper** [prápər | própə] 形 妥当な、固有である
コロ proper noun (固有名詞)
コロ in a proper way (ちゃんとしたやり方で)

派 **properly** 副 適切に、ちゃんと
コロ sit properly (ちゃんと座る)
Make sure that the sick are properly looked after.
(病人が適切に世話を受けられるようにしなさい) 慶應義塾大学

**1212 adequate** [ædikwət] 形 適切な、十分な

反 **inadequate** 形 不適切な

派 **adequacy** 名 適切さ、妥当性

**1213 moderate** [mádərət | mɔ́d-] 形 適度な、お手頃な 動 和らげる
Moderate exercise will do you good.
(適度な運動は体に良いでしょう) 東京大学

派 **moderation** 名 適度、緩和

**1214 fit** [fit] 形 サイズが適した、地位にふさわしい

**1215 suit** [súːt | sjúːt] 動 服装が似合う、食べ物・気候が適する
I don't think that blue dress suits her.
(あの青い服が彼女に似合うとは思わない) 中央大学
コロ go with A (Aに調和する)
Which dressing goes with this kind of salad?
(この種類のサラダにはどちらのドレッシングが合いますか) 明海大学

**1216 match** [mætʃ] 動 調和する 名 試合
コロ match colors (色を合わせる)

## 1217 adapt [ədǽpt] 動 適合させる、順応する（＋to, for）

でた! Languages, like species, are highly adapted to their environments.
（言語は、種と同じように高度に環境に順応している） 関西学院大学

派 **adaption** 名 適合

派 **adaptable** 形 適応できる（＋to, for）

## 1218 adjust [ədʒʌ́st] 動 調整する、適合させる、順応する（＋to）

コロ adjust A to B（AをBに適合させる）

でた! Children need special help adjusting to different cultures.
（子供達が異文化に順応するためには、特別な助けが必要である） 関西学院大学

派 **adjustment** 名 調節、適応

UNIT 96 適切・調整

Chapter5 Intention

# UNIT 97 不足・十分

**STEP 1** 過去問を解く

## 1

Jim's wife thinks Jim hasn't spent <u>sufficient</u> time with their son.

東海大学

1. enough
2. efficient
3. early
4. late

## 2

There is evidence that the ancient Egyptians, Greeks, and Romans were right-handed, but if you go far enough back in history, the evidence for right-handedness becomes <u>scant</u> and indirect.

大阪大学

1. important
2. various
3. definite
4. insufficient

## 3

Because the storm had left so many people homeless, there was a (　　) of beds at the shelter.

南山大学

1. decrease
2. failure
3. lacking
4. shortage

## 4

The police released the suspect due to (　　) of evidence.

青山学院大学

1. insufficient
2. lack
3. scarce
4. short

## STEP 2 正解を見抜く

### 1

Jim's wife thinks Jim hasn't spent enough time with their son. 　　正解 ①

**訳** ジムの妻は、ジムが彼らの息子と十分な時間を過ごしていないと考えています。

- **enough** 形 十分な
- **efficient** 形 効率的な
- **early** 形 早い
- **late** 形 遅い

> sufficientの語源はsuf（下に）+fic（作る）＝下に作った物で足りる＝十分な

### 2

There is evidence that the ancient Egyptians, Greeks, and Romans were right-handed, but if you go far enough back in history, the evidence for right-handedness becomes insufficient and indirect. 　　正解 ④

**訳** 古代エジプト人、ギリシャ人、ローマ人達は右利きだったと示唆する証拠はあるが、歴史をずっと遡ってみると、右利きであったという証拠は不十分で間接的なものになってくる。

- **important** 形 重要な
- **various** 形 様々な
- **definite** 形 明確な
- **insufficient** 形 不十分な

### 3

Because the storm had left so many people homeless, there was a shortage of beds at the shelter. 　　正解 ④

**訳** その台風のせいで非常に多くの人々が家を失ったので、避難所のベッドが足りなくなった。

- **decrease** 名 減少
- **failure** 名 失敗
- **lacking** 形 足りなくて
- **shortage** 名 不足

### 4

The police released the suspect due to lack of evidence. 　　正解 ②

**訳** 警察は証拠不足を理由として容疑者を釈放した。

- **insufficient** 形 不十分な
- **lack** 名 不足
- **scarce** 形 少ない
- **short** 名 不足

> lack of A（Aの不足）

## STEP 3 連鎖式に語彙を増やす 97

### 1219 sufficient [səfíʃənt] ア 形 十分な
でた! The teenagers seemed to lack sufficient calcium.
（その十代の若者達は十分なカルシウムを摂っていないようだった） 早稲田大学

類 **enough** [ɪnʌ́f] 形 十分な

反 **insufficient** 形 不十分な

類 **deficient** [dɪfíʃənt] 形 不足した

派 **sufficiency** 名 十分

### 1220 shortage [ʃɔ́ːrtɪdʒ] 名 不足
コロ shortage of water（水不足）
でた! WHO proposed solutions to the global shortage of health care workers.
（世界保健機関は世界の医療関係者不足の解決法を提案した） センター試験

派 **short** 名 不足 形 短い
コロ be short of A（Aが不足している）
でた! We were short of food.
（私たちは食料が不足している） 駒澤大学
コロ run short of A（Aが不足する）
でた! He is running short of money.
（彼は金欠である） 亜細亜大学
コロ run out of A（Aが不足する、Aが切れる、尽きる）
でた! They seemed to have run out of fuel.
（彼らは燃料が切れたようだ） 東京理科大学
コロ fall short of A（Aが達しない）
でた! Sometime technology falls short of its promises.
（科学技術は時に、期待される結果に及ばないこともある） 青山学院大学

### 1221 lack [lǽk] 名 不足 動 欠ける
でた! Most of the world's poor lack the energy for the basic necessities of life.
（世界中の貧しい人々の多くは、基本的な生活必需品のエネルギーが不足している） 千葉工業大学

派 **lacking** 形 欠けて
でた! The mathematician was lacking in communication skills.
（その数学者はコミュニケーション能力に欠けていた） TOEFL

派 **wanting** 形 欠けている

### 1222 defect [díːfekt | dɪfékt] 名 欠点、欠陥

**defective** 形 欠陥のある
- defective products（欠陥商品）

1223 **scarce** [skéərs] 形 少ない、乏しい

派 **scarcely** 副 ほとんどない

派 **scarcity** [skéərsəti] 名 不足

In spite of the scarcity of good data, investigators continued their search.
（良好なデータが不足していたにも関わらず、調査官は研究を続けた） 獨協大学

UNIT 97 不足・十分

Chapter5 Intention

# UNIT 98　増加・減少　STEP 1 過去問を解く

## 1

( ) sea levels and the increase in greenhouse gases are the result of our actions.

東京理科大学

1. Adding
2. Decreasing
3. Overflowing
4. Raising
5. Rising

## 2

The force which makes objects fall is ( ).

早稲田大学

1. mass
2. weight
3. magnetism
4. gravity

## 3

Recently there has been a ( ) in the number of students talking history at this school, while computer science has become much more popular.

英語検定2級

1. benefit
2. fiction
3. decline
4. mixture

## 4

This should <u>alleviate</u> the pain; if it does not, we shall have to use stronger drugs.

上智大学

1. endure
2. lighten
3. humiliate
4. maneuver
5. worsen

## STEP 2 正解を見抜く

### 1

Rising sea levels and the increase in greenhouse gases are the result of our actions.

正解 ⑤

**訳** 海面上昇と温室効果ガスの増加は、我々の活動の結果です。

- **add** 動 加える
- **overflow** 動 あふれ出る
- **rise** 動 上がる
- **decrease** 動 減少する
- **raise** 動 上げる

> riseは自動詞で（上がる）
> raiseは他動詞で（上げる）

### 2

The force which makes objects fall is gravity.

正解 ④

**訳** 物体を落下させる力は引力である。

- **mass** 名 塊
- **weight** 名 重量
- **magnetism** 名 磁力
- **gravity** 名 重力、引力

### 3

Recently there has been a decline in the number of students talking history at this school, while computer science has become much more popular.

正解 ③

**訳** コンピュータサイエンスが人気になっている一方で、最近では学校で歴史の授業を受講する学生の数が減少している。

- **benefit** 名 利益
- **decline** 名 減少
- **fiction** 名 作り事
- **mixture** 名 混合

> declineの語源はde（下に）
> ＋cline（傾く）＝減少する

### 4

This should lighten the pain; if it does not, we shall have to use stronger drugs.

正解 ②

**訳** これで痛みが和らぐはずです。そうでなければ、もっと強い薬を使わざるを得ないでしょう。

- **endure** 動 耐える
- **humiliate** 動 恥をかかす
- **maneuver** 動 策略を用いる
- **worsen** 動 悪化させる
- **lighten** 動 軽くする

> alleviateの語源はal（〜に向かって）
> ＋lev（軽い）＝軽くする、和らげる

UNIT 98 増加・減少

Chapter5 Intention

## STEP 3 連鎖式に語彙を増やす 98

**1224 increase** [inkríːs] 🅰 　動 増える　名 増加
- increase by 50%（50%増える）　be on the increase（増加している）
- Crime is certainly on the increase in many of our big cities.（犯罪は、大都市の多くで確かに増加している）〔慶應義塾大学〕

**1225 add** [ǽd]　動 加える、追加する、増す（＋to）
- The novel added to his reputation.（彼の小説は彼の名声を増した）〔東京外国語大学〕

派 **addition**　名 増加、足し算
- in addition to A（Aに加えて）

派 **additional**　形 追加の

**1226 augment** [ɔːgmént]　動 増加する

**1227 soar** [sɔ́ːr]　動 急上昇する

**1228 grave** [gréiv]　形 重大な　名 墓場

派 **graveyard**　名 墓地

派 **gravity** [grǽvəti]　名 重力、引力、重大さ
- realize the gravity of the situation（状況の重大さに気が付く）

**1229 tomb** [túːm] 発　名 墓

類 **bury** [béri] 発　動 埋める、埋葬する

派 **burial** [bériəl] 発　名 埋葬

> bully（いじめ）と混同しないように注意。

**1230 burden** [bə́ːrdn]　名 重荷、負担　動 重荷を負わせる
- tax burden（税負担）

● 語源 **lev**（軽い）

**1231 relieve** [rilíːv]　動 和らげる、取り除く
- She learned that talking about one's troubles relieves some of the pain.（悩みを話すと辛さが幾分和らぐことを彼女は学んだ）〔香川大学〕

派 **relieved**　形 安心した
- I was relieved to find someone who speaks Japanese.（日本語を話す人を見つけてほっとした）〔明治学院大学〕

派 **relief**　名 安心

> It was a great relief to hear that my father's presentation went all right.
> (父のプレゼンがうまくいったと聞いて安心した) 立命館大学

## 1232 elevator [éləvèitər] 名 エレベーター
派 elevate 動 上げる

## 1233 alleviate [əlíːvièit] 動 軽減する
コロ alleviate the pain（痛みを和らげる）
派 alleviation 名 軽減

## 1234 light [láit] 形 軽い
派 lighten 動 軽くする

## 1235 tiny [táini] 形 とても小さい

## 1236 lessen [lésn] 動 減らす
派 less 形 より少ない
コロ Less is more.（より少ないことは、より豊かなこと）

## 1237 lower [lóuər] 動 低くする
コロ lower one's blood pressure（血圧を下げる）
派 low 形 低い

## 1238 slight [sláit] 形 僅かな
コロ slight difference（僅かな違い）
派 slightly 副 僅かに

## 1239 decline [dikláin] 動 減少する、断る　原義 de（下に）+ cline（傾く）

## 1240 decrease [dikríːs] 動 減少する
コロ decrease the speed（スピードを減らす）　コロ be on the decrease（減少している）

## 1241 reduce [ridjúːs | -djúːs] 動 減らす
コロ reduce weight（体重を減らす）　コロ cut down（減らす）
派 reduction [ridʌkʃən] 名 減少

## 1242 shrink [ʃríŋk] 動 縮める、縮む　活 shrink-shrank-shrunk
> Woolen clothes shrink in hot water.
> (ウール素材の服はお湯につけると縮む) 京都外国語大学

派 shrinkage 名 収縮、縮小

## 1243 diminish [dimíniʃ] 動 減らす、減少する

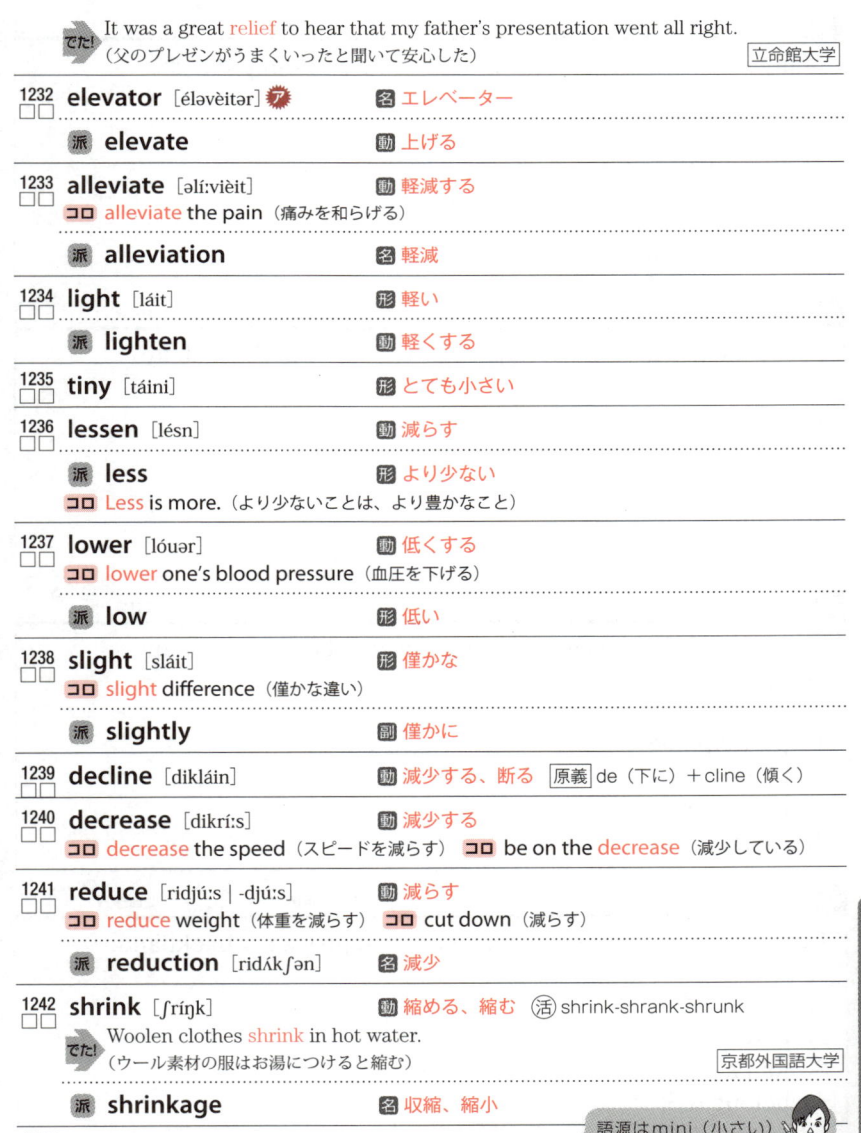

語源はmini（小さい）+ish（動詞化語尾）

Chapter5 Intention

# UNIT 99 参加・部分

## STEP 1 過去問を解く

### 1

Many students are (　　) in voluntary work in the local community.

学習院大学

1. excluded
2. involved
3. joined
4. participated

### 2

Everyone in the room is required to (　　) in this debate.

英語検定2級

1. express
2. arrange
3. participate
4. fulfill

### 3

The Olympic Games were a huge success because so many countries (　　).

センター試験

1. participated
2. played in
3. represented
4. took part in

### 4

I want to (　　) tennis club so I can improve my backhand.

慶応義塾大学

1. enroll
2. enter
3. join a
4. belong to

## STEP 2 正解を見抜く

### 1

Many students are involved in voluntary work in the local community.

正解 ②

訳 多くの学生達が地域社会におけるボランティア活動に参加している。

- **exclude** 動 除外する
- **involve** 動 巻き込む
- **join** 動 加わる
- **participate** 動 参加する

be involved in A（Aに関与している、参加している）

### 2

Everyone in the room is required to participate in this debate.

正解 ③

訳 その部屋の人は皆、この討論に参加しなければなりません。

- **express** 動 表現する
- **arrange** 動 整える
- **participate** 動 加わる
- **fulfill** 動 （約束などを）果たす

participateの語源はpart（部分）+cip（取る）+ate（動詞化語尾）＝全体の一部を取る＝参加する

### 3

The Olympic Games were a huge success because so many countries participated.

正解 ①

訳 オリンピック大会は非常に多くの国々が参加したので大成功でした。

- **participate** 動 参加する
- **played in** 〜の中で遊ぶ
- **represent** 動 代表する
- **take part in** 参加する

so以下の文章に目的語がないため他動詞のparticipateを選びます

### 4

I want to join a tennis club so I can improve my backhand.

正解 ③

訳 私のバックハンドが上達できるように、テニスクラブに入会したいと思います。

- **enroll** 動 入会する
- **enter** 動 入る
- **join** 動 参加する
- **belong to** 〜に所属する

tennis clubには冠詞のaが必要なのでjoin aが正解です

UNIT 99 参加・部分

Chapter5 Intention | 415

## STEP 3 連鎖式に語彙を増やす

### ● 語源 part（部分）

**1244 part** [páːrt] 　　名 部分

- Measurement is an essential part of science.
（測定は科学の本質的な部分である） 〔青山学院大学〕
- コロ take part in A （Aに参加する）
- I have to take part in a meeting.
（私は会議に参加しなければならない） 〔関東学院大学〕

**1245 partial** [páːrʃəl] 　　形 部分的な、不公平な

- 反 **impartial** 　　形 公平な
- 派 **impartiality** 　　名 公平、不偏、公明正大
- Judges are known for their impartiality.
（陪審員は公明正大で知られている） 〔TOEFL〕

**1246 particle** [páːrtikl] 　　名 破片、分詞、微量

- コロ a particle of A （少量のA）
- Particles of dust can destroy electronic instruments.
（ほこりの粒子は電子機器を破壊しうる） 〔TOEFL〕

**1247 portion** [pɔ́ːrʃən] 　　名 部分、分け前

- 派 **proportion** 　　名 割合、比率
- In Los Angeles, the proportion of Spanish speakers is more than half.
（ロサンゼルスではスペイン語を話す人の割合は、半分以上である） 〔立命館大学〕
- 類 **section** [sékʃən] 　　名 部分、新聞の欄、部門、課

**1248 apart** [əpáːrt] 　　副 ばらばらに、離れて

- 派 **apartment** 　　名 アパート

**1249 participate** [pɑːrtísəpèit] 　　動 参加する（＋in）

- He is trying to get the students to participate.
（彼は学生に参加させようとしている） 〔TOEFL〕
- 類 **join** [dʒɔ́in] 　　動 加わる
- I'm disappointed that you can't join us.
（あなたが加わることが出来なくて私はがっかりです） 〔青山学院大学〕

**派 participation** 名 参加

でた！ Some citizens vote or engage in more active forms of participation.
（投票をしたり、より積極的な参加に関わっている市民もいる）
東京大学

**派 participant** [pɑːrtísəpənt] 名 参加者

## 1250 particular [pərtíkjulər] 形 特定の

コロ in particular（特に）　コロ be particular about A（Aに関して好みがうるさい）

**派 particularly** 副 とりわけ

**派 particularity** 名 特徴、特定性

## 1251 party [pάːrti] 名 パーティー、集まり、政党

でた！ We take it for granted that political parties are vital to modern political life.
（私たちは政党が現代の政治世界にとって不可欠なものであるということを当然と思っている）
早稲田大学

## 1252 departure [dipάːrtʃər] 名 出発

でた！ I informed them of my intended departure.
（私は予定していた出発について彼らに知らせた）
関西学院大学

**反 arrival** [əráivəl] 名 到着

**派 depart** 動 出発する

でた！ Japanese trains are famous for departing and arriving exactly on time.
（日本の列車は時間通りに出発し到着することで有名である）
東北学院大学

**反 arrive** 動 到着する（＋at）

## 1253 department [dipάːrtmənt] 名 部門、デパートの売り場、大学の学部・学科

コロ department of education（教育学部）

でた！ He is in charge of the men's clothing department.
（彼は紳士服売り場の担当です）
上智大学

## 1254 involve [inválv | -vɔ́lv] 動 巻き込む、関与させる、伴う

コロ be involved in A（Aにかかわる）

でた！ Some parents are actively involved in their children's education.
（子供の教育に積極的にかかわる親もいる）
慶應義塾大学

**派 involvement** 名 関与

UNIT 99 参加・部分

Chapter5 Intention　417

# UNIT 100 勝敗・平等

**STEP 1 過去問を解く**

## 1

More than 100 students will (　　) in the city's English speech contest this year.

英語検定2級

1. compete
2. analyze
3. pretend
4. defend

## 2

The soccer team from Melbourne was missing two of its best players, so it was no surprise that the team was easily (　　) in the game.

英語検定2級

1. resigned
2. blessed
3. envied
4. defeated

## 3

We (　　) our opponents by three goals to nothing.

武蔵大学

1. beat
2. damaged
3. fought
4. pleased
5. won

## 4

Job opportunities for men and women should be (　　).

学習院大学

1. same
2. one
3. common
4. equal

## STEP 2 正解を見抜く

### 1

More than 100 students will compete in the city's English speech contest this year.  
正解 1

**訳** 今年、100人以上の学生が、市の英語弁論大会で参加するでしょう。

- **compete** 動 競争する
- **analyze** 動 分析する
- **pretend** 動 〜のふりをする
- **defend** 動 防御する

> competeの語源はcom（共に）＋pet（求める）＝共に求め合う＝競争する

### 2

The soccer team from Melbourne was missing two of its best players, so it was no surprise that the team was easily defeated in the game.  
正解 4

**訳** メルボルンから来たサッカーチームは、2人の最も良い選手が欠場だったので、チームが試合で簡単に負けたのは、驚きではありませんでした。

- **resign** 動 辞職する
- **envy** 動 うらやむ
- **bless** 動 祝福する
- **defeat** 動 負かす

### 3

We beat our opponents by three goals to nothing.  
正解 1

**訳** 我々は相手に3対0のゴールで打ち勝った。

- **beat** 動 打つ
- **damage** 動 ダメージを与える
- **fight** 動 戦う
- **please** 動 喜ばせる
- **win** 動 勝つ

### 4

Job opportunities for men and women should be equal.  
正解 4

**訳** 男女の雇用機会は均等であるべきだ。

- **same** 形 同じ
- **one** 名 1つ
- **common** 形 共通の
- **equal** 形 等しい

> equalの語源はequ（等しい）

UNIT 100 勝敗・平等

Chapter5 Intention

## STEP 3 連鎖式に語彙を増やす 100

- 語源 bat（戦う）

**1255 battle** [bétl]　動 戦う

コロ battle field（戦場）

類 **match** [mætʃ]　名 試合　動 調和する

**1256 combat** [kəmbǽt, kámbæt | kɔ́mbæt, kʌ́m-]　動 戦う　名 戦闘

debate about（一般的な事柄を討論する）
debate on（専門的な事柄を討論する）

**1257 debate** [dibéit]　動 討論する（+ about, on）

**1258 argue** [áːrgjuː]　動 議論する、主張する

派 **argument**　名 議論、主張

**1259 dispute** [dispjúːt]　動 論争する、口論する　名 論争、口論

**1260 discuss**　動 議論する

aboutは付かない

派 **discussion**　名 議論

**1261 controversy** [kántrəvə̀ːrsi | kɔ́n-]　名 論争（+ over）

でた！ There remains a controversy over how strong the family is.
（家族の絆がどれだけ強いかという論争が残っている）
〔東京外国語大学〕

派 **controversial**　形 論争の、論争の余地がある

でた！ The use of helmets is one of the most controversial issues in the sport.
（ヘルメットの使用はスポーツにおいて最も論争の余地がある問題の一つである）
〔明治大学〕

**1262 overcome** [òuvərkʌ́m]　動 打ち勝つ、克服する
活 overcome-overcame-overcome

コロ overcome obstacles（障害に打ち勝つ）

でた！ With more patience, you could have overcome the hardship.
（もう少し忍耐力があったら、その苦難に打ち勝てたかもしれない）
〔東京国際大学〕

コロ get over A（Aを乗り越える）

**1263 beat** [bíːt]　動 打つ、連打する

**1264 defeat** [difíːt]　名 負け、敗北　動 打ち負かす、破る

でた！ My favorite soccer team was badly defeated in the final match.
（私の好きなサッカーチームは最終戦でひどく打ち負かされた）
〔早稲田大学〕

**1265 struggle** [strʌ́gl]　動 戦う（+ with）

**1266 victim** [víktim]　名 犠牲者、被害者

> Those who kill themselves are, in a sense, victims of this society.
> （自殺をする人たちは、ある意味では、この社会の犠牲者だ） 成蹊大学

**派** **victimize** 動 犠牲にする

1267 **opponent** [ápəzit, -sit | ɔ́p-] 発 名 敵、対戦相手

**類** **rival** [ráivəl] 名（賞や順位を巡って競う）相手、ライバル

**類** **enemy** [énəmi] 名（危害を与えてくる）敵

1268 **conflict** [kənflíkt] 名 紛争、対立

> The American Civil War was the bloodiest conflict in American history.
> （アメリカ南北戦争は米国史上で最も血だらけの争いでした） 中央大学

1269 **quarrel** [kwɔ́:rəl | kwɔ́r-] 名 口論、喧嘩

> What brought about the quarrel between them?
> （何が彼らのけんかの原因だったの） 横浜市立大学

1270 **friction** [fríkʃən] 名 摩擦
コロ trade friction（貿易摩擦）

1271 **victory** [víktəri] 名 勝利

1272 **championship** [tʃǽmpiənʃip] 名 選手権大会

1273 **triumph** [tráiəmf] 発 名 大勝利

● 語源 **pet**（求める）

1274 **compete** [kəmpí:t] 動 競争する、競う（＋with）
原義 com（共に）＋pete（求める）

> Developing countries can compete with developed countries in the new economy.
> （新しい経済体制で発展途上国は先進国と競うことができる） 慶応義塾大学

**派** **competition** 名 競争、コンペ

> "Friendship first、competition second" is a common motto in China.
> （「友情第一、競争第二」は中国のよく知られたモットーだ） 関西学院大学

**派** **competitive** [kəmpétətiv] 形 競争的な
コロ competitive society（競争社会）

> Finding one's own way in today's competitive business environment is difficult.
> （今日の競争的なビジネスの環境では、自分自身の道を見いだすことは難しい） TOEFL

| 1275 | **appetite** [ǽpətàit] | 名 食欲 |

| 1276 | **competent** [kámpətənt \| kɔ́m-] | 形 有能な |

- 派 **competence** 名 能力、適性
- コロ communicative competence（コミュニケーション能力）

● 語源 **equ**（等しい）

| 1277 | **equal** [íːkwəl] | 形 等しい 動 等しい |

でた! Six times seven is equal to forty-two.
（7 × 6 = 42） 〔関西外国語大学〕

でた! I thought I was good at tennis, but I am equal to you.
（私はテニスが上手だと思っていたが、あなたと同じくらいである） 〔上智大学〕

- 派 **equality** 名 平等

でた! In Sweden and Denmark, emphasis is placed on gender equality at work.
（スウェーデンやデンマークでは、職場での男女平等が重視されている） 〔明治学院大学〕

| 1278 | **equivalent** [ikwívələnt] | 形 等しい、相当する |

| 1279 | **equation** [ikwéiʒən \| -ʃən] | 名 方程式 |

- コロ solve an equation（方程式を解く）

| 1280 | **equip** [ikwíp] 発 | 動 備え付ける、装備する、搭載する |

- コロ equip A with B（AにBを備え付ける）

でた! The cars will be equipped with a variety of sensors.
（その車には様々なセンサーが搭載されるでしょう） 〔TOEFL〕

- 派 **equipment** 名 装置、設備

| 1281 | **furnish** [fə́ːrniʃ] | 動 供給する、家具を備え付ける |

- コロ furnish A with B（AにBを備え付ける）
- 派 **furniture** [fə́ːrnitʃər] 名 家具

# INDEX

## A

- ability ... 062
- able ... 062
- abnormal ... 259
- abolish ... 330
- abolition ... 330
- abortion ... 376
- abrupt ... 234
- absence ... 132
- absent ... 132
- absolute ... 396
- absolutely ... 396
- absorb ... 090
- absorption ... 090
- abstain ... 153
- abstract ... 396
- abstraction ... 396
- absurd ... 319
- absurdity ... 319
- abuse ... 384
- accelerate ... 071
- acceleration ... 071
- accept ... 294
- acceptance ... 294
- accident ... 368
- accidental ... 368
- accidentally ... 368
- accommodate ... 063
- accommodation ... 063
- accompaniment ... 048
- accompany ... 048
- accomplish ... 141
- accomplishment ... 141
- accord ... 381
- account ... 231
- accumulate ... 211
- accumulation ... 211
- accuracy ... 361
- accurate ... 361
- accusation ... 247
- accuse ... 247
- accustom ... 136
- achieve ... 141
- achievement ... 141
- acknowledge ... 078
- acknowledgement ... 078
- acquaint ... 049
- acquaintance ... 048
- acquire ... 082
- acquisition ... 082
- act ... 157
- action ... 157
- active ... 157
- activity ... 157
- adapt ... 405
- adaptable ... 405
- adaption ... 405
- add ... 412
- addict ... 091
- addiction ... 091
- addition ... 412
- additional ... 412
- adequacy ... 404
- adequate ... 404
- adjust ... 405
- adjustment ... 405
- administer ... 210
- administration ... 210
- admirable ... 283
- admiration ... 283
- admire ... 283
- admission ... 295
- admit ... 295
- adopt ... 137
- adoption ... 137
- advance ... 071
- advantage ... 071
- advent ... 140
- adverb ... 114
- advertise ... 348
- advertisement ... 348
- advocacy ... 187
- advocate ... 187
- affair ... 286
- affect ... 357
- affection ... 357
- affirm ... 049
- affirmation ... 049
- affirmative ... 049
- affluence ... 357
- affluent ... 357
- afford ... 227
- affordable ... 227
- aggression ... 070
- aggressive ... 070
- agree ... 295
- agreement ... 295
- agricultural ... 032
- agriculture ... 032
- aid ... 353
- aim ... 377
- alarm ... 326
- alien ... 339
- alike ... 401
- allergy ... 124
- alleviate ... 413
- alleviation ... 413
- allocate ... 170
- allocation ... 170
- allow ... 295
- allowance ... 295
- alter ... 349
- alternate ... 349
- alternately ... 349
- alternative ... 349
- amateur ... 206
- ambassador ... 186
- ambition ... 141
- ambitious ... 141
- ambulance ... 125
- amuse ... 074
- amusement ... 074
- amusing ... 074
- analysis ... 389
- analyst ... 389
- analyze ... 389
- ancestor ... 037, 365
- ancestry ... 037, 365
- ancient ... 263
- anger ... 045
- angry ... 045
- animal ... 036
- anniversary ... 263
- annoy ... 302
- annoyance ... 302
- annual ... 263
- annually ... 263
- anticipate ... 377
- anticipation ... 377
- antipathy ... 045
- anxiety ... 303
- anxious ... 303
- apart ... 416
- apartment ... 416
- apologize ... 310
- apology ... 310
- apparent ... 396
- apparently ... 396
- appeal ... 307
- appealing ... 307
- appear ... 396
- appearance ... 396
- appendix ... 053
- appetite ... 422
- applicant ... 067
- application ... 067
- apply ... 067
- appoint ... 175, 267
- appointment ... 175, 267
- appreciate ... 238
- appreciation ... 238
- appreciative ... 238
- apprehend ... 250
- appropriate ... 404
- approval ... 295
- approve ... 295
- architect ... 215
- architectural ... 215
- architecture ... 215
- area ... 171
- argue ... 420
- argument ... 420
- aristocracy ... 187
- arm ... 326
- army ... 326
- arrest ... 250
- arrival ... 417
- arrive ... 417
- article ... 107
- artificial ... 016
- ascertain ... 254
- ascribe ... 373
- ashamed ... 303
- assemble ... 211, 400
- assembly ... 211, 400
- assert ... 049
- assess ... 356
- assessment ... 356
- assimilate ... 400
- assimilation ... 400
- assist ... 353
- assistance ... 353
- assistant ... 353
- associate ... 182
- association ... 182
- assurance ... 254
- assure ... 254
- asterisk ... 079
- astronaut ... 079
- astronomy ... 079
- atmosphere ... 024
- atmospheric ... 024
- attach ... 128
- attachment ... 128
- attain ... 141, 152
- attainment ... 152
- attempt ... 381
- attend ... 132
- attendance ... 132
- attention ... 132
- attitude ... 040
- attorney ... 242
- attract ... 306
- attraction ... 307
- attractive ... 307
- attribute ... 373
- attribution ... 373
- audience ... 218
- audio ... 218
- audition ... 218
- auditorium ... 218
- augment ... 412
- author ... 107
- authority ... 107
- authorize ... 107
- autobiography ... 099
- availability ... 384
- available ... 384
- avoid ... 166
- avoidable ... 166
- avoidance ... 166
- aware ... 086
- awareness ... 086
- awful ... 315

## B

- background ... 206
- ballot ... 190
- ban ... 323
- bankrupt ... 234
- bankruptcy ... 234
- barren ... 033
- base ... 195
- basic ... 195
- bath ... 036
- bathe ... 036
- battle ... 420
- bear ... 094
- beat ... 420
- beg ... 194
- begger ... 194
- beginning ... 279
- behave ... 040
- behavior ... 040
- belong ... 338
- belongings ... 338
- beneficial ... 223
- benefit ... 223
- bill ... 227
- bind ... 163
- biodiversity ... 348
- biography ... 099
- birth ... 036
- book ... 175
- border ... 334
- bother ... 302
- boundary ... 334
- brave ... 381
- bravery ... 381
- budget ... 227
- build ... 214
- building ... 214
- burden ... 412
- bureau ... 187
- bureaucracy ... 187
- bureaucratic ... 187
- burial ... 412
- bury ... 412
- business ... 202

423

## C

| Word | Page |
|---|---|
| calamity | 028 |
| calligraphy | 099 |
| campaign | 190 |
| cancel | 266 |
| cancer | 124 |
| candidate | 190 |
| candle | 190 |
| capability | 063 |
| capable | 063 |
| capacity | 062 |
| captive | 294 |
| captivity | 294 |
| capture | 294 |
| career | 206 |
| carriage | 163 |
| carsick | 163 |
| case | 368 |
| casual | 368 |
| casualty | 368 |
| catastrophe | 028 |
| catastrophic | 028 |
| cause | 198 |
| caution | 314 |
| cautious | 314 |
| cease | 330 |
| ceaseless | 330 |
| celebrate | 239 |
| celebrated | 239 |
| celebration | 239 |
| cell | 148 |
| cellphone | 148 |
| center | 090 |
| centipede | 174 |
| century | 262 |
| certain | 254 |
| certainly | 254 |
| certainty | 254 |
| certificate | 255 |
| certification | 255 |
| certify | 254 |
| championship | 421 |
| chance | 364 |
| chandelier | 190 |
| chaos | 167 |
| chaotic | 167 |
| charge | 227 |
| charm | 307 |
| charming | 307 |
| chat | 149 |
| chief | 195 |
| choice | 344 |
| choose | 344 |
| chronic | 129 |
| chronological | 263 |
| circulate | 121 |
| circulation | 121 |
| circumstance | 020 |
| civil | 032 |
| civilization | 032 |
| claim | 258 |
| clash | 029 |
| clever | 063 |
| client | 218 |
| climate | 024 |
| clue | 389 |
| cognition | 078 |
| cognitive | 078 |
| coincide | 368 |
| coincidence | 368 |
| coincident | 368 |
| collaborate | 203 |
| collaboration | 203 |
| collapse | 028 |
| colleague | 048 |
| collect | 211, 344 |
| collection | 211, 344 |
| collective | 344 |
| colonial | 032 |
| colonize | 032 |
| colony | 032 |
| combat | 420 |
| combination | 211 |
| combine | 211 |
| comedy | 314 |
| come of age | 037 |
| comfort | 327 |
| comfortable | 327 |
| comic | 315 |
| command | 179 |
| commence | 279 |
| commencement | 067, 279 |
| commit | 372 |
| commitment | 372 |
| commodity | 036 |
| common | 259 |
| community | 183 |
| commute | 163 |
| commuter | 163 |
| companion | 048 |
| companionship | 048 |
| company | 048 |
| comparable | 401 |
| comparative | 401 |
| comparatively | 401 |
| compare | 400 |
| comparison | 400 |
| compassion | 091 |
| compel | 326 |
| compensate | 226 |
| compensation | 226 |
| compete | 421 |
| competence | 422 |
| competent | 422 |
| competition | 421 |
| competitive | 422 |
| complain | 393 |
| complaint | 393 |
| compliment | 238 |
| complimentary | 238 |
| component | 393 |
| compose | 074, 392 |
| composer | 074 |
| composite | 393 |
| composition | 074, 393 |
| compound | 393 |
| comprehend | 082 |
| comprehensible | 082 |
| comprehension | 082 |
| comprehensive | 082 |
| compress | 291 |
| compression | 291 |
| comprise | 259 |
| compromise | 353 |
| compulsion | 326 |
| compulsory | 326 |
| conceal | 111 |
| concealment | 111 |
| concede | 295 |
| conceivable | 295 |
| conceive | 294 |
| concentrate | 090 |
| concentration | 090 |
| concept | 294 |
| conception | 295 |
| concern | 286 |
| concerning | 286 |
| concise | 360 |
| concrete | 396 |
| condition | 020 |
| conditional | 020 |
| conduct | 144 |
| conductor | 144 |
| confer | 210 |
| conference | 210 |
| confess | 247 |
| confession | 247 |
| confide | 380 |
| confidence | 380 |
| confident | 380 |
| confidential | 380 |
| confirm | 049 |
| confirmation | 049 |
| conflict | 421 |
| conform | 218 |
| conformity | 218 |
| confuse | 298 |
| confusion | 298 |
| congratulate | 239 |
| congratulation | 239 |
| congress | 187 |
| conquer | 194 |
| conquest | 195 |
| conscious | 086 |
| consciously | 086 |
| consciousness | 086 |
| consecutive | 271 |
| consensus | 044 |
| consent | 044 |
| consequence | 198, 270 |
| consequent | 270 |
| consequently | 270 |
| conservation | 029 |
| conservative | 029 |
| conserve | 029 |
| consider | 079 |
| considerable | 079 |
| considerably | 079 |
| considerate | 079 |
| consideration | 079 |
| consist | 259 |
| consistence | 259 |
| consistent | 259 |
| conspicuous | 397 |
| constellation | 079 |
| constitute | 187 |
| constitution | 187 |
| constitutional | 187 |
| constraint | 323 |
| constrict | 322 |
| construct | 214 |
| construction | 214 |
| consult | 103 |
| consume | 384 |
| consumer | 384 |
| consumption | 384 |
| contact | 128 |
| contagious | 128 |
| contain | 153 |
| contaminate | 028 |
| contamination | 028 |
| contemporary | 262 |
| content | 153 |
| continent | 270 |
| continental | 270 |
| continue | 270 |
| continuity | 270 |
| contract | 307 |
| contradict | 102 |
| contradiction | 103 |
| contradictory | 103 |
| contrary | 401 |
| contrast | 401 |
| contribute | 373 |
| contribution | 373 |
| control | 210 |
| controversial | 420 |
| controversy | 420 |
| convenience | 311 |
| convenient | 310 |
| convention | 136 |
| conventional | 136 |
| conversation | 148, 348 |
| converse | 149, 348 |
| conversion | 230 |
| convert | 230 |
| convey | 163 |
| convict | 250 |
| conviction | 250 |
| convince | 352 |
| convincing | 352 |
| cooperate | 202 |
| cooperation | 202 |
| cooperative | 202 |
| cope | 385 |
| corporate | 202 |
| corporation | 202 |
| correspond | 311 |
| correspondence | 311 |
| corrupt | 234 |
| corruption | 234 |
| cost | 226 |
| cough | 124 |
| council | 210 |
| count | 053 |
| countryside | 182 |
| courage | 381 |
| courageous | 381 |
| court | 246 |
| courteous | 319 |
| courtesy | 319 |
| co-worker | 048 |
| crash | 029 |
| create | 140 |
| creation | 140 |
| creative | 140 |
| creativity | 140 |
| creature | 140 |
| credible | 380 |
| credit | 380 |
| credulous | 380 |
| crew | 048 |
| crime | 250 |
| criminal | 250 |
| crisis | 314 |
| criterion | 259 |
| critical | 393 |
| critic | 393 |
| criticism | 393 |
| criticize | 393 |
| crop | 033 |

| Word | Page |
|---|---|
| crowd | 167 |
| crowded | 167 |
| crucial | 191 |
| crush | 029 |
| cultivate | 032 |
| cultivation | 032 |
| cultural | 032 |
| culture | 032 |
| cure | 121 |
| curiosity | 307 |
| curious | 307 |
| currency | 230 |
| current | 230 |
| currently | 230 |
| custom | 136 |
| customer | 218 |
| customize | 136 |
| customs | 136 |

## D

| Word | Page |
|---|---|
| damage | 258 |
| danger | 314 |
| dangerous | 314 |
| deadline | 266 |
| deal | 385 |
| debate | 420 |
| debt | 234 |
| decade | 262 |
| decency | 319 |
| decent | 319 |
| decently | 319 |
| decide | 360 |
| decision | 360 |
| declaration | 111 |
| declare | 111 |
| decline | 298, 413 |
| decrease | 413 |
| dedicate | 372 |
| dedication | 372 |
| defeat | 420 |
| defect | 408 |
| defective | 409 |
| defend | 247 |
| defense | 247 |
| defensive | 247 |
| deficient | 408 |
| deficit | 235 |
| define | 396 |
| definite | 396 |
| definitely | 396 |
| definition | 396 |
| degrade | 070 |
| degree | 070 |
| deject | 299 |
| dejected | 299 |
| delay | 167 |
| deliberate | 377 |
| delicious | 083 |
| deliver | 163 |
| delivery | 163 |
| demand | 194 |
| demanding | 194 |
| demerit | 071 |
| democracy | 186 |
| democratic | 187 |
| demonstrate | 110 |
| demonstration | 110 |
| denial | 393 |
| deny | 393 |
| depart | 417 |
| department | 417 |
| departure | 417 |
| depend | 052 |
| dependable | 052 |
| dependence | 052 |
| dependent | 052 |
| deposit | 231 |
| depress | 290 |
| depressed | 290 |
| depression | 290 |
| deprivation | 250 |
| deprive | 250 |
| derivation | 017 |
| derivative | 017 |
| derive | 017 |
| descend | 037, 365 |
| descendant | 037, 365 |
| descent | 037, 365 |
| describe | 098 |
| description | 098 |
| descriptive | 098 |
| desert | 033 |
| deserted | 033 |
| deserve | 029, 239 |
| designate | 175, 345 |
| designation | 175, 345 |
| despair | 310 |
| desperate | 310 |
| desperation | 310 |
| despise | 283 |
| destination | 369 |
| destiny | 369 |
| destroy | 029 |
| destruction | 029 |
| destructive | 029 |
| detach | 128 |
| detachment | 128 |
| detain | 153 |
| detect | 250 |
| detection | 250 |
| detective | 250 |
| detention | 153 |
| determination | 360 |
| determine | 360 |
| develop | 141 |
| development | 141 |
| device | 141 |
| devise | 140 |
| devote | 372 |
| devotion | 372 |
| diabetes | 124 |
| diabetic | 124 |
| diagnose | 125 |
| diagnosis | 125 |
| dictate | 102 |
| dictation | 102 |
| dictator | 102 |
| dictionary | 102 |
| differ | 401 |
| difference | 401 |
| dignity | 282 |
| digress | 071 |
| digression | 071 |
| diminish | 413 |
| diplomacy | 187 |
| diplomat | 187 |
| disability | 062 |
| disable | 062 |
| disadvantage | 071 |
| disagree | 295 |
| disappoint | 267 |
| disappointment | 267 |
| disapprove | 295 |
| disaster | 028 |
| disastrous | 028 |
| discern | 334 |
| discerning | 334 |
| discipline | 058 |
| disclose | 111 |
| disclosure | 111 |
| discourage | 381 |
| discouragement | 381 |
| discriminate | 334 |
| discrimination | 334 |
| discuss | 420 |
| discussion | 420 |
| disease | 124 |
| dismiss | 207 |
| dismissal | 207 |
| disobey | 218 |
| dispense | 226 |
| displace | 170 |
| display | 110 |
| disprove | 255 |
| dispute | 420 |
| disqualify | 255 |
| disrupt | 234 |
| disruption | 234 |
| distance | 157 |
| distant | 156 |
| distinct | 335 |
| distinction | 335 |
| distinctive | 335 |
| distinguish | 335 |
| distinguished | 335 |
| distract | 306 |
| distraction | 306 |
| distress | 322 |
| distribute | 373 |
| distribution | 373 |
| district | 183 |
| disturb | 306 |
| disturbance | 306 |
| diverse | 348 |
| diversify | 348 |
| diversity | 348 |
| divide | 334 |
| division | 334 |
| divorce | 036 |
| docile | 058 |
| doctrine | 058 |
| dogma | 058 |
| domestic | 339 |
| domesticate | 339 |
| dominance | 339 |
| dominant | 339 |
| dominate | 339 |
| domination | 339 |
| doom | 369 |
| dormitory | 339 |
| doubt | 251 |
| doubtful | 251 |
| downgrade | 070 |
| drought | 024 |
| drug | 120 |
| dry | 024 |
| dubious | 251 |
| due | 266 |
| durable | 094 |
| duration | 094 |
| during | 094 |
| duty | 222 |

## E

| Word | Page |
|---|---|
| eager | 091 |
| eagerly | 091 |
| eagerness | 091 |
| earn | 222 |
| earthquake | 028 |
| ecological | 020 |
| ecology | 020 |
| economical | 227 |
| ecosystem | 020 |
| edit | 107 |
| edition | 107 |
| editor | 106 |
| educate | 058 |
| education | 058 |
| educational | 058 |
| effect | 357 |
| effective | 357 |
| efficiency | 357 |
| efficient | 357 |
| effort | 327 |
| elaborate | 203 |
| elaboration | 203 |
| elect | 190, 344 |
| election | 190, 344 |
| element | 195 |
| elementary | 195 |
| elevate | 413 |
| elevator | 413 |
| embarrass | 302 |
| embarrassment | 302 |
| embassy | 186 |
| embrace | 040 |
| emerge | 353 |
| emergence | 353 |
| emergency | 353 |
| emergent | 353 |
| emigrant | 041 |
| emigrate | 041 |
| emission | 295 |
| emit | 295 |
| emotion | 044, 156 |
| emotional | 045, 156 |
| emphasis | 090 |
| emphasize | 090 |
| employ | 206 |
| employee | 206 |
| employer | 206 |
| employment | 206 |
| enable | 062 |
| encounter | 369 |
| encourage | 381 |
| encouragement | 381 |
| encyclopedia | 107 |
| end | 377 |
| endanger | 314 |
| endangered | 314 |
| endangerment | 314 |
| endeavor | 327 |
| endless | 270 |
| endurance | 094 |
| endure | 094 |
| enemy | 421 |
| enforce | 327 |
| enforcement | 327 |
| engage | 287 |
| engagement | 287 |
| enough | 408 |
| enroll | 066 |

425

| Word | Page |
|---|---|
| enrollment | 066 |
| ensure | 254 |
| enter | 066 |
| enterprise | 202 |
| entertain | 152 |
| entertainment | 152 |
| enthusiasm | 090 |
| enthusiastic | 091 |
| entitle | 255 |
| entrance | 066 |
| environment | 020 |
| environmental | 020 |
| environmentally | 020 |
| epidemic | 129 |
| epoch | 263 |
| equal | 422 |
| equality | 422 |
| equation | 422 |
| equip | 422 |
| equipment | 422 |
| equivalent | 422 |
| era | 263 |
| erect | 215 |
| erection | 215 |
| erupt | 234 |
| eruption | 234 |
| escape | 166 |
| essence | 191 |
| essential | 191 |
| establish | 214 |
| establishment | 214 |
| estate | 338 |
| esteem | 282 |
| estimate | 227 |
| eternal | 275 |
| eternity | 275 |
| evaluate | 356 |
| evaluation | 356 |
| event | 140 |
| eventually | 275 |
| evidence | 255 |
| evident | 255 |
| evocation | 198 |
| evoke | 198 |
| evolution | 071 |
| evolutionary | 071 |
| evolve | 071 |
| exact | 360 |
| exactly | 360 |
| exaggerate | 090 |
| exaggeration | 090 |
| examination | 388 |
| examine | 388 |
| examinee | 388 |
| examiner | 388 |
| exceed | 365 |
| except | 294 |
| exception | 294 |
| exceptional | 294 |
| excess | 365 |
| excessive | 365 |
| exchange | 349 |
| excite | 307 |
| exciting | 307 |
| exclude | 330 |
| exclusion | 330 |
| exclusive | 330 |
| exhaust | 021 |
| exhausted | 021 |
| exhaustion | 021 |
| exhibit | 110 |
| exhibition | 110 |
| exist | 141 |
| existence | 141 |
| expand | 171 |
| expect | 376 |
| expectancy | 376 |
| expectant | 376 |
| expectation | 376 |
| expecting | 376 |
| expedition | 174 |
| expenditure | 226 |
| expense | 226 |
| expensive | 226 |
| experience | 389 |
| experiment | 389 |
| expert | 389 |
| expertise | 389 |
| explain | 111 |
| explanation | 111 |
| explicit | 397 |
| explode | 106 |
| exploit | 141 |
| exploitation | 141 |
| exploration | 388 |
| explore | 388 |
| explorer | 388 |
| explosion | 106 |
| explosive | 106 |
| export | 162 |
| expose | 392 |
| exposure | 392 |
| express | 290 |
| expression | 290 |
| expressive | 290 |
| extend | 133, 171 |
| extension | 133, 171 |
| extensive | 133, 171 |
| extent | 171 |
| extinct | 335 |
| extinction | 335 |
| extinguish | 335 |
| extract | 306 |
| extraction | 306 |
| extraordinary | 259 |

## F

| Word | Page |
|---|---|
| facilitate | 063 |
| facility | 063 |
| factor | 198 |
| faculty | 063 |
| faith | 373 |
| faithful | 373 |
| fake | 017 |
| fame | 356 |
| familiar | 137 |
| famine | 124 |
| famous | 356 |
| fancy | 291 |
| fare | 227 |
| fascinate | 307 |
| fascinating | 307 |
| fascination | 307 |
| fashion | 133 |
| fashionable | 133 |
| fatal | 369 |
| fatality | 369 |
| fate | 369 |
| fear | 314 |
| fee | 227 |
| fertile | 033 |
| fertility | 033 |
| fertilize | 033 |
| fertilizer | 033 |
| fever | 124 |
| fiction | 107 |
| film | 156 |
| final | 279 |
| finale | 279 |
| finalize | 279 |
| finance | 227 |
| financial | 227 |
| fine | 251 |
| finish | 279 |
| fire | 207 |
| firm | 049 |
| first | 279 |
| fit | 404 |
| flame | 207 |
| flammable | 207 |
| flatter | 238 |
| flattery | 238 |
| flight | 174 |
| flood | 025 |
| flourish | 235 |
| flourishing | 235 |
| flow | 356 |
| flu | 124, 357 |
| fluency | 357 |
| fluent | 357 |
| fluently | 357 |
| focus | 090 |
| fog | 025 |
| fool | 319 |
| foolish | 319 |
| forbid | 323 |
| force | 327 |
| forces | 327 |
| forcible | 327 |
| forecast | 102 |
| foreign | 339 |
| foresee | 377 |
| foresight | 377 |
| forever | 274 |
| form | 058 |
| formal | 058 |
| former | 263 |
| formula | 058 |
| formulate | 058 |
| formulation | 058 |
| fortunate | 365 |
| fortune | 365 |
| fossil | 021 |
| foster | 059 |
| found | 214 |
| foundation | 215 |
| freight | 163 |
| friction | 421 |
| fright | 315 |
| frighten | 315 |
| frightening | 315 |
| fuel | 021 |
| fulfill | 141 |
| fulfillment | 141 |
| function | 157 |
| functional | 157 |
| fund | 215 |
| fundamental | 215 |
| furious | 045 |
| furnish | 422 |
| fury | 045 |
| fusion | 298 |

## G

| Word | Page |
|---|---|
| gain | 263 |
| gather | 211 |
| gathering | 211 |
| gender | 145 |
| gene | 145 |
| general | 145 |
| generally | 145 |
| generate | 145 |
| generation | 145, 263 |
| generator | 145 |
| genetic | 145 |
| genius | 145 |
| gentle | 145 |
| gentleman | 145 |
| germ | 129 |
| gifted | 063 |
| glacier | 021 |
| glance | 389 |
| glimpse | 388 |
| goal | 377 |
| gossip | 356 |
| govern | 186 |
| governance | 186 |
| government | 186 |
| governor | 186 |
| grade | 070 |
| gradual | 070 |
| gradually | 070 |
| graduate | 066 |
| graduation | 067 |
| graffito | 099 |
| grain | 033 |
| grant | 083 |
| grasp | 083 |
| grateful | 238 |
| gratitude | 238 |
| grave | 412 |
| graveyard | 412 |
| gravity | 412 |
| grief | 310 |
| grieve | 310 |
| grow | 058 |
| grown-up | 037 |
| growth | 058 |
| guarantee | 254, 287 |
| guard | 287 |
| guardian | 287 |
| guest | 218 |
| guilt | 251 |
| guilty | 251 |

## H

| Word | Page |
|---|---|
| habit | 136 |
| habitat | 136 |
| habitation | 136 |
| habitual | 136 |
| halt | 330 |
| harassment | 302 |
| harm | 314 |
| harmful | 315 |
| harsh | 322 |
| harvest | 032 |
| hate | 345 |
| hazard | 314 |
| hazardous | 314 |
| hemisphere | 024 |
| heritage | 274 |
| hesitant | 318 |

| Word | Page |
|---|---|
| hesitate | 318 |
| hesitation | 318 |
| hide | 111 |
| hierarchy | 187 |
| hinder | 306 |
| hire | 206 |
| holy | 372 |
| homicide | 361 |
| honest | 282 |
| honesty | 282 |
| honor | 282 |
| honorable | 282 |
| horrible | 315 |
| horror | 315 |
| hospital | 125 |
| hospitality | 125 |
| hospitalize | 125 |
| hotel | 125 |
| hug | 041 |
| human | 037 |
| humanity | 037 |
| humble | 283 |
| humbly | 283 |
| humid | 024 |
| humidity | 024 |
| humiliate | 283 |
| humiliation | 283 |
| hurt | 258 |
| hydrogen | 021 |
| hypothesis | 389 |
| hypothetical | 389 |

## I

| Word | Page |
|---|---|
| identical | 078 |
| identification | 078 |
| identify | 078 |
| identity | 078 |
| idle | 318 |
| idleness | 318 |
| ignorance | 078 |
| ignore | 078 |
| ill | 124 |
| illegal | 242 |
| illiterate | 098 |
| illness | 124 |
| illustrate | 110 |
| illustration | 110 |
| image | 291 |
| imaginable | 291 |
| imaginary | 291 |
| imagination | 291 |
| imaginative | 291 |
| imagine | 291 |
| imitate | 291 |
| immature | 037 |
| immediate | 262 |
| immediately | 262 |
| immigrant | 041 |
| immigrate | 041 |
| immigration | 041 |
| immortal | 121 |
| immune | 129 |
| immunity | 129 |
| impartial | 416 |
| impartiality | 416 |
| impatient | 125 |
| impediment | 174 |
| implicit | 397 |
| impolite | 319 |
| import | 162 |
| importance | 162 |

| Word | Page |
|---|---|
| important | 162 |
| importation | 162 |
| impose | 222, 392 |
| imposition | 223, 392 |
| impossible | 062 |
| impress | 290 |
| impression | 290 |
| impressive | 290 |
| improve | 141 |
| improvement | 141 |
| impulse | 157 |
| inaccuracy | 361 |
| inadequate | 404 |
| incentive | 157 |
| incident | 368 |
| incidental | 368 |
| incidentally | 368 |
| include | 223 |
| inclusion | 223 |
| inclusive | 223 |
| income | 222 |
| inconsistent | 259 |
| inconvenience | 311 |
| inconvenient | 311 |
| incorporate | 202 |
| incorporation | 202 |
| increase | 412 |
| incredible | 380 |
| indebted | 234 |
| indefinitely | 396 |
| independence | 052 |
| independent | 052 |
| independently | 052 |
| indicate | 102 |
| indication | 102 |
| indifference | 286 |
| indifferent | 286 |
| indignity | 282 |
| indispensable | 195, 226 |
| individual | 334 |
| induce | 352 |
| inducement | 352 |
| induction | 352 |
| indulgence | 059 |
| inefficient | 357 |
| inevitability | 167 |
| inevitable | 167 |
| inevitably | 167 |
| infamous | 356 |
| infancy | 356 |
| infant | 356 |
| infect | 128 |
| infection | 128 |
| infectious | 128 |
| inflation | 357 |
| influence | 357 |
| influential | 357 |
| inform | 078 |
| informal | 058 |
| information | 079 |
| infuse | 298 |
| inhabit | 136 |
| inhabitant | 136 |
| inherit | 274 |
| inheritance | 274 |
| initial | 279 |
| initiate | 279 |
| initiative | 279 |
| inject | 299 |
| injection | 299 |

| Word | Page |
|---|---|
| injure | 258 |
| injury | 258 |
| innate | 016 |
| innocence | 251 |
| innocent | 251 |
| innovate | 278 |
| innovation | 278 |
| innovative | 278 |
| inquire | 195 |
| inquiry | 195 |
| inscribe | 098 |
| inscription | 098 |
| insecticide | 361 |
| insight | 179 |
| insignificance | 191 |
| insignificant | 191 |
| insist | 258 |
| insistence | 258 |
| insistent | 258 |
| inspect | 388 |
| inspection | 388 |
| install | 141 |
| installation | 141 |
| instinct | 040 |
| instinctive | 040 |
| institute | 214 |
| institution | 214 |
| instrument | 074 |
| insufficient | 408 |
| insult | 283 |
| insulting | 283 |
| insurance | 254 |
| insure | 254 |
| intact | 128 |
| integral | 128 |
| integrate | 128 |
| integration | 128 |
| integrity | 128 |
| intellect | 063 |
| intellectual | 063 |
| intelligence | 063 |
| intelligent | 063 |
| intend | 133 |
| intention | 133, 377 |
| intentional | 133, 377 |
| intentionally | 133, 377 |
| interact | 202 |
| interaction | 202 |
| interactive | 202 |
| interest | 222 |
| interfere | 306 |
| interference | 306 |
| intermediate | 262 |
| international | 016 |
| interpret | 103 |
| interpretation | 103 |
| interpreter | 103 |
| interrupt | 234, 306 |
| interruption | 234, 306 |
| intersection | 167 |
| intervene | 306 |
| intervention | 306 |
| interview | 179 |
| introduce | 144 |
| introduction | 144 |
| introductory | 144 |
| intuition | 179 |
| invade | 306 |
| invalid | 125, 243 |
| invaluable | 239 |

| Word | Page |
|---|---|
| invasion | 306 |
| invent | 140 |
| invention | 140 |
| invest | 231 |
| investigate | 388 |
| investigation | 388 |
| investment | 231 |
| investor | 231 |
| invisible | 178 |
| involve | 417 |
| irrelevant | 286 |
| irritable | 302 |
| irritate | 302 |
| irritation | 302 |
| isolate | 278 |
| isolation | 278 |
| issue | 302 |
| itinerary | 174 |

## J

| Word | Page |
|---|---|
| jail | 250 |
| join | 416 |
| journey | 174 |
| judge | 246 |
| judgment | 246 |
| junior | 067 |
| jury | 246 |
| justice | 246 |
| justification | 246 |
| justify | 246 |

## K

| Word | Page |
|---|---|
| keen | 091 |
| keenly | 091 |
| kind | 079 |
| knowledge | 078 |

## L

| Word | Page |
|---|---|
| labor | 203 |
| laboratory | 203 |
| lack | 408 |
| lacking | 408 |
| lament | 310 |
| landscape | 179 |
| lately | 263 |
| latest | 278 |
| latter | 263 |
| laugh | 040 |
| laughter | 040 |
| launch | 279 |
| law | 242 |
| lawful | 242 |
| lawsuit | 247 |
| lawyer | 242 |
| laziness | 318 |
| lazy | 318 |
| league | 372 |
| lean | 133 |
| learn | 083 |
| learning | 083 |
| lecture | 345 |
| leftover | 274 |
| legal | 242 |
| legend | 099, 345 |
| legendary | 099, 345 |
| legislate | 242 |
| legislation | 242 |
| legitimacy | 242 |
| legitimate | 242 |
| less | 413 |
| lessen | 413 |

| letter | 098 |
| --- | --- |
| liability | 133 |
| liable | 133 |
| light | 413 |
| lighten | 413 |
| lightning | 025 |
| likely | 133 |
| limit | 323 |
| limitation | 323 |
| line | 148, 334 |
| literacy | 098 |
| literally | 098 |
| literary | 098 |
| literate | 098 |
| literature | 098 |
| local | 170 |
| locate | 170 |
| location | 170 |
| logic | 259 |
| logical | 258 |
| loneliness | 279 |
| lonely | 279 |
| low | 413 |
| lower | 413 |
| loyal | 242 |
| loyalty | 242 |
| lure | 352 |
| luxury | 235 |

## M

| machine | 157 |
| --- | --- |
| maintain | 152 |
| maintenance | 152 |
| major | 066 |
| majority | 066 |
| malnutrition | 125 |
| manage | 210 |
| management | 210 |
| manager | 210 |
| manicure | 174 |
| mankind | 037 |
| mansion | 274 |
| manual | 145 |
| manufacture | 145 |
| manuscript | 099 |
| marriage | 036 |
| marry | 036 |
| marvel | 283 |
| marvelous | 283 |
| master | 082 |
| match | 404, 420 |
| material | 020 |
| matter | 302 |
| mature | 037 |
| maturity | 037 |
| means | 227 |
| mechanic | 157 |
| mechanism | 157 |
| medical | 120 |
| medication | 120 |
| medicine | 120 |
| medieval | 262 |
| medium | 262 |
| meeting | 210 |
| memorial | 086 |
| memorize | 086 |
| memory | 086 |
| mention | 103 |
| merciful | 310 |
| mercy | 310 |
| merge | 353 |

| merger | 353 |
| --- | --- |
| merit | 071 |
| middle | 262 |
| midnight | 262 |
| migrant | 041 |
| migrate | 041 |
| migration | 041 |
| military | 326 |
| minister | 186 |
| ministry | 186 |
| miracle | 283 |
| miraculous | 283 |
| mirror | 283 |
| mischief | 319 |
| misconception | 259 |
| miserable | 310 |
| misery | 310 |
| misleading | 259 |
| missile | 295 |
| mission | 295 |
| missionary | 295 |
| misunderstand | 259 |
| mobile | 148 |
| moderate | 404 |
| moderation | 404 |
| modern | 263 |
| modest | 283 |
| modification | 349 |
| modify | 349 |
| moist | 024 |
| moisture | 024 |
| monitor | 210 |
| monopolize | 338 |
| monopoly | 338 |
| mortal | 121 |
| mortality | 121 |
| motion | 156 |
| motivate | 157 |
| motivation | 157 |
| motive | 157 |
| move | 156 |
| movement | 156 |
| movie | 156 |
| moving | 307 |
| murder | 250 |
| murderer | 250 |
| museum | 074 |
| music | 074 |
| musical | 074 |
| mutual | 202 |
| mutually | 202 |
| myth | 372 |

## N

| naive | 016 |
| --- | --- |
| nation | 016 |
| national | 016 |
| nationalism | 016 |
| nationality | 016 |
| native | 016 |
| natural | 016 |
| nature | 016 |
| naughty | 319 |
| navigate | 326 |
| navigation | 326 |
| navy | 326 |
| necessary | 195 |
| necessity | 195 |
| negative | 049 |
| neglect | 344 |
| negligence | 344 |

| negligent | 344 |
| --- | --- |
| neighbor | 036 |
| neighborhood | 036 |
| nod | 040 |
| nonsense | 044 |
| norm | 259 |
| normal | 259 |
| notice | 397 |
| noticeable | 397 |
| nourish | 125 |
| nourishment | 125 |
| novel | 278 |
| novelty | 278 |
| nowadays | 263 |
| nuclear | 326 |
| nucleus | 326 |
| nuisance | 302 |
| nurse | 125 |
| nurture | 059, 125 |
| nutrition | 125 |
| nutritious | 125 |

## O

| obedience | 218, 243 |
| --- | --- |
| obedient | 218, 243 |
| obese | 124 |
| obesity | 124 |
| obey | 218, 243 |
| object | 393 |
| objection | 393 |
| objective | 393 |
| obligation | 326 |
| obligatory | 326 |
| oblige | 326 |
| observance | 029, 243 |
| observation | 029, 243 |
| observe | 029, 243 |
| obsolete | 278 |
| obstacle | 306 |
| obtain | 153 |
| obtainable | 153 |
| obvious | 396 |
| obviously | 397 |
| occasion | 364 |
| occasional | 364 |
| occasionally | 364 |
| Occidental | 017 |
| occupation | 338 |
| occupied | 166, 338 |
| occupy | 338 |
| occur | 230 |
| occurrence | 230 |
| offspring | 037 |
| old-fashioned | 278 |
| operate | 121 |
| operation | 121 |
| opponent | 421 |
| opportunity | 364 |
| oppose | 392 |
| opposite | 392 |
| opposition | 392 |
| oppress | 290 |
| opt | 344 |
| option | 344 |
| optional | 344 |
| ordinary | 259 |
| organ | 120 |
| organic | 121 |
| organism | 121 |
| organization | 211 |
| organizational | 211 |

| organize | 211 |
| --- | --- |
| Oriental | 017 |
| orientation | 017 |
| origin | 016 |
| original | 017 |
| originality | 017 |
| originate | 017 |
| outcome | 198 |
| outlook | 376 |
| output | 144 |
| outrage | 045 |
| outrageous | 045 |
| outstanding | 397 |
| over | 279 |
| overcome | 420 |
| overdue | 266 |
| overseas | 339 |
| oversee | 210 |
| owe | 234 |
| own | 338 |
| owner | 338 |
| oxygen | 021 |

## P

| pact | 187 |
| --- | --- |
| pain | 251 |
| painful | 251 |
| parasite | 129 |
| parliament | 187 |
| part | 416 |
| partial | 416 |
| participant | 417 |
| participate | 416 |
| participation | 416 |
| particle | 416 |
| particular | 417 |
| particularity | 417 |
| particularly | 417 |
| party | 417 |
| passenger | 218 |
| passion | 091 |
| passionate | 091 |
| passive | 157 |
| passport | 162 |
| pastime | 152 |
| patent | 141 |
| path | 167 |
| patience | 125 |
| patient | 125 |
| pavement | 167 |
| pedal | 174 |
| pedestrian | 167, 174 |
| pedicure | 174 |
| pedometer | 174 |
| peer | 048 |
| penalize | 251 |
| penalty | 251 |
| pendant | 052 |
| pendulum | 052 |
| pension | 226 |
| perceive | 294 |
| perception | 294 |
| peril | 314 |
| perilous | 314 |
| permanent | 207, 274 |
| permanently | 207, 274 |
| permission | 295 |
| permit | 295 |
| perplex | 302 |
| perplexing | 302 |
| persist | 258 |

428

| | | | |
|---|---|---|---|
| persistence 258 | prejudice 246 | prophecy 338 | reception 294 |
| persistent 258 | prescribe 121 | prophesy 102 | recognition 078 |
| perspective 376 | prescription 121 | prophet 102 | recognize 078 |
| persuade 352 | presence 132 | proportion 416 | reconcile 361 |
| persuasion 352 | present 132 | proposal 392 | recover 121 |
| pesticide 361 | preservation 029 | propose 392 | recovery 121 |
| petroleum 021 | preservative 029 | proposition 392 | recruit 207 |
| phenomenon 028 | preserve 029 | prosecute 247 | recruitment 207 |
| phone 148 | president 186 | prosecution 247 | reduce 413 |
| picture book 107 | press 290 | prospect 376 | reduction 413 |
| pill 120 | pressure 290 | prosper 235 | refer 103 |
| pity 303 | prestige 356 | prosperity 235 | reference 103 |
| place 170 | prestigious 356 | prosperous 235 | refrain 153 |
| placement 170 | pretend 132 | protect 029 | refusal 298 |
| plague 124 | pretense 132 | protection 029 | refuse 298 |
| planet 079 | prevail 129 | protest 393 | regard 287 |
| poem 107 | prevalence 129 | protestant 393 | regarding 287 |
| poet 107 | prevalent 129 | prove 255 | regardless 287 |
| poetry 107 | prevent 140 | proverb 114 | region 171 |
| point 267 | prevention 140 | provide 179 | regional 171 |
| policy 186 | preventive 140 | province 170 | regret 303 |
| polite 318 | previous 263 | provision 179 | regrettable 303 |
| politely 319 | previously 263 | provoke 198 | reign 186 |
| politeness 319 | price 238 | public 106 | reinforce 327 |
| political 186 | priceless 238 | publication 106 | reinforcement 327 |
| politician 186 | print 107 | publicity 106 | reject 299 |
| politics 186 | prior 345 | publish 106 | rejection 299 |
| poll 190 | priority 345 | publisher 106 | relate 286 |
| pollute 028 | prison 250 | punctual 267 | relation 286 |
| pollution 028 | privacy 106 | punctuality 267 | relationship 286 |
| popular 106 | private 106 | punish 251 | relative 286 |
| popularity 106 | privilege 242 | punishment 251 | relatively 286 |
| populate 106 | probability 062 | purchase 227 | relevant 286 |
| population 106 | probable 062 | purpose 377 | reliability 053 |
| port 162 | probably 062 | pursue 195 | reliable 053 |
| portability 162 | problem 302 | pursuit 195 | reliance 053 |
| portable 162 | procedure 365 | puzzle 302 | relief 413 |
| porter 162 | proceed 364 | puzzling 302 | relieve 412 |
| portion 416 | proceeding 365 | | relieved 412 |
| position 393 | process 137, 365 | **Q** | religion 372 |
| positive 393 | procession 365 | qualification 255 | religious 372 |
| possess 338 | produce 144 | qualify 255 | reluctance 318 |
| possession 338 | product 144 | quarrel 421 | reluctant 318 |
| possibility 062 | production 144 | quest 194 | rely 053 |
| possible 062 | productive 144 | question 194 | remain 274 |
| posterity 037, 365 | productivity 144 | questionnaire 194 | remainder 274 |
| postgraduate 067 | profession 206 | queue 334 | remark 397 |
| postpone 266, 392 | professional 206 | quotation 107 | remarkable 397 |
| postponement 392 | profit 223 | quote 107 | remarkably 397 |
| postscript 099 | profitable 223 | | remedial 120 |
| posture 393 | progress 070 | **R** | remedy 120 |
| potential 063 | progressive 070 | radiation 021 | remind 086 |
| pour 025 | prohibit 323 | rage 045 | reminder 086 |
| povpcation 198 | prohibition 323 | rainfall 025 | remote 156 |
| practical 385 | project 299 | raise 058 | removable 156 |
| practice 385 | projection 299 | range 171 | removal 156, 330 |
| praise 238 | projector 299 | rational 258 | remove 156, 330 |
| precaution 314 | prominence 397 | reality 083 | renown 356 |
| precious 238 | prominent 397 | realization 083 | renowned 356 |
| precise 360 | prominently 397 | realize 083 | replace 170 |
| precisely 360 | promise 175 | realm 171 | represent 110 |
| precision 360 | promising 175 | reap 033 | representation 110 |
| predict 102 | promote 156 | rear 059 | representative 110 |
| predictable 102 | promotion 156 | reason 199 | reproduce 144 |
| prediction 102 | prompt 352 | reassurance 254 | reproductive 144 |
| prefecture 170 | promptly 352 | reassure 254 | republic 107 |
| prefer 345 | proof 255 | recall 086 | reputation 356 |
| preference 345 | proper 404 | receipt 294 | request 194 |
| pregnancy 376 | properly 404 | receive 294 | require 194 |
| pregnant 376 | property 338 | recent 263 | requirement 194 |
| | | recently 263 | |

429

| Word | Page |
|---|---|
| requisite | 194 |
| research | 389 |
| resemblance | 400 |
| resemble | 400 |
| reservation | 029, 175 |
| reserve | 029, 175 |
| reserved | 029 |
| residence | 036 |
| resident | 036 |
| residential | 036 |
| resign | 207 |
| resist | 095 |
| resistance | 095 |
| resistant | 095 |
| resolution | 361 |
| resolve | 361 |
| resource | 017 |
| respect | 282 |
| respectable | 282 |
| respectful | 282 |
| respective | 282 |
| respectively | 282 |
| respond | 311 |
| response | 311 |
| responsibility | 311 |
| responsible | 311 |
| restoration | 049 |
| restore | 049 |
| restrain | 323 |
| restrict | 322 |
| restriction | 322 |
| result | 198 |
| retain | 152 |
| retention | 152 |
| retribution | 373 |
| retrospect | 376 |
| retrospective | 376 |
| reveal | 111 |
| revenue | 222 |
| reverse | 348 |
| reversible | 348 |
| review | 178 |
| revise | 178 |
| revision | 178 |
| revival | 087 |
| revive | 087 |
| revolution | 348 |
| revolutionary | 348 |
| revolve | 348 |
| reward | 239 |
| rewarding | 239 |
| rhythm | 075 |
| ridicule | 283 |
| ridiculous | 283 |
| ripe | 037 |
| ripen | 037 |
| risk | 314 |
| risky | 314 |
| ritual | 373 |
| rival | 421 |
| roar | 041 |
| rob | 250 |
| robbery | 250 |
| rotate | 349 |
| rotation | 348 |
| row | 270 |
| royal | 107 |
| royalty | 107 |
| rude | 319 |
| rudeness | 319 |
| ruin | 029 |
| rule | 137 |
| rumor | 356 |
| run | 210 |
| rural | 183 |

## S

| Word | Page |
|---|---|
| sacred | 372 |
| sacrifice | 372 |
| safe | 231 |
| safety | 231 |
| salary | 222 |
| satisfaction | 153 |
| satisfy | 153 |
| saying | 114 |
| scarce | 409 |
| scarcely | 409 |
| scarcity | 409 |
| scare | 315 |
| scary | 315 |
| scatter | 211 |
| scene | 179 |
| scenery | 179 |
| schedule | 266 |
| scissors | 360 |
| scorn | 283 |
| scream | 041 |
| scribble | 099 |
| script | 099 |
| section | 416 |
| secure | 231 |
| security | 231 |
| seed | 033 |
| seek | 194 |
| select | 344 |
| selection | 344 |
| semiconductor | 144 |
| senior | 067 |
| seniority | 067 |
| sensation | 044 |
| sensational | 044 |
| sense | 044 |
| sensibility | 044 |
| sensible | 044 |
| sensitive | 044 |
| sensitivity | 044 |
| sentence | 246 |
| sentiment | 044 |
| sentimental | 044 |
| separate | 334 |
| separately | 334 |
| sequel | 270 |
| sequence | 270 |
| sequential | 271 |
| serendipity | 369 |
| servant | 029 |
| serve | 029 |
| service | 029 |
| settle | 361 |
| set up | 214 |
| severe | 322 |
| shade | 025 |
| shadow | 025 |
| shame | 303 |
| shameful | 303 |
| share | 334 |
| shelter | 036 |
| short | 408 |
| shortage | 408 |
| shower | 024 |
| shrink | 413 |
| shrinkage | 413 |
| sidereal | 079 |
| sight | 179 |
| sightseeing | 179 |
| signature | 191 |
| significance | 191 |
| significant | 191 |
| significantly | 191 |
| signify | 191 |
| silly | 319 |
| similar | 400 |
| similarity | 400 |
| simulate | 400 |
| simulation | 400 |
| simultaneous | 400 |
| simultaneously | 400 |
| sin | 250 |
| skill | 063 |
| slight | 413 |
| slightly | 413 |
| smart | 063 |
| soar | 412 |
| soccer | 182 |
| sociable | 182 |
| social | 182 |
| society | 182 |
| sociologist | 182 |
| sociology | 182 |
| soil | 033 |
| soldier | 327 |
| solitaire | 279 |
| solitary | 279 |
| solitude | 279 |
| solo | 279 |
| solution | 361 |
| solve | 361 |
| sometimes | 364 |
| sorrow | 310 |
| sorry | 310 |
| sort | 079 |
| source | 017 |
| sow | 033 |
| span | 263 |
| specialist | 066 |
| specialize | 066 |
| specialty | 066 |
| species | 037 |
| specific | 396 |
| specify | 396 |
| spectacle | 179 |
| spectacular | 179 |
| spectator | 218 |
| speculate | 376 |
| speculation | 376 |
| spend | 226 |
| sphere | 024 |
| spoil | 059 |
| spoilage | 059 |
| sponge | 311 |
| sport | 162 |
| spread | 129 |
| stand | 094 |
| standard | 259 |
| stare | 389 |
| starvation | 124 |
| starve | 124 |
| stereotype | 246 |
| stick | 137, 335 |
| sticky | 335 |
| stimulate | 157 |
| stimulus | 157 |
| stock | 049 |
| store | 049 |
| strain | 323 |
| strategy | 128 |
| strength | 322 |
| strengthen | 322 |
| stress | 090, 322 |
| stressful | 322 |
| stretch | 322 |
| strict | 322 |
| strictly | 322 |
| strong | 322 |
| structure | 214 |
| struggle | 420 |
| stupid | 319 |
| stupidity | 319 |
| subject | 066 |
| subjective | 066, 393 |
| subscribe | 099 |
| subscription | 099 |
| subsequence | 271 |
| subsequent | 271 |
| subsequently | 271 |
| subsidize | 227 |
| subsidy | 227 |
| substance | 020 |
| substantial | 020 |
| substitute | 349 |
| suburban | 183 |
| succeed | 271, 364 |
| success | 271, 364 |
| successful | 271, 364 |
| succession | 271, 364 |
| successive | 271, 364 |
| sue | 247 |
| sufficiency | 408 |
| sufficient | 408 |
| suicide | 360 |
| suit | 247, 404 |
| suitable | 247, 404 |
| supervise | 210 |
| supervisor | 210 |
| supply | 021 |
| support | 353 |
| supporter | 353 |
| suppress | 290 |
| suppression | 290 |
| surplus | 235 |
| surround | 020 |
| surrounding | 020 |
| survey | 388 |
| survival | 087 |
| survive | 087 |
| suspect | 251 |
| suspend | 053, 330 |
| suspense | 053 |
| suspension | 053, 330 |
| suspicion | 251 |
| suspicious | 251 |
| sustain | 152 |
| sustainable | 152 |
| sweat | 040 |
| sympathetic | 045 |
| sympathize | 045 |
| sympathy | 045 |
| symptom | 120 |
| syndrome | 125 |
| synthesis | 389 |
| synthesize | 389 |

## T

| tactics | 128 |
| tale | 107 |
| talent | 063 |
| talented | 063 |
| taste | 083 |
| tasty | 083 |
| tax | 222 |
| tear | 040 |
| telegram | 148 |
| telephone | 148 |
| telescope | 148 |
| television | 148, 148 |
| temper | 045 |
| temperament | 045 |
| temperature | 024 |
| tempo | 262 |
| temporal | 262 |
| temporarily | 207 |
| temporary | 207, 262 |
| tempt | 307 |
| temptation | 307 |
| tend | 132 |
| tendency | 132 |
| tender | 132 |
| tense | 132 |
| tension | 132 |
| tent | 132 |
| term | 048, 263 |
| terminal | 048 |
| terminate | 048 |
| terminology | 048 |
| terrible | 315 |
| terribly | 315 |
| terrify | 315 |
| terrifying | 315 |
| territorial | 170 |
| territory | 170 |
| terror | 315 |
| the Diet | 187 |
| theoretical | 385 |
| theory | 385 |
| therapist | 120 |
| therapy | 120 |
| threat | 315 |
| threaten | 315 |
| thrive | 235 |
| thriving | 235 |
| thunder | 025 |
| thunderstorm | 025 |
| time | 262 |
| tiny | 413 |
| token | 191 |
| tolerance | 094 |
| tolerant | 094 |
| tolerate | 094 |
| tomb | 412 |
| tone | 075 |
| touch | 128 |
| touching | 307 |
| tour | 174 |
| tourism | 174 |
| trace | 017 |
| tradition | 136 |
| traditional | 136 |
| traffic | 167 |
| tragedy | 315 |
| tragic | 315 |
| transfer | 162, 207 |
| transform | 349 |
| transformation | 349 |
| transfuse | 120 |
| transfusion | 120 |
| translate | 103 |
| translation | 103 |
| transmission | 295 |
| transmit | 295 |
| transplant | 120 |
| transplantation | 120 |
| transport | 162 |
| transportation | 162 |
| travel | 174 |
| treat | 121 |
| treatment | 121 |
| treaty | 187 |
| trend | 133 |
| trial | 246 |
| tribute | 373 |
| trigger | 198 |
| trip | 174 |
| triumph | 421 |
| trouble | 302 |
| troublesome | 302 |
| trust | 380 |
| trustworthy | 380 |
| tune | 075 |
| turbulence | 163 |

## U

| unable | 062 |
| unavoidable | 166 |
| unbelievable | 380 |
| uncertain | 254 |
| unconscious | 086 |
| uncover | 111 |
| undergo | 389 |
| undergraduate | 067 |
| understand | 082 |
| unemployment | 206 |
| unfamiliar | 137 |
| unfortunate | 365 |
| unfortunately | 365 |
| unpredictable | 102 |
| unwilling | 318 |
| upgrade | 070 |
| upset | 303 |
| urban | 183 |
| urge | 352 |
| urgency | 352 |
| urgent | 352 |
| usage | 103 |
| use | 384 |
| utensil | 036 |
| utility | 384 |
| utilization | 384 |
| utilize | 384 |

## V

| vacancy | 166 |
| vacant | 166 |
| vacation | 166 |
| vaccine | 129 |
| vacuum | 166 |
| vague | 397 |
| vaguely | 397 |
| vagueness | 397 |
| vain | 166 |
| valid | 242 |
| validate | 243 |
| validity | 243 |
| valuable | 239 |
| value | 239 |
| vanish | 166 |
| vanity | 167 |
| variety | 349 |
| various | 349 |
| vary | 349 |
| vehicle | 167 |
| verb | 114 |
| verbal | 114 |
| verdict | 246 |
| victim | 421 |
| victimize | 421 |
| victory | 421 |
| view | 178 |
| viewpoint | 376 |
| violate | 243 |
| violation | 243 |
| violence | 243 |
| violent | 243 |
| virus | 129 |
| visible | 178 |
| vision | 178 |
| visit | 178 |
| visual | 178 |
| visualize | 178 |
| vital | 191 |
| vitality | 191 |
| vivid | 087 |
| vividly | 087 |
| vocabulary | 103 |
| volcano | 028 |
| volume | 075 |
| vote | 190 |
| voyage | 174 |

## W

| wage | 222 |
| wanting | 408 |
| warn | 314 |
| warning | 314 |
| wealth | 235 |
| wealthy | 235 |
| weapon | 326 |
| weather | 024 |
| welfare | 183 |
| wheat | 033 |
| widespread | 129 |
| will | 318 |
| willing | 318 |
| wisdom | 063 |
| wise | 063 |
| withdraw | 231 |
| withdrawal | 231 |
| withstand | 095 |
| witness | 255 |
| work | 157 |
| workforce | 206 |
| worry | 303 |
| worship | 282 |
| worth | 239 |
| worthless | 239 |
| worthy | 239 |
| wound | 258 |

## Y

| yawn | 040 |
| yell | 041 |
| yield | 145 |

● 著者紹介

**嶋津幸樹** Koki Shimazu

平成元年(1989年)生まれ。海外進学塾 EUGENIC 主宰。山梨学院大学附属高等学校英語科卒、青山学院大学文学部英米文学科卒、オックスフォード大学 ELT 研修修了。専門は応用言語学、語彙習得理論、英語教育学。高校時代から海外進学塾を創設し、これまでに指導してきた生徒は 500 名以上。山梨県一の超人気英語塾に成長。最先端英語教育を実践し、数多くの国内大学合格者、海外大学合格者を輩出している。塾名の EUGENIC とは「優れたものを生みだす」という意味。

| | |
|---|---|
| 英文校正 | Josip Psihistal |
| カバーデザイン | 花本浩一 |
| 本文デザイン/DTP | 朝日メディアインターナショナル株式会社 |
| 本文イラスト | 田中斉 |
| 音声録音・編集 | (財) 英語教育協議会 (ELEC) |
| ナレーション | Rachel Walzer |
| | Josh Keller |
| | 水月優希 |

---

## 過去問で覚える英単語スピードマスター 必勝2000

平成 25 年 (2013 年) 8 月 10 日　初版第 1 刷発行

| | |
|---|---|
| 著　者 | 嶋津幸樹 |
| 発行人 | 福田富与 |
| 発行所 | 有限会社 J リサーチ出版 |
| | 〒166-0002　東京都杉並区高円寺北 2-29-14-705 |
| | 電　話 03(6808)8801(代)　FAX 03(5364)5310 |
| | 編集部 03(6808)8806 |
| | http://www.jresearch.co.jp |
| 印刷所 | 株式会社　シナノパブリッシングプレス |

ISBN978-4-86392-145-0　禁無断転載。なお、乱丁・落丁はお取り替えいたします。
© 2013 Koki Shimazu, All rights reserved.